Jazz Composition and Arranging in the Digital Age

Richard Sussman
and
Michael Abene

OXFORD
UNIVERSITY PRESS
New York

OXFORD
UNIVERSITY PRESS

Oxford University Press, Inc., publishes works that further
Oxford University's objective of excellence
in research, scholarship, and education.

Oxford   New York
Auckland   Cape Town   Dar es Salaam   Hong Kong   Karachi
Kuala Lumpur   Madrid   Melbourne   Mexico City   Nairobi
New Delhi   Shanghai   Taipei   Toronto

With offices in
Argentina   Austria   Brazil   Chile   Czech Republic   France   Greece
Guatemala   Hungary   Italy   Japan   Poland   Portugal   Singapore
South Korea   Switzerland   Thailand   Turkey   Ukraine   Vietnam

Copyright © 2012 by Oxford University Press

Published by Oxford University Press, Inc.
198 Madison Avenue, New York, New York 10016
www.oup.com

Oxford is a registered trademark of Oxford University Press

Library of Congress Cataloging-in-Publication Data

Sussman, Richard.
  Jazz composition and arranging in the digital age / Richard Sussman and Michael Abene.
      p. cm.
  Includes bibliographical references and index.
    ISBN 978-0-19-538099-6 (alk. paper) – ISBN 978-0-19-538100-9 (alk. paper)
  1. Arrangement (Music) 2. Composition (Music) 3. Jazz–Instruction and study.
  4. Instrumentation and orchestration (Band) 5. Musical notation–Computer programs.
  I. Abene, Mike. II. Title.
    MT73.5.S87 2011
      781.65'13–dc22   2010053107

1 3 5 7 9 8 6 4 2

Printed in the United States of America
on acid-free paper

Jazz Composition and Arranging
in the Digital Age

Contents

Preface and Acknowledgments by Richard Sussman • xiii

Preface by Michael Abene • xv

Music Examples—Recording Credits • xvii

Companion Website Audio Examples: Track List • xix

How to Use This Book and the Companion Website • xxiii

SECTION ONE: OVERVIEW AND BASIC INFORMATION

1 Introduction: Philosophical and Aesthetic Considerations • 3

2 Music in the Digital Age: A Brief Overview of MIDI and
Music Software • 5

    2-1 Overview of MIDI • 6

    2-2 MIDI 101 • 7

    2-3 MIDI Messages • 8

    2-4 An Overview of Music Software • 9

    Chapter Summary • 13

3 Basic Information on Instrument Ranges and Transpositions • 15

    3-1 The Brass Section • 16

    3-2 The Woodwind Section • 22

    3-3 The Rhythm Section • 27

4 Fundamental Musical Considerations • 33

    4-1 Balance • 33

    4-2 Economy • 34

    4-3 Focus • 34

    4-4 Contrast and Variety • 34

    4-5 Tension and Release • 34

    4-6 Unity • 35

5 Introduction to Music Notation Software • 37

    5-1 A Brief Historical Overview • 37

    5-2 Finale and Sibelius • 39

    5-3 Music Notation Software Basics • 40

    5-4 MIDI Playback and Editing • 47

    5-5 Music Preparation Basics • 50

    Chapter Summary • 53

SECTION TWO: ARRANGING FOR SMALL ENSEMBLE
(3–6 HORNS + RHYTHM SECTION)

6 **Overview of Small Ensemble Writing: Rhythm and Rhythmic Notation/Preparing the Score** · 57

  6-1 Jazz Rhythm Basics · 57

  6-2 Rhythmic Pulse and Style · 58

  6-3 Jazz Syncopation and Notation (Melodic Rhythm) · 59

  6-4 Swing Feel (Melodic Rhythm) · 62

  6-5 Harmonic Rhythm · 63

  6-6 Score Preparation · 63

    Chapter Summary · 64

    Exercises · 64

7 **Melody and Motivic Development (3–4 Horns)** · 67

  7-1 Basic Melodic Considerations: Melodic Shape and Motion · 67

  7-2 Melodic Motives and Phrase Structure · 69

  7-3 Techniques of Motivic Development · 71

  7-4 Basic Types of Musical Texture · 74

  7-5 Applying the Techniques of Melodic Development to an Arrangement · 76

    Chapter Summary · 79

    Exercises · 79

8 **Basic Harmonic Concepts (3–4 Horns)** · 81

  8-1 Chords Built by Thirds and Chord Scales · 82

  8-2 Vertical Harmony: Basic Principles of Jazz Chord Voicings · 86

  8-3 Horizontal Harmony · 87

  8-4 Standard Jazz Voicing Positions · 90

  8-5 Modal Concepts of Jazz Chord Voicings · 96

  8-6 Melodic Motion and Voice Leading · 98

    Chapter Summary · 100

    Exercises · 100

9 **Reharmonization of Approach Tones (3–4 Horns)** · 105

  9-1 Reharmonization of Approach Tones · 105

  9-2 Repeated Notes, Static Harmony, and Voice Leading · 111

    Chapter Summary · 116

    Exercises · 116

10 **Melodic Reharmonization and Counterpoint (3–4 Horns)** · 119

  10-1 Techniques of Melodic Reharmonization · 119

  10-2 Independent Counter-melodies and Polyphony · 126

    Chapter Summary · 129

    Exercises · 129

11 **Form and Planning the Arrangement/Instrumentation** • 131

11-1 Concept and Direction • 131

11-2 Improvisation and Form • 133

11-3 Basic Elements of Form • 133

11-4 Outlining and Graphing the Form • 137

11-5 Instrumentation and Outlining the Form • 138

11-6 Intros • 140

11-7 Transitions/Kickers • 142

11-8 Background Parts • 144

11-9 Codas/Endings • 146

Chapter Summary • 147

Exercises • 147

12 **Dynamics and Articulation/Brass Mutes** • 149

12-1 Dynamics • 149

12-2 Brass and Woodwind Articulations and Phrasing • 150

12-3 Muted Brass • 155

Chapter Summary • 158

Exercises • 159

13 **The Rhythm Section** • 161

13-1 Piano/Guitar • 161

13-2 Bass • 163

13-3 Chord Symbols and Abbreviations • 164

13-4 Drums • 165

13-5 General Considerations • 166

13-6 Rhythm Section Styles • 169

Chapter Summary • 170

Exercises • 170

14 **Completing the 3- to 4-Horn Arrangement** • 171

14-1 Adding a Recap and Ending • 171

14-2 Score and Part Layouts and Music Spacing • 172

14-3 Proofreading and Part Transpositions • 172

14-4 Printing the Parts and the Score • 173

14-5 Sample 4-Horn Arrangement and Analysis:
"Bill Bossa" (Richard Sussman) • 174

Chapter Summary • 185

Exercises • 185

15 **Notation Software: Generating Parts, Page Layout,
and Printing** • 187

15-1 Finale • 189

15-2 Sibelius • 193

15-3 Printing the Parts and the Score • 195

Chapter Summary • 195

Exercises • 196

16 Arranging for 5–6 Horns: Harmony and Chord Voicings • 197

16-1 Standard Chord Voicings for 5–6 Horns • 198

16-2 Reharmonization of Approach Tones for 5–6 Horns • 204

16-3 Repeated Notes, Static Harmony, and Voice Leading for 5–6 Horns • 206

16-4 Five and Six Note Close Position Voicings and Use of the Sus 4 and Natural or Augmented Eleventh • 206

Chapter Summary • 208

Exercises • 209

17 Form and Planning the Arrangement (5–6 Horns) • 213

17-1 Elements of Form (5–6 Horns) • 213

17-2 Woodwind and Brass Doubles and Muted Brass • 213

17-3 Instrumentation and Outlining the Form (5–6 Horns) • 214

17-4 Intros, Transitions/Kickers, Background Parts, Codas/Endings • 216

17-5 Laying Out the Score: Workflow Concepts • 222

Chapter Summary • 222

Exercises • 223

18 The Soli and the Shout Chorus • 225

18-1 The Soli Section • 225

18-2 Analysis of Soli Examples 18-1A and 18-1B • 230

18-3 The Shout Chorus • 230

18-4 Analysis of Shout Chorus Example 18-2 • 233

18-5 Recorded Examples of Solis and Shout Choruses for 5–7 Horns • 233

Chapter Summary • 234

Exercises • 235

19 Completing the 6-Horn Arrangement • 237

19-1 Adding a Recap and an Ending • 237

19-2 Score and Part Layouts/Transpositions/Proofreading/ Printing • 238

19-3 Six-Horn Arrangement and Analysis: "On a Misty Night" (Tadd Dameron/arr. Willie Smith) • 238

19-4 Six-Horn Arrangement and Analysis: "Minor Infraction" (Michael Abene) • 247

Chapter Summary • 259

Exercises • 260

**SECTION THREE: ARRANGING FOR LARGE JAZZ ENSEMBLE
(8 BRASS, 5 REEDS, AND RHYTHM)**

20 Overview of Large Ensemble Writing • 263

    20-1 Overview and Historical Perspective • 263

    20-2 Basic Principles and Considerations • 265

    20-3 The Expanded Sound Palette • 265

    20-4 Laying Out the Score • 266

    20-5 Selecting a Tune for a Big Band Arrangement • 267

    20-6 Recommended Listening • 268

        Chapter Summary • 269

        Exercises • 270

21 Unison and Octave Writing/Monophonic Texture • 271

    21-1 Melodic Considerations • 271

    21-2 Combining the Instruments: Considerations of Timbre, Register,
        and Tessitura • 272

    21-3 Melodic Phrase Structure • 274

        Chapter Summary • 278

        Exercises • 281

22 Concerted Writing for Brass • 283

    22-1 Overview of Concerted Writing for Brass • 283

    22-2 Review of Basic Harmonic and Voicing Principles
        (Vertical Harmony) • 284

    22-3 Application of Basic Voicing Principles to 8 Brass • 284

    22-4 Reharmonization of Approach Tones, Repeated Notes, and Voice
        Leading for 8 Brass • 286

    22-5 Voicing Considerations If the Melody Is in the Low
        Mid-Register (*8 Brass*) • 286

    22-6 Voicing Considerations If the Melody Is in the Mid-Upper Register
        (8 Brass): "The Basie Sound" • 288

    22-7 When To Use Open Position Voicings • 294

    22-8 Software Considerations • 295

        Chapter Summary • 297

        Exercises • 297

23 Concerted Writing for Saxes/Combining Brass and Saxes • 299

    23-1 Standard Voicing Techniques for Saxes • 299

    23-2 Combining Brass and Saxes: Constant and Variable Coupling • 301

    23-3 Summary of Basic Principles of Combining Brass and Saxes:
        "The Basie Sound" • 310

    23-4 Reharmonization of Approach Tones, Repeated Notes, and Voice
        Leading for 5 Saxes • 311

Chapter Summary • 311

Exercises • 312

24 Big Band Instrumental Subdivisions • 315

24-1 Contrasting the Brass and Sax Sections • 315

24-2 Cross-Sectional Instrumental Subdivisions • 320

Chapter Summary • 324

Exercises • 324

25 Form and Planning the Arrangement • 327

25-1 Elements of Form • 327

25-2 Instrumentation and Outlining the Form (Big Band) • 328

25-3 Laying Out the Score and Workflow Concepts • 330

25-4 Observations on the Creative Process • 331

25-5 Workflow Analysis of "Cross Section" • 332

Chapter Summary • 337

Exercises • 337

26 Modern Harmonic Concepts and Voicing Techniques • 339

26-1 Chords by Fourths • 340

26-2 Upper-Structure Triads • 345

26-3 Polytonal Sounds • 348

26-4 Other Types of Modern Chord Structures • 348

26-5 Clusters and Spread Voicings • 349

Chapter Summary • 352

Exercises • 352

27 More on Modern Harmony and Melodic Reharmonization • 355

27-1 Constant Structures • 356

27-2 Parallel Five-Voice Structures • 357

27-3 Modern Techniques of Melodic Reharmonization • 358

27-4 Independent Countermelodies and Polyphony with
Modern Harmonies • 361

Chapter Summary • 362

Exercises • 363

28 Woodwind and Brass Doubles and Mutes • 365

28-1 Woodwind and Brass Doubles • 365

28-2 Woodwind Doubles, Dynamics, and Balance • 367

28-3 Woodwind and Brass Doubles and Mutes: Homogeneous
Combinations • 368

28-4 Woodwind and Brass Doubles and Mutes: Mixed Combinations • 372

28-5 Orchestral Colors Within the Big Band • 379

28-6 More Instrumental Subdivisions and Color Combinations • 379

Chapter Summary • 381

Exercises • 382

29 Line Writing and Polyphony · 383

29-1 Basic Principles of Line Writing · 383

29-2 Line-Writing Procedure · 384

29-3 Increasing or Decreasing the Number of
Harmonized Voices: "Lineaology" · 393

29-4 Additional Examples of Polyphonic Big Band Writing · 396

Chapter Summary · 402

Exercises · 402

30 The Soli Section (Big Band) · 405

30-1 Basic Principles and Method for Creating the
Soli Section · 406

30-2 Analysis of "Analycity" Soli by Richard Sussman
Examples 30-1A, B, and C · 410

30-3 Analysis of "Swangalang" Sax Soli by Bob Mintzer · 411

30-4 Analysis of "Memories of Lives Past" Mixed-Section Soli
by Michael Abene · 413

Chapter Summary · 416

Exercises · 416

31 The Shout Chorus (Big Band) · 417

31-1 Basic Characteristics of the Shout Chorus · 417

31-2 Analysis of "Unithology" Shout Chorus by Richard Sussman · 418

31-3 Analysis of "Get a Handel on It" Shout Chorus by
Richard Sussman · 423

31-4 Analysis of "Uncertainty" Shout Chorus by Michael Abene · 426

Chapter Summary · 431

Exercises · 432

32 Arranging for Vocalists and Instrumental Soloists · 433

32-1 Basic Principles for Accompanying a Soloist · 433

32-2 Principles Specific to Vocalists/The Importance
of the Lyric · 435

32-3 Analysis of "Who Cares?" by Michael Abene · 438

Chapter Summary · 451

Exercises · 451

33 Completing the Big Band Arrangement · 453

33-1 Adding a Recap and an Ending · 453

33-2 Score and Part Layouts/Transpositions/Proofreading/
Printing · 454

33-3 Analysis of "Fletcher" by Richard Sussman · 454

33-4 Analysis of "Uncertainty" by Michael Abene · 463

33-5 Analysis of "Art of the Big Band" by Bob Mintzer · 472

Chapter Summary · 482

Exercises · 483

34 Summary of Music Notation Software Techniques · 485

34-1 Summary of Music Notation Techniques and Features · **485**

34-2 Comparison of Finale and Sibelius · **487**

34-3 Additional Software Tips · **488**

34-4 Using a Sequencer in Conjunction with Notation Software · **488**

34-5 Where Do We Go from Here? · **490**

Chapter Summary · 49I

Appendices (on the Companion Website)

A. Summary of Basic Arranging and Voicing Principles

B. Recommended Recordings for Further Study

C. Recommended Reading for Further Study

Index · 493

Preface and Acknowledgments
by Richard Sussman

I would like to acknowledge several of the great jazz arrangers and authors who have preceded us and provided valuable information and insights into the process of creating a jazz arranging text. At the top of the list is Don Sebesky, one of the great jazz arrangers of our time and author of the invaluable text *The Contemporary Arranger* (Alfred Publishing Co., 1974). I bought this book and took Don's class back in the late 1970s. Don's book has been a permanent fixture on my piano or writing desk for over 30 years. Although the original focus of Don's book is on "orchestrating for the recording medium," the basic information provided on the individual instruments, voicing techniques, and combining orchestral colors is still valid today. Of special significance to me are Chapter One: Basics, and Chapter Nine: General Advice. I still assign these two chapters as required reading for all of my undergraduate arranging and composition students on the first day of classes. With Don's permission, we'll be borrowing some important concepts from his first chapter, in Chapter 4 of this book.

Second, I'd like to acknowledge my first arranging teacher and collaborator, Michael Abene. In 1976, shortly after arriving in New York City, I got a call to join Lionel Hampton's band. I soon realized I had a great opportunity to write for the band, but, not having had a traditional music education, I didn't know the first thing about how to write an arrangement for big band. All of my prior efforts had been focused on learning jazz piano and writing for small groups. I asked several people in my circle to recommend an arranging teacher. The consensus was a unanimous: "Call Mike Abene!" Mike's lessons were practical and inspiring. He's since established himself as one of the preeminent jazz arrangers in the world. We've stayed in touch over the years, and for the past 10 years have been colleagues on the jazz faculty at Manhattan School of Music. It's an honor for me to have this opportunity to collaborate with him.

Two other books deserve special mention: *The Complete Arranger* by Sammy Nestico (Fenwood Music, 1993) and *Inside the Score* by Rayburn Wright (Kendor Music, 1982). Any jazz musician who's ever played in a jazz big band or listened to the classic Count Basie recordings of the 1960s is familiar with the wonderful jazz writing of Sammy Nestico. Although his book is not organized as a step-by-step "How to" of jazz arranging, it is filled with excellent musical examples and recordings from Sammy's library, complete with valuable analyses and anecdotes. It's written with a warm and generous tone, and I recommend it wholeheartedly to any serious student of jazz arranging at any level.

Ray Wright's *Inside the Score* has remained *the* authoritative treatise on jazz arranging since its publication in 1982. Again, although not organized as a "step-by-step" textbook, Ray's brilliant and insightful analyses of the music of Sammy Nestico, Thad Jones, and Bob Brookmeyer provide essential reading and study for anyone interested in this subject.

I would also like to acknowledge the many great jazz composers and arrangers of the 20th and 21st centuries, whose contributions to the repertoire have been, and continue to be, a source of inspiration for all of us: Duke Ellington, Fletcher Henderson, Gil Evans, Eddie Sauter, Bill Finnegan, Frank Foster, Benny Carter, George Russell, Quincy Jones, Sammy Nestico, Thad Jones, Bob Brookmeyer, Bob Mintzer, Jim McNeely, Maria Schneider, and many, many others, with a special acknowledgment to another of my teachers, the late, great Manny Albam.

I would like to thank Norm Hirschy and the staff at Oxford University Press for all their help in preparing this text (and especially to Norm for coming up with the original concept for the book). Thanks to Scott Wendholdt, Matt Haviland, Bill Kirchner, Mike Richmond, and Jay Azzolina for their help with instrument ranges and descriptions. Thanks to Russ Anixter and Don Rice for their help with the sections on music preparation. I'd also like to give special acknowledgments to Jay Dorfman and Dan Jamieson, and Mavis Kallestad for their invaluable assistance with the Sibelius and Finale software sections, respectively.

I'd like to extend a very big thank you to Bob Mintzer, Joe Lovano, Jim McNeely, and Randy Brecker for permission to use their outstanding music as examples in the book and website. I'd also like to extend a special acknowledgement to Bill Krasilovsky for his invaluable assistance in securing copyright permissions for some of the other music examples.

Thanks to Dae Bennett and the entire staff at Bennett Studios and especially to recording and mixing engineer Al Perrotta. Thanks also to John Guth for his help with the final mastering process. For their help with producing the recording sessions, I'd like to acknowledge Scott Reeves and Rich DeRosa (also thanks to Rich for his editorial comments and suggestions). Thank you to Chuck Schiermeyer for his many constructive comments and suggestions and for providing a student's perspective on the work. Thank you to Bill Kirchner and Dean Pratt for their vast knowledge of the jazz big band repertoire and invaluable help in compiling the expanded listening lists for the website. Also, a special word of appreciation should go to Justin DiCioccio, chair of the Jazz Arts program at Manhattan School of Music, and to all the wonderful student musicians from that program for their work on the accompanying recorded examples.

Finally, I'd like to acknowledge all of my composition and arranging students at Manhattan School of Music, whose inexhaustible supply of energy and creativity never ceases to amaze and inspire me.

Preface by Michael Abene

I have known Richard Sussman for over 30 years, first as a student and later as a colleague at Manhattan School of Music. He's not only a great arranger and composer but also an excellent and dedicated teacher. I was honored and excited when Richard asked me to be involved in the organization of this book. Excitement turned into panic when he asked me to write a preface.

Except for one year of piano lessons when I was a child living in Brooklyn, and later on when asking the advice of people like John LaPorta, Clem DeRosa, and other musicians I had met over the years, I am self-taught as a pianist and arranger/composer. My father was a guitarist and had many recordings of big bands and small groups. What captured my interest was the Benny Goodman band and those wonderful arrangements of people like Fletcher Henderson and Jimmy Mundy. The thought of a group of musicians playing written arrangements and sounding so wonderful intrigued me to no end.

When my family moved to Farmingdale, Long Island, after I graduated early from parochial school, I was totally knocked out by my high school dance band, under the direction of one of the most forward-thinking jazz educators at the time, Marshall Brown. I finally met young people who I had something in common with. I auditioned for the band, but my sight-reading was atrocious, so I spent that summer teaching myself to read music and composing and arranging by transcribing Count Basie charts. I spent so much time at the piano that my uncle who lived with us paid me to stop playing! My first arrangement was the standard "Back in Your Own Backyard." It was terrible, and sounded like a bad 1920s version. This was a very embarrassing situation, but I learned a lot that day. I still continue to sometimes find myself in embarrassing situations, and I continue to learn something from them!

I have been privileged to work with some great musicians over the years, both as a player and an arranger, and this has been my "education." Although there are many arrangers/composers from whom I have learned, my all-time favorites are Duke Ellington, Billy Strayhorn, George Russell, Gil Evans, and Gary McFarland. I had the pleasure and fun of working with Gary both as an arranger and keyboard player.

The most important part of learning arranging is to have your music played, preferably by live musicians, and to listen to their feedback, both negative and positive. I am as excited and inquisitive today as I was when I was first starting out, and I'm still always searching. There is nothing else I can imagine myself doing.

Use the principles and techniques presented in this book as a foundation to help you get started, and as a jumping-off point. This is only the beginning. The most important thing is *always* to move forward and to work with artists who challenge you, no matter what the genre. *Never* get complacent. Explore, EXPLORE, *EXPLORE*!

Music Examples—Recording Credits

Recorded and mixed at Bennett Studios, Englewood, New Jersey, June 2010.

Produced by Richard Sussman (unless otherwise noted).

All music composed, arranged, and conducted by Richard Sussman unless otherwise noted. (© 2011 Richard Sussman Music)

Recording and mixing engineer—Alessandro V. Perrotta

Mastering engineer—John Guth

Musicians

Small Groups

Alto sax—Andrew Gould

Tenor sax—Jonathan Ragonese

Baritone sax—Danny Rivera

Trumpets—Jonathan Barnes, Matt Holman

Trombone—Eric Miller

Piano—Jarrett Cherner

Bass—Jeff Koch

Drums—Jake Goldbas

Big Band

Reed 1—Andrew Gould—alto sax, soprano sax, flute, clarinet

Reed 2—Matt Chiasson—alto sax, soprano sax, flute, clarinet

Reed 3—Jonathan Ragonese—tenor sax, soprano sax, flute, clarinet

Reed 4—Sam Ryder— tenor sax, flute, clarinet

Reed 5—Danny Rivera—baritone sax, bass clarinet

Trumpet/flugelhorn—Paul Stadolka, Jonathan Barnes, Pablo Masis, Russell Moore, Richard Polatchek

Trombones—Eric Miller, Josh Holcomb, Matt Musselman

Bass Trombone—Jacob Garchik

Piano—Jarrett Cherner

Bass—Desmond White

Drums—Joe Saylor

Additional Musicians

Steve Slagle—flute, alto flute

Jay Brandford—soprano saxophone, alto saxophone

Jay Rattman—clarinet, soprano saxophone, alto saxophone
Bruce Eidem—trombone
Isaac Kaplan—trombone

Ex. 11-1

"Waiting"—*The Richard Sussman Quintet Live at Sweet Rhythm* (Origin Records, 2010); recorded live at Sweet Rhythm, New York City, June 2003

Tom Harrell—trumpet
Jerry Bergonzi—tenor saxophone
Richard Sussman—piano
Mike Richmond—bass
Jeff Williams—drums

Ex. 29-5 A and 29-5B

"One For Thad", composed and arranged by Richard Sussman – The Manhattan School of Music Jazz Orchestra, directed by Justin DiCioccio, 2001

Ex. 30-3

"Memories Of Lives Past", composed and arranged by Michael Abene – The WDR Big Band, featuring Dick Oatts on Soprano Saxophone, directed by Michael Abene, 2005

Exs. 33-1A, 33-1B, 33-1C

"Fletcher", composed and arranged by Richard Sussman—The Pratt Brothers Big Band —*Groovy Encounters* (Amosaya Music, 1997); recorded at Rudy Van Gelder Studios, 1997

Ex. 31-3 and 33-2

"Uncertainty", composed and arranged by Michael Abene – The Manhattan School of Music Jazz Orchestra, directed by Justin DiCioccio, 2003

Companion Website Audio Examples: Track List

All examples composed and arranged by Richard Sussman except as noted.

1.	Ex. 7-5	Oct/Unison 3 Horns + Rhythm "I Could Write a Book"[1]	0:29
2.	Ex. 7-6A and B	Tessitura—"I Could Write a Book"[1]	0:17
3.	Ex. 8-3	Example Tune Analysis—"Analycity"	3:58
4.	Ex. 8-4A-1–6	Standard Jazz Voicing Positions—3 Horns "I Could Write a Book"[1]	0:51
5.	Ex. 8-4B-1–6	Standard Jazz Voicing Positions—4 Horns "I Could Write a Book"[1]	0:51
6.	Ex. 8-6-1–4	Types of Melodic Motion—3 Horns "My Romance"[1]	0:38
7.	Ex. 9-1-1–5	Reharmonization of Approach Tones—4 Horns "My Romance"[1]	0:47
8.	Ex. 9-2A	Reharmonization of Approach Tones—4 Horns "Analycity"	0:34
9.	Ex. 9-2B	No Reharmonization of Approach Tones— 4 Horns "Analycity"	0:34
10.	Ex. 9-3-1–5	Repeated Notes—"Tautology"	0:51
11.	Ex. 11-1	Modifying the Blowing Changes—"Waiting"	1:20
12.	Ex. 11-3-1–6	Intros—4 Horns—"Have You Met Miss Jones?"[1]	1:15
13.	Ex. 11-4-1–4	Kickers/Transitions—4 Horns "Have You Met Miss Jones?"[1]	0:41
14.	Ex. 11-5-1–4	Background Parts—4 Horns "Have You Met Miss Jones?"[1]	0:57
15.	Ex. 12-1	Brass and Woodwind Articulations	1:58
16.	Ex. 12-1A-1–5	Brass and Woodwind Articulations Comparison	0:44
17.	Ex. 12-2A	"I've Got the Articulations and Dynamics Blues" (with articulations)	0:27
18.	Ex. 12-2B	(without articulations)	0:27
19.	Ex. 12-3A	Trumpet Mutes	0:58
20.	Ex. 12-3B	Trombone Mutes	0:52
21.	Ex. 13-2A	"I've Got the Rhythm Section Notation Blues" (with rhythm section support)	0:27

1 Composed by Rodgers & Hart, arranged by Richard Sussman.

22.	Ex. 13-2B	"I've Got the Rhythm Section Notation Blues" (without rhythm section support)	0:27
23.	Ex. 14-2	"Bill Bossa" 4-Horn Arrangement	4:09
24.	Ex. 16-1A-1–6	Standard Jazz Voicing Positions—5 Horns "I Could Write a Book"[1]	0:48
25.	Ex. 16-1B-1–6	Standard Jazz Voicing Positions—6 Horns "I Could Write a Book"[1]	0:51
26.	Ex. 16-1C-1–3	Brass and Sax Sections—6 Horns "I Could Write a Book"[1]	0:24
27.	Ex. 16-2-1–5	Reharmonization of Approach Tones—6 Horns "My Romance"[1]	0:47
28.	Ex. 16-3	Mixed Voicing Positions – 5 Horns "There Will Never Be Another You"[2]	0:57
29.	Ex. 17-1-1–6	Intros—6 Horns—"Have You Met Miss Jones?"[1]	1:10
30.	Ex. 17-2-1–4	Kickers—6 Horns—"Have You Met Miss Jones?"[1]	0:38
31.	Ex. 17-3-1–4	Background Parts—6 Horns "Have You Met Miss Jones"[1]	0:54
32.	Ex. 18-1A	Soli—Unison/Octaves—"Analycity"	0:17
33.	Ex. 18-1B	Soli—Voiced—"Analycity"	0:17
34.	Ex. 18-2	Shout Chorus—"Analycity	0:17
35.	Ex. 19-2	"Minor Infraction" (complete)*	3:24
36.	Ex. 21-1A-1–3	Unison and Octaves (High Unison)	0:32
37.	Ex. 21-1B-1–4	Unison and Octaves (Low Unison)	0:43
38.	Ex. 21-1C-1–11	Unison and Octaves (Octaves)	1:56
39.	Ex. 21-3	Unison and Octave Scoring—"Unithology"	0:51
40.	Ex. 22-2	Brass Voicing Examples—8 Brass "Dancing on the Ceiling"[1]	0:31
41.	Ex. 22-3A	Brass Voicing Examples - 8 Brass "12-Bar Blues" **Style #1**	0:24
42.	Ex. 22-3B	Brass Voicing Examples - 8 Brass "12-Bar Blues" **Style #2**	0:24
43.	Ex. 22-3X-1–3	Brass Voicings Common Mistakes "12-Bar Blues"	0:32
44.	Ex. 22-4	Brass Voicing Examples – 8 Brass "Dear Old Stockholm"[3]	1:29
45.	Ex. 23-2A-1–2	Combining Brass and Saxes—"Constant Coupling"	0:20
46.	Ex. 23-2B-1–2	Combining Brass and Saxes—"Variable Coupling"	0:21

---

* Composed and arranged by Michael Abene © Giggles Music.

2 Composed by Harry Warren and Mack Gordon, arranged by Richard Sussman © Richard Sussman Music.

3 Traditional, arranged by Richard Sussman © Richard Sussman Music.

47.	Sol. 23-1A-1–2	Exercise 23-1A Solution	0:19
		"Combining Brass and Saxes"	
		Constant Coupling	
48.	Sol. 23-1B-1–2	Exercise 23-1B Solution	0:19
		Variable Coupling	
49.	Sol. 23-1C-1–2	Exercise 23-1C Solution	0:20
		Constant and Variable Coupling	
50.	Ex. 23-3	Combining Brass and Saxes	0:23
		"12-Bar Blues"	
51.	Ex. 23-4	Combining Brass and Saxes	1:30
		"Dear Old Stockholm"[3]	
52.	Ex. 24-1	"Riffology"	0:25
53.	Ex. 24-2	"Fletcher" Intro/Head	0:49
54.	Ex. 24-3B	"Cross-Section" Score	0:17
55.	Ex. 24-4	Cross-Sectional "Unithology"	0:14
56.	Ex. 25-1	"Cross-Section" First Draft	0:16
57.	Ex. 26-2	"Ivories Tower"	
		Intro mm. 13-22	0:18
58.	Ex. 26-3	"Upper Structure Triads"	0:22
59.	Ex. 26-4	"Clusters"	0:22
60.	Ex. 26-5	"Spreads"	0:22
61.	Ex. 28-1A–D	Woodwind Doubles	0:57
62.	Ex. 28-2A–I	"Brass Colors 1"	1:41
63.	Ex. 28-3A–D	"Brass Colors 2"	0:45
64.	Ex. 28-4A	"Ivories Tower" Letter "B"	
	and B	A - **Flute & Open Trumpet**	
		B - **Flute & Trumpet in Harmon**	0:35
65.	Ex. 28-5 A-C	"Analycity"	
		A- Four Flutes in Unison	
		B- Three Flutes in Unison with Piccolo 8va	
		C- Four **Flutes** + Bs Clar & Muted Brass	0:51
66.	Ex. 28-6	"Exercise In Flutility"	0:41
67.	Ex. 28-7	"Ivories Tower" Intro	0:31
68.	Ex. 28-8A–C	"Ivories Tower" Soli	1:51
69.	Ex. 29-1E-F	Line Writing Solutions—"Linealogy"	0:30
70.	Ex. 29-2A	Rhythmically Independent Lines —"Linealogy"	0:15
71.	Ex. 29-2B	Line Writing with Brass Added—"Linealogy"	0:14
72.	Ex. 29-3	Increasing/Decreasing Voices—"Linealogy"	0:14
73.	Ex. 29-4	Cascade Effect—"Linealogy"	0:14
74.	Ex. 29-5A	"One for Thad" Head	0:23
75.	Ex. 29-5B	"One for Thad" Fugue	0:34
76.	Ex. 30-1B	Sax Soli Unison/Oct—"Analycity"	0:17
77.	Ex. 30-1C	Sax Soli Voiced—"Analycity"	0:17

78.	Ex. 30-3	"Memories of Lives Past"—Ensemble*	1:09
79.	Ex. 31-1C	"Unithology"—Shout Chorus	0:17
80.	Ex. 31-2	"Get a Handel on It"— Shout Chorus	0:27
81.	Ex. 31-3	"Uncertainty"—Shout Chorus	0:49
82.	Ex. 33-1A	"Fletcher"—Intro/Head	0:49
83.	Ex. 33-1B	"Fletcher"—Kicker	0:16
84.	Ex. 33-1C	"Fletcher"—Head Out	0:37
85.	Ex. 33-2	"Uncertainty"—Head *	1:45

How to Use This Book and the Companion Website

Overview

This book is about writing and arranging jazz music that is to be performed by real people playing acoustic instruments in various-size ensembles. It is *not* primarily about music technology or software. Most of the content consists of an examination of traditional musical principles that deal with melody, harmony, rhythm, orchestration, and form.

The book is intended to function as an introductory text on jazz arranging and composition, although we believe that much of the information presented would also be of interest to intermediate and advanced students as well as professionals. Many areas of jazz harmony are examined (Chapters 8, 9, 10, 26, 27). However, you should be familiar with basic concepts of jazz harmony in order to understand and benefit fully from the material presented.

The focus throughout most of the book is more on the arranging and instrumentation of existing material rather than on the composition of original tunes or larger works. However, we believe that the musical concepts presented are equally applicable to the composition of original material, hence the title, *Jazz Composition and Arranging in the Digital Age*.

What distinguishes this book from countless others on the same topic that have preceded it is that the material is presented from the perspective of doing much, if not all, of the creative work using music notation and other types of music software. We are in the "Digital Age"! Computers of all shapes and sizes, smart phones, the Internet, etc., have permeated all areas of our lives. Jazz and other forms of acoustic music are alive and well, but computers have become indispensable tools in the creation and realization of the music.

In an effort to provide you with a background and foundation in the effective use of some of these tools, we've included several chapters that do focus primarily on the software itself. Chapter 2 provides a brief overview of MIDI and music software, including some historical background. Chapter 5 presents an introduction and overview of the most important features and concepts central to the use of the two currently most popular music notation software programs: Finale and Sibelius. Chapter 5 also includes a summary of some basic principles of music preparation applicable to any music, whether hand-copied or computer generated.

Chapter 15 provides a more detailed look at one of the most important areas of music preparation, an area most likely to be fraught with errors—score and parts layout—including music spacing and printing the score and parts. In order to achieve satisfying readings and performances, it's essential that the music be properly notated and legible. Finally, Chapter 34 provides a summary of music software as applied to jazz arranging, with a brief look toward the future.

At the end of most chapters, we've provided "Software Tips," with software information and shortcuts relevant to the musical material presented in that chapter. Frequently, the text will consist of a brief synopsis, with more detailed information provided on the companion website. This is done not only to save paper, but also to avoid one of the pitfalls of writing about technology in general. Because of the rapid pace of technological change, something printed today may be out of date in 6 months or a year. The website provides us with an easily updatable format for keeping our software tips in sync with advances and upgrades to the various software programs.

None of the chapters or sections focusing on the two notation programs are intended to function as detailed tutorials or reference guides for either program. That's beyond the scope of this book. However, we do hope to provide you with enough information and background to overcome some of the most common obstacles and problems inherent in music software, which may otherwise tend to impede the creative process. Our motto throughout the book is "Technology is a means to an end, not an end in itself." Our goal is the mastery of specific musical techniques necessary for the creation of music.

To attain the greatest benefit from this book, you should do the various exercises using notation software, then print out the parts and have them played by real players. We say over and over throughout the book that MIDI playback, although useful for many purposes, is *never* a substitute for live performers playing acoustic instruments.

The symbol ◊ will be used to indicate paragraphs of special importance, sometimes accompanied by "Important!" or "Please Note:" This symbol will also be used to indicate the "Software Tips" at the end of most chapters as follows: ◊ Software Tip!.

Important technical and musical terms will be italicized when used for the first time. In various spots throughout the book, when a particular point illustrates a key concept from Chapter 4, it will be indicated at the end of a section in the following manner: (*Balance*), (*Contrast and Variety*), etc.

How This Book Is Organized

Section One—Overview and Basic Information (Chapters 1–5)

This section provides an introduction and overview of some philosophical, aesthetic, and musical considerations (Chapters 1 and 4) as well as the overview of software considerations (Chapters 2 and 5) mentioned earlier. Chapter 3 provides basic information on instrument ranges and transpositions, indispensable to any book on this topic.

Section Two—Arranging for Small Jazz Ensemble (3–6 Horns + Rhythm Section) (Chapters 6–19)

This section is designed to be adaptable for use as a syllabus for the fall semester of a first-year conservatory or college-level course in jazz arranging and composition. The basic approach is to begin with an exposition of fundamental concepts of rhythm, melody, harmony, chord voicings, instrumentation, and form, as applied to arranging for small ensembles: first for 3–4 horns (1 trumpet, 1 or 2 saxes, 1 trombone), then for 5–6 horns (2 trumpets, 1 trombone, 2–3 saxes), plus a 3- to 4-piece rhythm section consisting of piano, bass, drums, and guitar (optional). Most chapters contain musical examples, many of which are available as audio recordings and/or software files on the companion website. The end of most chapters contains musical exercises and software tips illustrating the application of music notation software to the topic at hand.

Basic harmonic and voicing concepts will be presented first within the context of 3–4 horns + rhythm, then 5–6 horns + rhythm, and finally, in Section Three, for full jazz big band. In addition to the many original music examples written for this book, some examples of fundamental principles will be based on familiar tunes, such as "I Could Write a Book" and "My Romance" (reprinted by permission). By using the same familiar material, first with the smaller ensembles and then repeated for the large ensemble, we hope to reinforce your understanding of these concepts. Chapter 15 focuses on music notation techniques involving music spacing, layout, and printing of parts and scores.

Section Three—Arranging for Large Jazz Ensemble (8 Brass, 5 Reeds + Rhythm) (Chapters 20–34)

This section is designed to be adapted for use as a syllabus for the spring semester. Musical techniques and principles presented in Section Two are reviewed and applied to writing for a larger ensemble, the standard 17-piece jazz big band consisting of 8 brass, 5 saxes, and 4 rhythm. As in Section Two, most chapters contain musical examples, many of which are available as audio recordings and/or software files on the companion website. The end of most chapters also contains musical exercises and software tips illustrating the application of music notation software to the topic at hand. Chapter 34 provides a summary of music software techniques.

The Companion Website

The companion website provides a valuable resource available to purchasers of the book. It contains information and musical examples integral to understanding the information presented in the book. There are five different types of files available on the website:

1. Audio recordings of many of the printed musical examples in the book are available for streaming or download in mp3 format. Any musical example in the book with a corresponding audio recording on the website will have the symbol ⊙ displayed above its title.

2. Software files in Finale, Sibelius, or Standard MIDI File format of some of the printed musical examples, exercises, and templates in the book, are available for download from the website. Any musical example with a corresponding software file on the website will have the symbol 🖥 displayed above its title.

3. Several musical examples presented as piano reductions, or in abbreviated fashion, in the text, are available as full scores as pdf format files on the website. Any musical example with a corresponding expanded score on the website will have the symbol 🖥 displayed above it's title.

4. Many of the "Software Tips" presented at the ends of chapters, as well as in sections of Chapter 15, will have more detailed information available on the website. Any Software Tip with more detailed information on the website, will have the symbol 🖥 displayed above its title, as well as the phrase statement "Refer to the companion website for more detailed information" at the paragraph's end.

5. There are several appendices on the website only:
   Appendix A is a "Summary of Basic Arranging and Voicing Principles."
   Appendix B is an expanded "List of Recommended Scores and Recordings for Further Study."
   Appendix C is an expanded "List of Recommended Reading for Further Study."

To access any of these files, simply log in to the website and under "Resources" click on the appropriate chapter number.

The companion website address is www.oup.com/us/jazzcomposition. You may access the site using username Music2 and password Book4416.

Overview and Basic Information

Introduction
Philosophical and Aesthetic Considerations

Music has a life of its own! It is our responsibility as composers, arrangers, and players to discover the true, optimum potential of a musical idea and to nurture it to fruition through the application of our innate talents and acquired technical skills. We arrived at this precept by sheer intuition at an early age and have held it as a guiding principle and deeply felt conviction throughout all of our many musical endeavors over the years. If you try to take a musical idea and force it in a direction it doesn't want to go, the music may sound acceptable to some, but, for you as a creative artist, the result will always be somehow less than satisfying.

The main purpose of this book is to provide the aspiring jazz composer/arranger with a set of proven technical principles and guidelines that will assist with the realization of that lofty goal—the creation of music. Not bad or mediocre music, but good, even great, heartfelt music—one of the crowning expressive capabilities of the human spirit. And great music, of any style, like any art form, cannot be reduced to a set of rules or formulas. It is a unique and intangible means of communicating the full range of human emotions, through sound, on a very deep level. It is truly a universal language.

Without getting too metaphysical, we feel it's necessary to share some of our thoughts about the process of musical creation. Otherwise, the rest of the material in this book would be presented out of context. Granted, different people have varying degrees of musical talent. But we firmly believe that anyone with a modicum of talent, and the willingness to acquire the necessary technical skills through hard work and discipline over a period of years, can gain access to that inner (or outer, depending on your perspective) universal source of artistic creation. It is an indescribable, indefinable "something," which we all have access to and which can serve as a beacon to guide us in the process of making the difficult decisions that are necessary to bring our musical ideas to their best possible realization. Sometimes, too much intellectualizing about the music or the application of technical facility without listening with your "inner ear," can actually impede this process.

A good analogy is that of the composer as an explorer or gem polisher. Once you've discovered that initial three- to five-note motive or the basic concept for an arrangement of an existing or original tune, your job is to polish it and nourish it, to bring it to its greatest potential fulfillment. Does this mean there is only one possible solution to any musical problem? No! There are usually many directions that can be taken with satisfactory results. However, we do believe there is usually one "true" or "ideal" culmination inherent in any musical idea, and that is what we should strive for. That's where the techniques, principles, and experience come into play. The more of that you have, the easier it becomes to attain or approach that ideal. However, a mastery of all the knowledge, techniques, and tricks in the world, without a little bit of soul, will *not* result in the creation of good music.

Any serious composer/arranger must learn how to evaluate and critique their own work. This requires a real commitment to maintaining one's musical integrity and can be accomplished only through concentration, focus, and listening to what you've written with your "inner ear." "Music does not exist on paper."* With time, practice, and experience, you will come to trust your musical instincts and to follow them, but you must first develop the ability to listen objectively and to hear what you're writing.

One way to develop this ability is to listen to and analyze as much music as possible. Listening lists are provided throughout this book to assist in that process. Also, one of the best ways to really get inside any piece of music, whether it's an improvised solo or a written arrangement, is to transcribe it. There will be important transcription assignments throughout this course of study.

There have been several great TV interviews by Charlie Rose with Quincy Jones over the years where Quincy has made reference to his belief in the spiritual quality of musical creation. To paraphrase him: *We are terminals for a much higher power—it's not about us. We all have access to it. You just need to learn how to get out of your own way and let that force go to work.* Sometimes we can be our own worst enemies—in musical creation, as in life.

What unites us all—the authors of this book, all musicians everywhere (young, old, good, bad), music educators, music students, and you, the readers of this book—is our love for music. We hope that some of the principles and techniques presented here will help you on the wonderful journey of exploration that lies ahead of you. Study, analyze, experiment, listen, create—and enjoy!

---

* Sebesky, *The Contemporary Arranger*.

Chapter **2**

Music in the Digital Age

A Brief Overview of MIDI and Music Software

Welcome to the Digital Age! First of all, it's important to emphasize that this book is fundamentally intended as a text on jazz composition and arranging for acoustic instruments, *not* for synthesizers or electronics. Many of the basic musical principles presented here, except for those dealing with specific musical styles, have not changed significantly in the past fifty years. However, the musical material is presented within the context of using computers and music software as the primary tools for composing, arranging, and assembling musical ideas.

From our perspective, the computer and software function in the same way as a pencil and score pad. Of course, there may be a little bit more of a learning curve to mastering Finale or Sibelius than to using paper and pencil. However, once you understand the software basics, it becomes increasingly easier to use, and there are significant advantages to working with music notation software in terms of economics, workflow efficiency, making revisions, and printing of parts and scores. We strongly recommend that you take a few minutes to read and thoroughly understand the material presented in this chapter and the subsequent chapters focusing on music software (Chapters 5, 15, and 34).

So what exactly do we mean by *digital*, and what does it have to do with music? Let's begin by defining a couple of basic terms that inevitably pop up in any discussion of MIDI or audio recording software: *analog* and *digital*. For our purposes, *analog* can be defined as "represented by continuous fluctuations in voltage, with an infinite number of values between minimum and maximum." *Analog* means the "real world" (phonograph records, reel-to-reel and cassette tapes, microphones, speakers, light dimmers, film cameras, and motion pictures). *Digital* can be defined as "quantized into discrete steps and represented by binary code, with a finite number of values between minimum and maximum." *Digital* means computers or the "virtual world" (CDs, DVDs, mp3s, minidisks, iPods, all forms of digital music downloads, digital cameras).

As we move into the 21st century, advances in electronics and computer technology continue to have a significant impact on the composition, performance, notation, and recording of music. In order to understand and utilize this new technology properly, we must first recognize that the basic elements of music—melody, harmony, rhythm, form, timbre (orchestration), and expressiveness—and the ways in which we as human beings (the listeners) respond and react emotionally to music remain fundamentally the same. However, the means with which we are able to deal with those elements have changed dramatically over the past 25 years.

This is especially true in the areas of music composition, arranging, notation, and recording and to a somewhat lesser extent in the area of performance. Music sequencers and notation software enable us to create and notate music in any style, experience "instant replay" with the click of a mouse, make changes quickly and easily (without having a desktop covered with rubber eraser shavings and broken pencils), create professional-looking scores and parts, and even create fairly convincing demos of music written primarily for acoustic instruments. In addition, the modern composer/arranger has access to a vast sound palette consisting of realistic acoustic samples with a wide range of dynamics and articulations as well as to an extraordinary array of electronic sounds, which can be modified and shaped to suit one's taste.

2-1 Overview of MIDI

A detailed history and examination of electronic music and MIDI is beyond the scope of this book. However, a brief overview of MIDI and MIDI software can provide an effective backdrop for understanding how to achieve the most musical and practical results in utilizing the notation software we'll be examining. Although it's quite possible to function in any music notation program or MIDI sequencer without really understanding anything about the inner workings of MIDI, there is a definite advantage to knowing a little bit about what's going on "behind the scenes" of the software interface. This knowledge can prove to be invaluable when dealing with the expressive, dynamic, and more advanced features of the software as well as when troubleshooting the occasional bugs and crashes that will inevitably occur when working in this medium.

MIDI (Musical Instrument Digital Interface) was first developed in the early 1980s, primarily as a means of establishing a standard by which musical devices made by different manufacturers could communicate with each other. After a period of negotiation between the leading American and Japanese synthesizer manufacturers, the original MIDI 1.0 specification (MIDI 1.0 spec) was published in 1982. The primary initial application of MIDI was to connect two or more synthesizers together so that you could create layered sounds or switch quickly from one sound to another in live performance.

It's important to understand that MIDI is both an *interface* (a means of transferring data between different types of devices) and a *protocol* (a set of technical rules about how information should be transferred and received using computers—in other words a kind of basic language or code for constructing music-related software).

By 1985, virtually all professional and consumer electronic instruments and keyboards contained MIDI implementation. As microprocessors and personal computers became more powerful, the MIDI manufacturers and software developers continued to discover new and more powerful ways of applying the MIDI standard. History may perceive the "golden age" of the MIDI interface to be roughly from 1985 to 2005.

The extraordinary power of the latest (and future) generation of computers has led to an interesting development. The typical *MIDI studio* (project studio used by composers) of the 1980s and '90s consisted of racks of keyboards, MIDI modules, effects processors, mixing consoles, and multitrack tape decks. This is being replaced by project studios consisting of one keyboard connected via USB to an array of computers utilizing *virtual instruments* (software programs designed to function as sound sources) and employing *digital audio* recording technology to record electronic as well as acoustic sounds, and notation software to create scores and parts using traditional music notation. The trend is toward keeping everything in the digital domain until the final mastering process.

So, although MIDI modules and cables (MIDI as an interface for transferring data) seem to be disappearing from the project studio, MIDI software is thriving! MIDI as a protocol, still based on the original MIDI 1.0 spec, continues to provide the foundation on which the current generation of most music software is built. Before proceeding further, it would be useful to have an understanding of some of the basic principles contained in the MIDI spec as well as a familiarity with some common types of MIDI and music software in widespread use today.

2-2 MIDI 101

The fundamental concept underlying MIDI is that any musical event can be expressed in terms of a series of commands, and data attached to those commands. For example, a typical command might be Note On, and the data attached to that command would be the pitch of the note and how much force was used to strike the key of the MIDI keyboard (referred to as *attack velocity* in MIDI terminology). Since music occurs over time, we also need a clock, or "metronome," to indicate the start time and duration of the notes and the tempo of the music.

The commands and data used to express musical events are transferred from one device to another (or from one piece of software to another within a computer) as binary code, referred to as *MIDI messages*. An essential feature of MIDI is that musical messages may be sent simultaneously on 16 independent, polyphonic channels without interfering with each other. For example, the piano part may be assigned to channel 1, the bass to channel 2, and the trumpets to channel 3.

If a MIDI device is set to receive on channel 1, it will respond to messages being transmitted on channel 1 and ignore all others. The "Golden Rule" of MIDI is that "the *transmit channel* and the *receive channel* must match" for a MIDI device to respond to an incoming MIDI message. Almost all professional MIDI devices (MIDI keyboards, various types of MIDI controllers, software, and virtual instruments) allow the user to set the MIDI transmit and receive channels to a number from 1 to 16.

2-3 MIDI Messages

For our purposes, the most important MIDI messages, and the only ones relevant to music notation software, are Note On, Note Off, Control Change, Pitch Bend, and Program Change. These are referred to as *MIDI channel voice messages*. Channel voice messages contain all information associated with musical performance and may be assigned to 16 independent, polyphonic channels. These are the nuts and bolts of all MIDI software programs, and, although commonly hidden from the user in programs like Finale and Sibelius, they are always present in the background, making the software work.

Each channel voice message consists of a command (the most important being Note On) and one or two pieces of data attached to the command (e.g., the pitch of the note and its attack velocity). At the end of the duration of a MIDI note, when you let go of the key, a Note Off message is generated automatically. Other musical events, such as the use of a sustain pedal, mutes, crescendos or decrescendos and the application of vibrato, glissandos, or other inflections and expressive techniques, can be expressed with MIDI commands such as Control Change, Pitch Bend, and Program Change.

One type of MIDI message of particular importance to any musician or composer/arranger is the Control Change. These messages lump together various controllers (such as faders, knobs, wheels, joysticks, and pedals) associated with musical expression and dynamics. The following are the most important MIDI controllers.

> a. *Controller 1—Modulation* (range from 0 to 127): usually applied with a modulation wheel (mod wheel) or by pushing the joystick forward on the front panel of a keyboard. It should be noted that with MIDI or

synthesizers, the term *modulation* has nothing to do with key change; it refers to applying an effect such as vibrato or tremolo to the sound.

b. *Controller 7—MIDI Volume* (0–127): usually associated with an external volume pedal or fader or a virtual fader in the software's mixing board.

c. *Controller 10*—Panning (0–127)—panning left or right in the stereo field. Generally, values for controller 10 are displayed so that 0 = panned in the middle, –63 = panned hard left, and +64 = panned hard right.

d. *Controller 64—Sustain Pedal* (Switch controller, On or Off): usually associated with an external sustain pedal.

The more you know about attack velocity, note duration, control changes, pitch bend, and program changes, the more effectively you will be able to make use of the expressive features of any music notation software, such as dynamics and articulation markings, during MIDI playback of the music. Behind every crescendo is a controller 7 (MIDI volume) change; behind every accent, an increase in attack velocity; and behind every "Mute" or "Open" marking is a MIDI program change or its equivalent.

It's especially important to understand the difference between controller 7 and attack velocity in terms of controlling MIDI volume. Controller 7 is "pure volume," with a range of values from 0 to 127. It affects *only* the volume of the sound. Attack velocity is generally programmed so that as you strike a key harder, the sound gets louder and also adds overtones, causing the sound to get brighter in timbre (as is the case with acoustic instruments in the real world). Changing attack velocities only works when notes are being attacked. If you need to apply a crescendo or decrescendo to a sustained note or chord, you *must* use controller 7.

One other specific MIDI message deserves to be mentioned. Occasionally, a Note Off message may get lost or deleted, with a resultant *stuck note*, which will keep playing indefinitely. MIDI provides an All Notes Off command to cause all notes to stop sounding, available in the MIDI/Audio Menu in Finale or in the Play menu ("⇧ O") in Sibelius.

2-4 An Overview of Music Software

Following is a list and description of some common types of music software in use today.

a. *The MIDI or digital audio sequencer*: A virtual multitrack recorder, used for composing and recording music produced by MIDI synthesizers, samplers, virtual instruments, and acoustic instruments and voices. The user interface is usually designed to resemble a traditional analog tape recorder and track list. (The term *sequencer* derives from the fact that the original sequencers were simply a series of oscillators, or sound generators, which could be tuned to different pitches, connected to a clock source, and programmed to play a repeating, ostinato-like sequence of notes or melodic figure.) The early versions of this type of software (MIDI sequencers) could work only with digital sound sources, so you couldn't add a real violin, trumpet, or vocal to your sequence (*examples*: early versions of Performer, Logic, Cubase, Sonar, and Reason).

Most MIDI sequencers have evolved into *digital audio sequencers*, which allows the ability to add tracks of real audio along with the MIDI tracks. In addition, they provide the capacity to use *virtual instruments* as sound sources as well as a wide variety of other audio effects, or "*plug-ins*," such as reverbs, delays, compressors, and equalizers, which can be applied to the audio and virtual instrument tracks (*examples*: Digital Performer, Logic Pro, Cubase, Sonar, Reason Record, Ableton Live). Some programs, such as Ableton and Reason, also favor "loop-based" interfaces, which allow the user to work with prerecorded audio loops or loops recorded while performing live (Ableton) along with traditional audio and MIDI tracks.

b. *Digital audio recording and editing software (digital audio workstations, or DAWs)*: These programs are designed to function as virtual multi-track recording studios for recording and mixing live music performance or as postproduction tools for mixing TV shows and films. Most digital audio sequencers can also function as DAWs, but not all DAWs necessarily include MIDI sequencing capabilities (*examples*: Pro Tools, Logic Pro, Digital Performer, Cubase, Sonar, Fairlight, Sound Forge).

c. *Music notation software*: These programs are designed primarily to give one the ability to create professional-looking scores and parts and to print them out for use in live performances. They can also function as a virtual score pad for the composer. The user interface is designed to represent a traditional music score, with tools to insert notes, rests, and other musical symbols. Most notation programs also include rudimentary sequencers for MIDI playback of the music (*examples*: Finale, Sibelius, Score).

d. *Editor librarian software*: These programs have two functions. First, they can function as a means of storing and organizing many banks of sounds for traditional MIDI synthesizers (hence *librarian*). Second, they can function as virtual editing modules (hence *editor*) for a synthesizer, where the interface is designed to display a virtual panel of knobs and sliders controlling the sound parameters of that synth. With the gradual decline in the usage of MIDI hardware synthesizers and modules, the importance and popularity of traditional editor librarian software seems also to be diminishing.

e. *Samplers, sample libraries, and virtual instruments (VIs)*: A *sampler* is a device that can digitally record (*sample*) the sound of an acoustic or electronic instrument, or sound effect, in different registers and then

arrange, or *map*, the samples so that they can be triggered by a MIDI keyboard or other controller. Since the audio source can be an actual recording of a real acoustic instrument, for instance, a violin or an oboe, the sound quality is capable of much greater realism than that of older electronic synthesizers. Samplers and the *sample libraries* (orchestral, percussive, electronic, SFX, etc.) that have been developed to work with them have revolutionized the MIDI composer's sound palette over the past 20 years.

Originally, samplers were hardware modules or keyboards, similar in appearance to other MIDI synthesizers (*examples*: Synclavier, Fairlight, Akai S6000, Roland S760, Kurzweil K2600, Emu Emulator IV). Over time, various third-party companies developed comprehensive libraries of sounds that could be purchased on CDs or DVDs for use with the various samplers.

As computers have become more and more powerful, the hardware samplers and synthesizers that were commonplace only a few years ago have generally been replaced by virtual samplers and instruments. These are software programs that actually turn the computer into a sound-generating device that can mimic the hardware devices of the previous generation of technology. For the most part, these virtual instruments (VIs) and samplers have been designed to function as *plug-ins* operating within a *host* sequencer or notation program. For sound sources, they rely on the vast array of libraries of sampled sounds and sound-generating algorithms that exist entirely within the computer and its various hard drives. Each instance of a VI opened as a plug-in is referred to as an *instantiation*. The number of virtual instruments you can have open, or instantiated, at any time is a function of the speed and power of your computer's *CPU* (central processing unit) and the amount of *RAM* available in the computer.

Virtual Instruments are often modeled after some form of traditional analog or digital synthesizer or sample player (Virtual Moog, Pro 53, FM8, Kontakt 3, ESX 24) or are newly designed powerful hybrid synthesizers (Omnisphere, Absynth, Massive). Some VIs are designed to resemble and imitate specific acoustic instruments (Akoustik Piano, Ivory, B4, Elektrik Piano), and some focus specifically on drum and percussion sounds and sampled loops (Stylus RMX, Battery 3, Storm Drums). Many large orchestral sample libraries originally developed for use in the hardware samplers and sample players of the 1990s are now available as VIs (The VSL Instrument, EastWest Quantum Leap Play, Garritan Personal Orchestra).

f. *Sound-designing environments (SDEs)*: At the high end of sound-generating software are sophisticated programs such as Max/MSP, KYMA, Reaktor, and pd, which provide an environment enabling users essentially to design and create their own electronic instruments or *effects processors*. These instruments can then be used to create any sound imaginable, to manipulate and transform recorded acoustic sounds, or to enable interactive musical performances by live players with computer-generated or -processed acoustic sounds. This type of software tends to be favored by contemporary classical electronic composers.

g. *Music education software (computer-assisted instruction, or CAI)*: A vast and wonderful array of educational software is available for educators and students of all ages and levels. This includes programs in music history, theory, ear training, introduction to orchestral instruments, and composition (*examples*: Sibelius Educational Suite, Auralia, Music Ace, Morton Subotnick's "Creating Music" series).

At the time of this writing (December 2010), there have been recent, significant breakthroughs and advances in the area of music software, partly resulting from the ongoing development of computer technology and the increase in computer processing capabilities and speed. There has also been significant research and development into new types of music software interfaces and programming environments, most notably OSC (Open Sound Control), which is "a protocol for communication among computers, sound synthesizers, and other multimedia devices that is optimized for modern networking technology."* OSC has managed to overcome some of the deficiencies in the older MIDI 1.0 spec, such as a slow transmission rate and relatively coarse resolution. Meanwhile, the MIDI Manufacturers Association (MMA), has been developing a new "MIDI HD" (High Definition) protocol that would "provide greater resolution in data values . . . (and lead to) more expressive products, improved ease of use, and new and innovative applications."** Either of these new systems or something similar could eventually replace MIDI 1.0 as a protocol for writing music software, including music notation software.

However, our goal in the following chapters is to focus primarily on the application of current notation and sequencing software to the compositional process and on the ways in which this software can be utilized to assist in both the creative and practical aspects of producing jazz compositions and arrangements for small and large ensembles. Software will be employed both as a pedagogical tool (in the form of examples and exercises) and as a practical tool, illustrating how many composers and arrangers are using these techniques successfully in the real world today. There will also be several chapters devoted exclusively to the creative use of music technology and software.

Finally, it's important always to keep our perspective with regard to our ultimate goal—the creation of music! Technology can be very fascinating and

---

* opensoundcontrol.org
** www.midi.org

seductive in its own right, and it is certainly a worthwhile pursuit. However, for us—the professional musicians and composers, serious music students, music educators, and music hobbyists—technology is a means to an end, not an end in itself. Music technology can be a tremendously powerful tool in the creative process. It can also be a terrible distraction, especially when you've got a deadline and things start crashing or bugging out. There is always a solution or workaround for the technical problem! Maintain your perspective and keep your focus on that final goal—the beauty and artistry of the music itself.

Chapter Summary

In this chapter, we provided a brief overview of the history and inner workings of MIDI. We also defined some of the most important types of MIDI messages and some other important technical terms. Finally, we examined some of the common types of MIDI software in use today.

Chapter 3

Basic Information on Instrument Ranges and Transpositions

Before beginning the study of arranging or orchestration for various combinations of musical instruments, it is essential to have a solid understanding of the ranges, transpositions, timbral characteristics, and performance attributes of these instruments. Since this book deals primarily with composing and arranging for small and large jazz ensembles, we'll limit our examination of the basics to those instruments most commonly associated with modern jazz ensembles.

1. The *Brass section*: B♭ trumpet, B♭ flugelhorn, tenor trombone, bass trombone, French horn (F), tuba.
2. The *Woodwind section*: soprano, alto, tenor, and baritone saxophones, "C" flute, alto flute, piccolo, B♭ clarinet, B♭ bass clarinet.
3. The *Rhythm section*: piano, electric piano, electric organ, synthesizers, acoustic and electric guitar, acoustic and electric bass, drum set, mallet instruments (vibes, marimba, xylophone, steel drums, etc.), and assorted other percussion instruments (shaker, tambourine, cowbell, congas, etc.)

If you're interested in exploring the sonorities of other instruments, such as the string section, orchestral woodwinds, orchestral percussion, and other keyboard instruments, then consult one of the many fine books on orchestration currently available (e.g., Adler, Kennan, Rimsky-Korsakov, Sebesky).

A word on transposing instruments: An instrument is considered to be a transposing instrument if it's written pitch is different from concert pitch (the note actually sounding when played). The most common transpositions in use today are B♭, E♭, F, and G. The following simple chart illustrates how this principle works.

Transposition	Written Pitch	Concert Pitch (Sounding)	Instruments
B♭	C	B♭—Major second below written pitch	trumpet, flugelhorn, clarinet, soprano saxophone
B♭	C	B♭—Major ninth below written pitch	tenor saxophone, bass clarinet
E♭	C	E♭—Major sixth below written pitch	alto saxophone
E♭	C	E♭—Major sixth + 1 octave below written pitch	baritone saxophone
F	C	F—Perfect fifth below written pitch	French horn, English horn
G	C	G—Perfect fourth below written pitch	alto flute

3-1 The Brass Section

In a typical jazz ensemble, the brass section consists primarily of trumpets (often doubling on flugelhorns), trombones (tenor and bass), and an occasional tuba. Sometimes French Horns are also available, for added richness and color. All members of the brass family share the following common characteristics.

1. They have a relatively bright timbre, with all of the overtones present.[1]
2. They have a great deal of dynamic range, from a warm and mellifluous tone when played quietly, to a capacity for tremendous power and forcefulness at full volume.
3. They have a fair amount of technical facility at fast tempos, although skips of larger intervals tend to be more difficult to execute than with woodwinds.
4. Playing any brass instrument, especially in the upper register or for long periods of time, can be very demanding physically. It's important to give your brass players (especially the lead players) frequent rests.
5. It's also important to give brass jazz soloists at least 4–8 bars of rest both before and after playing an extended improvised solo. This is for psychological as well as physical reasons. Jazz soloists need to feel free to access that unique creative zone necessary for improvising. This can require a few seconds to mentally prepare for the beginning of a solo (e.g., there's no need to include the 4th trumpet in an ensemble section immediately preceding their solo). Similarly, knowing that they need to focus on a written part immediately following an improvised solo may force these

---

1 Even though the tenor trombone, bass trombone, and tuba appear to have a darker timbre than the trumpet or French horn, upon analyzing the overtone structures produced by these instruments, one discovers that all of the partials in the natural overtone series are present in brass instruments, which is *not* the case with woodwinds. It is this unique overtone structure that enables us to distinguish the "brassy" quality of a bass trombone or tuba from that of a bass clarinet or baritone sax in the same register.

players to start thinking about the next entrance near the end of a solo, thereby limiting their creative capacity. There's also a purely logistical aspect to this principle. In some concert settings, the trumpet or trombone soloists are expected to leave the section and come center stage to play their solo. In this case they would need more time—at least 16–32 bars—to walk from their seats to the microphone and back.

B♭ Trumpet

The B♭ trumpet is a transposing instrument sounding a whole step lower than written. The timbre of the trumpet can range from dark and mellow in the lower register to bright and aggressive in the high register. It is the most powerful, penetrating, and flexible instrument of the brass section. As a section, trumpets can sound good voiced in unison, octaves, close position, semi-open position or clusters, blending well with other brass instruments or saxophones. The timbre of the trumpet can be modified dramatically by inserting a variety of different mutes into the bell.

B♭ Flugelhorn

The flugelhorn is a transposing instrument, written exactly like the trumpet. The range of the flugelhorn is theoretically the same as the trumpet's. However, for practical purposes its most useful range would typically not extend beyond (written) G or A above the staff when writing for a section. Although lacking the power and range of the trumpet, its timbre is warmer and more intimate, making it very useful as a contrasting color, especially in softer sections or ballads. It sounds good as a solo instrument or in a section with other flugels or trumpets (open or muted). The flugelhorn is always played open, without a mute.

Tenor Trombone

The tenor, valve, and bass trombones, although technically pitched in B♭ (with the slide all the way in, the notes of the harmonic series based on B♭ can be played), are all nontransposing instruments, written in the bass clef. The timbre of the tenor trombone can range from dark and mellow in the lower register, to bright and aggressive in the high register. Although not quite as agile as the trumpet, the slide trombone possesses a surprising amount of technical facility in all registers, except the very high and low ends of the horn. There are seven slide positions, each producing a complete overtone series. Example 3-1 shows the notes produced by each slide position and presents a list of possible glissandos. The only real technical limitation occurs when moving between low notes available only in first and second positions to and from those available only in sixth and seventh positions (Ex. 3-1). Some tenor trombones have

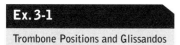

Ex. 3-1

Trombone Positions and Glissandos

Positions

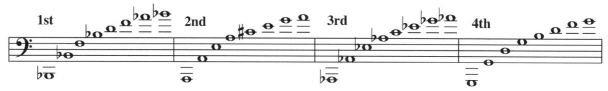

Possible Glissandos (to and from these notes and any note in between)

Difficult (without F Extension)

From any of these ——————— to any of these

extra tubing with a trigger mechanism similar to the bass trombone (sometimes called an *F extension*), which significantly helps to overcome these technical difficulties.*

As a section, trombones can sound good voiced in unison, octaves, close position, semi-open, open position, or clusters. They blend well with trumpets, French horns, or saxophones, or they can stand alone as a section. The timbre of the trombone can also be modified dramatically by inserting a variety of different mutes into the bell.

18

Valve Trombone

The three-valve system has been applied to trombones. Although the valves provide greater technical facility at fast tempos, intonation problems, a somewhat "stuffy" tone, and the absence of that most distinguishing characteristic of trombones—the slide—has resulted in a general avoidance of this instrument by both classical and jazz players. Probably the best-known proponent of the valve trombone, both as a jazz soloist and section player, is Bob Brookmeyer.

Bass Trombone

The bass trombone is a nontransposing instrument, written exactly as the tenor trombone. It is constructed with additional tubing, often referred to as a *trigger* or *extension*, which makes it possible to play all the notes in between low E1 and B♭0 as well as all the pedal tones down to the low E0.[2] It is similar in timbre and technical facility to the tenor trombone. However, because of its larger bore and trigger mechanism, its greatest strength and unique feature is its extreme depth and power in the low register, providing a solid harmonic foundation for the entire ensemble. It is generally not desirable to write for the bass trombone in the upper register (above the staff), because that range is handled much more effectively by the tenor trombone.

French Horn

The French horn is a transposing instrument, pitched in F; it sounds a perfect fifth lower than written. Most notes are written in the treble clef, except when descending into the lowest register (written G below middle C and lower). It is not a standard member of the typical jazz big band since it lacks some of the forcefulness and facility of trumpets and trombones. It also overlaps the register of the trombones, making it nonessential from a harmonic perspective. However, its unique and beautiful timbre and its ability to blend equally well with either brass or woodwinds make it a desirable addition to the jazz ensemble when warranted.

The timbre of the French horn can be modified by a technique known as *stopping*. The hand is inserted deep into the bell, blocking the airflow and producing either a soft, distant tone or a harsh, metallic tone when blown more forcefully. This effect is indicated by writing "+" over the note, or "stopped" for a longer passage, and "open" for the resumption of normal tone. A similar effect can be produced by inserting a straight mute into the bell.

---

2 In standard MIDI terminology, middle C = C3, C an octave lower = C2, C two octaves lower = C1, etc. This terminology is useful when describing the ranges of the instruments. (This standard is not universally accepted. Some manufacturers designate middle C as "C4").

Tuba

The tuba is a nontransposing instrument written in the bass clef. It comes in a variety of sizes, but the most common (in the world of jazz and marching bands) is the BB♭ (B♭ contrabass tuba—although the fundamental tone is B♭, like the tenor and bass trombones, this instrument is notated in concert pitch). Technically the BB♭ tuba is capable of producing pedal from Bb-1 (the lowest B♭ on the piano) all the way down to E-1. However, for practical purposes, the low end of the tuba's range could be safely placed at F0 (Ex. 3-2A). The tuba has a full, deep tone but with a softer edge and warmer timbre than the bass trombone. It is most commonly used in a jazz context as an alternative to the bass trombone, providing a contrasting color for the low end and foundation of the brass section. The tuba can also function effectively as a solo voice in the middle to upper registers. It is also often used as the bass voice in traditional Dixieland jazz bands. The timbre of the tuba can be modified by inserting a straight mute into the bell. Many professional bass trombonists also double on tuba.

EX. 3-2A

Instrument Ranges and Transpositions: Brass

Brass:

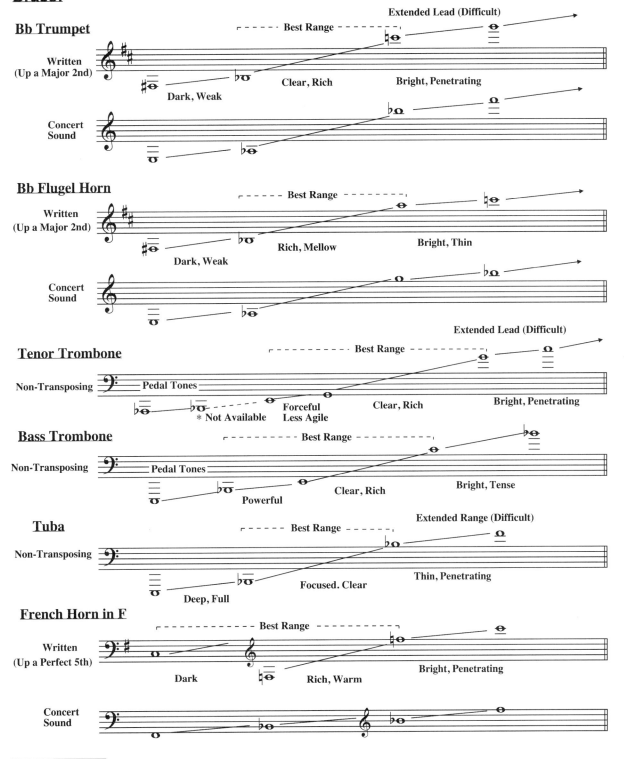

* The notes between low E and low B♭ are not available on the tenor trombone without the F extension. The pedal tones from low B♭ (B♭0) all the way down to E0 are available but are not really practical for section writing.

3-2 The Woodwind Section

In a typical jazz ensemble, the woodwind section consists primarily of soprano, alto, tenor, and baritone saxophones, with those players often doubling on various flutes and clarinets and occasionally on piccolo. Once in a while a double reed (orchestral woodwind), such as an oboe, an English horn, or a bassoon, makes an appearance, but not nearly as often as we might encounter a French horn or tuba.

Saxophones are the primary woodwind instruments in most jazz ensembles (except for Dixieland bands, which feature the clarinet). Compared to other woodwinds, they generally have a brighter timbre and a greater ability to project and blend with brass. Saxes sound good voiced in unison, octaves, close or semi-open position, open position, clusters, and of course as solo voices. The standard jazz big band saxophone section consists of two altos, two tenors, and one baritone sax.

All members of the woodwind family share certain common characteristics.

1. They have a relatively darker, warmer timbre compared with the brass family, with some overtones missing from the partial structure.[3]
2. They have a great deal of dynamic range but in general are softer, with less projecting power (with the possible exception of the piccolo), than brass instruments.
3. They have a great degree of technical facility at fast tempos, executing scalar passages and skips of larger intervals with more ease than the brass.
4. Playing most woodwinds does not require as much physical exertion as playing brass instruments. Double-reed instruments are generally more demanding than single-reed instruments and flutes. However, as an arranger/orchestrator you must still be conscious of any wind player's need to breathe, and must remember to leave space for them to rest throughout the course of an arrangement
5. All saxophones, clarinets, and flutes, including the baritone sax and bass clarinet, are written in the treble clef. Of the standard orchestral woodwinds, only the bassoon is written in bass clef (or tenor clef).
6. It's important to give woodwind jazz soloists at least 4–8 bars of rest both before and after playing an extended improvised solo, and before giving them a written ensemble part to play, for the same reasons as mentioned earlier with regard to brass players.

---

3 Even though the flute, piccolo, clarinet, and oboe can appear to have a bright, even piercing quality in the upper registers, upon analyzing the overtone structures produced by these instruments, one discovers that certain partials may be missing or sounding at different volumes when compared to brass instruments. It is the unique overtone structure and method of tone production that give each instrument of the orchestra its unique and identifiable timbre.

Ex. 3-2B

Instrument Ranges and Transpositions: Saxophones

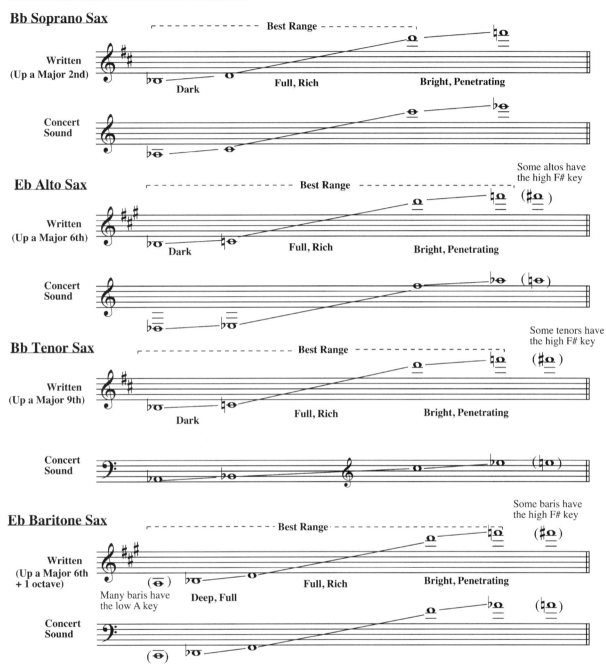

B♭ Soprano Sax

The B♭ soprano sax is a transposing instrument which sounds a whole step lower than written. The timbre of the soprano sax ranges from full and rich in the low to mid-register, to bright and penetrating in the high register. Although not an "official" member of the standard jazz big band sax section, the soprano can be used as an effective contrast to the alto as the lead voice of the sax section. It is also effective as an improvised solo voice, as popularized by the great John Coltrane.

E♭ Alto Sax

The E♭ alto sax is a transposing instrument which sounds a major sixth lower than written. The timbre of the alto sax ranges from full and rich in the low to mid-register, to bright and penetrating in the high register. Along with the tenor sax, it is the most flexible and versatile of the saxophones. The lead alto generally functions as the lead voice of the saxophone section. Many alto players also double on soprano sax, flute, clarinet, and occasionally on piccolo.

B♭ Tenor Sax

The B♭ tenor sax is a transposing instrument which sounds a major ninth lower than written. The timbre of the tenor sax ranges from full and rich in the low to mid-register, to bright and penetrating in the high register. Along with the alto sax, it is the most flexible and versatile of the saxophones. Many tenor players also double on soprano sax, flute, and clarinet.

E♭ Baritone Sax

The E♭ baritone sax is a transposing instrument which sounds an octave and a major sixth lower than written. The timbre of the baritone sax ranges from deep and full in the low register to bright and penetrating in the high register, although it can be somewhat thin and piercing in the extreme upper register. In the low register, the baritone sax provides a powerful foundation for the sax section and (along with the bass trombone) for the entire ensemble. Many baritone saxes have the low "A" key, producing a low "C" two octaves below middle C. Essential for funk and R&B (à la Tower of Power), this option often seems to be avoided by jazz purists. Many bari players also double on bass clarinet.

"C" Flute

Flutes come in a variety of sizes and register, the most common being the "C" flute. The timbre of the flute can range from clear and transparent in the low to mid-register to bright and penetrating in the high register. The flute blends well with saxes, other woodwinds, and muted brass. However, it is relatively weak in the low register and has difficulty projecting over the full band in its lower octave. As a general rule, we don't recommend scoring the flute lower than C above middle C, unless used as a solo voice (or very well miked). Flutes also sound good as a section or mixed with clarinets, saxes, or brass, voiced in unison, octaves, close position, or clusters. In the upper register (above the staff) the flute projects easily over saxes, other woodwinds, and brass. Flutes and piccolos possess a great degree of technical facility, capable of executing extremely fast scalar runs, arpeggios, repeated notes, trills, and skips of larger intervals with relative ease.

Alto Flute

The alto flute is a transposing instrument, pitched in G which sounds a perfect fourth lower than written. It has a particularly beautiful and mellow timbre, which is most effective when used as a solo voice or in a section with other flutes and clarinets. Unfortunately, this instrument has very limited projection, and generally does not blend well with saxes or open brass. It is not practical to use the alto flute in the upper register (above the staff); that range is handled much more effectively by the "C" flute.

Piccolo

The piccolo is a concert-pitched instrument which sounds an octave higher than written. Although soft and weak in the low register, the piccolo has a bright, piercing quality in the upper register, capable of projecting over an entire orchestra. The piccolo can be used quite effectively to reinforce a lead flute line by doubling it an octave higher. It can also be used to impart a happy, lighthearted feeling to an arrangement.

B♭ Clarinet

The B♭ clarinet is a transposing instrument which sounds a whole step lower than written. It has the most extensive range of any woodwind instrument. The timbre of the clarinet can range from dark and rich in the lower (chalumeau) register, to clear and bright in the upper to middle (clarino or clarion) register, to shrill and piercing in the highest (altissimo) register. As a section, clarinets sound good voiced in unison, octaves, close or semi-open position, open position, and clusters. They blend well with saxophones, other woodwinds, and brass. The clarinet can be used effectively as the lead voice over a sax section (the "Glenn Miller" sound). A striking, "orchestral" contrast to the sax section can be provided by a woodwind section, with doublers playing two flutes, two clarinets, and bass clarinet.

Like flutes, clarinets possess a great degree of technical facility, capable of executing extremely fast scalar runs, arpeggios, repeated notes, trills, and skips of larger intervals with relative ease. The only technical limitation of the clarinet is the pale, weak timbre of the "throat tone" register (written G to B♭ within the staff) and a difficulty for doublers in executing fast passages directly over the "break" between B♭ and B natural (created by the nature of the fingering system used on the clarinet).

Ex. 3-2C

Instrument Ranges and Transpositions: Woodwinds

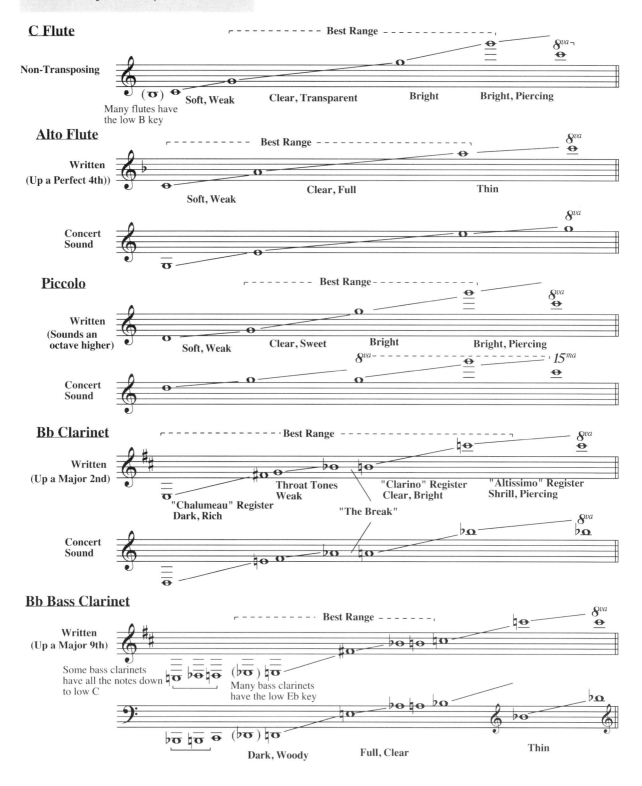

B♭ Bass Clarinet

The B♭ bass clarinet is a transposing instrument which sounds a major ninth lower than written. Technically, it is similar to the B♭ clarinet, sounding an octave lower. The timbre of the bass clarinet ranges from dark and woody in the low register, to full and clear in the mid-range, to somewhat thin and shrill in the upper register. Its most effective use in a jazz context, is as a contrast to the baritone sax for the low end of the jazz reed section. Its penetrating and unique timbre makes it also effective as a solo voice in the low to mid-register. It is not practical to use the bass clarinet in the upper register (above the staff), because that range is handled much more effectively by the B♭ clarinet.

3-3 The Rhythm Section

In a typical jazz ensemble, the rhythm section consists of acoustic piano, bass (acoustic or electric), drums, and electric guitar (optional). This can typically be modified or expanded through the use of electric piano, electric organ, synthesizers, acoustic guitars, mallet instruments (most commonly vibes or marimba), and assorted percussion instruments. More details on the specific characteristics of these instruments and on the methods of notating for them will be covered in Chapter 13.

Piano

The piano has the widest range of any acoustic instrument. Its primary functions in a jazz ensemble are to flesh out chord voicings within the rhythm section, comp behind soloists, play written or improvised melodic lines, lend rhythmic and harmonic support to horn figures, and occasionally help support bass lines through unison or octave doublings in the left hand. The piano also works in conjunction with the bass, drums, and guitar to create the fundamental jazz rhythmic pulse and feel, which forms the foundation of rhythmic drive and momentum for the entire ensemble. Although pianists will find a great deal of difference between the sound of a Bosendorfer, Steinway D, Yamaha C3, or Kawai upright, these factors seem to have little bearing on the way piano parts are conceived and written by composers or arrangers of any style.

Electric Piano/Electric Organ/Synthesizer

The most popular true electric pianos were the Fender Rhodes and the Wurlitzer. Although it's still possible to find an authentic Fender Rhodes and, to a lesser extent, Wurlitzer, in recording studios and performance venues these instruments have largely been replaced by synthesizers. This is because of the synthesizer's greater portability and its fairly realistic approximations of the original Rhodes and Wurlitzer sounds. The standard Wurlitzer EP had 64 keys, with a range from A0 to C6.[2] The Fender Rhodes came in the popular 73-key model, with a range from E0 to E6, or a full 88-key model.

The most popular synthesizer controllers today generally come with 61 keys, having a range from C1 to C6. This is similar to the standard five-octave range of the pipe organ and Hammond electric organ. Many synthesizers are also available in 76-key and 88-key models. Obviously it's important for an arranger to know the range of a particular keyboard instrument when scoring for it. There are many varieties and models of modern synthesizers, each with a unique and extensive sound palette. The contemporary synthesizer player also generally has access to an even more extensive library of sounds available as virtual instruments on a laptop computer. Synthesizer sounds can generally be grouped into 15–16 distinct categories. As an arranger, it is best to suggest the general sound quality desired (e.g., "airy pad" or "aggressive lead") and to leave the specific patch selection to the player.*

The Hammond organ is also still available, and has frequently been used effectively as a rhythm section and solo instrument in a jazz setting. However, like electric pianos, today it is generally replaced by a synthesizer, for the same reasons as mentioned earlier.

Guitar

The guitar comes in a wide variety of models, both acoustic and electric, each with a distinctive timbral quality. All guitars are concert-pitched instruments, written in the treble clef, and sounding an octave lower than written. All guitars also have the same range, basic six-string tuning (E-A-D-G-B-E, from lowest to highest), and fundamental method of tone production (plucking the strings with a pick or with the fingers). The 12-string guitar simply adds an extra string for each of the basic six. The doubled, bottom four strings of the 12-string guitar (E, A, D, G) are tuned in octaves, while the top two strings (B and E) are tuned in unisons. The electric guitar has a built-in pickup for amplification. There are a wide array of devices available for altering the timbre of the electric guitar. These include reverbs, digital delays, distortion devices, wah-wah pedals, equalizers, and amp simulators.

The skilled arranger should become familiar with the distinctive characteristics of the most common varieties of guitars, such as the acoustic 6-string nylon, steel string, and 12-string guitars, as well as the most popular models of electric guitar, such as the Fender Stratocaster and Gibson hollow-body. The acoustic and electric guitar function in a jazz ensemble in much the same way as the piano, as described earlier.

---

* Some synthesizer patches sound an octave lower or higher than played. It's up to the individual keyboard player to determine the appropriate register.

As with most stringed instruments, natural and artificial harmonics are available on acoustic and electric guitars. By placing the fingers at precise positions on the neck of the guitar, it's possible to cause certain overtones to sound, usually the second partial (one octave above the fundamental) or the fourth partial (two octaves above the fundamental), instead of the fundamental pitch. The result is a delicate and pure sound quite different from the normal guitar tone, which can be used effectively for contrast. There are several ways of notating harmonics, but the simplest is to write the actual pitch desired with a small circle above the notes indicating that they are to be played as harmonics. The method of tone production (natural or artificial) is left to the player's discretion.

Bass

The acoustic and electric bass are both concert-pitched instruments, written in the bass clef, and sounding an octave lower than written. Like guitars, all basses have similar ranges and methods of tone production, with the electric bass containing a pickup for amplification, similar to the electric guitar. The standard tuning of the four-string bass (acoustic or electric) is E-A-D-G (from lowest to highest). Some electric and acoustic basses have a fifth string, extending the range downward to low B. Some acoustic four-string basses have a *C extension*, which extends the lowest string down as far as low C, an octave below the lowest note on the cello. Less common is the six-string electric bass guitar (tuned B-E-A-D-G-C, from bottom to top).

The method of tone production for electric basses is to pluck the strings with a pick or with the fingers (as with guitars). The acoustic bass may be plucked with the fingers (pizzicato) or bowed (arco), utilizing techniques similar to those of other members of the orchestral string section. The primary functions of the bass in a jazz setting are to provide the harmonic foundation for the entire ensemble and to work in conjunction with the piano, guitar, and drums to create the fundamental jazz rhythmic pulse and feel. The bass can also be used effectively to play written or improvised melodic lines.

In a jazz group, the acoustic bass is generally played pizzicato, by plucking the strings, although the bow can also be used to produce a full arco sound for sustained notes, slow sections, or ballads. Double stops are possible, the most commonly played being those involving a perfect fourth or fifth. Natural and artificial harmonics are also available, and these can be especially effective on the electric bass. Bass harmonics are notated in a similar manner as for the guitar. The skilled arranger should become familiar with the different types of electric basses, such as fretted or fretless, as well as their various techniques for tone production (e.g., fingered, picked, and slapped).

Drum Set

The standard jazz drum set consists of a pedal bass drum, snare drum, several tom toms, pedal hi-hat cymbals, and a variety of ride and crash cymbals. The primary function of the drums is to work in conjunction with the piano, guitar, and bass to create the fundamental jazz rhythmic pulse and feel of the ensemble. The jazz drummer is also called on to support rhythmic figures played by the horns, to play drum fills in between accented figures, and to play improvised drum solos. The drummer, more than any other rhythm section player, dictates the rhythmic drive of the band and is expected to be familiar with a variety of common rhythmic styles, including straight-ahead swing, various Latin and Brazilian styles, rock, funk, and broken-time feels.

Percussion Instruments

The jazz drummer is occasionally called on to play a variety of percussion instruments, such as shakers, tambourines, cowbells, woodblocks, and triangle. It is much more desirable and effective to have a specialized percussionist play these instruments as well as others, such as the congas, bongos, timbales, and bell tree. Adding a percussionist to the jazz rhythm section can give a tremendous energetic boost to the overall rhythmic feel and provide an array of interesting rhythmic colors not available in the standard drum set.

Mallet (Pitched Percussion) Instruments

It is valuable for the jazz arranger to be aware of the sound and ranges of the various mallet instruments. The vibraphone (vibes), marimba, steel drums, xylophone, and glockenspiel have all been used on occasion in a jazz context. Many professional percussionists will be familiar with some of these instruments. The function of mallet instruments is to provide another color for highlighting melodic figures, playing written or improvised melodic lines, and (vibes and marimba) working in conjunction with the piano and guitar to flesh out the harmonic chord structure of the rhythm section.

Ex. 3-2 D

Instrument Ranges: Rhythm Section

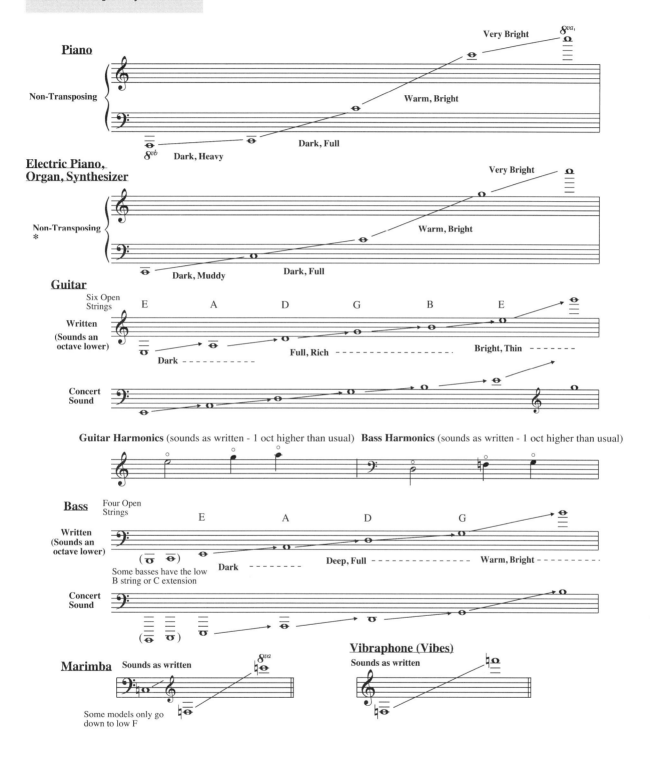

Chapter 4

Fundamental Musical Considerations

In addition to a thorough knowledge of the ranges, characteristics, and technical parameters of the instruments of a jazz ensemble, the aspiring jazz composer/arranger needs to have an understanding of some fundamental musical considerations applicable to almost all musical styles. In Chapter One of *The Contemporary Arranger*, Don Sebesky points to four basic factors "essential to the construction of a good arrangement: balance, economy, focus, and variety."* In addition, we'd like to add the concepts of tension and release, expectation and surprise, symmetry and asymmetry, and unity.

4-1 Balance

The concept of *balance* in music can be applied to any of the fundamental areas of music: melody, harmony, rhythm, form, and instrumentation (timbre). For example, when applied to vertical harmony, a well-balanced jazz big band chord voicing could be one where the chord tones are distributed in an even fashion. Normally this would place the root on the bottom, the third and the seventh of the chord in the low to mid-register, with wider intervals at the bottom and smaller intervals at the top of the voicing. Upper chord tones (ninths, elevenths, and thirteenths) and altered chord tones would normally appear in the mid- to upper register, and there would be no skips of larger than a major sixth between any two adjacent chord tones except for the bottom two voices. This sense of vertical harmonic balance is derived from the distribution of tones in the natural overtone series.

---

* Sebesky, *The Contemporary Arranger*.

When applied to form, *balance* could refer to a musical form that begins with a clear melodic or harmonic statement, develops logically to a climax about two-thirds to three-fourths of the way through the piece, and then drops in intensity to a clear recapitulation of the theme with a short coda.

4-2 Economy

Economy refers to the principle of getting your musical message across as efficiently as possible. This means eliminating anything from your score that is not absolutely essential for its optimum realization. Think of a score as an organic entity, with every note and section having significance and impact in relation to the rest. A good composer or arranger must learn to be objective about his or her work and develop the ability to edit, cut, or revise anything that's not contributing to the overall success of the score. Sometimes "Less is more."**

4-3 Focus

In most music, even in the most complex contemporary classical compositions, there are generally no more than three main areas of focus at any given time, which we refer to as *foreground*, *middleground*, and *background*. It's the arranger's or orchestrator's task to draw the listener's attention to the appropriate primary focus (foreground) at any point within the arrangement.

4-4 Contrast and Variety

The concept of *contrast and variety* in music can also be applied to any of the fundamental areas of melody, harmony, rhythm, form, and instrumentation. For example, if you score the "A" section of a tune for the saxophones, it might be a nice contrast to bring in the trombones on the bridge and the full band for the last "A" section. This would also create a well-balanced form for the instrumentation of the head. If we hear too much similarity in any area, we tend to get bored and the music loses its focus and impact.

4-5 Tension and Release

As a piece of music unfolds over time, there is always a flow of tension and release of tension related to the expression of human emotions and feelings within the music. Certain specific musical techniques serve to increase or decrease tension. For example, harmonic dissonance, deceptive cadences, increased melodic motion or skips of large intervals, crescendos, and accelerandos all tend to increase tension. Consonance, full cadences, slower melodic

---

** Sebesky "The Contemporary Arranger".

motion or stepwise motion, decrescendos, and ritardandos tend to provide a release of tension in the music.

Tension and release, expectation and surprise, and *symmetry and asymmetry* all refer to the intermingling of melody, harmony, rhythm, and instrumentation within the larger musical form. The concept of *symmetry and asymmetry* is usually applied to melodic and harmonic phrase structure; this will be examined in detail in Chapters 7 and 8. It's generally a good idea to strive for a balance between expectation and surprise and symmetrical and asymmetrical phrase structure. This way the music acquires an appropriate amount of emotional tension and release necessary for the optimum musical expression. Contrast and variety, elements of surprise, and asymmetry all can create tension within a musical composition, which must be balanced by a certain amount of release of tension. However, if the music is constantly changing, surprising, and asymmetrical, this can actually have the reverse effect. Continuous tension can become boring, turning into too much release and throwing the music out of balance. The listener is then left with nothing to hold onto, causing the music to become unfocused and dull. This brings us to the concept of *unity*.

4-6 Unity

In addition to the foregoing elements, in order for a musical composition to convey a sense of beauty and expressiveness, unifying elements must be present, enabling the listener to absorb the totality of the musical experience within a familiar frame of reference. This can be accomplished through the repetition and development of thematic, harmonic, rhythmic, and timbral elements throughout the composition.

All of these fundamental concepts (balance, economy, focus, contrast and variety, tension and release, and unity) will be examined in greater detail in later chapters in conjunction with our study of the specific musical elements of melody, harmony, rhythm, form, and instrumentation.

Chapter 5

Introduction to Music Notation Software

5-1 A Brief Historical Overview

Modern music notation software can trace its origins to research done by composers Leland Smith and John Chowning at the Stanford University Artificial Intelligence Laboratory, beginning in 1967 and continuing through the 1970s and 1980s. This research led to the development of the Score Music Publishing System by San Andreas Press, which was probably the first professional-quality computer-based music notation system.

With the advent of personal desktop computers in the early 1980s and the release of the MIDI 1.0 spec in 1982, many software developers began to explore the possibilities of perfecting a viable music notation program for the consumer market. The first commercially available product, Professional Composer, was introduced in 1984 for the Macintosh platform by Mark of the Unicorn (MOTU), which also developed the groundbreaking MIDI sequencer Performer, now Digital Performer. Some other pioneers in the development of MIDI sequencers, including Opcode (Vision—now defunct), C-Lab (Notator, the forerunner of Logic), and Steinberg (Cubase), also worked on developing music notation software. Ultimately, all of these companies opted to prioritize their MIDI sequencing software, with the eventual addition of digital audio recording functionality, choosing to incorporate basic music notation capabilities within the sequencer.

Essentially, the development of notation software parallels that of desktop publishing software, given the similarity of graphic complexities and challenges to be solved by the programmers. Some of the difficulties inherent in the development of music notation software include the large number of symbols needed (many more than in the alphabet), the problems of visually representing synchronized, polyphonic elements, the complexity of some of the specific elements of notation (e.g., cross-staff beaming, alternate notation), and the fact that music notation has a visual, aesthetic aspect that is difficult to reduce to simple algorithmic formulas.

In 1985, San Andreas released an MS-DOS–compatible version of Score for the PC. By the early 1990s, Score had been perfected to the extent that it could effectively compete with traditional music-engraving systems and began to be adopted by serious music publishers, such as Schirmer and Hal Leonard. Score dominated the music publishing industry through the 1990s and is still in widespread use today as a music-engraving tool, but it was never successfully marketed to the professional or educational music consumer community. Although it is certainly an extremely capable product, it remains virtually unused outside the music publishing industry.

The first successful consumer-oriented notation program appeared with the introduction of Finale, for the Macintosh platform, in 1988. A Windows version appeared a few years later. By 1990, with the introduction of version 2.5 for the Mac, Finale had developed into a very powerful notation program, with serious music-engraving capabilities. However, the user interface, similar to a tool-based graphics program, was fairly cumbersome, with a steep learning curve. Despite the difficult interface, Finale dominated the music notation market throughout the 1990s and into the early 2000s.

Finale's first serious competition appeared with the release of the London-based Sibelius for Windows in 1998 and for the Macintosh in 1999. (Sibelius had originally been developed for the now-defunct British Acorn computer platform in 1993.) Sibelius immediately attracted attention due to its more user-friendly interface, and it has continued to challenge Finale through the introduction of innovative features such as Linked Parts (Sibelius 5, now also available in Finale) and Magnetic Layout and Rewire capabilities (Sibelius 6). In 2006, Sibelius was purchased by Avid Technology, the leading professional video-editing manufacturer and parent company of Digidesign, maker of Pro Tools, the leading professional audio mixing/editing system.

To a great extent due to the success of their chief competitor and rival, Finale has made vast improvements in its feature set, and the user interface has become much more flexible and user friendly over the past several years. Although several impressive, competing notation programs have emerged in recent years, at the time of this writing (December 2010), the field continues to be dominated by Finale and Sibelius, now both with similar feature sets as well as comparable interfaces. For this reason, the material in this and subsequent chapters will be presented within the context of these two software platforms.

5-2 **Finale and Sibelius**

Both Finale and Sibelius are very powerful and complex programs, and it's beyond the scope of this book to offer detailed instruction on basic or advanced functions in either program. There are no "software tutorials" here (with one exception—because of its importance and the amount of confusion often surrounding this topic, some details of page layout and generating and printing parts will be covered in Chapter 15). For additional details, you'll need to consult the online Help manuals or various supporting books available for each program, such as *Mastering Sibelius 5* by Marc E. Schonbrun, *Sibelius: A Comprehensive Guide to Sibelius Music Notation Software* by Tom Rudolph and Vince Leonard, *Finale: An Easy Guide to Music Notation* by Thomas E. Rudolph, and *The Finale Projects* by Tom Carruth.

This chapter provides an outline of the basic types of software techniques you'll need to be familiar with in order to accomplish the jazz arranging goals set forth in this book. Our focus will be more on the global challenges to be confronted while engaged in the creative process of composing and arranging music using notation software and on the need to keep your perspective while doing this. All downloadable music examples will be available in several formats on the companion website. In addition, Software Tips for both formats will be provided at the end of most chapters. We'll return to some specific issues pertaining to the software in Chapter 15 and to a summary of software-related issues in Chapter 34.

Despite the fierce competition between the two companies (Finale and Sibelius) as well as the ongoing debate between the two loyal user bases, there are actually many similarities between the two interfaces, which each rely heavily on the use of keyboard/mouse shortcuts. Both programs feature two primary ways of viewing the music: "Scroll View" and "Page View" in Finale (View Menu > Scroll View or Page view, or "⌘-E" Mac or Control-E Win, to toggle between the two), which correspond to "Panorama View" and "Score View" in Sibelius (View > Panorama or "⇧-P" to toggle between the two). In each program, certain functions are more easily performed in one or the other view. Consult your program manuals for details. Finale also now offers a "Studio View," which enables you to record a live audio track along with the instrument staves, especially useful if you're doing a chart for a vocalist or an instrumental soloist.

The most basic function, note entry, can be accomplished in both programs either with the computer keyboard and mouse alone or in conjunction with a MIDI keyboard (Simple or Speedy Entry in Finale, Note Input in Sibelius) or by playing the notes to a click in real time, sequencer style (Hyperscribe in Finale, Flexi-time in Sibelius). Most Finale professionals seem to favor "Speedy Entry"; Sibelius users tend to develop a personal style of note input that combines aspects of several of the input methods.

39

Although note entry is relatively straightforward in both programs, even on this basic level there are many keyboard/mouse shortcuts that can only be learned with practice over time. For example, in Finale, pressing the * key on the numeric keypad displays or hides a courtesy accidental, and the "9" key changes the enharmonic spelling of a note in Speedy Entry. In Sibelius, pressing Return (Mac) or Enter (Windows) on the main keypad toggles the spelling of a note. For courtesy accidentals, use the Sibelius (fifth) Keypad window and select the parenthesis symbol. This accounts for some of the resistance to switching programs on the part of users who have mastered one platform. If you've spent a fair amount of time becoming proficient in learning the shortcuts and tricks on one platform, why switch and go through the learning curve all over again?

As previously stated, the focus of this book is on the musical techniques needed for writing music for large and small jazz ensembles and on using music notation and sequencing software as tools for achieving this goal. Both Finale and Sibelius provide excellent functionality for accomplishing this creative goal as well as the means for printing professional-looking scores and parts.

◊ **A note on writing about technology and software, and some general advice:** The rate of technological development has progressed to a dizzying pace in recent years. Both Finale and Sibelius seem to be coming out with major upgrades once a year, sometimes with changes to the look of the interface as well as important new feature sets and software shortcuts. In order to avoid the necessity of a new edition of our book every year to keep pace with this change, we will be presenting primarily general concepts in the print version of the book and only those software procedures that have become firmly entrenched in the various interfaces. More detailed and easily updatable software tips will be presented on the companion website, which will be updated every 6–12 months. As with most Mac and PC software, keyboard/mouse shortcuts are displayed on the right side of the pull-down menus in both programs.

You should also prioritize becoming familiar with using the online Help functions, which are quite powerful in both programs. Join the user groups of either platform. Many problems and questions can be solved in the online forums. Finally—keep that tech support hotline phone number handy, and don't hesitate to use it. There will be times when you will need it!

5-3 Music Notation Software Basics

Following is a list of some of the basic notation techniques necessary for creating music scores and parts in any style and where to find them in Finale (2010/11) or Sibelius (6).

◊ **Please Note:** In general, for the following techniques (and in the Software Tips throughout the book), the Command key on a Mac (⌘) is equivalent to the Control key on Windows, the Option key on a Mac is equivalent to the Alt key on Windows, and control-clicking on a Mac is the same as right-clicking on a PC, in both Finale and Sibelius.

1. *Start a New Score*: Both Finale and Sibelius provide easy methods for creating a new score from a large selection of templates (referred to as Manuscript Papers in Sibelius) provided with the software. It's also important to know how to create and customize your own templates for future use. Use "Setup Wizard" in Finale, and File Menu > New in Sibelius ("Start a New Score"). Once you've created your own templates, you no longer need to use the "Setup Wizard" or "Start a New Score."

2. *Program and Document Preferences*: Both Finale and Sibelius provide the ability to choose from a variety of available music and text fonts as well as setting preferences for the positioning of various music symbols, such as clefs, key and time signatures, note flags and beaming, accidentals, rests and multimeasure rests, and grace notes. It's also possible to set preferences for how the score appears while you're working on it, including the ability to zoom in and out. Use Finale Menu > Preferences (Mac) > or Edit Menu (Win) > Program or Document Options, and the View Menu in Finale. Use Sibelius Menu > Preferences, and the magnifying glass (Zoom) tool in Sibelius.

3. *Note Entry*: In addition to being able to enter notes at the correct pitch and rhythmic value, it's essential to know how to change the enharmonic spelling of a note, add courtesy accidentals, adjust the beaming of eighth and sixteenth notes, change the stem direction of notes on a staff, create tuplets, and change the value of rests where needed (e.g., from two eighth rests to one quarter rest). In Finale, use "Simple or Speedy Entry" for most basic note entry functions. Use "Layers" 1–4 to create up to four independent polyphonic lines on any staff. Use the Tuplet Tool for creating and adjusting the appearance of any type of tuplet. In Sibelius use the "Keypad" window (actually a multilayered tool palette referred to as "Keypad 1-5") to access all rhythmic values. Use the third keypad to break and group beams into nonstandard groups. The equivalent of Finale's "Layers" in Sibelius is "Voices," and they function in a similar manner. To create tuplets in Sibelius, choose Tuplets from the Create menu.

4. *Key Signatures*: To indicate the beginning key signature of a piece as well as to *modulate*, or change to a different key at any point within the piece, use the Key Signature Tool in Finale, and press "K" in Sibelius (Create > Key Signature).

5. *Time Signatures*: To indicate the beginning time signature of a piece as well as to change meter at any point within the piece, use the

Time Signature Tool in Finale, and press "T" in Sibelius (Create > Time Signature).

6. *Clefs*: To indicate the beginning clef of any staff, use the Staff Tool > Staff Attributes > Select First Clef in Finale, and House Style > Edit Instruments > Edit Instrument > Notation Options in Sibelius. To change clefs on any staff at any point within the piece, use the Clef Tool in Finale, and press "Q" in Sibelius (Create > Clef).

7. *Staves and Staff Attributes*: To add or delete staves from a score as well as to name a staff, assign a transposition (if it's for a transposing instrument), determine what musical elements will be displayed or hidden on any staff (e.g., measure numbers, staff name, chords), designate alternate notation (e.g., for percussion or guitar parts), and create staff groups (for instrumental sections, such as saxes, trumpets), use the Staff Tool and Staff Attributes dialogue box in Finale. In Sibelius, press the "I" key to open the Instruments dialogue box, where you can add, delete, or change the order of instruments in a score. Instrument transpositions are applied automatically when you add instruments to a score in Sibelius. Elements within the staves can be displayed or hidden in the Properties window.

8. *Instrumental Doubles and Transpositions*: It's also essential to know how to change the transposition on a given staff in the event that an instrumental double is called for and how to indicate the change (e.g., switching from E♭ alto sax to flute) at any point within a piece. This is accomplished by using Staff Styles from the Staff Menu in Finale, and Create > Other > Instrument Change in Sibelius.

9. *Copy-and-Paste Editing*: To perform basic cut, copy, and paste editing functions, similar to those in a word processor, including accessing the Edit Filter (Edit Menu > Edit Filter or ⇧-opt-⌘-F in Finale), and to perform music-specific editing operations such as Transpose and "Explode" or "Implode" Music (see the Chapter 9 Software Tip), in Finale use the Selection Tool and Edit menu. Use the Utilities menu for Transpose, Explode Music, and Implode Music. All of the Copy and Paste functions in Sibelius are found in the Edit menu. Use the *Simple Filter* (Edit > Filter) or the *Advanced Filter* (Edit > Filter > Advanced Filter) to select specific items to be edited. Music-specific editing functions in Sibelius, such as Transpose and Explode Music, are found in the Notes menu.

10. *Music Spacing and Page Layout*: It's absolutely essential to know how to properly adjust the music spacing, measure width, number of measures per system, number of systems per page, distance between staves (for multistave systems in a score), distance between systems, page size and orientation (portrait or landscape), as well as page and system margins so that the music is clearly legible. Although the default

settings in both programs will space the music automatically, it can sometimes be advantageous to turn off that function and space the music manually.

In Finale, use Fit Measures, Music Spacing, and Update Layout from the Utilities menu for all basic music-spacing functions. Go to Finale Menu > Preferences (Mac) > or Edit Menu (Win) > Program Options > Edit, and uncheck "Automatic Update Layout" and "Automatic Music Spacing." Use the Measure Tool to adjust measure widths, if necessary, to fine-tune the appearance of the music *after* applying the music-spacing commands. (Applying "Update Layout" to a region will undo any manual adjustments you've made to measure width using the Measure Tool.) Use the Staff Tool to adjust the distance between staves in a score. Use the Page Layout Tool for adjusting the distance between systems, number of systems per page, page size and orientation and to adjust page and system margins and all other page layout issues.

Much of the music-spacing issues you might encounter in previous versions of Sibelius are eliminated in version 6 with the addition of the "Magnetic Layout" feature, a customizable set of collision management functions. Go to Layout > Magnetic Layout Options to adjust these settings, or uncheck Magnetic Layout to turn it off. Use Layout > Break and Layout > Format to adjust the number of measures on each system or the number of systems per page. If you find there is just too much on the page, go to Layout > Document Setup to increase or decrease margin widths.

◊ **Important**! When changing the page orientation from portrait to landscape, or vice versa, in both Finale and Sibelius it's necessary to change the page orientation in "Page Setup" from the "File Menu" as well as in the "Page Layout Menu" (Finale) or File > Page Setup (Sibelius). If you don't change the orientation in both places, it won't work! In Finale there is a Preference which enables you to avoid this extra step. Go to Finale Menu > Program Options > Save and Print, and check the box next to "Use Finale's Page Orientation Instead of the Printer's Page Orientation." (The only other exception to this rule is if you have a wide-format printer and want to print two 8-½ x 11 pages on 11 x 17 tabloid size paper.) For more details on music spacing and layouts, refer to Chapter 15.

11. *Dynamics, Expressions, Articulations*: To add and position dynamic expressions of any type, including slurs, hairpin crescendos, and all articulation markings, in Finale use the Expression Tool for text expressions (e.g., *p*, *mp*, *f*, *cresc.*, *ritardando*, mutes, indications of tempo and feel). Select the Expression Tool and double-click anywhere to open the Expression Selection dialogue box to select an existing

expression or create a new one. From within the Expression Selection dialogue box, take advantage of Finale's "Assign" and "Edit Categories" functions for determining which staves in a score and which parts the expressions will appear on (especially useful for rehearsal letters and tempo changes). In the revamped Expression Tool (Finale 2009), any marking in the Tempo Marks, Tempo Alterations, and Rehearsal Marks categories will now do the following:

- Automatically appear in the top staff of your score only (or in larger scores, on the top staff and once again halfway down your score page).
- Automatically appear in all of the parts.

(You can change these settings by clicking on the Edit Categories Button and setting up a new Score List.)

With the other expression categories (Show All, Dynamics, Expressive Text, Technique Text, and Misc.), expressions appear only in the staff or staves to which you assign them by double-clicking on a staff or by using the Assign To Staves option (lower right corner of the Expression Selection dialogue box).

Finale 2010 also now has automatic rehearsal letters. Using the Expression Tool, hold down *Metatool* (see the "Tip" at the end of this section for a definition of *Metatool*) "M" (or "A" for a handwritten or jazz font template), and click in a measure to enter an automatic rehearsal letter attached to that measure. (They will start with letter "A" and will automatically be sequenced correctly and automatically update if you delete one.) If you prefer to have sequential numbers or measure numbers for your rehearsal marks, double-click on the measure where you want the rehearsal marks to begin. In the Rehearsal Marks category, select the default rehearsal letters (or create a new one), and click the Edit button to change the look, font size, and/or enclosure shape. Uncheck "Use Rehearsal Marks Category Fonts" to change the font and/or font size. Select from the available "Use Auto-Sequencing Style" drop-down menu options.

Use the Smart Shape Tool for slurs, hairpins, brackets, and similar symbols. Select the desired shape from the Smart Shape Palette, and double-click and drag anywhere to insert the shape. Use the Articulation Tool for accents, staccato, tenuto, fermatas, and all other articulations. Click on a note to open the Articulation Selection dialogue box, or use one of the many predefined shortcuts ("a"-click for accent, "s"-click for staccato, etc.). You can also create your own shortcuts, or *Metatools* (consult the online Help).

In Sibelius (as in Finale), expressions and shapes must always be "attached" to a note or rest (although the note or rest can be hidden if you don't want it to appear on the score). Select the note or rest first, then go to Create > Text > Expression) for text expressions that appear under a note or to Create > Text > Technique for technique text that appears above a note. Click where you want the expression or technique to appear. Control-click on the blinking cursor to open a drop-down menu of available expressions, or you can simply type in the text. All of the text commands to which Sibelius will respond are listed in the Dictionary (Play > Dictionary).

12. *Chord Symbols*: To add chord symbols to a rhythm section part or jazz soloist part, use the Chord Tool in Finale, and Create > Chord Symbol in Sibelius.

13. *Alternate Notation*: To apply slash or rhythmic notation to rhythm section parts or other parts playing chord changes, percussion notation to percussion parts, one- and two-bar repeat signs, etc., use Staff Styles from the Staff Menu in Finale, and the Notes area of the Properties window in Sibelius.

14. *Measure Attributes*: To add, insert, or delete measures, create double or final bar lines, or assign and edit measure numbers, use the Measure Tool in Finale. The Selection Tool may also be used for adding, inserting, or deleting measures. Using the Selection Tool, double-click on any measure to select a "Measure Stack" (Shift-click to select more than one measure). Control click or right-click anywhere in the selected region to open a contextual menu where you can select "Insert Measure Stack" or "Delete Measure Stack."

    In Sibelius, measures can be added or inserted by using the Create menu, Create > Bars. To delete existing measures in Sibelius, Control-click (Windows) or ⌘-click (Mac) in a bar to select a measure stack, and then press Delete on your keyboard. Measure numbers in Sibelius are generally controlled in House Style > Engraving Rules.

15. *Repeats*: To create repeat signs, including 1st and 2nd endings, segnos, and coda signs, use the Repeat Tool in Finale. In Sibelius, use the Create menu, Create > Barlines to select beginning or ending repeat bar lines. Use Create > Lines ("L") to open the Lines dialogue box to select 1st and 2nd endings, etc.

16. *Page, Staff, and Note Resizing*: To resize a page, staff, or individual notes, use the Resize Tool in Finale. This can also be accomplished in the Page Layout Menu > Resize Page or Resize Staff System. In Sibelius, resize pages using Layout > Document Setup, and resize individual elements, such as notes, using either the Properties window or the House Style > Engraving Rules settings.

17. *Text Blocks and Lyrics*: To add text blocks of any type in Finale, use the Text Tool. You may also use the Expression Tool for this purpose, especially if it's relatively short text that's going to be repeated throughout a

45

piece (e.g., "Solo Break," "Play Backgrounds 2nd X Only") For titles, composer name, page numbers, etc., use File Info from the File menu and "Inserts" from the Text Tool menu. For lyrics, use the Lyric Tool.

Almost all text in Sibelius, including title, composer name, and lyrics, is created by using the Create > Text menus. See #11 above for details regarding text expressions. For rehearsal letters, use Create > Rehearsal Mark (⌘-R/Mac or Control-R/Win), and click where you want the symbol to appear. Sibelius numbers pages automatically following default engraving rules. To change the appearance of a page number, go to Create > Other > Page Number Change. To edit various default text settings, use the House Styles menu, House Styles > Engraving Rules, Edit All Fonts, Edit Text Styles, Default Positions, etc.

18. *Special Functions*: For specialized, detailed editing, such as adjusting stem length, beam angle and height, and repositioning of accidentals, use the Special Tools Tool in Finale. For similar functions in Sibelius, use House Style > Engraving Rules.

19. *Generating and Printing Parts*: Until fairly recently, in both Finale and Sibelius, parts were extracted from scores as separate files. This meant that if a change was made on a part, it would have to be manually duplicated on the score in order to keep the score and parts compatible, making file management extremely cumbersome. It also meant that many part layout edits would have to be duplicated for each extracted part, although time could be saved by doing the layouts for an entire section where the layouts would be similar. Another option, still favored by many professional copyists, is to create separate part templates for each instrument of an ensemble and then to copy and paste individual staves from the score into the part template. However, this still leaves you with the necessity of duplicating changes made to parts or scores in order to keep them compatible.

All of this was revolutionized a few years ago with the introduction of Dynamic Parts in Sibelius 4, which was followed shortly by "Linked Parts" in Finale 2007. It's now possible to generate parts from a score and to print everything out while keeping everything within the same file. This means that a change made on a part will automatically be reflected in the score, and vice versa.

There are still some glitches to watch out for that may require manual adjustment of certain items on individual parts (e.g., with text blocks and measure numbers in Finale or with text placement in Sibelius), but in general it's a huge improvement over the previous system. In both programs, you still have the option of extracting parts as separate files by going to File > Extract Parts (Finale), or Parts Window > Extract Parts (Sibelius). To print the score or parts in either program, simply go to File > Print, and select which elements you want to print.

◊ For more detailed instructions on page layouts, music spacing, and printing parts and scores, refer to Chapter 15.

◊ Many of the Tool-based techniques just listed for Finale are also now accessible from the Selection Tool Contextual Menus by Control- or right-clicking on a measure and selecting from the drop-down (contextual) menu. It's also possible to access certain tools (from the Selection Tool) by simply clicking on a particular symbol (e.g., click on a clef to access the Clef Tool, click on a chord symbol to access the Chord Tool, etc.). Click on the Escape key to return to the Selection Tool at any time.

◊ "Metatools" in Finale are "macros," or keyboard short cuts for mouse, menu, and dialog box actions that can dramatically speed things up and enable you to enter certain markings very quickly. Up to 36 metatools can be programmed for the following items: Articulations, Chord Symbols, Expressions, Key Signatures, Time Signatures, Selection, Repeats, and Tuplets.

5-4 MIDI Playback and Editing

Both Finale and Sibelius provide easy, straightforward capabilities for MIDI playback of scores. In both programs, the playback controls resemble those of a traditional tape recorder, similar to any MIDI sequencer. In fact, the playback functions of both programs are MIDI sequencers, incorporated into the notation software. When you hit Play, the notes send *Note On* messages at the appropriate pitch and attack velocity. *Note Off* messages are sent at the end of the note durations. Dynamic markings such as *p, f, and cresc* and hairpins generate *controller 7* data, or changes in attack velocity, affecting the volume of the sound generated; and markings such as "cup mute," "open," "flute," and "alto sax" send MIDI *Program Change* messages or *"Key Switches"* (a newer variation on program changes). Refer to Sections 2-2 and 2-3 for more details on MIDI messages.

Both programs also now come bundled with fairly respectable sample libraries (Finale with Garritan Instruments for Finale, using the Garritan Aria Player, and Sibelius with Sibelius Sound Essentials, utilizing the Native Instruments Kontakt Player). Both programs also provide the ability to access additional third-party virtual instruments, such as Native Instruments Kontakt 4 (the complete sample player, *not* the same as the scaled-down "Kontakt Player"), the VSL Ensemble, and EastWest Play. Although it's possible to work quite effectively using the factory sounds provided, MIDI playback can be significantly enhanced by adding one or more of the available third-party instruments, which come with much larger sample libraries of superior quality and with a greater variety of instruments and instrumental inflections and articulations.

Finale has a "MIDI/Audio" menu, which allows you to select whether Finale will play back using internal sounds ("Play Finale Through Audio Units"—Mac, or VST—Windows) or external sounds ("Play Finale Through MIDI"). In either case, you will need to tell Finale which MIDI instruments or VIs you have available in the MIDI/Audio menu > Device Setup window, and assign the staves of your score to the appropriate instruments in the Instrument List window, accessible either from the MIDI/Audio menu or the Window menu.

Also available from the MIDI/Audio menu are MIDI/Audio interface options (if you're using an external MIDI interface or audio card/interface), MIDI Thru options ("Smart" or "Fixed Channel" are the most useful), and, of course, the all-important "All Notes Off" command. You will also need to set the tempo and deal with any tempo changes that occur throughout the piece. Tempo changes can now easily be attached to Text Expressions in Finale. Just double-click on any text expression. When the Expression Selection dialogue box opens, click on Edit, select the Playback tab, and choose the desired effect from the drop-down menu. There is also a separate Tempo Tool for handling tempo changes in a more detailed manner. Detailed tempo changes can also be accomplished with the MIDI Tool in Finale.

In Sibelius, MIDI playback instrument sounds are assigned by going to Play > Playback Devices, which opens the Playback Devices dialogue box. Clicking on the Configuration tab allows you to select from a list of preset *configurations* (either factory presets or ones you create) that will address *sound sets*. For example, a full installation of Sibelius 6 includes a configuration called "Sibelius Essentials, 16 sounds (Kontakt)." This configuration will initialize the Kontakt player to play back up to 16 channels of sounds, and those sounds will be from the Sibelius Essentials set. When Sibelius starts, it scans for newly installed sound sets, so if you create a new sound set, make sure that you quit and restart Sibelius. All available virtual instruments and MIDI devices will appear in the list at the left of the Playback Devices window. You can create custom configurations by initializing new devices (select them from the list and click "Activate") or by de-initializing devices you don't want to use. If you create a new configuration, be sure to save it with a new name.

Both Finale and Sibelius also offer a variety of options for improving the feel of MIDI playback, which can tend to sound stiff and mechanical. To make playback sound more "human" and expressive in Finale, open the Playback Controls window from the Windows menu, and click on the arrow in the lower left corner of the Playback Controls window (Mac), or double-click on the Playback Controls speaker icon (Win) to access the "Human Playback" styles, "Human Playback Preferences," and "Playback/Record" options. Here you can choose from a variety of preset styles or, for greater control, select a percentage of "Swing Feel" (see Sections 6-1 and 6-3 for a detailed explanation of Swing Feel), and select preferences for how Finale MIDI playback will respond to specific expressions and articulations.

In Sibelius, similar settings can be accessed in several places. Use Play > Transform Live Playback to make general adjustments to velocities and timings in relation to how they were recorded from your MIDI instrument in Flexi-time recording. Use Play > Performance to adjust stylistic elements such as swing feel and reverb on playback. Finally, in Sibelius 6 you can use "Live Tempo" to record a tempo track in real time and attach it to the score, allowing for extremely variable and more realistic tempo changes during playback. See the Sibelius 6 manual or online Help for step-by-step directions on the use of this function.

Finale also has a MIDI Tool, which provides access to detailed editing of note durations, attack velocities, continuous data (control changes such as controller 7 volume, controller 1 modulation, pitch bend, and channel pressure), program changes, and tempo changes. The Tempo Tool may also be used for handling detailed editing of tempo changes. MIDI parameters in Sibelius are generally handled through musical markings. However, fine details can be adjusted in the Mixer window (press "M" to open this window). Attack Velocities can be displayed and edited by going to View > Live Playback Velocities. You can adjust these individually, or you can go to Play > Transform Live Playback to change MIDI velocities globally. This type of detailed MIDI editing is generally necessary if you want to create a more musical, expressive MIDI demo of the music.

Unfortunately, the MIDI editing capabilities in both Finale and Sibelius are still (as of December, 2010) relatively cumbersome compared to those in a dedicated sequencer such as Digital Performer, Logic, or Cubase. Although both Finale and Sibelius have mixing boards, which do a fairly good job of recording MIDI volume (controller 7), what's missing is a MIDI Graphic Editor, available in all professional sequencers. This type of window gives you much greater control, not only of controller 7 and velocities, but of many other types of MIDI continuous data that can be used to add expression to a MIDI performance. It's also much easier to adjust note durations and articulations in a Graphic Editor window. For that reason, if you really need a good sounding MIDI mockup of the score, it's highly recommended that you do that work in the sequencer, *not* in the notation program.

It's easy to transfer files from one program to another as *Standard MIDI Files* (File Menu > Save As > Format—MIDI File in Finale, and File Menu > Export > MIDI File in Sibelius). However, this is not an ideal situation, since it requires you to do some of the work twice. There are also some specific issues that need to be carefully managed when exporting MIDI files from a sequencer or notation program. We'll provide more details on this topic in Chapters 15 and 34.

All of this may soon become moot due to a recent breakthrough in Sibelius 6 (2009), which enables Sibelius to function in *"Rewire"* mode concurrently with a sequencer of your choice. Rewire is a function that allows two or more MIDI applications to be open and to interact with each other simultaneously on

49

the same computer. This could potentially provide us with the best of both worlds, enabling you to do detailed, expressive MIDI editing in the sequencer and detailed notation editing in the notation program at the same time. Also, since the purchase of Protools and Sibelius by Avid, Sibelius has been incorporated as the notation window in the Protools sequencer. This gives the user the ability to do the type of editing described above, if you choose to do all of the work in Protools. However, at the time of this writing, the MIDI functionality in Protools still leaves something to be desired, and there are still some glitches in the notation implementation that need to be worked out.

5-5 Music Preparation Basics

In order to ensure the maximum legibility of computer-generated parts and scores, it's important for anyone working with a notation program to be familiar with certain conventions normally used by professional music copyists and engravers. As stated previously, a detailed study of music preparation is beyond the scope of this book. For additional information on this topic, we recommend *The Art of Music Copying* by Clinton Roemer (1984, currently out of print, but used copies are available on Amazon.com), *The Essential Dictionary of Music Notation* by Tom Gerou (1996), *The Norton Manual of Music Notation* by George Heussenstamm (1987), *Teach Yourself the Art of Music Engraving and Processing* by Ted Ross (1987), or *Music Notation—Preparing Scores and Parts* by Matthew Nicholl and Richard Grudzinski (2007).

Understanding the following basic conventions and using them consistently will not only make your scores and parts look more professional but will definitely save a lot of time (and eye strain) and result in more accurate readings of your music at rehearsals, performances, and recording sessions.

1. *Score Layout*: Jazz big band scores with fewer than 20 staves, as well as scores for smaller ensembles, are almost always formatted in *landscape orientation*, ideally with eight measures per score page whenever possible. Orchestral scores with more than 20 staves should be formatted in *portrait orientation*, with four measures per page. Scores, whether in portrait or landscape orientation, should be printed on both sides of the page so that they can be bound "book style" on the left edge. Scores may be printed on 8½ x 11–size paper, but for performances, we recommend the larger, legal size (8½ x 14) or tabloid size (11 x 17).

2. *Score Staff Arrangement*: With jazz scores for six or more horns, including standard jazz big band, put the saxes (reeds) on top, then the trumpets, then trombones, with the rhythm section on the bottom (refer to the various Templates provided in the chapter 5 "Resources" section on the companion website). With ensembles of two to five horns, it's OK to put the trumpets on top and arrange the other instruments in order of register, with alto and tenor saxes in the middle

and trombone or baritone sax below. The rhythm section staves should still be on the bottom of the score (refer to the Template examples on the website).

3. *Parts Layout*: Parts should *always* be in *portrait orientation,* with four measures per system when possible. Generally there should be 8–10 systems per page, depending on the page size. When preparing parts, it's very important to make sure that page turns are manageable for each player. Ideally, page turns should be preceded by or followed by at least one or two measures of rest. Sometimes this will mean putting only four or five systems on a page instead of eight. Parts pages should *always* be taped so that the parts open "accordion style," to avoid having pages fly off the music stands. Each part page should clearly display the *page number, part name,* and *composition name* in the page header. Part pages may be printed on standard 8½ x 11 letter-size paper.

4. *Number the Measures*

   a. Number every measure of the score in a large font size below the bottom (drum) staff. With larger ensembles (big bands, orchestral scores), also display measure numbers in the middle of the score (e.g., between the saxes and trumpets or between the trumpets and trombones), and leave a little extra space between staves to do this.

   b. Number the first measure of each system with a smaller font size for the parts.

5. *Use Rehearsal Letters* (A, B, C, D, etc.—generally enclosed in square boxes) to indicate the beginnings of important musical sections (e.g., the head, bridge, first solo, soli section). Measure numbers enclosed in a square box may be used instead of rehearsal letters (e.g., "17" instead of "A," "65" instead of "B"). Rehearsal letters (or measure numbers), in a large font size, should be placed above the top score staff or above the part staff at the beginning of the new section. It's advisable to display rehearsal letters *not* on every staff of the score but only on the top staff or top staff of each section to avoid a cluttered appearance. Coda signs, segnos, and some other global expressions, such as indications of tempo and style, should also be displayed only on the top staff or the top staff of each section to avoid clutter.

6. *Alignment*: Whenever possible, have the beginnings of important sections, double bar lines, rehearsal letters, and repeat signs align with the left and right margins of score pages and with the left and right margins of part systems. In other words, if you have a six-bar intro, you might consider making that the first score page (consisting of only six bars) and starting page 2 with letter "A," rather than starting "A" as bar 7 of the first page. Similarly, if you have an extra two bars at the end of the head, you might consider putting 10 bars on that page so that the first bar

of the next section aligns with the left margin. Some of these types of decisions depend on how many notes are in each measure. With fewer notes, it's easier to squeeze more measures onto a page or system.

7. *Courtesy Accidentals*: The use of courtesy accidentals can be somewhat subjective, but we believe it's always better to err on the side of too many rather than too few. One generally universal rule, if there's an accidental (e.g., an A♭ in the key of C major) in one measure followed by the natural note in the next measure (e.g., A natural), is *always* to insert a courtesy accidental (even though technically the bar line cancels the A♭). Similarly, if you have a string of A♭s (in C major) spread over several bars followed by an A natural several bars later, we still recommend inserting the courtesy A natural.

8. *Parts and Score Layout Consistency*: All measure numbers, rehearsal letters, repeat signs, segnos, and coda signs (the "road map") *must* be the same for *all* parts and the score!

The underlying principle behind all of this is to make the music as legible and easy to read as possible. If there's an especially notey section, you might limit the part system to three or even two measures instead of four. Whatever you do, don't try to save paper by squeezing too many bars onto a score page or part system. Following these basic rules will ensure smooth and efficient rehearsals and performances of your music.

◊ **A Note About Concert vs. Transposed Scores:** There is an ongoing controversy among jazz, pop, classical, and film and TV composers and arrangers about the relative merits of concert vs. transposed scores. A *concert score* displays the notes of transposing instruments at the pitches actually sounding, whereas a *transposed score* displays the notes as they would appear in the individual parts. The chief disadvantage of a concert score is that it forces you to put the low saxophones in the bass clef or to use many ledger lines, which can be very confusing to a conductor reading the score. It can also lead you to make mistakes regarding the actual ranges of the instruments and the relative tessitura of the parts.

On the other hand, it certainly can be much easier for the beginner, or even the seasoned arranger, to interpret the vertical harmonies with a concert score. That obstacle can be overcome fairly easily with a little practice. In fact, using almost any music notation program begs the question, since it's possible to compose in concert and then change to transposed format with a few clicks of the mouse. However, we believe there are significant advantages to working in a transposed score, and we recommend that the aspiring jazz composer/arranger make an effort to compose and read scores in this format. If you get to a particularly harmonically complex section, you can always turn off the transposed staves momentarily or do a concert sketch of the section. It's not cheating!

Chapter Summary

This chapter presented a basic introduction to music notation software, beginning with a brief historical overview, followed by a comparison of the two currently leading programs in use, Finale and Sibelius. We provided an outline of basic notation techniques necessary for creating music scores and parts in either software platform. We also examined some important features regarding MIDI playback and editing in both Finale and Sibelius. Finally, we outlined some basic principles of music preparation essential to creating professional-looking and legible scores and parts.

Arranging for Small Ensemble (3–6 Horns + Rhythm Section)

Overview of Small Ensemble Writing

Rhythm and Rhythmic Notation/Preparing the Score

We'll begin our study of jazz composition and arranging by examining arranging techniques for the small jazz ensemble, first with 3–4 horns + rhythm, and then with 5–6 horns + rhythm. In many ways the small jazz ensemble has served as a source of innovation and creativity for jazz over the years, from Louis Armstrong's Hot 5 and Hot 7 to the quintets and sextets of Charlie Parker, Miles Davis, Art Blakey, Horace Silver, and numerous others on up to the present day.

◊ Starting with the smaller group of 3–4 horns, followed by 5–6 horns later in this section, allows us to focus more carefully on some of the musical fundamentals common to writing for ensembles of any size. So, although most of these techniques will be illustrated first within the context of the smaller ensemble, this does not mean their application is in any way restricted to the small ensemble. These fundamental principles will be reviewed and, with some simple modifications, easily applied to the larger ensembles covered in Section Three. We've found it especially useful to end this section with the 5- to 6-horn ensemble, which can be approached as a "small" big band, in preparation for writing for the larger ensemble.

6-1 Jazz Rhythm Basics

Rhythm is possibly the most fundamental aspect of music. It is also the distinctive approach to elements of rhythm that form some of the most essential defining aspects of jazz. Without a proper understanding and appreciation of the unique qualities of jazz rhythm, it would be impossible for anyone to write an effective and convincing jazz composition or arrangement.

Rhythm plays a defining role in jazz in four distinct ways.

1. Jazz has a unique, underlying rhythmic pulse, usually provided by drums, percussion, and the other rhythm section instruments.

2. There is a particular emphasis in jazz on certain types of rhythmic syncopation as applied to melody, harmony, and the rhythmic pulse. This quality of jazz can be traced all the way back to the jazz of the early 20th century, to the 19th century African American precursors to jazz, and to its origins in the indigenous music of West Africa. This emphasis on syncopation has evolved into a kind of rhythmic lexicon not found in Western classical music, although some contemporary classical composers have certainly borrowed from these jazz rhythmic elements (Copland, Stravinsky, Bartok, and Adams, to name a few).

3. There is a unique, jazz interpretation of eighth and sixteenth notes known as *swing feel*. In the case of eighth notes, this involves delaying every second eighth note in a melodic passage so that its placement occurs somewhere in between the mathematically correct ("legitimate") eighth note and the third triplet in a group of eighth-note triplets. In the case of sixteenth notes, this same principle would be applied to every second and fourth sixteenth note. In general, more of a "triplet" feel will suggest an older style of jazz (from the 1920s and '30s), and more of an "even-eighth-note" feel will suggest a more modern style (beginning with the 1960s and '70s). However, the exact placement of the "swung" eighth note is a personal matter determined by the individual player, writer, or conductor. In fact, it is one of the unique expressive techniques available to any jazz performer.

4. There is a rhythm to the motion of the harmony or chord changes; this is referred to as *harmonic rhythm*.

6-2 Rhythmic Pulse and Style

There are many rhythmic styles available to the jazz composer/arranger and rhythm section players. These can range from a medium-tempo, straight-ahead swing feel, to a burning funk-fusion groove, to a mellow bossa nova or jazz waltz. The sources for these various rhythmic styles originate in such diverse locations as western and eastern Europe, Africa, the West Indies, India, the Middle East, Asia, and Latin American countries, including Brazil. The contemporary jazz arranger should be familiar with the most common types of rhythmic styles or grooves, in various meters and tempos, including:

1. Straight-ahead jazz swing
2. Jazz waltz

3. Jazz ballad
4. Modern, even-eighth-note "broken time" feel
5. Funk/fusion
6. Rhythm and blues (R&B)
7. Rock/pop
8. Hip-hop, drum and bass, trance, techno, etc.
9. Various "Latin" styles, such as salsa, cha-cha, and mambo
10. Various "Brazilian" styles, such as bossa nova and samba

There are many more possibilities, including combinations of two or more different styles. It's also important for the jazz arranger to understand the subtle differences between various types of swing feel, such as the difference between a groove played by Art Blakey, Max Roach, Tony Williams, or Elvin Jones. In fact it can be useful to make reference to a particular drummer when indicating the desired rhythmic feel on a drum part (e.g., "Philly Joe Jones" swing feel). Not only does knowledge of many types of rhythmic styles give the jazz arranger a wider rhythmic palette to choose from, but very often an arranger may be called on to write an arrangement of a standard tune in a particular style, for example, "Autumn Leaves" as a samba. Of course the best way to acquire this familiarity is to listen to as much music in as many different styles as possible. So—there's your first assignment. Please continue this exercise for the rest of your life!

6-3 Jazz Syncopation and Notation (Melodic Rhythm)

According to the *Concise Oxford Dictionary of Music*, syncopation "is achieved by accenting a weak instead of a strong beat, by putting rests on strong beats, by holding on over strong beats, etc."* In jazz there is a definite propensity to accent the *upbeat* (beats 2 and 4 in 4/4 meter or the second eighth note of a beat), as opposed to the *downbeat* (beats 1 and 3 in 4/4 or the first eighth note of a beat). Applying the principles of *balance* and *contrast and variety* from Chapter 4, you should be careful not to use too much syncopation. Sometimes, after a long string of syncopated eighth notes, landing with a strong accent on "1" can be much more dramatic than continuing the syncopation.

Once again, the best way to acquire an understanding of good jazz syncopation is through listening. For those of us who grew up listening to jazz, syncopation and swing are as natural as breathing. However, for those who grew up with a strict classical background or in another setting where jazz was not part of the musical environment, jazz syncopation and swing feel can be some of the most difficult concepts to grasp.

---

* *Concise Oxford Dictionary of Music* (New York: Oxford University Press, 1980).

Creating and Notating Syncopated Rhythms

What follows are some general principles and rules for creating and notating syncopated jazz rhythms.

1. A melody written predominantly with quarter notes and half notes can be syncopated by shifting notes forward or backward by an eighth or sixteenth note or by shifting an accented note from the first or third beat to beat 2 or 4 and through the use of triplets.

2. Anticipations are generally more effective than delays.

3. Correct Notation and Beaming of Syncopated Material: In 4/4 meter, think of an imaginary bar line in the middle of the measure so that the third beat is always clearly visible, and notate your syncopated rhythms accordingly, making beat 3 always visible. The result will greatly facilitate sight-reading and the performance of your music. The only exceptions are very simple rhythms, such as quarter note–half note–quarter note. This rule also applies to the beaming of eighth notes. In most cases you shouldn't beam eighth notes across the third beat. There is a certain "commonsense" quality to this important notational rule. Once you understand it, it can easily be applied to 3/4, 6/8, and other meters. The general principle is to keep your notation as simple and clear as possible. Here's another rule regarding beaming: It's generally better *not* to beam eighth notes in groups of four over an eighth rest (the default setting in Finale).

   Break the beam manually ("/" in Speedy Entry), or change the beaming preferences in Document Options > Beams. On the other hand, sixteenth notes *should* generally be beamed across sixteenth rests (see Ex. 6-1c). It's also usually a good idea not to beam three eighth notes preceded or followed by an eighth rest, because this can easily be mistaken for an eighth triplet when sight-reading (Ex. 6-1c, bar 4).

4. When writing a note of short duration on the beat, it's common practice in jazz notation to write a quarter note with a dot over it rather than an eighth note followed by an eighth rest, even if that's technically the correct rhythmic value desired. Any experienced jazz player (including most college-level students) will interpret the staccato quarter note as an eighth note followed by a rest. Again, the underlying principle is to make the music as easy to sight-read as possible. More rests in a part tend to make it appear more complicated.

5. Example 6-1e illustrates a common problem that often occurs with default settings of certain notation programs when inputting syncopated rhythms. Simply apply the principle of "Less is more"—in other words, don't notate a phrase with more notes than are necessary. It's much easier to read a dotted quarter note than an eighth note tied to a quarter note.

Example 6-1 illustrates a simple quarter-note/half-note melody that has been syncopated by using eighth-note displacement or triplets, as described in item 1. Example 6-1a shows the syncopated phrase notated correctly, as described in item 3, with beat 3 clearly visible. Example 6-1b illustrates the same passage notated incorrectly. Example 6-1c illustrates correct and incorrect eighth-note beaming based on the same principle. Example 6-1d illustrates the correct jazz notation of short notes on the beat described in item 4. We'll return to this point in Chapter 12 when discussing the correct use of articulations. Example 6-1e illustrates the correct notation for syncopated rhythms and ties.

Ex. 6-1

Syncopation and Correct Notation

All Quarters & Half Notes

a. Syncopated Rhythms- Correct Notation (Beat 3 is visible)

Created by shifting notes by
an 1/8th note & using triplets

b. Syncopated Rhythms - Incorrect Notation

Wrong Notation - Beat 3 NOT Visible

c. Beaming

d. Short Notes On the Beat

Not Recommended
(harder to read)

Better
(easier to read)

Not Recommended
(4th bar of Ex. 6-1c)

Better

e. Syncopated Rythms and Ties

61

6-4 Swing Feel (Melodic Rhythm)

The word *swing* has two very distinct meanings in the world of jazz.

1. It can be a complimentary, descriptive adjective. If the music swings, then the improvised solo, composition, or performance is good, organic, expressive, and musical.

2. It can refer to a very specific interpretation regarding the performance of eighth and sixteenth notes, as described earlier. In addition to delaying the second eighth note and the second and fourth sixteenth notes in a passage, placing a slight accent on the upbeats rather than on the downbeats is another characteristic of swing feel.

It's this second definition that concerns us here. Any jazz musician, from student to seasoned professional, will instinctively interpret a series of eighth or sixteenth notes toward a triplet feel, with varying degrees of emphasis, unless specifically instructed in the music not to do so with a marking such as "Even Eighth Feel." On the other hand, classically trained musicians will generally interpret the same passage literally, playing rhythmically correct eighth and sixteenth notes.

This can create serious interpretive problems when writing for an ensemble, such as a studio orchestra, where you will encounter a mix of musicians coming from both jazz and classical backgrounds. Unless the strings and other orchestral players have specific experience performing jazz (as in the top Hollywood and European studio orchestras or Broadway pit orchestras) or there is a dynamic conductor with jazz experience, it can be very difficult to get the orchestral players to "swing" in sync with the jazz players. This is a problem that persists to the present day. In such situations, when you have artistic freedom, we recommend writing in an "even eighth note" style rather than a jazz swing style or having the strings play much slower rhythms along with syncopated rhythms by the jazz musicians.

Most sequencers and notation programs provide the capability to add a variety of differing intensities of swing feel to eighth and sixteenth notes, in order to impart a jazz feel to MIDI playback. The degree of resolution or subtlety varies from program to program. If 100% swing equals actual triplets (turning the second eighth note into the third note of the triplet), then generally somewhere between 10% and 60% swing applied to eighth notes or sixteenth notes (depending on the program) will achieve a satisfactory simulation of a jazz feel on playback. Of course, this won't sound as good as what real players would do, because no human being could possibly delay every second eighth note by exactly the same amount!

◊ **Beware of relying too heavily on MIDI playback for an assessment of your music!** Unless you're willing to spend many, many extra hours tweaking every note, there will always be a slightly mechanical feel with the application of a MIDI tool such as Quantization with Swing Feel.

When used properly, however, many of the techniques and tricks we will be examining can help you achieve much more musical-sounding MIDI files. Remember: A computer is a powerful tool, but it is still a machine and does not possess the expressive capabilities of human beings.

6-5 Harmonic Rhythm

Harmonic rhythm refers to the rate at which chord changes occur and is usually related to the melodic phrase structure and form of the piece. An understanding of the relationship between harmonic rhythm and melodic phrase structure is essential to the development of a jazz arrangement. We'll be taking a closer look at harmonic rhythm in Chapters 7 and 8.

6-6 Score Preparation

We end this chapter with a few words about preparing a score. For now, through Chapter 14, we'll be working with the 3–4 Horns + Rhythm Concert Score Templates, which place the trumpet on the top staff and the other horns below the trumpet in order of register, notated in their *concert* pitch. Basically, we're still thinking of this group as a large combo, so it makes sense to do it this way. In this case it's acceptable to lay out the score staves with trumpet (the upper register) on top, sax or saxes in the middle, and trombone (the lower register) on the bottom. With ensembles consisting of 5–6 horns or larger, we'll follow the customary practice of putting the saxes and any other woodwinds above the brass.

For the rhythm section, it's customary always to put the piano part in a grand staff in the score, even if there's nothing written in the bass clef. However, in the printed piano part, the bass clef staff would be deleted if it contained no notes. We recommend the following layout for the placement of rhythm section staves: If you have a guitar part, place it above the piano staff. Place the bass staff below the piano staff, with the drums on the bottom staff. This is not an absolute rule, and you may encounter variations of the placement of rhythm section staves depending on the preferences of a particular orchestra, conductor, or arranger. We'll get into more of the specific techniques of notating for the rhythm section in Chapter 13.

Various templates ("manuscript paper" in Sibelius) are available on the companion website (in the Resources > Templates section) for various-size ensembles, with or without guitar, for use in the arranging exercises in the following chapters. Use one staff for each horn, grand staff for piano, and one staff each for guitar, bass, and drums.

For the upcoming exercises, please use the following instrumentation:

3 horns = trumpet, alto sax or tenor sax, trombone

4 horns = trumpet, alto sax, tenor sax, trombone

Use the 3 or 4 Horns + Rhythm Concert Score Template available on the website as a template for your 3- to 4-horn arrangements in upcoming chapters.

Chapter Summary

You should now be familiar with some of the basic rhythmic concepts of jazz, including rhythmic pulse and style, jazz syncopation and notation, and swing feel. We also introduced the concept of harmonic rhythm and talked a little bit about some ways of simulating swing feel using MIDI software. We concluded this chapter with a few words about laying out the score for 3–4 horns plus rhythm arrangements.

◊ **Software Tip!** Make sure you know how to switch between transposed and concert score views. It's simple in either program. In Finale, the default view is "Transposed Score." To view in concert pitch, go to Document > Display in Concert Pitch. In Sibelius, the default is "Concert Score." To view as a transposed score, go to Notes > Transposing Score (shortcut Ctrl-⇧-T/WIN or ⌘-⇧-T/Mac), or just click on the "Transposing Score" button (the two flats) in the toolbar. When viewing a jazz score in concert pitch, you'll need to put the baritone sax (and occasionally the second tenor sax) in the bass clef to avoid having an excessive number of ledger lines. Consult the Software Tips on the companion website for more details.

Exercises

1. Import the following MIDI files from the website into your sequencer or notation program. Use the best piano or brass samples you have for playback.

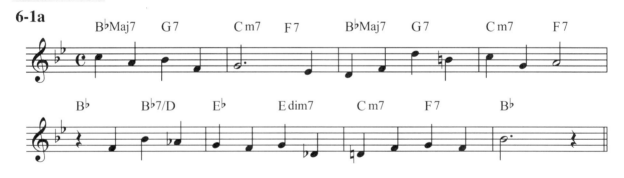

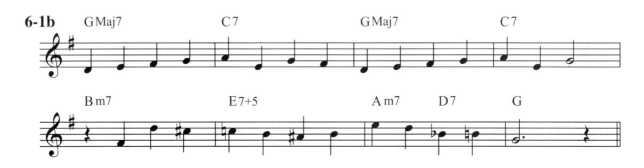

- Using the same notes, create a syncopated feel by shifting notes forward or backward by an eighth note and by using triplets.

- If you have the option, try applying varying degrees (between 10% and 40%) of swing feel to the lines. See if you can hear the difference between *no* swing feel and 10% swing feel. Experiment with percentages of swing greater than 40%.

- If you're working in a sequencer like Digital Performer or Logic, applying swing feel to eighth notes with a Quantization Grid Value of sixteenth notes will only delay every second and fourth sixteenth note (which aren't there if you didn't play sixteenths) and will *not* effect the second eighth note. So in this exercise, if you want to hear the effect of the sequencer's swing feel, make sure you select the grid value to be eighth notes. Triplets or any tuplet must be quantized separately. If you use triplets in the exercise, do *not* try to quantize them to eighth notes!

- Experiment with increasing slightly the attack velocity of eighth-note upbeats, to emphasize the swing feel. This can be done in the Event List or Graphic Editor of your sequencer. Usually, placing an accent over a note in a notation program increases the attack velocity of the note, although often the default values are rather extreme. You may need to find the preferences for "playback of accents" and adjust it down so that the result is not so jarring.

- Make sure the music is notated properly, with beat 3 always clearly visible and with the proper beaming of eighth notes. Print out, play, and analyze the results.

2. Take a recording of 8–16 bars of a Basie shout chorus from the 1950s or '60s. Transcribe the melody and rhythm of the brass section, taking care to use proper rhythmic notation. Do the same with any of the examples from the Small Ensemble Listening List.

3. Get together with a good rhythm section, and play some standard tunes using other than typical rhythmic feels, for example, "Giant Steps" as a ballad or a bossa nova, "Lover Man" as a samba, "Softly As in a Morning Sunrise" as a waltz.

Small Ensemble Listening List

1. "*Meet the Jazztet*"—MCA, 1960. Personnel: Art Farmer—tpt, Benny Golson—ts, Curtis Fuller—tbn, McCoy Tyner—pno, Addison Farmer—bs, Lex Humphries—dr
   a. "It's All Right with Me"
   b. "Blues March"

2. Oliver Nelson—"The Blues And The Abstract Truth"—Impulse, 1961. Personnel: Freddie Hubbard—tpt, Oliver Nelson—as, ts, arr/cp, Eric Dolph—as, fl, George Barrow—bari sx, Bill Evans—pno, Paul Chambers—bs, Roy Haynes—dr.
   a. "Stolen Moments"
   b. "Hoe Down"

3. *McCoy Tyner*—"*Expansions*"—Blue Note, 1968. Personnel: McCoy Tyner—pno, Woody Shaw—tpt, Gary Bartz—as, Wayne Shorter—ts, Ron Carter—cello, Herbie Lewis—bs, Freddie Waits—dr
   a. "Peresina"
   b. "Vision"

4. Art Blakey & the Jazz Messengers—*"Ugetsu"—Riverside,* 1963. Personnel: Freddie Hubbard—tpt, Curtis Fuller—tbn, Wayne Shorter—ts, Cedar Walton—pno, Jymie Merritt—bs, Art Blakey—dr
   a. "Ping Pong"
   b. "Ugetsu"

5. Cannonball Adderly—"The Cannonball Adderley Sextet in New York"—Riverside, 1962. Personnel: Cannonball Adderley—as, Nat Adderley—cornet, Yusef Lateef—ts, fl, oboe, Joe Zawinul, pno, Sam Jones—bs, Louis Hayes—dr
   a. "Gemini"
   b. "Dizzy's Business"

6. *"Nancy Wilson/Cannonball Adderley"—Capitol, 1962* (use of voice as a third horn). Personnel: Nancy Wilson—voc, Cannonball Adderley—as, Nat Adderley—cornet, Joe Zawinul—pno, Sam Jones—bs, Louis Hayes—dr
   a. "Never Will I Marry"
   b. "Old Country"

7. *Ray Charles—"Ray" (Motion Picture Soundtrack), Warner Brothers (originally recorded on Atlantic and ABC/Paramount, 1957–76). Personnel: Ray Charles— pno & voc, David "Fathead" Newman—ts, 2 tpts, bari, bs, dr
   a. "Hard Times" (1961)
   b. "Maryann" (1955)
   c. "Night Time Is the Right Time" (1958). (Marjorie Hendricks—voc)

8. *Earth, Wind, & Fire—"The Best of," Columbia, 1974–81 (EWF with five-piece horn section)
   a. "Fantasy" (1977)
   b. "September" (1978)
   c. "Can't Hide Love" (1975)

Please refer to Appendix B on the companion website, "Recommended Recordings for Further Study," for a more comprehensive listening list.

---

* Why include Ray Charles and Earth, Wind, & Fire as listening examples in a book geared toward jazz composition and arranging? First of all, many younger students of jazz will have opportunities and an interest in writing in pop or rock idioms. It's valuable for all to be exposed to the sound of 3–6 horns in musical contexts other than "straight-ahead" jazz. Most of the musical techniques explored in this book can be applied to this type of music as well. Second, it's just great music, and the horn writing, especially in EWF, is superb. Also, Ray Charles was an accomplished jazz improviser, on both piano and alto sax, and Maurice White, the founder of EWF, played drums with the Ramsey Lewis Trio for two years before moving to Los Angeles to form EWF.

Chapter 7

Melody and Motivic Development (3–4 Horns)

7-1 Basic Melodic Considerations: Melodic Shape and Motion

What makes a good melody good? How can we analyze melodies we've written in order to improve them? What specific techniques are available to us for the process of melodic development? How can we apply these principles to jazz arrangements for three to four horns or larger ensembles?

First of all, let's acknowledge something often overlooked in the study of jazz theory. The fundamental harmonic and melodic language of jazz (as well as rock and pop) music is derived primarily from Western European tonal music— from about 1750 up to the early 20th century. Now, it's certainly true that significant melodic and harmonic innovations and modifications have been introduced by jazz composers and players since the early 1900s. Most notably, these include the *blues scale* and the acceptance of the *dominant seventh chord*, with all of its possible alterations, as a consonant rather than dissonant (or unstable) harmonic element. In fact, there has been a fundamental reinterpretation of the concepts of consonance and dissonance and a predilection for certain scale modes (Dorian, Phrygian, etc.) and *synthetic scales* (diminished, altered dominant, etc.) not common in classical music. We'll examine some of these concepts in greater detail in this and later chapters.

However, the underlying foundation for all of this is derived from the European tonal system. That includes basic concepts of dominant harmony, the major and minor scales and their modes, and underlying concepts of melodic, harmonic, and formal development. Most jazz historians seem to agree that jazz is the result of a fusion of European harmonic and melodic concepts with African rhythmic and melodic elements. In fact, many of the principles that apply to good writing from the periods of traditional classical, romantic, and early modern classical music, may also be applied to good jazz writing, and vice versa. This is certainly true in the case of melody.

Most good melodies, classical or jazz, generally have an interesting melodic shape. In other words, the line tends to change directions within a melodic phrase. Similarly, there is generally a contrast between stepwise or scalar motion with skips of larger intervals. In Ex. 7-1a, in the first example, which has a relatively uninteresting melodic shape, the line of pitches simply ascends and then descends, and the largest interval is that of a major third. In the second example, which uses the same pitches and general melodic contour, the melody changes direction several times, and there are a number of skips of larger intervals, which make this melody much more musical as a result. In Ex 7-1b, the different types of melodic motion are illustrated.

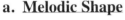

a. Melodic Shape

Uninteresting

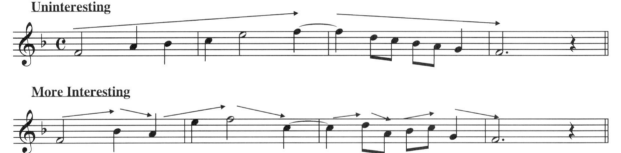

More Interesting

b. Melodic Motion

Scalar (step-wise)

Skips of larger intervals

Combined

7-2 Melodic Motives and Phrase Structure

Most Western melodies, including blues melodies, are constructed from short *melodic motives* (two to five notes), which are then combined and developed to form longer musical phrases (usually one to four bars). These phrases are then combined to create a basic structure, such as an AABA or ABA song form, similar to the *exposition* section of a classical piece in *sonata form*. Very often, phrase structures fall into a pattern of *antecedent* and *consequent* phrases. A brief melodic analysis of the first 16 bars of "I Could Write a Book" by Rodgers and Hart will illustrate some of these concepts (Ex. 7-2):

Analysis

Pickup and m. 1 = motive **a**.

mm. 2–3 = motive **b** (notes 1–3 of **b** are a rhythmically altered, transposed inversion of the last three notes of **a**; notes 2–4 of **b** are a rhythmically altered, transposed, retrograde of the last three notes of **a**).

mm. 4–5 = **b** developed through repetition.

mm. 6–8 = **b¹** = **b** developed: The m6 skip from E to C in bar 5 is an augmentation of the E–G skip in bars 4 and 5, in terms of both pitch and duration. The rhythmic augmentation creates a new rhythmic motive (♩ ♩ ♩) that reoccurs in mm 10 and 14. The last two notes E to G also reflect the E–G skip in mm 4 and 5. The melody ends on the sustained

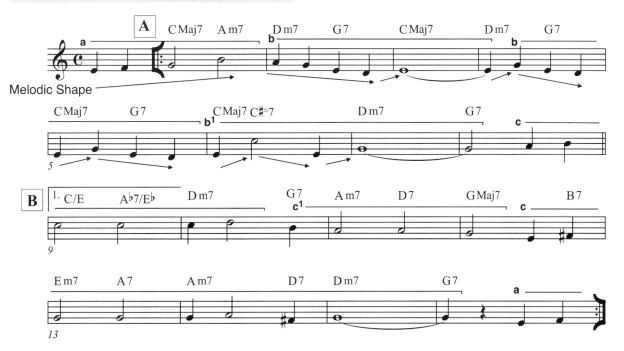

Ex. 7-2

Melodic Analysis: "I Could Write a Book" by Rodgers & Hart

G, the dominant scale degree of C, coinciding with and reinforcing the *half cadence* to G7 (V7) in m. 8. We could also make a case for designating mm. 6–8 as a new motive. The last two notes of bar 8 (A–B) resemble the stepwise motion of **a** as well as beginning the **c** motive. In fact we could also make an argument that **c** is merely an extension and development of **a**.

mm. 8–10 = motive **c**: We've chosen to designate this as a new motive since it seems to have a distinctive quality of its own as well as a new harmonization (C/E– A♭7, etc.). The rhythmic motive from bar 6 is repeated in mm 10 and 14, providing unity.

mm. 10–12 = '**c¹**' = '**c**' inverted and altered rhythmically.

mm. 12–16 = **c** repeated, transposed, and extended, once again ending on the dominant scale degree with a half cadence to the V7 chord G7.

The melodic motives are indicated by lowercase letters: **a, b, c,** etc. The larger sections of the form are indicated by capital letters: **A, B, C,** etc. Notice that the entire **A** section consists of only two motives: **a** (ascending) and **b** (descending). The motives are then combined, developed, and rearranged to form the eight-bar **A** section of the tune. Please bear in mind that musical analysis is itself subjective and that a given passage can often be interpreted in many different ways. Throughout this book we will use musical analysis and our interpretations of various passages as tools for understanding the compositional process better rather than as academic exercises.

The first four bars of "I Could Write a Book" could be viewed as an antecedent phrase and the second four bars as consequent, which the listener hears in relation to each other. We could also make a case that **a** is the antecedent and **b** the consequent phrase. There is always more than one possible analysis of a given musical passage. The important thing is not so much whether or not your analysis is "correct" but whether or not it helps you understand the music better. The **B** section of the tune really consists of just one motive, **c**, which is itself similar to **a**. We chose to refer to this as a new motive, **c**, because of the reharmonization and the way it develops over the following six measures. Notice the simple melodic shape of bars 1–2, which becomes more complex and jagged in bars 4–7. Also note the contrast of melodic motion throughout (stepwise vs. skips of larger intervals).

Let's now introduce the concepts of *symmetrical* (regular or parallel) and *asymmetrical* (irregular) phrase structure. By *symmetrical* we mean balanced or complementary phrase structure, where there are generally the same number of bars (one, two, three, etc.) in both the antecedent and consequent phrases or some other "balanced" arrangement of the phrases (e.g., two two-bar phrases followed by a four-bar phrase). By *asymmetrical* we mean any other weighting, such as one bar of antecedent and three bars of consequent phrasing, or 1-1/2 bars of antecedent followed by 2-1/2 bars of consequent phrasing.

We will be referring to these concepts frequently throughout the book. In general, an asymmetrical phrase structure leads to an increase in tension, and a symmetrical phrase structure leads to a release of tension (*tension and release*).

Notice how the **A** section of "I Could Write a Book" has an asymmetrical melodic phrase structure in relation to the regular harmonic rhythm (phrase structure of the chord changes): one bar of **a** followed by four bars of **b** and three bars of **b**[1]. By contrast, the **B** section has a symmetrical melodic phrase structure: two bars of **c**, two bars of **c**, four bars of **c**. Also notice how the melodic shape and motion of **B** is more subdued (more repeated notes and stepwise motion) than that of **A** (a more complex melodic shape, with skips of larger intervals) (*contrast and variety*).

In general, Western music, whether classical, jazz, or pop, has a "pull" toward regular or symmetrical phrase structure in the area of form, just as it has a "pull" from V to I in the area of harmony. We would like to propose that an analysis of the best music (whether Mozart, Louis Armstrong, John Coltrane, or Stravinsky) will reveal a tendency toward irregular or asymmetrical melodic phrase structure and that too much regular or parallel phrase structure will result in inferior and less interesting music. Ultimately, the best melodies will have a combination of symmetrical and asymmetrical melodic phrase structure.

One additional consideration when analyzing a melody is its overall range and register. Notice that the melody of "I Could Write a Book" ascends to a B in bar 1 and a C in bar 6 and reaches its peak on a D in bar 10. This creates a gradual increase in intensity to the high point in bar 10, which overlaps the form of the tune. This is followed by a decrease in tension as the melody descends back to E in bar 16.

7-3 Techniques of Motivic Development

Now that we've examined the principles of melodic shape and motion, let's take a look at some of the common methods for developing melodic motives. It should come as no great surprise that many of the same techniques found in most traditional classical theory books can also be applied quite effectively to the development of jazz melodies. Some of these techniques include:

1. Repetition.
2. Transposition.
3. Rhythmic alteration (syncopation).
4. Inversion (inverting the pitches or playing the melody upside down).
5. Retrograde (playing the notes backwards).
6. Retrograde inversion (combining techniques 4 and 5).

7. Augmentation and diminution (intervallic—increasing or decreasing the intervals).

8. Augmentation and diminution (time—increasing or decreasing the note durations)

9. Extension or embellishment.

10. Truncation or simplification.

Although many of us tend to associate terms such as *retrograde* and *retrograde inversion* with the complex serial compositional techniques of 20th century classical music, we find, on taking a closer look, that these same techniques are often used instinctively by the jazz improviser. As jazz composers and arrangers, an understanding and awareness of these techniques can help us achieve our goals of creating more interesting and "swinging" melodies. Play through the examples in Ex. 7-3 and note how they all sound somehow related to the original melody of "I Could Write a Book."

Ex. 7-3

Techniques of Melodic Alteration and Development: "I Could Write a Book" by Rodgers & Hart

1. Repetition(+ Rhythmic Alteration)

2. Rhythmic Alteration (Syncopation)

3. Transpostion (within the scale)

4. Inversion (Diatonic)

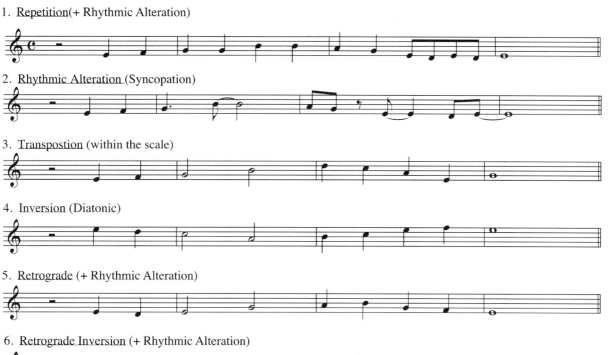

5. Retrograde (+ Rhythmic Alteration)

6. Retrograde Inversion (+ Rhythmic Alteration)

7. Augmentation (Intervallic)

8. Augmentation (Time)

9. Diminution (Intervallic)

10. Diminution (Time)

11. Extension (Embellishment)

12. Truncation (Simplification)

7-4 **Basic Types of Musical Texture**

We'll conclude this chapter with a quick look at the various types of musical texture. Once again, we'll be borrowing some terms from classical music. We'll then be in a position to begin applying some of these ideas to actual musical exercises. The traditional classical definitions have been modified slightly in order to apply these principles more effectively to a jazz context.

a. *Monophonic*: Melody in unison or octaves only, with or without octave displacement. Since your first assignment involves an exercise in monophonic writing, let's take a closer look at some techniques to make this type of texture sound as musical as possible.

1. Change the timbre (instrumentation) of the melody periodically to create contrast and variety.

2. Overlap melodic phrases when switching from one instrument to another to create smoother transitions.

3. Try using rhythm section instruments (piano, bass, guitar) as melodic choices.

4. Always be conscious of the relative *tessitura* (relative intensities of the different instruments in different registers) of the instruments you're working with when making choices regarding unison or octave placement of the melody.

b. *Homophonic*

1. Melody over chordal accompaniment (sustained pads or rhythmic comping).

2 Melody voiced in *rhythmic unison*.

c. *Polyphonic*

1. Melody with a *countermelody*.

2. *Free counterpoint* (two or more voices moving independent of each other).

Example 7-4 illustrates *monophonic, homophonic,* and *polyphonic* textures. Note that *monophonic* always means *only* unison or octaves. The commonality between the two types of *homophonic* texture is the fact that in each case there is only one distinct melody line, supported by some type of accompaniment. *Polyphonic* means two or more lines moving independent of each other.

Ex. 7-4

Basic Musical Textures: "I Could Write a Book" by Rodgers & Hart

1. Monophonic

2a. Homophonic - Melody Over Chords

2b. Homophonic - Melody Voiced in Rhythmic Unison (with bass line)

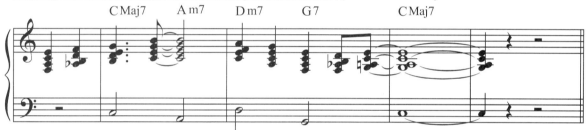

3. Polyphonic - Free Counterpoint

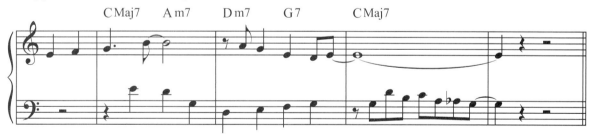

7-5 Applying the Techniques of Melodic Development to an Arrangement

The melodic principles and techniques of motivic development discussed in this chapter can obviously be useful when composing an original tune or composition. These techniques are also powerful tools for the arranger desiring to bring a personal interpretation and expressive touch to the arrangement of a standard or pop tune, or a jazz standard. One of the most common and useful initial steps for creating an arrangement of a nonoriginal tune is first to create a modification of the original melody. Use the techniques presented here, especially rhythmic alteration, to create a personal statement of the melody suitable for the ensemble and context for which you're writing.

If you're writing an instrumental arrangement of a song written by another composer, it's also a good idea to be aware of the lyric content of the song, if there are lyrics. Knowing the lyrics can suggest an interpretation and direction for an arrangement that might otherwise be overlooked.

Many of the greatest jazz improvisers have held the conviction that it's essential to know the lyrics of a song in order to interpret and improvise on it properly. The same can be said for writing an arrangement.

Example 7-5 illustrates scoring the melody of "I Could Write a Book" in monophonic texture for 3 horns and rhythm while also applying some of the techniques of motivic development to the melody.

◊ A word about *tessitura*: All acoustic instruments sound brighter and more intense in their upper registers. This is especially true in the case of wind instruments (brass and woodwinds) and the human voice, where it literally requires more physical force to create a sound in the instruments' upper register. So, for example, if you have a trumpet and a trombone both playing a G above middle C in unison, the trumpet will be in its low to mid-register, whereas the trombone will be in its upper register. Therefore the trombone will sound more intense and is likely to overpower the trumpet. The trumpet and trombone in octaves would be much more balanced in this respect. The basic principle is: "In most cases, the intensity of the lower parts should not exceed that of the higher ones."*

◊ Remember that most of the "rules" presented in this book are meant to be guidelines, not principles written in stone. There are some situations where the unison doubling of trumpet and trombone presented in Ex. 7-6 would be perfectly acceptable. It doesn't sound bad. It's just a different color not typically used in a straight-ahead jazz setting, with the trombone masking the normally more prominent sound of the trumpet. For example, the rock band Chicago used this sound quite effectively on many recordings.

---

* Don Sebesky, *The Contemporary Arranger*, p. 44.

Ex. 7-5 Oct/Unison 3 Horns + Rhythm "I Could Write a Book"

by Rodgers & Hart
arr. by Richard Sussman

Concert Score

Example 7-6 provides two illustrations of the relative tessitura of instruments in unison or octave scoring. In the first example, with the trumpet and trombone in unison, the trombone is in its upper register and is too high and intense relative to the mid-range of the trumpet. The second example, in octaves, is much more balanced, with each instrument in its middle register.

Ex. 7-6

Tessitura: "I Could Write a Book" by Rodgers & Hart

Concert Score

a. Trombone too high in relation to Trumpet

b. Trumpet & Trombone in octaves is more balanced in terms of register

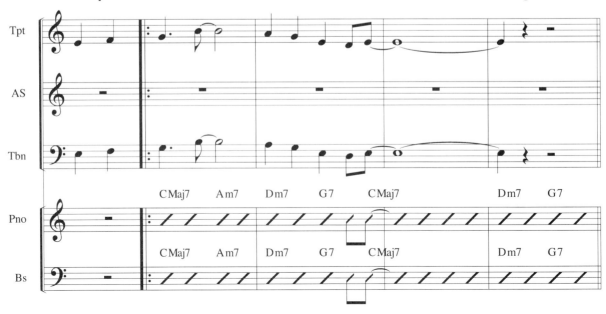

Chapter Summary

You should now be familiar with some fundamental concepts of melody, including melodic shape and motion, melodic motives, techniques of motivic development, symmetrical and asymmetrical phrase structure, and the three types of basic musical texture: monophonic, homophonic, and polyphonic. However, it's important to understand that there is much more to writing a good melody than following these rules. Whenever you're writing, whether it's a simple exercise in this book or your next symphony, always listen with your inner ear and your heart, and always strive to reach that creative source to which we all have access.

◊ Software Tip! For best results, when using MIDI playback in any of the musical examples in this and the following chapters, be sure to *disable MIDI playback of chords* if you're working in Finale. The only exception is if the example is a lead sheet with only a single melody line with chord symbols. Sibelius does not play back chord symbols entered as text into a score. Refer to the website for more details.

Exercises

1. Listen to as much small group jazz as possible (refer to the Listening List at the end of Chapter 6). Get the sound of those instruments in your "inner ear." As you listen, try to pick out examples of the different types of melodic shapes and the difference between symmetrical and asymmetrical phrase structure. Try to hear the difference between monophonic, homophonic, and polyphonic textures. Take notes, and write down anything that piques your interest, even if you don't know the specific musical technique being used. Whenever you hear something that really grabs your attention, transcribe it!

Use "Speedy Entry" in Finale or "Note Input" in Sibelius for the following exercises.

2. Compose several four- to eight-bar melodies, with or without chord changes, illustrating principles of good melodic shape and motion, techniques of motivic development, and regular and irregular phrase structure. (Use the Lead Sheet Template.)

3. Write a modification of the melody to "I Could Write a Book," "My Romance," or a similar standard. (Use the Lead Sheet Template.)
   • Use a single staff with chord symbols.
   • Experiment with any of the techniques of melodic development discussed in this chapter, but focus on rhythmic alteration.

4. Arrange your modified melody for three horns and rhythm. *Use the 3 Horns + Rhythm Concert Score Template*: For now, just put the chord changes and accents for the rhythm section on the piano treble clef staff. Make sure to observe the correct instrument ranges for each instrument as well as the principles of tessitura discussed in this chapter.

- Write the arrangement for trumpet, alto or tenor sax, and trombone.
- For now, *use only solo, unison, or octaves*. Refer to Section 7-4 for ideas on how to make this assignment musically interesting.
- Be conscious of the principles outlined earlier regarding the relative range and intensity of the instruments.

5. Print out the score and parts, including three to four copies of the rhythm section parts for Exercise 4. Be sure to observe correct transpositions for the horn parts. Play and analyze the results.

◊ **Important Software Tip!** It's essential that you know how to generate parts and how to print both the score and the individual parts of your arrangements. Jazz scores should be printed in *landscape* orientation, with eight bars per page whenever possible. Parts should be printed in *portrait* orientation, with four bars per staff whenever possible.

Make sure you know how to adjust the number of measures per staff and the spacing of staves. You should also be familiar with the methods for spacing the music properly. Please consult the online manuals for Finale or Sibelius, or refer to Chapter 15 of this book for more details on these functions.

Chapter 8

Basic Harmonic Concepts (3–4 Horns)

The study of jazz harmony is a vast undertaking that can easily encompass a lifetime of work. However, a thorough understanding of some of the basics, equivalent to a first-year college course in jazz harmony, is a prerequisite for understanding many of the concepts presented in this book. We've chosen to include some of these fundamental harmonic principles in this and the following chapter, because we feel they are so essential to the jazz arranger.

A primary goal in this second section of the book is to provide techniques for accomplishing one of the most basic tasks in writing a jazz arrangement: harmonizing a melody line for three or more brass and woodwind instruments, in other words, choosing which notes to assign to the voices accompanying a melody so that they support the melody in a musical manner, consistent with the chord symbols or underlying harmony of the moment. In this and the following chapter, we'll be presenting these concepts in the context of writing for 3–4 horns, later in this section for 5–6 horns, and in Section 3 for full big band (13 horns).

In the interests of presenting the material in an organized, concise, easy-to-understand, and easily referenced fashion, we've attempted to consolidate some fundamental principles and rules regarding jazz voicings. Many of these principles apply to writing for ensembles of any size, but some are actually more easily understood and applied when writing for larger ensembles and are noted as such. Also, some of the rules may not make much sense until you actually begin the process of writing. We'll refer back to these basic principles later in this section in the chapters on writing for 5–6 horns and again in Section 3 when discussing techniques for arranging for the large jazz ensemble.

Also, so as not to overwhelm you with too much information in this one chapter, we've postponed the important discussion of *approach tone reharmonization* until the next chapter. For the examples and exercises in this chapter, we've stuck to the simplest, or *diatonic*, solutions for harmonizing a melody, utilizing only notes of the most basic major, minor, and dominant chord scales. Finally, it's important always to keep the following important concept in mind as you proceed through this book and, hopefully, continue beyond it.

◊ **"The Rules" are presented to help you quickly make effective arranging decisions that will have stylistic integrity. Following "The Rules" while doing the exercises in this book will help you to build a foundation of knowledge and techniques that should enable you to make better musical choices. However, in the creative arts, "Rules are made to be broken," and ultimately your choices should be determined by what you hear and by your own creative instincts!**

◊ Beginning with Ex. 8-4A and in many subsequent examples, we'll be illustrating some basic principles in a piano *grand staff* "sketch" format, with the intended instruments labeled on the left. It's important that you understand that each horizontal line is intended to be played by the individual instruments indicated exactly as if it were written in a *full score* format.

8-1 Chords Built by Thirds and Chord Scales

According to traditional classical music theory, an *interval* is any two notes sounded simultaneously or in sequence. A *chord* can be defined as any simultaneous or arpeggiated combination of three or more notes. Chords and the way they interact form the basis of our harmonic language. A *chord voicing* is any arrangement of chord tones or distribution of those notes among various instruments that results in the sounding of a particular chord. To understand better how to create effective chord voicings when writing a jazz arrangement, it's useful first to review and expand on some essential aspects of jazz harmony.

Conventional jazz harmony is based primarily on the concepts of the *diatonic major and minor scales, chords built by thirds,* and *dominant harmony.* Following are some fundamental principles of jazz harmony.

a. *Building chords by thirds* refers to the common practice of starting with the chord root and adding notes derived from the major or minor scale at the interval of a major or minor third. Starting with the root, major or minor third, and perfect fifth to form a *triad*, we can then proceed to add the seventh, the ninth, the eleventh, and the thirteenth, with their various possible alterations.

b. We then arrive at the three fundamental *chord qualities*: *major, minor,* and *dominant*. In jazz harmony, *diminished* chords almost always function as part of a dominant seventh ♭9 chord.

c. Traditionally, *major* and *minor* chords have been defined as *consonant,* or stable—they are destination chords that can be resolved to. *Dominant* and *diminished* chords have been defined as *dissonant,* or unstable— they tend to want to resolve to a major or minor chord. Although, in jazz harmony the *dominant seventh chord* can occur as a consonant (stable) rather than dissonant (unstable) harmonic element, the traditional interpretations of major, minor, and dominant are still valuable for our purposes.

d. If we build chords by thirds starting on each note of the major or minor scale (it doesn't matter which form of the minor scale) and use *only* notes of the given scale to form those chords, we arrive at the concept of *scale-derived chords.* We can then define a *diatonic chord progression* as any chord progression consisting exclusively of scale-derived chords (Ex. 8-1).

e. *Dominant harmony* refers to what we like to call "The Law of Gravity" of harmony. It is that unique pull from the V7 (dominant seventh) chord to the I (*tonic*) chord, which provides the foundation for probably at least 75% of all standard, jazz, and pop chord progressions as well as most classical harmony from the Baroque period up to the early 20th century. It's important to understand that the term *dominant* can refer to chord progressions based around V-I root motion (dominant function) as well as to the dominant seventh chord itself. Dominant seventh chords are frequently, though not necessarily, a component of dominant harmony. Conversely, dominant seventh chords may also be used in passages not employing dominant function.

f. A *secondary dominant* chord can be defined as the dominant seventh (V7) chord of any *scale-derived chord* and may be indicated as V of ii, V of iii, etc. Although secondary dominant chords contain notes outside the range of the diatonic scale, it's useful to expand the definition of a diatonic chord progression to include secondary dominants as well as scale-derived chords (see Section 8-3). The concept of secondary dominants can in turn be expanded to include the ii-V of any scale-derived chord and represented as ii-V of ii, ii-V of iii, etc. (see Ex. 8-3).

g. The third and seventh degrees of a dominant seventh chord form the interval of a *tritone* (augmented fourth or diminished fifth). The unique instability of this interval and its tendency to want to resolve either inward or outward by half steps form the basis for the concept of *tritone substitution* in jazz harmony. A diminished seventh chord contains two tritones. The fact that a diminished seventh chord usually functions as a

83

dominant seventh ♭9 chord in jazz harmony forms the basis for the concept of *minor third substitution* (Ex. 8-2).

h. Every chord has one or more *chord scales* associated with it. A chord scale is a set of stepwise pitches related to and consistent with the sound of the vertical tones of a given chord. For example, in the case of any scale-derived chord, the most obvious chord scale would be the major or minor scale of I. The concept of chord scales is central to an understanding of *modal concepts of chord voicings*, which will be examined later in this chapter.

We'll take a look at some more modern concepts of chord voicings, such as *chords built by fourths, polytonal sounds,* and *non-functional harmony,* in Section 3 of this book. For now, we've got plenty of material to work with.

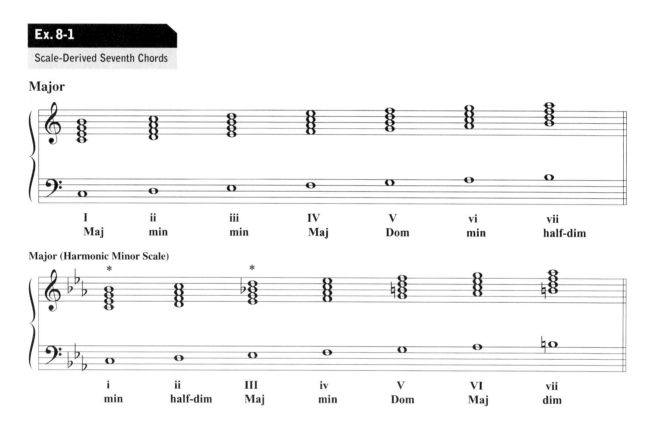

Ex. 8-1

Scale-Derived Seventh Chords

*Typically the i chord in minor will be a minor seventh chord, and the III chord in minor will be a Major seventh, not the min seventh (Δ7) or Maj 7+5, which would occur if we were adhering strictly to the notes of the harmonic minor scale. So this is really kind of a hybrid "Natural/Harmonic" minor scale. The traditional definitions of natural, harmonic, and melodic minor tend to become a little more flexible in jazz harmony, commonly using the minor seventh interval on the i and III chord, but the raised seventh on the V and vii chord. Similarly, in jazz harmony, the melodic minor scale will typically have the sixth and seventh scale degrees raised both ascending and descending, rather than lowered while descending as in the traditional classical definition of this term.

Ex. 8-2

Tritone and Minor Third Substitution

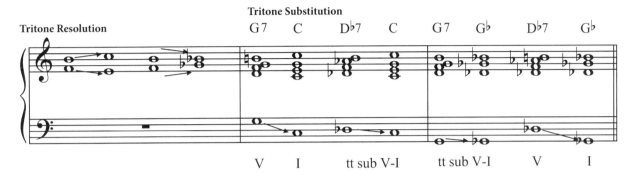

Any tritone has two possible resolutions, with each note moving either in or out by half steps. Any tritone can be contained within two possible dominant seventh chords, with roots a major third below either note of the tritone. Therefore, any dominant seventh chord has two possible resolutions. So the tritone F-B can have a root of G or D♭. If the root is G, we form a G7 chord, which can resolve down a fifth to C (V-I) or down a half step to G♭, depending on whether the notes of the tritone resolve inward or outward. This unique characteristic of the tritone interval forms the basis for *tritone substitution* in jazz harmony.

The Diminished Seventh Chord

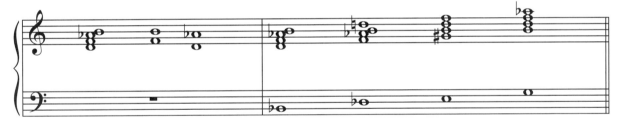

Any diminished seventh chord contains two tritones, each with two possible resolutions. Any diminished seventh chord also has any of four possible roots, each a major third below any note of the diminished seventh chord, forming dominant seventh ♭9 chords in each case. Each of these dominant seventh ♭9 chords thus has four possible resolutions. This phenomenon forms the basis for *minor third substitution* in jazz harmony. Another way of looking at the diminished seventh chord is to notice that it is made up of four m3 intervals. It is a "symmetrical" chord, where each inversion forms another diminished seventh chord. Another example of a "symmetrical" chord is the *augmented triad*, consisting of three major third intervals.

Minor Third Substitution (All Dominant seventh chords may contain the ♭9)

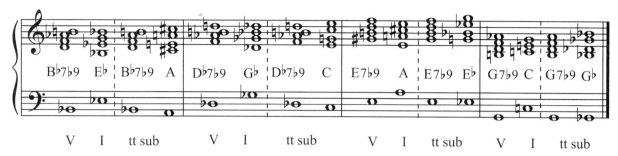

Tritone/Minor Third Substitution

ii	V	I
Fm7	B♭7	E♭
A♭m7	D♭7	G♭
Bm7	E7	A
Dm7	G7	C

Any ii chord can move to any V chord to any I chord.

8-2 Vertical Harmony: Basic Principles of Jazz Chord Voicings

Vertical harmony refers to the construction of chords consisting of various notes sounding simultaneously (appearing as a vertical column of notes on a score page). There are many possible chord voicings for any given chord symbol in jazz harmony. Following are some basic principles and rules for building effective jazz chord voicings.

a. The *primary chord tones* are the root, the third, the fifth, and the seventh. Of those, the most important in terms of defining *chord function* (chord quality) are the third and the seventh.

b. The *third and the seventh* of the chord are best placed in the *low to mid-register* (between C2 and E3), for greater strength in defining the chord quality and function.

c. The *perfect fifth* is the weakest and least important chord tone. It can be omitted from the voicing or used as a filler in any register.

d. The *upper structure chord tones* (ninth, eleventh, and thirteenth) as well as any available *altered tones* are *color tones*, useful for adding richness or tension to a chord voicing.

e. Primary chord tones tend to work best on the bottom of a chord voicing, and upper structure chord tones tend to work better in the upper register of a voicing. This follows the principle of the *natural overtone series*.

f. In "modern" jazz (1940 to present), the *chord root* is usually *not* part of the chord voicing played by the horns (except in *open position* or if it's the melody note, to avoid the interval of a major or minor second between the top two voices, or to create better voice leading in the inner voices by avoiding repeated notes or awkward skips). This is because the chord root functions best in the low register, as a harmonic anchor for the entire ensemble, and is normally played by the bass. The common practice of using the ninth instead of the root as a primary chord tone in constructing modern jazz chord voicings is one of the main techniques responsible for the fuller and richer-sounding chords associated with modern jazz harmony.

g. *Low interval limits* and *chord spacing*—When voicing for an instrumental ensemble:

1. Avoid intervals smaller than a major third more than one octave below middle C.

2. Avoid sixths and sevenths below low F on the bass clef (F1).

3. Placing larger intervals, such as octaves, sevenths, and tenths, on the bottom and smaller intervals higher up (a "pyramid"-shaped voicing) will create stronger and more balanced voicings (*balance*). This also follows the principle of the *Natural Overtone Series*.

h. Any available chord tone can be doubled or omitted.

i. *Rules are made to be broken.*

Another important concept to consider is the principle of *internal resonance*. This refers to the internal intervals present within any chord voicing.

a. The consonant intervals, major or minor *thirds* and *sixths*, provide richness and warmth.

b. The dissonant intervals, major or minor *seconds* and *sevenths*, and the *tritone* add tension and color.

c. Perfect *fifths* and *octaves* provide an open, transparent sound.

d. *Perfect* fourths have a distinctive, modern quality.

e. *Consonance* and *dissonance* can be thought of in terms of *chord density*. The more dissonant intervals in a chord, the more density and tension it will have. Fewer dissonant and more consonant intervals will result in a more transparent sound with less tension.

8-3 Horizontal Harmony

Horizontal harmony refers to the progression of harmony over time, or *chord progression* (appearing as a horizontal progression of chords or chord symbols on a score page). It's essential for a jazz arranger to have a thorough understanding of the chord progression of the tune or composition being arranged. Following are some important relevant considerations.

a. There are several primary types of chord progressions in jazz harmony:

1. *Diatonic*—based on diatonic scales and dominant harmony, centered around V-I and ii-V-I; any chord progression consisting predominantly of scale-derived chords or their corresponding secondary dominants (most standards and bebop tunes).

2. *Constantly modulating*—containing elements of diatonic and dominant harmony, but with a constant shifting of *tonal centers* ("Giant Steps," "Lazy Bird").

3. *Modal*—harmonies based more on *modes* of the diatonic scales, but without the emphasis on dominant harmony ("Impressions," "Milestones," "Transition").

4. *Non-diatonic or non-functional*—not based on diatonic scales and dominant harmony, but still having a tonal center (or centers), with chord roots often moving by major or minor thirds, seconds, and tritones ("Inner Urge," "The Sorcerer," "Pinocchio").

5. *Atonal*—no tonal center, with a conscious avoidance of any dominant or diatonic harmony (Ornette Coleman, Cecil Taylor).

b. A *tonal center* is a central pitch around which the chord progression seems to revolve. In a diatonic progression, the tonal center is the tonic (I), or the first note of the scale. Very often nondiatonic progressions still have implied tonal centers. So there's a big difference between what we're calling *nondiatonic* and *atonal*. Before beginning an arrangement, be sure to identify the primary tonal centers of the piece.

c. Identify any *modulations,* or shifts of tonal center.

d. Identify any particular types of chord structures that are fundamental to the nature of the chord progression (e.g., chords built by fourths or polytonal sounds).

When planning an arrangement, it's always a good idea to begin by analyzing the tune to be arranged from the perspectives of *form, harmony, melody,* and *style.* Be sure to analyze carefully the harmonic structure of the tune, and be able to identify the basic types of chord progressions and root motions present. A chord progression can consist of a combination of two or more of the foregoing categories. We will be focusing primarily on tunes with diatonic, modulating, and modal types of chord progressions in this section, saving the more complex nondiatonic and atonal types of progressions for Section Three. We've provided an example of a sample tune analysis for review in Ex. 8-3. We let the guys stretch out a little on this one. After all, this is a book about jazz. Hope you enjoy it! (Notice that the trumpet player takes a few rhythmic liberties in his jazz interpretation of the written notes on the lead sheet.)

Ex. 8-3

Example Tune Analysis: "Analycity" by Richard Sussman

Analysis

Form: AABA, indicated by: **A**

Key Centers/Modulations indicated by: **F:**

Harmonic Analysis: Roman numerals indicate scale degrees of the Diatonic Scale of Key Tonal Center.

Upper case = Major, Dom., Aug. Lower case = minor, diminished, 1/2 diminished.

Melodic motives indicated loosely by: **a** ―――――

XC = Chromatic Passing Chord

Note: Melodic Phrase Structure of "A" = aaba, of "B" = cdcd; Harmonic & Melodic Rhythm slow down at "B"

8-4 **Standard Jazz Voicing Positions**

At this point, we are concerned primarily with finding effective chord voicings for the brass and woodwind members of the ensemble, *not* the rhythm section, although some of these same principles could also be applied to writing for piano or guitar as well as strings or voices. When arranging for a small or large jazz ensemble, the most common, standardized voicing positions are *close position, semi-open* or *"drop-2" position,* and *open position.*

These are sometimes referred to as *"mechanical"* voicings because there are strict rules for their application. Some writers/authors also mention "drop-2 and 4," "drop 3," etc. We believe, however, that these other formulas are less useful and that if you understand "drop-2," you can easily expand that concept to include the other options. We're presenting these definitions here, but in some ways it's actually easier to use these voicings, in the strict sense, with more instruments available, as we'll see when we get to arranging for 5–6 horns later in this section.

◊ It's important to understand that the following definitions work best when applied to four or five note voicings of ninth chords built by thirds, containing the third, fifth, seventh, and ninth intervals of the chord, or thirteenth chords where the thirteenth replaces the fifth or seventh of the chord. We'll examine the use of natural or augmented elevenths, suspended fourths, and the possibility of five note close position voicings in Chapters 16 and 22.

◊ It's also important at this point to understand the difference between *Target Tones* and *Approach Tones,* a distinction that we'll revisit in greater detail in the following chapter. For now, *Target Tones* may be defined as those melody notes which are usually under chord symbols, often on strong beats, and of longer duration. *Approach Tones* are the melody notes in between *Target Tones.* In general, target tones should be harmonized with the chord tones of the given chord symbol, whereas approach tones may be harmonized from any notes of the chord scale associated with the chord symbol, or with other methods to be demonstrated in the next chapter. It's generally more important to avoid the chord root on target tones (see 1-c below), and acceptable to include the chord root on voicings of approach tones.

Here are some "rules" for *close, semi-open,* and *open position* voicings. (Please refer to Ex. 8-4A and 8-4B for musical illustrations of these principles.)

1. *Close Position and Drop-2:*
   a. Build the chord diatonically from the top (melody note) down by using the next available notes from the appropriate chord scale. The

appropriate chord scale will very often be the major or minor scale of I of the particular passage.

b. The most common "available" chord tone choices will be the third, the fifth, the seventh, and the ninth, although this may change depending on the melody note and the choice of altered chord tones. Very often the sixth (or thirteenth) may be substituted for the fifth or the seventh, and the root may sometimes be substituted for the ninth (see letter "c" below).

c. The root will usually *not* be contained in the chord voicing, unless it is the melody note or to avoid the interval of a second between the top two voices, or to create better voice leading in the inner voices by avoiding repeated notes or awkward skips.

d. Generally, try to avoid the interval of a major or minor second between the top two notes of the voicing because this can have the effect of obscuring the melody (it's OK to do once in a while).

The following two rules apply to ensembles with at least 4 or 5 horns (see Exs. 16-1A and 16-1B for illustrations of these rules).

e. If there are five or more voices playing, the melody is *always* doubled 8vb.

f. There will *always* be three, and *only* three, chord tones in addition to the melody.

2. *Close Position*:
a. The voicing is *always* contained within one octave.
b. The voicing always contains adjacent available chord tones (usually the third, the fifth, the seventh, and the ninth).

◊ This means that in the case of ninth chords, the intervals contained within the voicing will always consist of major or minor thirds and no more than *one* major or minor second. In the case of dominant thirteenths and major or minor 6/9 chords, the intervals contained within the voicing may consist of major or minor thirds, *one* perfect or augmented fourth and one or two major or minor seconds, depending on the inversion and whether or not the ninth is altered.

3. *Semi-open Position and Drop-2*:
a. *Semi-open position* is not as strictly defined as *close position* or *drop-2*. It refers to a voicing created by skipping some of the adjacent chord tones available for close position, thereby creating more space in the voicing. With only 3 horns, it's impossible to create an authentic drop-2 voicing in the traditional sense. To create a semi-open position voicing for 3 horns, simply skip down to the second, third, fourth, etc. available chord tone below the melody for your second or third voice (see Ex. 8-4A).

b. *Drop-2* is a specific type of semi-open position voicing that can be derived from close position voicings of 4 or more notes. For drop-2 voicings (4 or more horns), the second voice below the melody *always* drops one octave 8vb from close position (see Ex. 8-4B).

4. *Open Position*:

a. The voicing will be more spread out (generally over several octaves).

b. The chord root will frequently be in the lowest voice.

c. There can be five or more different chord tones present (when voicing for larger ensembles).

5. *All Voicings*:

a. In general, keep the relative positions of the instruments within the voicings the same (trumpet above sax, alto sax above tenor sax, etc.). In other words, don't cross voices unnecessarily unless you're doing so specifically to avoid repeated notes or to create independent contrapuntal lines.

b. Observe the standard *low interval limits* outlined earlier in this chapter.

c. In general, avoid having a gap of more than a major sixth between any two adjacent voices, except the bottom two voices, which can be separated by a seventh, an octave, or a tenth.

d. Always be aware of the relative tessitura of the instruments and the basic principle that "the intensity of the lower parts should not exceed that of the higher ones."*

◊ In this and all similar "sketch" examples in the book, it is always assumed that the chord roots will be played by the bass. Without the chord root, the voicings would sound incomplete. Listen to the recorded examples on the companion website to hear the full voicings.

◊ Note that with only three horns, it's often not possible to create full sounding voicings, including the third and seventh of the chords, using the strict definitions of close position and drop-2, as was the case with Ex. 8-4A. Ex. 8-4A-1 provides an example of how to remedy this situation by using semi-open position voicings, while still maintaining a tight "close position" sound.

---

* Sebesky, *ibid.*

Ex. 8-4A

Standard Jazz Voicing Positions—3 Horns: "I Could Write a Book" by Rodgers & Hart

1. **Close Position (Rhythmic Unison)**

Melody notes in between chord symbols are harmonized "Diatonically" with any notes from the Major Scale of I, or with indicated altered tones (♭9).

2. **Semi-Open Position (Rhythmic Unison)**

♭9 avoided for smoother melodic motion.

3. **Open Position (Rhythmic Unison)**

Tritone substitution used to create Contrary Motion between trumpet & trombone.

4. **Homophonic Texture - Melody Over Pads (Semi-Open Position)**

5. **Homophonic Texture - Melody Over Rhythmic Comping (Semi-Open Position)**

6. **PolyphonicTexture - Independant Counter Melody (Top 2 Voices Close Position)**

Tpt & TS

Ex. 8-4A-1

Alternate Voicings—3 Horns: "I Could Write a Book" by Rodgers & Hart

1. Semi-Open Position Provides 3rd & 7th of Each Chord

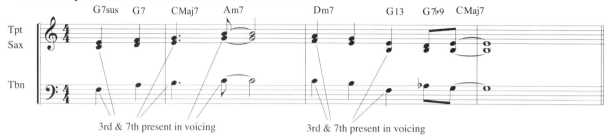

3rd & 7th present in voicing   3rd & 7th present in voicing

2. Semi-Open Position (Another Option)

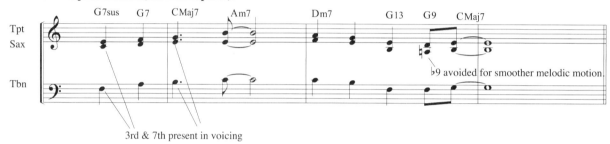

♭9 avoided for smoother melodic motion.

3rd & 7th present in voicing

Sometimes, applying the strict drop-2 formula to a four horn passage will result in unwanted parallel fifths and other voice leading problems discussed in section 8-6. Ex. 8-4B-1 provides an illustration of how to correct some problems in Ex. 8-4B by momentarily changing the voicing position (e.g., from drop-2 to close position and back). We'll re-examine some of these considerations in chapter 9 and later chapters dealing with voicing for the larger ensembles.

Play Examples 8-4A and 8-4B through *slowly* at a piano as well as listening to the recordings.

◊ Notice how much easier it is to create full-sounding close position, drop-2, and open position voicings with four notes rather than three.

Ex. 8-4B

Standard Jazz Voicing Positions—4 Horns: "I Could Write a Book" by Rodgers & Hart

1. Close Position (Rhythmic Unison)

Root used instead of 9th to avoid Maj 2nd interval between top two voices.

Melody notes in between chord symbols are harmonized "Diatonically" with any notes from the Major Scale of I, or with indicated altered tones (♭9).

2. Semi-Open Position - Drop 2 (Rhythmic Unison)

(Open Position)

The alto sax part from the Close Position voicing is dropped down an octave to become the trombone part. The other notes of the voicing remain intact, but the alto now plays what was the tenor part, and the tenor now plays what was the trombone part.

3. Open Position (Rhythmic Unison)

Tritone substitution used to create Contrary Motion between trumpet & trombone.

4. Homophonic (Melody Over Pads)

Semi-Open Position - - - - - - - - -   Close Position

5. Homophonic (Melody Over Rhythmic Comping)

Semi-Open Position - - - - - - - - -   Close Position

6. PolyphonicTexture - Independant Counter Melody (Top 3 Voices Close Position)

95

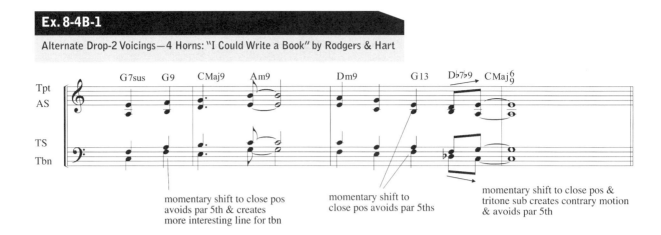

Ex. 8-4B-1

Alternate Drop-2 Voicings—4 Horns: "I Could Write a Book" by Rodgers & Hart

momentary shift to close pos avoids par 5th & creates more interesting line for tbn

momentary shift to close pos avoids par 5ths

momentary shift to close pos & tritone sub creates contrary motion & avoids par 5th

8-5 Modal Concepts of Jazz Chord Voicings

A useful analogy to the study of jazz harmony and arranging techniques is that of climbing up a ladder, one rung at a time. It's generally not advisable to attempt jumping directly from the first to the fifth rung. By acquiring an understanding of *standard jazz voicing positions*, you've jumped up to the second or third rung of the ladder. Now we're going to present another concept, which will not only take you up to the next rung, but hopefully keep you supplied with many more fresh voicing possibilities, as you proceed all the way up to the very top of the ladder. We call this *modal concepts of jazz chord voicings*.

Bearing in mind that the other principles of voicings presented in the preceding pages still apply, here's how modal concepts work.

a. We accept that there are three main chord qualities in jazz harmony: major, minor, and dominant.

b. Each of these three chord qualities has one or more possible chord scales or modes associated with it. Think of these chord scales, not in the traditional sense of scales as a stepwise progression of notes, often used mainly as a form of instrumental technical exercise, but as a *set of available notes* from which chords can be constructed.

c. To identify the primary chord scale for a particular chord, first build the chord by thirds, all the way up to the thirteenth. You'll wind up with seven notes extending over a range of two octaves: tonic, third, fifth, seventh, ninth, eleventh, and thirteenth. Simply "collapse" the seven notes into the range of one octave to form the appropriate chord scale.

d. It is possible to create effective chord voicings for any given chord by simply selecting any notes from the related chord scale and combining them, bearing in mind the principles regarding spacing, balance, density, consonance and dissonance, internal resonance, and the importance of placing the third and seventh of the chord in the low mid-register mentioned earlier in this chapter.

A comprehensive chart illustrating these principles is shown in Ex. 8-5. Play through the sample chord voicings of major, minor, and dominant seventh chords. For each voicing, first play the chord root (C), indicated in parenthesis under the bass clef staff. At a grand piano, hold the chord root down using the sostenuto pedal. With the chord root firmly established in the low register, any combination of notes from the C Lydian mode can function as a voicing for CMaj7, any combination of notes from C Dorian can function as a Cm7, etc.

Ex. 8-5

Modal Concepts of Jazz Chord Voicings

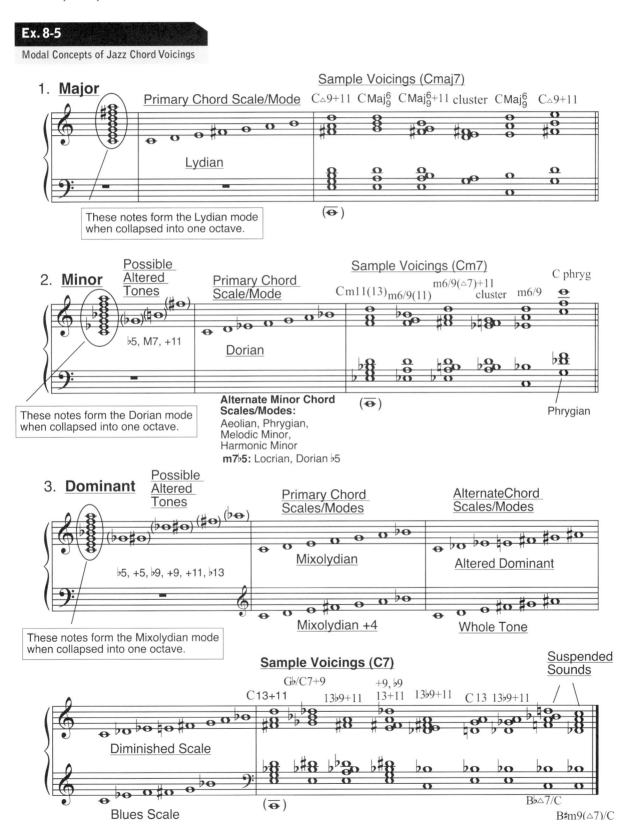

8-6 Melodic Motion and Voice Leading

We conclude this chapter with a look at some principles of *melodic motion* and *voice leading* as they relate to jazz harmony and chord voicings. When examining melodic motion consisting of two or more linear voices, we discover that there are four basic types of melodic motion (derived from classical species counterpoint):

a. *Parallel motion*—two or more voices moving in the same direction and keeping the same intervals between each of the voices.

b. *Similar motion*—two or more voices moving in the same direction but with the intervals between the voices changing.

c. *Oblique motion*—two or more voices moving, with one voice remaining static, playing repeated notes.

d. *Contrary motion*—two or more voices moving in opposite directions.

These principles are illustrated in Ex. 8-6. Please note that in this example it was nearly impossible to stick entirely to one type of melodic motion within the four-bar phrase and still keep the examples sounding musical. The type of melodic motion used is clearly indicated within each example.

We've found that it's useful to borrow a few more voice-leading principles from classical theory.

a. Move each voice as smoothly as possible from one chord to the next, using scalar motion or intervals of no greater than a perfect fourth wherever possible, unless there are skips of larger intervals in the melody line. In general, no inner voice should skip by an interval larger than that of the melody.

b. Parallel thirds and sixths work best in terms of internal resonance.

c. Avoid *parallel fifths* unless going for a special effect. Parallel fifths occur when two independent voices sounding a perfect fifth move to another perfect fifth by parallel motion.**

d. Avoid *exposed* or *hidden fifths* or *octaves* between the outer two voices, unless you're going for a special effect. Hidden or exposed fifths or octaves occur when two independent parts approach a perfect fifth or octave by similar motion.**

e. Try for contrary motion between the outer two voices or inner voices whenever possible.

f. Avoid crossing voices unnecessarily, except to avoid repeated notes or parallel or hidden fifths or octaves or when creating independent contrapuntal lines.

** It's not necessary to apply these rules from classical species counterpoint in a strict sense when writing for a jazz ensemble. However, we've discovered that avoiding parallel or hidden fifths or octaves invariably leads to better voicing solutions. We strongly recommend that if you are seriously interested in mastering the art of jazz arranging, you should consider taking a separate course in classical species counterpoint.

g. Try to make each inner voice as melodic as possible. Especially, try to avoid excessive repeated notes in an inner part, since this will make the part boring to the player. We can't emphasize this point enough.

◊ **The more interesting and musical the individual parts are for each player in an ensemble, the more musical and expressive the overall performance will be.**

Ex. 8-6

Types of Melodic Motion—3 Horns: "My Romance" by Rodgers & Hart

1. Parallel

Technically, this is diatonic or scalar parallel motion, since the intervals are adhering to the notes of a Bb major scale, as opposed to strict parallel motion, where each voice would move chromatically by exactly the same interval.

2. Similar

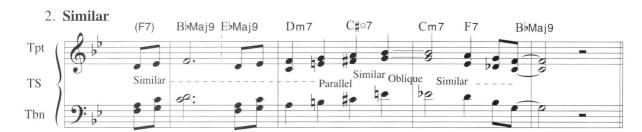

3. Oblique

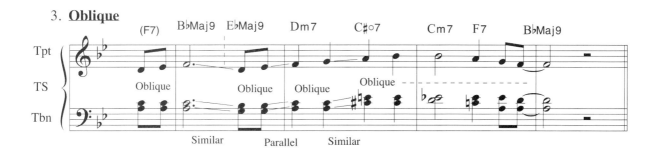

4. Contrary

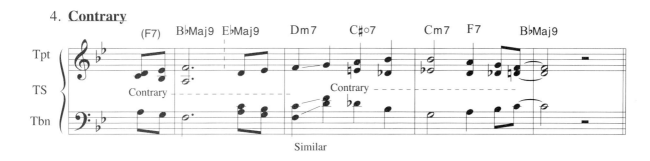

Chapter Summary

In this chapter, we reviewed some areas of jazz harmony that we believe are essential to the jazz arranger, with special focus on the properties of the tritone and diminished seventh chord, as well as tritone and minor third substitution. We then introduced the concepts of vertical and horizontal harmony and provided some basic principles and rules for creating good jazz chord voicings, including the rules pertaining to the standard jazz voicing positions: close position, semi-open position, drop-2, and open position.

We also presented the important and useful modal concepts of chord voicings. Finally, we discussed the various types of melodic motion and provided some principles for creating good voice leading. You should be familiar with all of the *italicized* terms and concepts defined or discussed earlier in this chapter or preceding chapters.

◊ When doing Exercises 4 & 5 below, be sure to harmonize notes under chord symbols, on strong beats of the measure, or of longer duration (*Target Notes*), with primary chord tones or tensions derived from the chord symbol. For now, stick to diatonic harmonizations (using only notes of the chord scale of I) of any approach tones or passing tones (as illustrated in Ex. 8-4A & B). We'll provide detailed definitions of target notes and approach tones, and examine additional techniques for approach tone harmonization in chapter 9.

Exercises

Continue to use the appropriate functions in your notation software for the following exercises, using the templates provided on the website. However, in certain cases, as with instrument transpositions, using the software can make things "too easy," resulting in a weakness in some area of your arranging skills. Please be sure to do Exercise 2 by hand, as indicated. We'll go into greater detail about how to print out professional-looking scores and parts in Chapter 15. For now, as much as possible, try to keep four bars per staff for the parts and eight bars per page for the scores.

1. Pick a tune you like of any 3- to 4-horn jazz recording. Listen to the recording in a focused way, and be able to describe what it is about the music that makes it sound great.
2. Pick any 32-bar standard or jazz standard. Copy out parts by hand, with the correct clefs and transpositions, of the melody, for B♭ trumpet, E♭ alto sax, B♭ tenor sax, trombone, guitar, and bass. Play, and check for mistakes.
3. Using modal concepts of chord voicings write five or six voicings for each of the three main chord qualities (major, minor, and dominant).

Use the Grand-Staff Piano Template provided on the website for this exercise. It can be useful to make this an ongoing exercise, eventually filling up several pages with possible voicings for each chord quality. When you find a voicing you really like, take it through a circle of fifths.

4. Voice the first eight bars of "My Romance" or a similar standard (one with a lot of stepwise motion) for 4 horns (trumpet, alto sax, tenor sax, and trombone) 3 times:
   a. In close position only.
   b. In drop-2 only.
   c. In open position only.

   Use the Grand-Staff Piano Template. Observe all the rules for these voicings outlined in this chapter, and don't cross any of the voices (trumpet always on top, then alto, tenor, and trombone on the bottom). Stick to diatonic harmonization of approach tones.

◊ Please note that it's a very valuable exercise to master the rules for each of the three basic standard voicing positions. However, in real life, you will rarely voice an entire passage exclusively with only one technique, choosing rather to move from one style to another, going with the ebb and flow of the music, and trusting to your musical instincts.

5. **Arranging Project 1:** Begin writing an arrangement for 3–4 horns (trumpet, alto and/or tenor sax, and trombone) + rhythm of "My Romance," "I Could Write a Book," or a similar standard tune (refer to the Recommended Standard Tunes list at the end of this chapter). Start by arranging just the head of the tune using voicing techniques discussed in this chapter. Stick to close, semi-open, or drop-2 voicing positions for this exercise (no roots in the chord voicings except as noted). Apply ideas from your modified melodies from the last chapter's assignment.
   - *First "A" Section (8 bars)—Homophonic:* Melody above pads or rhythmic comping.
   - *First "B" Section (8 bars)—Monophonic:* Solo instrument *or* any 2 horns in unison or octaves.
   - *Second "A" Section (8 bars)—Rhythmic Unison (homophonic):* Horns voiced in close or semi-open position using techniques discussed in this chapter.
   - *Second "B" Section (8 bars)—*First four bars: A different solo instrument, unison, or octaves (monophonic); second four bars: 3 or 4 horns in rhythmic unison as in the second "A" section (homophonic). Focus on the principles of chord voicings and contrasting types of melodic motion discussed in this chapter. Use the 3 or 4 Horns +

101

Rhythm Concert Score Template. For now, just put the chord changes and accents for the rhythm section on the piano treble clef staff. Make sure to observe the correct instrument ranges for each instrument as well as the principles of tessitura discussed in the preceding chapter.

- *For 3* Horns: Use trumpet, alto or tenor sax, and trombone.
- *For 4 Horns*: Use trumpet, alto sax, tenor sax, and trombone.

6. Print out your score and parts, including three to four copies of the rhythm section parts. Make sure to observe correct transpositions for the horn parts. Play and analyze the results. Whenever possible, do this for all exercises in this book.

◊ **Software Tip:** When doing Exercise 4, and in subsequent arranging exercises, try using the piano grand staff as a sketchpad to work out the horn voicings. Once you've got the voicings worked out, input the correct notes into each appropriate staff, and delete them from the piano staff.

Get into the habit of using the copy and paste, transpose, and similar functions in your software to speed things up. For example, if you want the trombone to double the alto sax an octave lower, input the notes into the alto staff, then copy and paste into the trombone staff, and transpose down an octave. This procedure, and all "Cut, Copy, and Paste" commands from the Edit menus, are similar in both Finale and Sibelius. Consult "Software Tips" on the companion website for more details.

◊ The following tunes are recommended for the initial exercises in this book because they contain qualities that lend themselves to the application of some of the basic principles and techniques we'll be presenting. The list is by no means comprehensive, and any songs with similar qualities would be suitable for the arranging exercises. These qualities include the following.

1. Medium-tempo to up-tempo swing feel in 4/4 meter.
2. Relatively simple, ii-V–based chord progressions (modulations are OK).
3. A greater percentage of stepwise and quarter-note/eighth-note motion (not too notey).
4. Relatively simple, standard song forms (AABA, ABAC, etc.).

Recommended Standard Tunes

All of Me

All the Things You Are

Alone Together

Autumn Leaves

But Not for Me
Dancing on the Ceiling
Days of Wine and Roses
Don't Get Around Much Any More
Have You Met Miss Jones
How Deep Is the Ocean?
How High the Moon
The Song Is You
I Love You
I Should Care
I'll Remember April
In a Mellow Tone
Invitation
Isn't It Romantic
It Could Happen to You
It's All Right with Me
Just Friends
Just in Time
Just One of Those Things
On Green Dolphin Street
Our Love Is Here to Stay
Out of Nowhere
Somebody Loves Me
Speak Low
The Night Has a Thousand Eyes
The Way You Look Tonight
You and the Night and the Music
You Stepped Out of a Dream

Jazz Standards
Fee-Fi-Fo-Fum
Four
In Your Own Sweet Way
Jeannine
Minority
Nica's Dream
Stablemates
Voyage
Whisper Not

Chapter 9

Reharmonization of Approach Tones (3–4 Horns)

In this chapter, we'll continue with our exploration of harmonic tools available to the jazz arranger, with special focus on the technique known as *reharmonization of approach tones*. We'll also examine some more principles of voice leading and techniques for improving the musicality of the inner voices (those parts below the melody).

9-1 Reharmonization of Approach Tones

When harmonizing a melody, it's important to distinguish between *target notes* and *approach tones*. Target notes tend to be longer or emphasized notes, usually the ones underneath chord symbols on a lead sheet, or at the end of a phrase, which can be harmonized directly by primary chord tones or tensions derived from the chord symbol. Approach tones, often referred to as *passing tones* in classical music theory, are the notes in between, often of shorter duration, leading to the target notes. In the preceding chapter, we dealt with approach tones by harmonizing them diatonically, which is one available option.

The concept of *reharmonization of approach tones* is critically important to any arranger, because it provides a means for creating much more colorful and lively harmonizations of a melody, which could otherwise be dull and static. Because the chords arising from these techniques resolve quickly back to the harmony of the target notes, the primary underlying harmony of the music is not disturbed. Don't confuse reharmonization of approach tones with *melodic reharmonization*, which we'll look at later, in Chapter 10. It should also be pointed out that the following techniques are most effective when the melody line is moving by scalar, or stepwise, motion.

Here are five useful techniques for reharmonization of approach tones.

1. *Diatonic*—When a melody moves diatonically to or from a target note using notes derived from a chord scale of the target note or of the tonal center of the passage, the approach tones may be harmonized using notes from those same chord scales.

2. *Dominant*—If the approach tone is a note or altered tone of a dominant or secondary dominant to the chord being approached, the approach tone may be harmonized by notes from the chord scale of this dominant or secondary dominant chord. The techniques of minor third and tritone substitution as well as changing color tones (natural or altered fifth, ninth, eleventh, and thirteenth) may also be applied to this method, providing many arranging options.

3. *Diminished seventh chords*—An approach tone may be harmonized by building a diminished seventh chord downward from the melody note. This technique almost always works, because the ambiguous and unstable nature of the diminished seventh chord seems to impart a healthy, forward motion to the line.

4. *Parallel (half-step/whole-step planing)*—If the approach tone moves by half step or whole step, ascending or descending, to or from a target note or another approach tone, it may be harmonized by moving the voicing of the target note backward or forward in parallel motion to the approach tone. This technique is sometimes referred to as *half-step or whole-step planing*. Although most commonly used with all voices moving in parallel motion, half-step and whole-step planing can also be effective when some voices move in contrary motion to the target note.

5. *Free reharmonization*—The approach tone is harmonized by any available chord, without using diatonic or dominant harmony, as long as it sounds good. (This is actually an illustration of non-diatonic, or non-functional, harmony, which we'll examine in more detail in Section 3.)

Listen to the recorded examples on the website and play through the music in Ex. 9-1 at a piano. The bass line is written in (with stems pointing down in the bass clef) for reference. Refer to the legend given at the end of this chapter to identify which notes are target notes and which techniques are being employed. Notice how each technique has a slightly different flavor. Diatonic, dominant, and diminished seventh chord techniques seem to have a more "traditional" sound (more release), whereas parallel and free reharmonization seem to sound more "modern" (more tension). The best results are obtained by mixing and matching the different techniques, based on which ones sound best for a particular passage (contrast and variety). Try to keep your choices balanced. For example, don't start out with a few free reharmonizations followed by eight bars of only diminished seventh chords. The harmonization of a melody may also be affected by changing the altered or color tones of a chord. We've chosen to designate these cases as **Alt** (altered tones) in the examples.

Ex. 9-1

Reharmonization of Approach Tones—4 Horns: "My Romance" by Rodgers & Hart

1. Diatonic

1. The approach tones are harmonized entirely by notes from the diatonic major scale of I (B♭ Major). The C♯ diminished seventh chord in bar 2 is labeled a target note because that chord is actually part of the original harmonization of this melody by Richard Rodgers. (In other words, Rodgers was aware of the "approach tone" quality of diminished seventh chords.) Changing the inversion, chord spacing, or diatonic color tones of a target chord also belongs in this category; such instances are labeled **D** in the examples.

2. Dominant

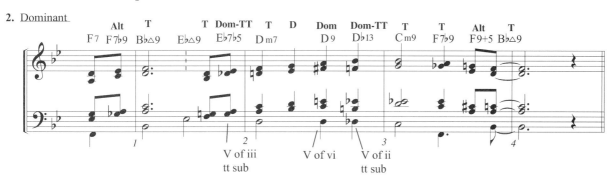

2. • Bar 1 - last chord = E♭7♭5 (secondary dominant—tritone sub V of iii).
   • Bar 2—third chord = D9 (secondary dominant—V of vi).
   • Bar 2—fourth chord = D♭13 (secondary dominant—tritone sub V of ii).
   • Pickup bar and last chord of bar 3—labeled **Alt**. Changing the altered tones of the dominant V7 chord (e.g., 9th to ♭9 or P5 to +5) adds color and also belongs in this category.

3. Diminished 7th

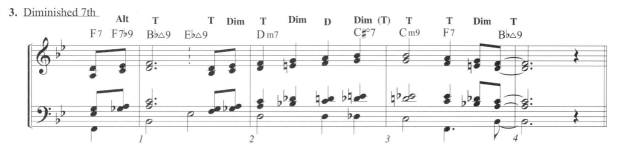

3. Pickup bar—second chord, bar 1—last chord, bar 2—second and fourth chords, and bar 3—third chord are all diminished seventh chords. It doesn't matter what the roots are.

107

4. Parallel

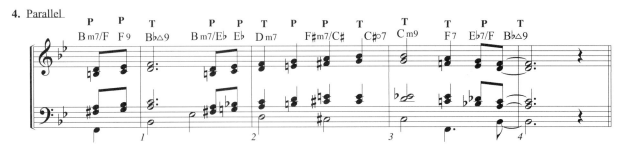

4. Pickup bar—both chords, bar 1—second and third chords, bar 2—second and third chords, and bar 3—third chord all utilize parallel reharmonization techniques.

5. Free Reharmonization

5. • Pickup bar, last chord = A♭m9.
   • Bar 1—last chord = A♭9.
   • Bar 2—second chord = Cm9(Maj 7), fourth chord = BMaj7.
   • Bar 3—third chord = G13♭9.
   • All examples of free (non-functional) reharmonization.
   • Also note the use of contrary motion in bar 3, beats 3 and 4.

The reference bass line represents a typical bass line, outlining the chord roots, which might be played by the bass. It's important to hear all of these examples referenced to the underlying harmony and chord roots.

Play these examples through *slowly* at a piano as well as listening to the recordings.

Example 9-2A provides an illustration of reharmonization of approach tones in a melodic passage scored for 4 horns, using a balanced variety of these techniques (balance). Example 9-2B illustrates the same passage with *no* approach tones reharmonized. Study and listen carefully to both examples, comparing the differences. Notice the excessive number of repeated notes in Ex. 9-2B, resulting in uninteresting, dull sounding inner voices. Also, notice that there's a fair number of chord roots contained in some of the voicings in Ex. 9-2A. This was done in the interest of producing more lyrical, melodic inner voices with good voice leading.

Ex. 9-2A

Reharmonization of Approach Tones—4 Horns: "Analycity," composed and arranged by Richard Sussman

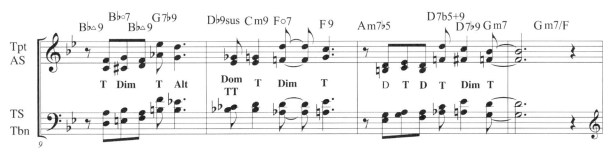

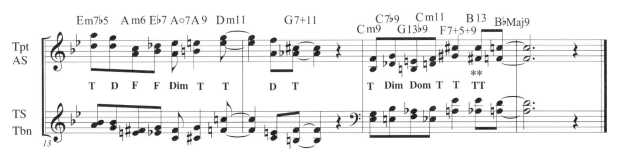

109

* m. 3, 3rd beat - Really Dominant Harmony - a voicing for Am11, the ii of Gm, giving us a ii-V-i to Gm

** m. 15, 4th beat - 1/2 Step Planing with 1 voice moving in contrary motion to the others.

◊ **Software Tip:** Examples 9-2A and 9-2B are available for download as Finale, Sibelius, or MIDI files on the companion website. There's a "Hidden" Bass Track in this file for MIDI Playback. Make sure you have a Bass sound selected for the Bass Staff in the Instrument List Window of Finale or the Instruments Window of Sibelius and Piano sounds selected for the other two staves to get the full effect.

Example 9-2B is the same as Ex. 9-2A, but with no approach tones reharmonized, for comparison.

Ex. 9-2B

No Reharmonization of Approach Tones—4 Horns: "Analycity," composed and arranged by Richard Sussman

A good method for working out the harmonizations of approach tones is first to label the target notes (T) and work out chord voicings for those notes. Then, *working backward* from the target note, decide on an appropriate reharmonization method from the five listed earlier. For example, see if the approach note can be harmonized by the secondary dominant of the target chord or if one of the other techniques sounds better. Once you've made your choice, fill in the other notes of the voicings, generally using close, semi-open, or drop-2 positions (save open position for final resolutions or *full tutti* sections requiring extra force and power). Finally, when you've completed voicing a passage, play through each part of the accompanying voices to make sure they all sound melodic and musical. If you find a line that has too many repeated notes or awkward melodic motion, make appropriate adjustments to the parts.

◊ In general, the techniques for reharmonization of approach tones just illustrated are applied to voicings for the brass and woodwinds and generally should also be reflected in the chord symbols used in the rhythm section parts. There are some situations where these techniques may *not* need to be reflected in the rhythm section parts, especially when the reharmonizations are diatonic or diminished seventh chords. Here the piano and bass will typically play notes associated with the "original" chord changes, unless serious dissonant clashes occur. In situations where there are a lot of chromatic and altered tones in the approach tone reharmonizations, it's usually advisable to write in *every* reharmonized chord symbol in the rhythm section parts. This is illustrated in Exs. 9-1 and 9-2A.

9-2 Repeated Notes, Static Harmony, and Voice Leading

When harmonizing a melody for any size ensemble, it's critically important to pay close attention to the linear, melodic quality of all instrumental voices underneath the melody line. It's easy, especially when first starting out, to focus on the vertical harmony of each chord and to lose track of the horizontal lines being created for the inner voices. One of the most common problems during this process is the accumulation of too many repeated notes in an accompanying part. Not only do repeated notes result in a less interesting melodic shape, but they can also create articulation problems for the players, causing the section to sound less unified. As stated at the end of the preceding chapter, the more interesting and musical the individual parts are for each player in an ensemble, the more musical and expressive the overall performance will be. Obviously, this should be an important concern for any writer.

There are several easy and effective methods for reducing the number of repeated notes, thereby creating more musical lines for the inner voices.

1. Change the spacing of the chord voicing (e.g., from close to semi-open position, or vice versa).

2. Choose alternate chord tones or tensions for the inner voices (e.g., substitute the sixth for the fifth, or use an altered fifth or ninth instead of the natural one).

3. Use strategic reharmonization of approach tones.

4. Crossing voices (e.g., the tenor sax moves momentarily above the alto, or the third trombone moves momentarily above the second in a big band arrangement), when used judiciously, can be a very effective way of keeping the inner voices melodically interesting. However, be careful *not* to cross voices unnecessarily, except to avoid repeated notes or parallel or hidden fifths or octaves or when creating independent contrapuntal lines, because this can create confusion within a horn section during a performance.

Example 9-3 illustrates the application of these techniques to a passage that was first harmonized in a manner resulting in too many repeated notes. Listen carefully to the recorded examples to hear how the motion of the inner voices affects the overall sound of the music. Example 9-3-4 (reharmonization of approach tones) is the most dramatic.

Pay special attention to Ex. 9-3-5, "Crossing Voices." The alto, tenor, and trombone lines cross each other a number of times to avoid repeated notes in each part. Play through the alto, tenor, and trombone parts separately (indicated by the crossing arrows), and compare how much more musical each part sounds than in the original example, Ex. 9-3-1. The X's indicate where the alto sax crosses below the tenor. Example 9-3-5, although almost identical harmonically to Ex. 9-3-1, sounds much livelier because of the cross-voicing motion of the inner voices. If you play this example as written, on the piano or on your sequencer, you won't hear any difference.

In Example 9-3, be sure to play through each individual line separately, beginning with the original passage with repeated notes. Care was taken, in creating the four solutions, not only to avoid repeated notes but also to avoid awkward tritone skips and parallel fifths. Nevertheless, we've left some repeated notes in, because it sounds OK to do so—in fact it can actually sound worse if you try to eliminate every single repeated note. Notice that in the last measure of Exs. 9-3-2 and 9-3-3 moving the trombone momentarily down to G♯ and then back up to A not only eliminates the repeated notes but also provides contrary motion between the outer two voices. The momentary absence of the primary-chord third A is not missed. In Ex. 9-1-5, the X under the AS notes indicates the alto part crossing under the tenor.

Ex. 9-3

Repeated Notes: "Tautology," composed and arranged by Richard Sussman

1. Original Passage With Repeated Notes

2. Changing the Spacing

3. Choosing Alternate Chord Tones

4. Reharmonization of Approach Tones

5. Crossing Voices

Static harmony refers to a situation where there is a fairly active melody harmonized by only one chord for several measures. A good example of this is the first four bars of "I'll Remember April." The same techniques employed for reharmonization of approach tones and avoiding repeated notes illustrated earlier can also be effectively applied when dealing with static harmony (Ex. 9-4).

In any event, always examine all parts and inner voices carefully to make sure there are no awkward skips, parallel fifths, or unnecessary crossing of voices. These types of problems can usually be fixed by changing the spacing of the chord voicing, simply switching the crossed voices, and following the principles for good voice leading outlined in the preceding chapter.

Please be aware that occasional repeated notes are OK, as you can see in the examples. It's only when you have strings of three or more repeated notes occurring throughout a part that it becomes a problem. Also, notice that we've ended all the examples of "I'll Remember April" with an interval of a major second between the top two voices, breaking one of the rules from Chapter 8

Ex. 9-4

Static Harmony: "I'll Remember April," by Johnston, Raye, and De Paul

1. Static Harmony & Accompaniment

2. Static Harmony with Diatonic Reharmonization (Close Position)

3. Static Harmony with Approach Tone & Melodic Reharmonization (Close Position)

(Section 8-4). Again, an occasional major or minor second between the top two voices is OK. It's only when there's a string of successive seconds that it can become a problem by tending to obscure the melody.

Example 9-5-1 is full of typical voicing mistakes commonly made by beginning arrangers. The alto, tenor, and trombone cross each other a number of times for no reason (indicated by brackets). This can result not only in bad voice leading (in this case a couple of awkward skips of a tritone and a minor sixth) but also in confusion among the players (e.g., when the trombone part suddenly appears *above* the saxes). Also, notice the parallel fifths between the trumpet and alto in the first measure, which stick out like a sore thumb. Example 9-5-2 shows the same passage with these mistakes corrected.

Ex. 9-5

Voice-Leading Considerations: "I'll Remember April," by Johnston, Raye, and De Paul

Concert Score

1. Mistakes

2. Better

Chapter Summary

In this chapter we continued our study of those elements of jazz harmony essential to the art of arranging. You should now be familiar with the important concept of reharmonization of approach tones. We also provided some useful techniques for dealing with repeated notes and static harmony.

◊ **Software Tip:** When doing the following Exercise 2, in Finale, try using the technique known as "Explode Music" in the Utilities menu. Work out the horn voicings on the top (Trumpet) staff, with a piano sound temporarily assigned to that staff. When you've got a section of the voicings worked out, select the entire region, using the Selection tool. Then go to Utilities > Explode Music. Make sure to assign a trumpet sound back to the trumpet staff before you attempt MIDI playback. A similar tool is available in Sibelius. Refer to the website for more details.

◊ **Software Tip:** If you want to get a more satisfying swing feel out of Finale for MIDI playback, first select "Jazz" for Human Playback Mode in the Playback Controls window. We then recommend scaling back the swing feel to about 30% to 60%. You can also apply swing feel to playback of Sibelius scores. Go to Play > Performance. Choose one of the available presets from the "Rhythmic Feel" drop-down menu.

Exercises

1. Arrange the first 16 bars of "My Romance," "I Could Write a Book," or a similar standard for 3–4 horns in close position or drop 2. Use the techniques for reharmonization of approach tones discussed in this chapter, avoiding repeated notes. Use the 3 or 4 Horns + Rhythm Concert Score Template.

2. **Arranging Project 1:** Continue working on the arrangement for 3–4 horns and rhythm of "My Romance," "I Could Write a Book," or a similar standard. Develop the arrangement begun in Chapter 8 by applying the principles of reharmonization of approach tones and voice leading discussed in this chapter. Pay special attention to avoiding the excessive use of repeated notes. Apply ideas from Exercise 1. Use the 3 or 4 Horns + Rhythm Concert Score Template.

◊ **Important:** The following legend explains the abbreviations used in Exs. 9-1 and 9-2A to indicate which type of approach tone reharmonization technique is employed. This legend applies throughout the book wherever there is an analysis of approach tone reharmonization.

Legend for Approach Tone Reharmonization

T—target note

P—parallel approach chord

D—diatonic approach chord

F—free reharmonization

Dom—dominant approach chord

TT—tritone substitution

SD—secondary dominant

Alt—altered tones

Dim—diminished seventh passing chord

Melodic Reharmonization and Counterpoint (3–4 Horns)

In this chapter we continue our exploration of jazz harmony with an examination of the techniques of *melodic reharmonization*. These techniques actually change the fundamental underlying harmony of a chord progression and are distinctly different in function from the *reharmonization of approach tones* discussed in the last chapter.

10-1 Techniques of Melodic Reharmonization

The original, *primary harmony,* or chord progression, of a tune may be altered at the arranger's discretion as a means of creating a fresh interpretation of a familiar melody by introducing new harmonic colors and as a way of creating contrast and variety within an arrangement. There is a wide range of techniques of melodic reharmonization available to any arranger, varying in intensity from mild to extreme. Care must be taken not to subject a melody to an inappropriate harmonization (one that sounds forced and unnatural) and also to be respectful of the original harmonizations of standard tunes by such esteemed composers as Gershwin, Ellington, and Rodgers. Any melodic reharmonization, as with any other element of music, should feel organic and natural and should serve to support and enhance the overall arrangement. In other words, reharmonize a melody only if you really hear it that way—*not* just to be hip or different.

Finally, we believe that melodic reharmonization is most effective when the arranger truly understands the original harmonization first and uses it as a point of departure or reference. This point is clearly illustrated in the "modern" reharmonization of "Autumn Leaves" provided in Ex. 10-2B.

Following are some common techniques of melodic reharmonization. To be consistent with our approach to harmony in this section, for now we'll focus mainly on the diatonic, dominant/functional, and modal techniques (techniques 1–12). We'll return to this list and examine the more modern techniques (numbers 13–17) in Section 3.

Techniques 3 and 4 are essentially the same as what we've already looked at with the reharmonization of approach tones. Technique 5 (dominant harmony), although one of the methods used with approach tones, can be utilized here as a way of reharmonizing a target note, thus changing the primary harmony, with a very different and more dramatic result.

At this point we would like to introduce the concept of a *primary chord,* or *target chord,* meaning a chord that occurs on a *target note* and is part of the original *primary harmonization* of the tune. The most useful of the following techniques, for our purposes at this stage, are likely to be numbers 5, 6, 7, and 8. These are the techniques (up to number 12) that will most effectively change the color of the primary harmony, as opposed to the approach tones or passing tones.

For a more comprehensive study of the techniques of melodic reharmonization, we refer you to the excellent *Handbook of Chord Substitutions* by Andy Laverne.

Techniques of Melodic Reharmonization

1. Simple diatonic reharmonization.
2. Additions or alterations of chord tones (interpretation of chord symbols).
3. Harmonization of additional melody notes (approach tones).
4. Diatonic or diminished seventh passing chords (approach tones).
5. Dominant harmony, including secondary dominants (can be used on primary, target notes, as well as with approach tones).
6. Changing chord quality.
7. Insertion of chords in between melody notes.
8. Tritone/minor third substitution.
9. Modulation.
10. Suspended sounds.
11. Pedal points.
12. Modal harmony.
13. Polytonal sounds (slash chords).
14. Non-functional harmony—arbitrary root motion or root motion by:
    a. Whole-step/half-step.
    b. Major/minor third/tritone.
15. Constant structures.
16. Any melody note can be harmonized by any chord root as:
    a. Chord tone.
    b. Altered chord tone or upper structure.
    c. Non-chord tone.
17. Atonal sounds.

Example 10-1 illustrates techniques 1–12 individually. Examples 10-2A and 10-2B illustrate the application of some of these techniques to a reharmonization of "Autumn Leaves."

Ex. 10-1

Techniques of Melodic Reharmonization: "Autumn Leaves" by Mercer, Prevert, and Kosma

1. Simple Diatonic

1. *Diatonic*: The primary chords are reharmonized using scale-derived chords or secondary dominants from the tonic scale.

2. Altered Chord Tones

2. *Altered chord tones*: Adding different alterations or tension tones to a chord can affect its impact significantly.

3. Harmonization of Additional Melody Notes

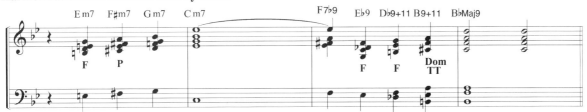

3. Harmonization *of additional melody notes*: Essentially the same as with reharmonization of approach tones.

4. Diatonic or Diminished 7th Passing Chords

4. *Diatonic or diminished seventh passing chords*: Essentially the same as with reharmonization of approach tones.

121

5. Dominant Harmony (Including Secondary Dominants)

5. *Dominant* harmony: In Example 10-1-5, we've used secondary dominant techniques, working backward from the target chord, in mm. 1 and 3. D9 = V of V of iv, D♭13 = V (tritone substitution) of iv. In bar 3, D♭7 = V (tritone substitution) of iv, C9 = V of V of III, and B9 = tritone substitution of V of III. These examples are all essentially the same as with reharmonization of approach tones. What's possibly more interesting is the substitution of E7+9 (V of ii in G minor) for the expected E♭Maj7 in bar 5. Also, notice that it's OK sometimes to change the melody notes to make them fit the reharmonization.

6. Changing Chord Quality

6. *Changing chord quality*: Changing the expected C minor to C7+9+11, the F7 to Fm9, and the B♭Maj7 to B♭13+11 can have a surprisingly dramatic impact.

7. Insertion of Chords In Between Melody Notes

7. *Insertion* of *chords between melody notes*: This technique can also have a surprisingly dramatic effect, especially when the harmonic rhythm of the tune is moving relatively slowly and when utilizing dominant harmony.

8. Tritone & Minor 3rd Substitution

8. *Tritone/minor* third *substitution*: Possibly the most familiar and effective of all of these techniques—described in detail in Chapter 8.

* Dominant sequence supported by descending chromatic bass line.

9. Modulation

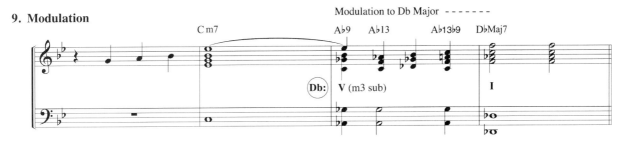

9. Modulation: As you can hear in Example 10-1-9, this can be overly dramatic; it should be used in moderation.

10. Suspended Sounds

10. *Suspended sounds*: Essentially a variation on changing chord quality or the use of a specific type of chord structure (very often resulting in chords built by fourths) for effect.

11. Pedal Points

11. *Pedal points*: Pedaling on the dominant (as illustrated—analyzing the first four bars in B♭) or another scale degree can provide an effective variation to the primary chord changes.

12. Modal Harmony

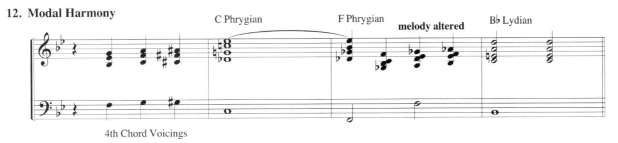

4th Chord Voicings

12. *Modal harmony*: There are many different interpretations of the term *modal harmony*. We've provided one in Example 10-1-12 by designating a mode instead of chord symbol for the chord changes. Very often a modal approach to harmony can lead to chords built by fourths, hence the fourth-chord voicings in the pickup measure. Notice the change of melody note in the last phrase, as in technique 5.

Ex. 10-2

Lead Sheet with Analysis: "Autumn Leaves" by Mercer, Prevert, and Kosma

In Ex. 10-2A we stretched things a little in m. 10 by using what's really a polytonal sound (technique 13), although the chord could also technically be analyzed as an alteration of F7 with the ♭9 in the bass. We've included Ex. 10-2B partly as a preview of things to come in Chapter 27. However, it's useful to notice now that even though we've ventured pretty far from the original chord changes, through the use of non-functional harmony and polytonal sounds, the reharmonization sounds accessible because we've made reference to the original harmonic structure through the V-I or implied V-I resolution from D7 to G minor in bars 7–8 and 15–16, as well as by preserving some of the original root motion.

Ex. 10-2A

Functional Reharmonization: "Autumn Leaves" by Mercer, Prevert, and Kosma

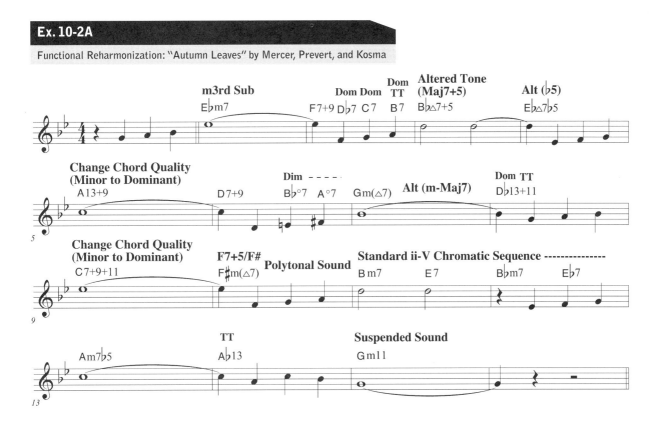

Ex. 10-2B

"Modern" Reharmonization: "Autumn Leaves" by Mercer, Prevert, and Kosma

10-2 Independent Counter-melodies and Polyphony

An in-depth study of counterpoint is beyond the scope of this book. However, counter-melodies and polyphony form an integral part of the palette of any competent jazz arranger. In fact, polyphonic techniques provide essential tools for adding excitement and color to a musical composition or arrangement. Here are a few basic principles to keep in mind when adding counter-melodies to an arrangement.

1. Apply the techniques and principles for constructing a good melody presented in Chapter 7.

2. Apply the principles of melodic motion and voice leading presented in Chapter 8.

3. Try to contrast the melodic shape and motion of the counter-melody with that of the primary melody (contrast and variety).

4. Try to arrive on consonant intervals at key harmonic destination points (target chords).

5. It can be useful to think of counter-melodies as being either *active* (fast) *or slow* or as being simply *fills* in between phrases of the primary melody (contrast melodic density).

6. Move the counter-melody during sustained notes or rests in the primary melody, and, conversely, pause the counter-melody when the primary melody becomes more active (balance).

7. Strive for contrary motion, especially between the lowest and highest voices, whenever possible.

8. In general, it's not a good idea to harmonize two or more independent melodic lines simultaneously. With polyphony, unisons and octaves work best in terms of orchestrating the different lines, or one voice may be harmonized, accompanied by one or more counter-melodies in unisons or octaves (focus).

Example 10-3 illustrates the use of counter-melodies in a 3-horn arrangement of "Autumn Leaves." Notice how the "active" counterpoint occurs mainly during pauses in the primary melody. The melody switches to the trombone momentarily in mm. 6–7 while the trumpet and sax pick up the counterpoint. We altered the melody notes slightly in m. 10 to fit the reharmonization. There are consonant intervals on all of the target chords. Remember, a tritone or dominant seventh chord may be considered to be consonant in jazz harmony, as may a major or minor ninth chord.

◊ The type of slow, linear counterpoint illustrated in mm. 9–10 is often referred to as "Guide Tones" because it "guides" the inner voice to important chord tones such as the third or seventh (the chord sevenths in m. 10—if we continued the line with a D on the downbeat of m. 11 it would be the chord third).

127

Ex. 10-3

Counterpoint—3 Horns: "Autumn Leaves" by Mercer, Prevert, and Kosma, arranged by R. Sussman

Concert Score

Chapter Summary

In this chapter we presented some valuable techniques for melodic reharmonization. You should now be familiar with and understand the difference between the important concepts of *reharmonization of approach tones* and *techniques of melodic reharmonization*. We also introduced some principles for constructing effective counter-melodies and polyphony.

◊ **Software Tip:** In the Chapter 7 Software Tip, we recommended that you disable Chord Playback in the Chord Menu in Finale. If you want to hear piano chords during MIDI playback, you'll get much better results by playing in the actual voicings using Speedy or Simple Entry. The notes will be hidden from view when you select Slash or Rhythmic Notation using the Staff Styles Tool (more about this in the next chapter). Another option (if you've got a written line in the piano part + chord symbols) is to put the chords in Layer 2 and hide the notes in that layer. In either case, the chords will play back even though they are hidden from view. It's also possible to hide entire staves with music in them, which will play back during MIDI playback. We've used these techniques in some of the MIDI examples available on the website (e.g., Exs. 9-2A and 9-2B).

Similar techniques are available in Sibelius. Consult the Software Tips on the website for more details on these functions. We recommend that you use these techniques when creating piano, guitar, and bass parts while working in either software platform *if* you want to experience satisfying MIDI playback of the music as you work.

Exercises

1. Reharmonize the first 16 bars of the tune you've selected for Arranging Project 1, using techniques discussed in this chapter. Use the Lead Sheet Template (Single Staff/Melody & Chord Symbols).

2. Compose a counter-melody to the melody of the tune. Use the Piano Grand Staff Template (two lines with chord symbols).

◊ 3. **Arranging Project 1:** Continue working on your arrangement for 3–4 horns and rhythm of a standard tune. Develop the arrangement by using elements of your reharmonization and counter-melody from Exercises 1 and 2. (*Hint*: Add a counter-melody during the first B section or bridge of the tune.) Refer to all principles of chord voicings, voice leading, and reharmonization of approach tones discussed so far in this book. Use the 3–4 Horns + Rhythm Concert Score Template.

Chapter 11

Form and Planning the Arrangement/ Instrumentation

We've now completed our initial study of the fundamental musical elements of rhythm, melody, and harmony—and established some principles and techniques applicable to these elements with regard to the process of jazz composition and arranging. It's now time to begin examining the process of assembling these building blocks in a logical, coherent, and musical manner. Our ultimate goal is a musical composition with a beginning, middle, and end that tells a story, develops in a unified and balanced manner, and results in a satisfactory musical experience for all involved—composer/arranger, performers, and listeners.

11-1 Concept and Direction

Before examining the specific building blocks of a musical arrangement, it's important to consider issues regarding the concept, direction, and style of a musical composition. When first approaching an arrangement of an original or existing tune, certain questions need to be asked and decisions made, or the music is likely to become rambling and unfocused.

What will the tempo, key signature, and meter be? Will there be tempo and/or meter changes or modulations throughout the arrangement? Should the basic rhythmic feel be straight-ahead jazz swing, even-eighths or broken time, funk, hip-hop, etc.? Will the underlying harmonies and voicings be based on dominant harmony, non-functional harmonies, more dissonant polytonal sounds, or atonal sounds—or a combination of all of these? How will the melody be treated in terms of phrase structure, rhythmic alteration, and articulations?

Will it be reharmonized? What is the size and instrumentation of the ensemble? How will the primary melody and accompanying parts be orchestrated? How will the overall form be constructed? Will there be improvised solos, backgrounds, transitions, and ensemble sections such as solis and shout choruses?

The list can seem endless and daunting to the beginner and seasoned professional alike. Very often, the hardest part is just getting started. Our best advice is to learn to trust your instincts, pick a direction, and just jump in and start writing! Nothing is written in stone, and you can always change direction if things don't seem to be working. As we said in Chapter 1, music has a life of its own. Once you get started, this phenomenon can kick in, and the music will lead you to ideas and directions that would never occur to you while staring at a blank page (or computer monitor).

It can be helpful to begin by simply choosing to emphasize one or two (or three) aspects of the music. Following is a list of some musical devices that can provide a unique twist or direction for an arrangement (see the Listening List at the end of this chapter for more details on the examples).

1. A particularly striking reharmonization of the melody (John Coltrane, "But Not for Me"; Bob Brookmeyer, "Willow Tree").

2. Choosing a different meter or feel for a familiar tune (e.g., "All the Things You Are" in 5/4 or "Giant Steps" as a waltz).

3. Choosing a unique and striking instrumentation for the melody (Thad Jones, "Three and One"—flugelhorn, baritone sax, and bass).

4. Choosing an unusual instrumentation for the ensemble (Herbie Hancock, "The Prisoner"—flugelhorn, flute, tenor sax/alto flute, bass clarinet, trombone, bass trombone, piano, bass, drums).

5. The use of a rhythmic vamp or hook as a unifying device (Cedar Walton, "Bolivia"; Gil Evans, "Summertime" from *Miles Davis' "Porgy and Bess"*; Michael Abene, "Who Cares?").

6. The use of blues-based harmonies and riffs (Neal Hefti/Count Basie, "The Kid from Red Bank," "Fantail").

7. Emphasizing odd or changing meters (many compositions by Russell Ferrante of the Yellowjackets).

8. Emphasizing a particular type of harmonic language or voicing structure (Bob Mintzer, *"Art of the Big Band"*—fourth chords and parallel constant structures; Bob Brookmeyer, "First Love Song"—clusters and spreads; Michael Abene, "Uncertainty"—fourth chords and parallel constant structures).

9. Emphasis on contrapuntal writing (Bill Holman, "You Go to My Head"; Jim McNeely, "Extra Credit").

10. Choosing a novel, unique approach to the form (Bill Holman, "Just Friends"—the entire opening portion of the chart is a unison soli for

the whole band; Earth, Wind & Fire—"Got To Get You into My Life"—
entirely new material introduces and frames the popular Beatles song;
Joshua Redman—"I'm an Old Cowhand"—the unusual, modern intro
becomes a contrapuntal bass line to the melody).

It's of critical importance to have a clear musical concept and direction
when beginning and while working on any musical composition or arrangement. A solid understanding of the general principles presented in Chapter 4
can be extremely helpful in maintaining musical focus, balance, and the
effective realization of your musical goals.

Finally, there seems to be an almost universal tendency, especially on the
part of beginners, to overwrite. Always remember that space and silence as well
as sound are part of music. Not everyone needs to be playing all the time!
Understanding the importance of principles such as balance, economy, focus,
and contrast and variety can often provide important clues to sustaining the
effectiveness of the music.

11-2 Improvisation and Form

One thing that often seems to get overlooked in discussions about jazz arranging techniques is the fact that improvisation is almost always a key element in
any jazz composition or performance. It's important for you to understand the
unique kind of energy and excitement that emanates from improvisation and to
ensure that the composed sections of an arrangement complement and support
the improvised sections in a unified manner.

Determining which instruments will play improvised solos, the order of
the solos, and the roll of background parts, are crucial decisions for the jazz
arranger. Very often some of these decisions will be based on knowledge of the
individual players in an established band, as was the case with the various bands
of Count Basie, Duke Ellington, Thad Jones & Mel Lewis, and many others.
Sometimes two or more soloists can play off each other, as with "tenor battles"
or any type of trading fours or eights, and sometimes entire sections, or even
the whole band, can improvise collectively, as at the end of the shout chorus to
Michael Abene's "Uncertaintly" (Ex. 31-3).

Ultimately, the most important consideration is that the composed and
improvised sections of any arrangement should feel integrated and unified, as
part of a greater musical whole. Ideally, the various sections of an arrangement
should flow together seamlessly and organically in a balanced and coherent
manner.

11-3 Basic Elements of Form

There are several different levels where considerations of musical form come
into play—some at a micro level, some macro, and some in between.

133

1. *Melodic phrase structure*—This refers to the length of and balance between melodic phrases on a micro level, antecedent and consequent, symmetrical and asymmetrical, examined in Chapter 7.

2. *Harmonic rhythm*—There is a form to the harmonic rhythm, or chord progression, of a jazz composition, both at a micro and a macro level. We examined the "micro" aspects of harmonic form in Chapter 8. How many chords are there per measure? Is the progression symmetrical or asymmetrical? What is the relationship of the harmonic rhythm to the melodic phrase structure? Are there modulations, and where do they occur?

   There is also a "macro" aspect to harmonic form. For example, there may be a shift (or several shifts) in key center, or modulation. Modulating up a half step, whole step, minor third, or more can be an effective device for building intensity when transitioning from one section of an arrangement to another, for example, into a *shout chorus* or *recap*. The jazz arranger may also choose to change the harmonic rhythm of the underlying chord progression as a means of providing contrast and variety to the development of an arrangement. Simplifying the chords of a tune with a complex chord progression for the blowing section and doubling or halving the duration of each chord are examples of this technique (see Ex. 11-1).

3. *Song form*—Songs, or *tunes*, still form the nucleus of a majority of longer jazz compositions and arrangements. Songs are generally anywhere from 12 bars (the blues) in length to 64 bars or more. Songs usually have clearly identifiable sections, which give structure and balance to the song through the repetition and development of certain sections; these can generally be designated as ABA, AABA, ABAC, etc. We examined some aspects of song form in Chapters 7 (Section 7-2, Ex. 7-2) and 8 (Ex. 8-3). There is generally (but not always) a contrast of melodic and/or harmonic material from one section of a song to another.

4. *Large form*—Any musical composition or arrangement *not* based on song form or consisting of two or more repetitions of the song has a larger, overall form, which gives structure to the music. It is this large form, or *compositional form*, with which we are primarily concerned in this chapter. Some compositional forms common in classical music include the following:

   a. *Sonata form*—exposition, development, recapitulation.

   b. *Rondo form*—ABACADAE, etc.

   c. *Theme and variations*—A, A1, A2, A3, A4, etc., where the "A" generally has a sectional form of its own, such as ABA.

   d. *Minuet*—usually a three-part form in ¾ meter, often the third movement of a classical symphony or concerto.

   e. *Through-composed*—not falling obviously into one of the previously listed sectional forms.

Ex. 11-1

Modifying the Blowing Changes: "Waiting" by Richard Sussman

135

"Waiting"

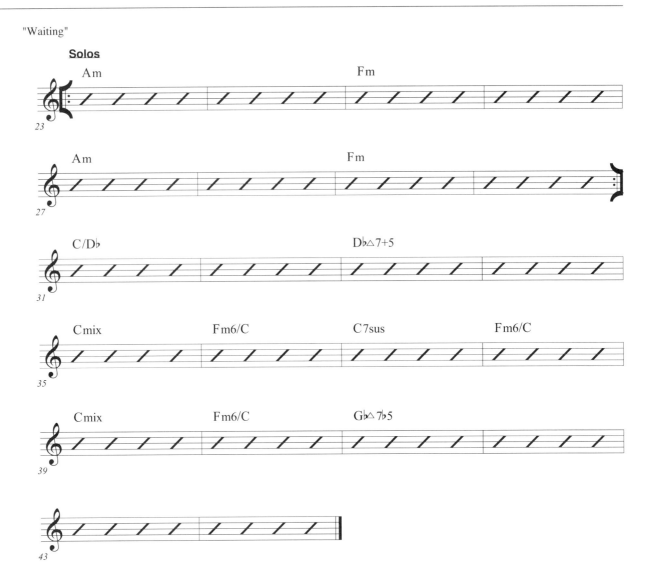

In this tune, the harmonic rhythm has been altered for the blowing section to provide greater freedom for the soloist. The "A" section has been extended to 16 bars instead of 8, and the chord changes of the middle 4 bars have been simplified.

In addition to the foregoing classical forms, larger, multimovement compositions, such as symphonies, sonatas, concertos, and suites, can be created in which the individual movements may consist of any (or none) of the listed forms.

By far the most common large form found in jazz is *theme and variations*, which is essentially what occurs when you play the head of a tune, improvise on repeated choruses of the tune, with or without interludes or transitions, and return to a recap of the head at the end (or not!). However, we encourage the aspiring jazz arranger *not* to feel restricted by the theme-and-variations structure common to jazz, but continually to look beyond that for ways to add interest and variety to a large-scale jazz composition.

The study of classical and contemporary classical music provides a vast resource for ideas pertaining to musical form (as well as to melody, harmony, rhythm, and orchestration). We encourage you to listen to and study the scores of the great classical composers, including those from the 20th century, such as Ravel, Stravinsky, Schoenberg, Berg, Webern, Bartok, Messiaen, Boulez, and Berio, among many others. The primary focus of this chapter is to examine techniques and devices for enhancing the overall, large form of a jazz arrangement.

11-4 Outlining and Graphing the Form

Any piece of music, regardless of style, whether composed or improvised, consists of an overall structure or form, which provides a framework for the development of the musical elements. Closer examination reveals the existence of smaller building blocks, which are assembled by the skilled composer/arranger in such a way as to create an organized ebb and flow of musical content, hopefully resulting in some form of gratifying emotional response on the part of the listener. A good piece of music, like life, has peaks and valleys, includes tension and release, builds to a climax or climaxes, has transitions and recapitulations and other unifying devices, and, above all, tells a story.

The following are the most common formal building blocks of a jazz arrangement.

1. *Introduction.*
2. *Exposition* (most commonly, but not necessarily, the *head* of a tune).
3. *Transitional passages* (kickers, interludes, etc.).
4. *Development*—In jazz, the development frequently consists of improvised solos, generally following a theme-and-variations format, and can also include *backgrounds* (played behind soloists), *solis* (composed sections played by two or more players, often designed to sound like improvised lines), *shout choruses* (forceful tutti sections generally occurring at climactic points in the arrangement), and any other type of compositional development of material derived from the exposition.
5. *Recapitulation* (or *recap;* in jazz, usually a reprise of the head or part of the head).
6. *Coda,* or *ending.*

Of course, entirely new material can be introduced into any musical composition at any point as long as it flows naturally and makes musical sense to do so. There's really no rule about this one. It's a matter of learning to trust your instincts and acquiring the ability to be sensitive to where the music wants to go, as described in chapter 1. For now we'll stick to items 1–6 in the preceding list.

It can be very useful to create a projected outline of the overall form of a musical composition or arrangement. Such an outline would indicate the manner in which the various sections could build and develop over time

137

through changes in instrumentation, melodic and harmonic content, and rhythm. The outline of an arrangement can also be displayed in graphic form, indicating the peaks and valleys and overall development of the chart. Having such an outline as a framework for development at the beginning can be a valuable tool for avoiding a common compositional pitfall: losing sight of the forest for the trees. Nothing is written in stone. You can always revise the outline as you proceed.

11-5 Instrumentation and Outlining the Form

One of the most powerful tools for developing musical ideas in an ensemble is through *instrumentation*—combining instrumental colors in various and contrasting ways. A useful technique for achieving variety in this area is to make a list of the different types of instrumental and textural color combinations (including the use of brass mutes and woodwind doubles) at your disposal for any given arranging assignment. For example, in the case of 4 horns (trumpet, alto sax doubling on flute, tenor sax doubling on clarinet, trombone) and rhythm section (piano, bass, and drums), we could arrive at the following possibilities for a melodic statement:

1. Any horn playing solo with the rhythm section.
2. Trumpet + alto sax in unison.
3. Trumpet + tenor sax in octaves.
4. Trumpet in Harmon mute + flute 8va.
5. Trumpet melody over chords played by the saxes and trombone.
6. Alto and tenor saxes in octaves, with a slow trombone counter-melody
7. Trumpet, alto, tenor, and trombone voiced in close or semi-open position, in rhythmic unison.
8. Piano and bass playing the melody, with rhythmic hits by the horns.

The list is endless, even for a small ensemble, and the possibilities increase exponentially as the size of the ensemble increases. Rather than trying to create an exhaustive list of all possible color combinations, it's probably more practical to start with just those combinations you think you may want to use for a given project. A sample outline of an arrangement for four horns and three rhythm of "My Romance" might look something like this:

Intro

    (4 bars) Four horns in rhythmic unison playing a figure derived from the end of the tune.

    (4 bars) Piano and rhythm section echo horn figure to set up the entrance of the melody.

Head

    First "A" section (8 bars)—trumpet melody above pads in saxes and trombone (homophonic).

138

First B section (8 bars)—tenor sax melody solo (monophonic).

Second "A" section (8 bars)—all four horns voiced in close or semi-open position, with trumpet on top (rhythmic unison—homophonic).

Second B section (8 bars)

First 4 bars—alto sax and trombone melody in octaves (monophonic).

Second 4 bars—all four horns in rhythmic unison, as previously.

Kicker (4 bars)—continuation, building from the previous 4 bars, all four horns in rhythmic unison leading into the first solo.

Alto solo (1 chorus/32 bars)—improvised solo + rhythm section.

Backgrounds (1 chorus/32 bars)—Alto solo continues, with background pads by muted brass.

Kicker (4 bars)—Same as previously to lead into a piano solo.

Piano solo (1 chorus/32 bars)—Improvised solo + rhythm section.

Backgrounds (1 chorus/32 bars)

The piano solo continues, with background pads by saxes.

Piano solo ends with a figure from the last 4 bars of the Intro.

Recap—D.S. to second half of Head:

Second "A" section (8 bars)—All four horns voiced in close or semi-open position, with trumpet on top (rhythmic unison—homophonic).

Second B section (8 bars)

First 4 bars—Alto sax and trombone melody in octaves.

Second 4 bars—All four horns in rhythmic unison, as previously.

Coda (8 bars)—Four 2-bar phrases derived from the Intro:

All four horns (2 bars).

Two horns (2 bars).

Rhythm section (2 bars).

Piano alone (2 bars).

Final chord—Everybody—PPP.

We've used contrasting instrumental colors and textures to create an arrangement that builds naturally, with peaks and valleys, and winds down at the end with a recap and a coda. This outline could be displayed graphically as shown in Ex. 11-2. (This technique of graphically representing the form of an arrangement has been used effectively by Rayburn Wright throughout his classic text *Inside the Score*.) Let's take a closer look at some of the specific structural components listed in our outline.

Ex. 11-2

Graph of "My Romance"

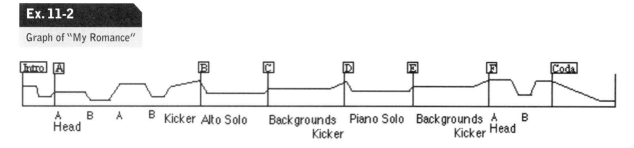

139

11-6 Intros

The *intro* (introduction) is generally a relatively short section (four to eight bars) that helps to set up and prepare the listener for the opening statement of the *exposition* (tune). On the other hand, musical introductions can be much longer than eight bars, or they can be dispensed with entirely, having the composition begin immediately with the exposition.

Following are examples of some common devices that can be used to construct intros that will lead naturally into the statement of a tune. These same musical devices can also be used to construct *transitions,* or *kickers,* between sections of an arrangement, or as *codas,* or *endings.* Any of these devices could be orchestrated in any number of ways—from a solo instrument, to rhythm section only, to full tutti.

1. *Vamps and pedals*—Rhythmic figures in the style of the tune, often over a I or V pedal.
2. *Material derived from the tune*—Constructing an intro from melodic, harmonic, or rhythmic material derived from the tune can be an effective unifying device.
3. *Turnarounds*—A common bebop harmonic device generally based on the progression iii-vi-ii-V. Possibly the most common type of intro, often used in arrangements for singers or in head arrangements, turnarounds can be made more harmonically interesting through the use of m3/tritone substitution or half-step sequences (Ex. 11-3-4, mm. 5-7 of the example).
4. *New material*—New melodic or harmonic material not contained in the tune can function as an intro to the tune. This technique is most effective if the material is brought back somewhere else in the arrangement (e.g., as a transition, a background part, a coda, or part of a shout chorus) to provide unity.
5. *Hooks*—Sometimes it can be colorful to come up with a distinctive musical motive, or *hook,* to use as a basis on which to build your statement of the tune. In such a case, this material can function effectively as an introduction to the arrangement.

Very often these techniques can be combined. For example, a vamp or pedal may be based on material from the tune, may contain new material, or may be based on a turnaround. In many cases the intro may simply be an improvised chorus (or more) by the rhythm section on the changes to the tune.

Example 11-3 illustrates these various techniques. Notice how, in each example, we end the intro on the V chord, in preparation for the entrance of the first statement of the tune starting on I. For more examples of different types of intros, refer to the Listening List at the end of this chapter.

Ex. 11-3

Intros—4 Horns: "Have You Met Miss Jones?" by Rodgers & Hart, arranged by R. Sussman

5. New Material

6. Hooks

11-7 Transitions/Kickers

Transitions, or *kickers,* like intros, are generally short passages (two to eight bars) that lead us from one primary section of an arrangement to another, for example, from the end of the head into the first improvised solo, or from one solo to another. Kickers can be entirely contained within the form of the tune, can overlap the double bar line (e.g., from the last four bars of one chorus to the first two bars of the next), or can be added as extensions to the standard song form (e.g., adding three bars at the end of a 32-bar head). Kickers can add spice to a jazz arrangement as they propel the band into an improvised solo, soli, shout chorus, or recap. Constructing a kicker from material derived from the tune or intro can be an effective unifying device. Example 11-4 illustrates some of these principles.

Ex. 11-4

Kickers/Transitions—4 Horns: "Have You Met Miss Jones?" by Rodgers & Hart, arranged by R. Sussman

1. Derived From Tune

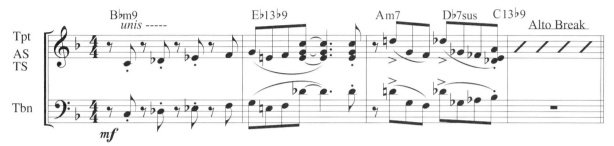

2. Derived From Tune (less obvious)

3. Derived From Intro (Pedal)

4. New Material

All examples begin at Bar 31 of the head.

11-8 Background Parts

Backgrounds give the jazz arranger an opportunity to add support and color behind an improvised solo. Generally, the most important rule pertaining to background parts is *Keep Them Simple!* The function of backgrounds is to support the improvised solo and to provide musical ideas with which the soloist can interact. If they become too complicated or loud, they can draw attention away from the solo and interfere with the soloist's ability to improvise. Background parts are generally given to a timbre that contrasts with that of the soloist (e.g., if there's a trumpet solo, the backgrounds might be played by the saxes; if there's a sax solo, the backgrounds might be played by muted brass). However, backgrounds can also be played by a mixed ensemble (e.g., two saxes, three muted brass) or any instrumental timbre, as long as they fulfill the function of supporting and not interfering with the soloist. Background parts commonly fall into one of the following four categories, illustrated in Example 11-5.

1. *Pads*—Sustained chords.
2. *Rhythmic comping*—Outlining the harmonies in a more rhythmic and syncopated fashion, similar to that of a piano or guitar part. There is often a temptation to fall into repeated, parallel patterns when writing rhythmic background parts, which can lead to predictable and somewhat boring results. A good way to avoid this is to strive for asymmetrical phrase structure in your backgrounds.
3. *Counter-melodies*—Generally slower-moving melodic lines that outline the harmonic motion (often as *guide tones*—see section 10-2) and provide a slow melodic backdrop to the soloist.
4. *Riffs*—Actually a special kind of jazz counter-melody, with faster and more syncopated motion than the type of counter-melody referred to in number 3. Riffs are repeated, simple, often bluesy, rhythmic melodic figures à la Horace Silver or Count Basie. Unlike rhythmic comping, described earlier, the essence of riffs are in fact their very predictable, parallel structure and repetitive nature.

   Occasionally, background parts can become much more active, creating more interplay and interaction between the ensemble and soloist. In this type of situation, the backgrounds should be cued into the soloist's part, so that he or she knows what to expect and how to interact with the ensemble.

Ex. 11-5

Background Parts—4 Horns: "Have You Met Miss Jones?" by Rodgers & Hart, arranged by R. Sussman

1) Pads

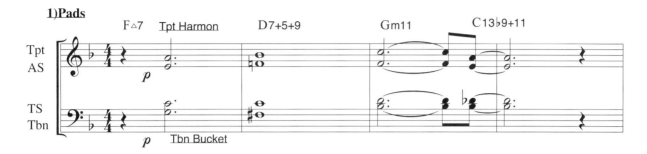

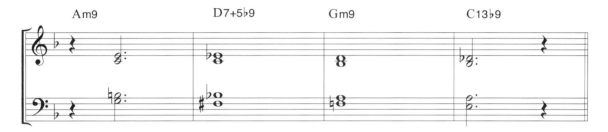

2) Rhythmic Comping

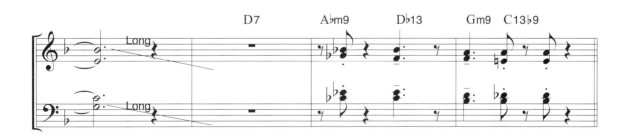

145

3) Counter Melody

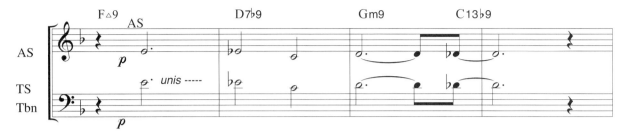

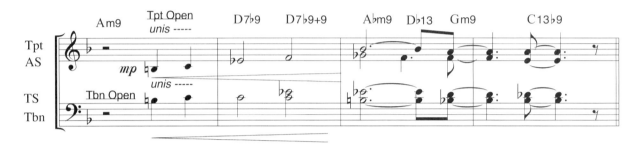

4) Riffs

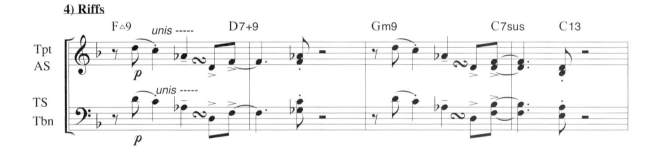

11-9 Codas/Endings

Any of the devices described in Section 11-6 can be used effectively as an ending, or coda. Sometimes the simplest and most effective way to end a chart is simply to repeat the last phrase of melody, with a slight ritard. Of course there are also many stock endings in the jazz lexicon, such as the classic "Basie" ending. However, a creatively constructed coda that relates organically to the rest of the chart, provides the arranger with an opportunity to tie everything together and make a closing statement. It's especially important because it's the last thing the listener will hear. It has often been said that the most important parts of any musical performance are the beginning and ending.

Chapter Summary

In this chapter, we discussed important issues relating to the concept and direction of an arrangement, as well as the unique function of improvisation in jazz. We then examined some fundamental principles of musical form and how they relate to planning and outlining an arrangement. We also provided some specific examples of techniques for constructing intros, transitions/kickers, background parts, and codas/endings.

◊ **Software Tip:** Make sure you understand how to insert measure stacks, add measures, create repeat signs that will properly affect MIDI playback, and insert expressions in whichever platform you're working. Check the website for more detailed instructions about these functions.

Exercises

Apply techniques discussed in this chapter to the following exercises.

◊ **Continue working on Arranging Project 1, the 3- to 4-Horn arrangement of a standard tune.**

1. Transcribe one or more of the intros from the Listening List that follows.
2. Add a four- to eight-bar *intro* to your arrangement.
3. Add a *kicker* to the end of the head leading into an improvised solo.
4. Choose which instrument will play the first improvised solo in your arrangement. Add 1 chorus of *background parts* to be played the second time only behind the soloist.

Listening List

(Some of these recordings are also in the Small Ensemble Listening List at the end of Chapter 6.):

1. *Vamps/pedals*
   a. "It's All Right with Me"—arr. by Benny Golson—*Meet the Jazztet* (1959), Argo. The intro contains new material that does not return in the arrangement.
   b. "Ping Pong"—Wayne Shorter—Art Blakey and the Jazz Messengers, *"Ugetsu" Art Blakey's Jazz Messengers at Birdland* (1963), Riverside. The vamp intro is actually part of the tune.
   c. "Room 608"—Horace Silver—Horace Silver, *The Best of Horace Silver* (1953), Blue Note. The pedal intro contains new material that returns as a coda.
2. *Derived from the tune*: "If You Could See Me Now"—arr. by Willie Smith—Joe Lovano, *52 Street Themes* (2000), Blue Note. The intro is derived from the melody of the tune.

3. *Turnarounds*: "Don't Be That Way"—arr. by Bob Brookmeyer—Terry Gibbs, *The Dream Band* (1959), Contemporary.

4. *New material*

   a. "On a Misty Night"—arr. by Willie Smith—Joe Lovano, *52 Street Themes* (2000). The intro contains new material that recurs in the background parts.

   b. "Got to Get You into My Life" —Lennon/McCartney, Earth, Wind & Fire, *The Best of Earth Wind, & Fire*, Vol. 1 (1977), Columbia. An amazing cover of the classic Beatles song, with a totally unique approach.

5. *Hooks*

   a. "You Go to My Head"—arr. by Bill Holman—Terry Gibbs, *Dream Band* (1959), Contemporary. The intro becomes a contrapuntal accompaniment to the melody.

   b. "I'm an Old Cowhand"—Joshua Redman, *Back East* (2007), Nonesuch. The very original, modern intro to this quaint, old standard becomes the bass line and establishes the vibe of the arrangement.

6. *Concept and direction*

   a. "But Not for Me"—John Coltrane, *John Coltrane Quartet* (1960), Capitol.

   b. "Willow Tree"—by Fats Waller, arr. by Bob Brookmeyer, Thad Jones/Mel Lewis, *Live at the Village Vanguard* (1967), Solid State.

   c. "Three and One"—Thad Jones, *Presenting Thad Jones/Mel Lewis and the Jazz Orchestra* (1966), Solid State.

   d. "The Prisoner"—Herbie Hancock, *The Prisoner* (1969), Blue Note.

   e. "Bolivia"—Cedar Walton, *Eastern Rebellion* (1975), Timeless.

   f. "Summertime"—George and Ira Gershwin, arr. by Gil Evans, Miles Davis, *Porgy and Bess* (1958), Columbia.

   g. "Who Cares?"—George and Ira Gershwin, arr. by Michael Abene, Patti Austin, *Avante Gershwin* (2007), Rendezvous.

   h. "The Kid from Red Bank," "Fantail"—by Neal Hefti, Count Basie, *The Complete Atomic Basie* (1957), Roulette.

   i. "Art of the Big Band"—Bob Mintzer, *Art of the Big Band* (1991), DMP.

   j. "First Love Song"—Bob Brookmeyer, Bob Brookmeyer composer, arranger, *The Mel Lewis Orchestra* (1980), Gryphon.

   k. "Uncertainty"—Michael Abene (available on companion website).

   l. "Extra Credit"—Jim McNeely, *The Vanguard Jazz Orchestra* (1997), New World Records.

   m. "Just Friends"—Bill Holman. *The Bill Holman Band, World Class* (1987), JVC.

Chapter 12

Dynamics and Articulation/Brass Mutes

Before completing our initial study of arranging for the small ensemble, it's important to examine some of the means for indicating expression, dynamics, and articulations in the score and the parts. The professional arranger must have a thorough understanding of these devices, including articulations and effects specific to many brass and woodwind instruments. The proper use of dynamics and articulations not only will make your scores and parts look professional but will also ensure that the performance of your music comes to life with appropriate expressiveness and feeling. You may have noticed that articulations and dynamics mysteriously appeared in the musical examples in the preceding chapter. After you've read the material in this chapter, go back and reexamine the examples in Chapter 11, paying special attention to how the notated articulations and expressions affect the sound of the music.

12-1 **Dynamics**

First of all, it's important to indicate the basic dynamic levels, including crescendos and diminuendos, of all the parts, using standard music notation. In general, brass instruments will tend to sound louder and project more than woodwinds, given the same dynamic indication. For example, if you want the brass and saxes to sound at the same volume, it's sometimes practical to mark the saxes one dynamic level higher than the brass (e.g., saxes *f*, brass *mf*, or saxes *mf*, brass *p*). This is usually more important in softer and more expressive sections and less so in loud, full tutti sections, such as a shout chorus. It's an equally important responsibility of the arranger to indicate appropriate levels for melodic (f) and background parts (p).

12-2 Brass and Woodwind Articulations and Phrasing

The following articulations are common to all jazz brass and woodwind instruments, and their correct use is essential to expressive interpretation of the music. Again, it's the responsibility of the arranger to indicate the proper articulations and phrasing. This can mean the difference between a musical passage coming to life and "swinging" or laying flat like a wet noodle. Listen to the recordings on the companion website of the following articulations, as well as the demo of brass mutes in the next section. The best way to truly understand these markings is to study scores and recordings to hear how they sound in a musical context. Listen to the examples on the companion website of the articulations used in a musical context as illustrated in Ex. 12-2. Listen to the difference between the two recorded versions, Ex. 12-2A "Played With Articulations & Dynamics," and Ex. 12-2B "Played Without Articulations & Dynamics." The bass and drum parts have been left incomplete on purpose. We'll address correct rhythm section notation in Chapter 13.

There is a certain amount of confusion and controversy among players and writers over the correct interpretation of certain articulations, particularly regarding short and long accents. If you talk to three different trumpet players, you may get three different interpretations for the symbol ^, and some may say that the symbols ≥ and > are irrelevant because a normal accent > is always played long, so > is contradictory, and a · is always accented.

Listen carefully to the recorded demonstrations of the articulations in Exs. 12-1 and 12-1A, as well as the demo of brass mutes in the next section. You should be able to hear the subtle differences between and logic of the various articulations. On the other hand, it's very likely that the first four versions of Ex. 12-1A demonstrating the effect of the various accent symbols would have sounded exactly the same had we not told the trumpet player to make a special effort to exaggerate the differences. Ex. 12-1A-5 illustrates the effect of slurs.

With jazz players, by far the most critical issue is invariably the duration of quarter notes. If the articulations aren't there, the inevitable question will arise: Should they be long or short? Eighth notes are much easier to interpret intuitively. If you're not a brass or reed player, it's a good idea to ask the advice of an experienced wind player regarding the articulations on a part. It can save a lot of time at a rehearsal or recording session.

Ex. 12-1

Brass and Woodwind Articulations

1. Tenuto **(Long)** - A line over a note indicates it is to be played to its full value.

2. Staccato **(Short)** - A dot over a note indicates it is to be clipped short, not played to its full value.

3. Accent **(Punch)** - A sideways V over a note indicates it is to be played with a forceful attack with a quick decay extending almost to its full value.

4. Long Accent - A sideways V over a line over a note indicates it is to be played with a forceful attack and played to its full value.

5. Short Accent - A sideways V over a dot over a note indicates it is to be played with a forceful attack and clipped short, not played to its full value.

6. Hat Accent - An upside down V over a note indicates it is to be played with a forceful and percussive attack with a short duration. There are two interpretations of this symbol in the recorded examples - the 1st short and percussive, the 2nd short and "fat".

7. Scoop or Short Gliss - A curved or straight line leading up to a note indicates a short gliss or scoop up to the actual pitch of the note.

8. Glissando - A long straight or wiggly line ascending to a note indicates a long upward gliss to the actual pitch of the note. Often "Gliss" or "Glissando" is written above the line.

9. Rip or Lip Gliss - A line descending to a note indicates a short gliss downward to the actual pitch of the note.

10. Plop - A quick slide down to a short, accented note from about a 5th above. Sounds almost like a kind of grace note.

151

11. Short Fall -A short curved or straight line descending from a note indicates a short downward gliss to a note of indeterminate pitch. It should be clearly labelled "SHORT".

12. Long Fall - A long straight or wiggly line descending from a note indicates a long downward gliss to a note of indeterminate pitch. It should be clearly labelled "LONG".

13. Doit - A curved or straight line ascending from a note indicates a short upward gliss to a note of indeterminate pitch.

14. Appoggiatura or Turn - A sideways S between 2 notes indicates the player is to rise quickly above and back down to the 1st note before descending to the 2nd note.

15. Bend - A wide U over a note indicates it is to be played on pitch, then bent flat, and then bent back up to pitch.

16. Shake - A wiggly line above or next to a sustained note indicates a shake, produced as a "Lip Trill" on brass instruments, and by trilling up a minor 3rd on woodwinds. It should be clearly labelled "SHAKE" and is generally used on sustained notes. *

17. Slur - A curved line over a group of adjacent notes indicates they are to be played "legato", in a smooth, connected line, usually in one breath, with only the 1st note being tongued.

18. Ghosted Notes - An X notehead or parantheses around the note head indicates the note is to be "swallowed" and played at an implied or ambiguous pitch.

152

*Only brass instruments play shakes. For a similar effect with woodwinds, write a trill or tremolo (Ex. 12-3, m. 6). For an example of brass shakes used effectively on short notes, check out the EWF version of "Got to Get You into My Life."

Ex. 12-1A

Comparison of Brass and Woodwind Articulations

Medium Swing

1.

2.

3.

4.

5.

153

Ex. 12-2A & B "I've Got The Articulations & Dynamics Blues"

Richard Sussman

12-3 Muted Brass

The sound of brass instruments may be modified through the use of a variety of mutes, which may be inserted inside the bell or placed outside of it. Most mutes are typically made of aluminum, brass, or copper. Since all mutes reduce the flow of air out of the bell, they modify the volume of the instrument, making it sound softer. Mutes also filter out certain overtones, thereby modifying the timbre of the instrument as well. Because all mutes obstruct the airflow, they make it harder to play and control the pitch in the extreme lower and upper registers. The arranger/orchestrator needs to adjust the practical range of brass instruments described in Chapter 3 when employing mutes. For harmon and cup mutes, a safe, practical range for trumpets would be from concert B♭ below the staff up to F or G above the staff; for trombones in cups, B♭ in the staff up to F above the staff would be safe. For straight and bucket mutes you can safely go a little higher—up to concert B♭ for trumpets and to high B♭ for trombones. Keep in mind that a strong lead player on either instrument will be able to go a little higher.

When writing for mutes, with the exception of hand-held mutes, such as plungers and hats, it's important to give the players ample time to insert and remove the mutes at the beginning and end of a muted passage—usually at least four to eight bars of rests at a medium tempo is desirable. It's equally important to prepare the player for the upcoming switch to mutes. To indicate the use of a particular mute, simply write on the part "To Harmon Mute," "To Cup Mute," etc. at least four to eight bars before the muted passage and then "Harmon Mute," "Cup Mute," etc. at the beginning of the muted passage. Write "Open" to indicate that the mutes are to be removed at the end of a passage.

We'll now take a look at (and listen to) the mutes most commonly used for trumpets and trombones in a jazz setting.

a. *Harmon mute*—One of the most common mutes used in jazz, the harmon mute consists of two parts: the main body and an adjustable hollow stem with a cup on the end. Although made for both trumpet and trombone, it is commonly used only for trumpets. Harmon mutes are held in place by a solid ring of cork, which forces all of the air to flow into the mute when it is inserted into the bell. The result is a characteristic metallic, buzzy sound. With the stem removed, the result is the classic "Miles Davis" sound of the 1950s and '60s. With the stem in place, a player can create a "wah-wah" effect by covering and uncovering the cup with the left hand.

b. *Straight mute*—The straight mute is most favored by classical composers, but it is also occasionally used in jazz settings. It is inserted into the bell of the instrument but allows some air to bypass the mute. The result is a soft but piercing sound, closer in timbre to an unmuted sound.

155

Straight mutes are commonly used with both trumpets and trombones as well as with French horns and tubas.

c. *Cup mute*—The cup mute, more favored by jazz players and arrangers, is similar in construction to the straight mute, but it has a large cup attached to the mute, which further deflects and dampens the sound. The result is a warmer, mellower sound than that of the harmon or straight mute, although edgier than that of the bucket mute. Cup mutes are commonly used by both trumpets and trombones.

d. *Bucket mute*—The bucket mute, also favored by jazz players and arrangers, is not inserted into the bell but is clipped to the bell's rim and contains a gauzelike material that muffles the sound. The result is a warmer, mellower sound, similar to, but a little louder and darker than, that of the cup mute. Because it is not inserted into the bell, the bucket mute allows more of the natural airflow of the instrument to pass around the mute, resulting in a timbre closer to the natural, open sound. This also makes it easier to play in the upper or lower registers.

e. *Derby mutes, or hats*—These mutes were originally actual bowler hats. Today they are typically made of metal or fiber. Derby mutes don't attach to the bell in any way. They are often mounted on stands in front of the trumpet and trombone players, to permit quick movement of the bell in and out of the hat, although they can also be held by hand over the bell of the instrument. Derby mutes sound similar to bucket mutes and are used today primarily for their showy and colorful appearance onstage.

f. *Plunger mutes*—Literally unused rubber toilet plungers, these mutes, like derbies, don't attach to the bell at all but are held in front of it by hand. By opening and closing the bell, the player can create the characteristic jazz "wah-wah" or "doo-wah" effect. By vocalizing or growling into the horn while playing, the player can produce the jazz "growl" effect. When writing for the plunger mute, the closed position is indicated with a "+" above the note, the open position with an "o", and "+-o" for the "wah" effect. Simply write "Growl" at the beginning of a passage if that is the desired effect. Buckets, hats, and plunger mutes may all be used by both trumpets and trombones.

g. *In stand*—When the bell of the instrument is directed downward into the music stand, instead of up and toward the audience as is normally done, the music stand itself becomes a kind of mute. The horns are still open, so the timbre isn't altered, but the sound is much softer, with less projection than usual. This is an extremely effective dynamic tool for the jazz arranger when desiring a softer brass sound without altering the timbre (as is the case with all mutes). It's also an effective option when there's no time in the music to insert or remove a mute. Simply write "In Stand" at the beginning of a passage where that effect is desired and "Open" at the end of the passage.

Brass mutes provide the arranger with a powerful tool for creating subtle shadings of timbre and color in an arrangement. When writing for a larger ensemble, you may use brass mutes within a section in a variety of different combinations (e.g., four trumpets, all in harmons or cups, two trumpets in harmons—two in cups, two trumpets in cups—one in harmon—one flugelhorn, etc., with similar options for the trombones and for combining trumpets and trombones). However, bear in mind that it's easier for the players in a section to maintain the proper balance within the section when they're all using the same kind of mute. Because some types of mutes are louder or softer than others, you may want to indicate different dynamic levels in the parts when mixing mutes (e.g., *p* for harmons and *mp* for cups). Obviously it's essential first to have a clear understanding of what each of the individual mutes sounds like. Please listen to the recorded examples of Ex. 12-3 (the melody from the first four bars of Ex. 12-2) on the companion website and view pictures of the various trumpet and trombone mutes illustrated in Ex. 12-4 (on the website).

Listen to the variations of Ex. 12-3 played first by the trumpet and then by the trombone using a variety of mutes. The "+, o" markings apply only to the examples of plunger mutes.

Ex. 12-3A Trumpet Mutes

1. Trumpet harmon mute.
2. Trumpet cup mute.
3. Trumpet straight mute.
4. Trumpet bucket mute.
5. Trumpet plunger mute.
6. Trumpet plunger mute (with growl).

Ex. 12-3B Trombone Mutes

1. Trombone cup mute.
2. Trombone straight mute.
3. Trombone bucket mute.
4. Trombone plunger mute.
5. Trombone plunger mute (with growl).

Ex. 12-4 Brass Mutes (photos on website)

Ex. 12-3

Brass Mutes

Medium Swing

mp

Chapter Summary

In this chapter we discussed the importance of indicating musical dynamics in both the score and the parts and examined some brass and woodwind articulations common in jazz writing. We also examined the use of brass mutes as dynamic and color devices.

◊ **Software Tip:** It can be time-consuming and tedious to achieve consistent musical MIDI playback of articulations and dynamics in a notation program. This generally involves adjusting the default program settings for how articulations and dynamics markings affect MIDI attack velocity, controller 7, and note duration. In a similar manner, if you choose third-party sample libraries, getting your tracks or staves to reflect the use of brass mutes through MIDI program changes or key switching is possible, but this can also be overly time-consuming. Consult the website for more details. Sometimes it's best to stay focused on the creative process and use your imagination. After all, that technique has proven quite effective for hundreds of years before the advent of personal computers!

◊ **Software Tip:** As with most Mac and PC software, keyboard/mouse shortcuts are displayed on the right side of the pull-down menus in both programs. Both programs contain many shortcuts and macros (keyboard equivalents for mouse, menu, and dialogue box actions) that will significantly increase your efficiency. One kind of macro, called *Metatools* (keyboard-mouse shortcuts), is built into Finale. These can be especially useful for inserting expressions and articulations into a score. Essentially this means you can press preassigned letter or number keys to designate the most common articulations and expressions. You can use the factory presets, or you can customize your own. "By using a Metatool to place an expression marking into the score, for example, you can bypass three

158

dialogue boxes and several mouse clicks. See the individual tool for instructions for programming Metatools."*

In Sibelius, the equivalent to Metatools can be found in the Expression Word Menu and on the Keypad. Consult the manual and online help for the many other shortcuts available in that program. Please go to the companion website for more details on how to program Metatools in Finale and Expression shortcuts in Sibelius.

◊ Don't forget our advice from the end of Chapter 2: It's important always to keep our perspective with regard to our ultimate goal—the creation of music! For us—the professional musicians and composers, serious students, music educators, and music hobbyists—technology is a means to an end, not an end in itself.

Exercises

Use techniques discussed in this chapter.

1. Study examples 12-1, 12-2, and 12-3 illustrating the use of brass and woodwind articulations and brass mutes. Refer to our audio and graphic files provided on the companion website.

2. **Continue working on Arranging Project 1, the 3- to 4-horn arrangement of a standard tune.** Add dynamics and articulations to the brass and sax parts. Experiment with using brass mutes for color (especially during background sections).

159

---

* Finale online Help.

Chapter 13

The Rhythm Section

In the rush to uncover the mysteries of arranging music for various assortments of brass and woodwind instruments, the aspiring arranger is sometimes prone to overlook the important functions of the rhythm section instruments and the correct notation of their parts. The *rhythm section*—piano, bass, drums, and (optional) guitar—provides the rhythmic foundation and driving force of any jazz ensemble. Very often the standard jazz rhythm section is augmented by an additional percussionist, usually specializing in an array of instruments such as congas, timbales, shakers, tambourines, and occasionally mallet instruments such as vibes and marimba. The percussionist can be viewed by the arranger as a source of rhythmic spice as well as of additional melodic colors provided by the mallet instruments.

Any successful jazz arranger has a responsibility to understand the functions and correct notation of the rhythm section instruments and to become familiar with the various types of rhythmic grooves and styles common to the jazz lexicon. Following are some basic principles relating to the function of the rhythm section instruments and the proper notation of their parts.

13-1 Piano/Guitar

The piano and guitar in a jazz ensemble function primarily to provide a harmonic backdrop for the band, fleshing out the notes of the underlying harmonies in conjunction with the bass and horns, to comp behind improvising soloists, to play improvised solos, and occasionally to play written melodic parts. The piano and guitar also work with the bass and drums to provide the rhythmic impetus and propulsion for the band. The following applies equally to acoustic or electric pianos, electric organs or synthesizers, and acoustic or electric guitars as used in a jazz rhythm section.

1. Chord symbols with slashes or slash noteheads (rhythmic notation) is the standard form of notation for piano and guitar.

2. Notation of altered tones and rhythms of chord symbols in the piano/guitar part should generally match those of the horn voicings and rhythms. Indicate the precise altered/tension tones to match those in the horn voicings (e.g., if there's a ♭9 in the horn voicing, be sure to write C7♭9, *not* C9, in the piano, guitar, and bass parts).

3. Write out specific chord voicings when necessary. If the horn voicings are particularly complex and dense, as may frequently occur in a big band shout chorus, it's sometimes best to simply have the piano and guitar tacet during that section. They won't be heard over a loud, full tutti brass section anyway.

4. Write out solo melodic lines or bass lines when desired.

5. Indicate the tempo, style, feel, dynamics, etc. at the beginning of the part.

6. Sometimes it can be helpful to write out one or two bars of a particular rhythm pattern or style with chord voicings at the beginning of a passage, followed by slashes and chord changes and the term "simile…."

7. It's customary to write the piano in grand staff in the score, even if nothing is written in the bass clef. In such a case, with nothing written in the bass clef, the actual part would be written only in treble clef. It's common for a piano part to switch between written sections in grand staff and sections with chord symbols and slashes in treble or bass clef only.

8. When writing for guitar, indicate what type of guitar is required (acoustic nylon or steel string, electric guitar, etc.) and any type of effect needed for electric guitar (overdrive, chorus, etc.).

9. The guitar sounds one octave lower than written.

Sometimes in a piano or guitar part it may be desirable to indicate a melodic line or the top notes of the voicings with chord symbols in a passage, leaving the precise note choices in the chords to the discretion of the player. This can make for easier sight-reading as well as addressing the fact that most writers (unless they're guitar players) are not as familiar with what's playable on a guitar fretboard as on a piano keyboard. This can be indicated by simply writing a single-note melodic line with chord changes above and the instruction "Voice Chords Underneath Melody" by extending the stems of the chords downward below the noteheads or by writing a few x noteheads on the stems under the melody notes (see Ex. 13-1(2b)).

Although the piano and guitar fulfill similar functions in the rhythm section, there are obvious differences in how they contribute to the sonority of an arrangement. The piano has a much greater range and versatility (both melodically and harmonically). However, the guitar is capable of providing some unique inflections (such as bending notes) and timbral options (through the use of electronic devices such as fuzz tones, wah-wah pedals, and other signal processors). Also, through amplification, the electric guitar is capable of much greater volume and power, providing a key component to the driving energy in a rock or funk groove.

Because both instruments are called on to improvise a harmonic backdrop based on chord symbols, it's essential that the chord symbols and altered tones be notated precisely and match exactly in each part, as they should with the horn voicings. The pianist and guitarist also need to listen carefully to each other in order to avoid rhythmic and harmonic clashes, which can result in a muddy and ineffective chordal accompaniment. A variety of simple techniques can accomplish this. For example, one instrument can play sustained chords while the other comps rhythmically, one can play a steady rhythm on the downbeats while the other plays a more syncopated rhythm on the upbeats, one can play a melodic line (with or without the horns) while the other plays chords, or they can take turns comping while the other lays out.

An experienced arranger can take control of this situation by indicating the type of part to be played in various sections (e.g., "play sustained chords," "comp rhythmically"), by writing out one to two bars of a rhythmic part followed by slashes and chord changes and the term "simile…", or by judiciously selecting who will comp in a given section by having the other part tacet. These instruments are an important part of the arranger's timbral palette, and their use should be considered carefully, just as you would consider when to include saxes or brass or full tutti. It can be quite effective to have the piano or guitar or both double a melodic line played by the horns.

13-2 Bass

The function of the bass (acoustic or electric) is to provide the harmonic foundation for the ensemble, generally playing the chord roots and stringing the notes together in a melodic fashion to create an improvised contrapuntal part underneath written and improvised parts played by the rest of the ensemble. The bass also works in conjunction with the drums, piano, and guitar to provide the basic rhythmic pulse for the band.

1. Chord symbols with slashes or slash noteheads (rhythmic notation) is the standard form of notation for acoustic and electric bass.
2. Notation of altered tones and rhythms of chord symbols in the bass part should generally match those of the horn voicings and rhythms. Indicate the precise altered/tension tones to match those in the horn voicings, as well as those played by the piano and guitar. However, there may be some situations where it's not necessary to notate all altered chord tones played by the horns in the bass part, since the underlying harmonic

foundation (chord roots) played by the bass won't be affected by the various alterations. This allows the bass part to be less cluttered and easier to read. There may also be situations where it's preferable for the bass to *not* support all rhythmic syncopations played by the horns, as this can have the effect of breaking up the groove and making the ensemble sound stiff (see Section 13-5).

3. Write out specific bass lines for harmonic or melodic purposes when necessary.

4. The bass can also be used effectively as a contrasting color for melodic statements, either alone or in conjunction with one or more horns (consider the classic Thad Jones chart on "Three and One").

5. Indicate the tempo, style, feel, dynamics, etc. at the beginning of the part.

6. Sometimes it can be helpful to write out one or two bars of a particular bass line or style at the beginning of a passage, followed by slashes and chord changes and the term "simile…."

7. Indicate what type of bass is required, acoustic upright or electric.

8. The bass sounds one octave lower than written.

13-3 Chord Symbols and Abbreviations

The following symbols and abbreviations are in common use and recognized by most professionals.

Major: Maj, MA, Δ
Minor: min, mi, m, –
Augmented: Aug, +
Diminished: dim, °
Half-diminished: ϕ, m7$\flat$5
Suspended fourth: sus 4
Minor/major seventh: m(Δ7), m9(Δ7), min(Δ7), min9(Δ7), m(Maj7), etc.
Add 2: add 2, (2)—common in pop music to indicate a major chord or open fifth with the second scale degree but no seventh.
Major sixth or 6/9: Maj6, Maj 6/9

Minor sixth or 6/9: min6, m 6/9

Be as precise and consistent as possible with the chord symbols you use in piano, guitar, and bass parts. Use the same symbol to indicate major (e.g., either Maj or Δ) or minor (e.g., min, m, -) within one piece of music. *Never* use M for major, because it can too easily be mistaken for minor. If you want a seventh or a ninth in the chord, write it that way (e.g., specify C Maj7 or C Maj9). Many jazz pianists and guitar players will reflexively tend to add ninths or other altered tones to major, minor, or dominant chords. Let them know if you don't want that by indicating "No 9th," etc.

Avoid using the common "dom 7 alt" symbol when writing for any size ensemble with horns, unless it's purely for a blowing section, because you'll never know what you're going to wind up with, and clashes with the horn voicings are inevitable. Always be specific with regard to altered chord tones, and make sure that the chord symbols in the rhythm section parts match what the horns are playing, as mentioned earlier. That means if you need a ♭9, +9, and +11, that's what you should write: C7♭9+9+11. Sometimes it can help to put some alterations in parentheses: C7♭9(+5). And sometimes, if the chord symbols start getting too complex, it's really best to write everything out in the piano or guitar part. You can write the piano voicing in the guitar part and ask the guitar player to grab as many notes as possible, or you can indicate which notes are most important.

13-4 Drums

The drums, or drum set, sometimes with the aid of an additional percussionist, function as the primary source of rhythmic propulsion for most jazz ensembles, working in conjunction with the bass, piano, and guitar, to create the fundamental rhythmic drive or groove of a jazz performance. The drums also function in a very important way to support rhythmic figures played by the rest of the ensemble, to play rhythmic fills where needed, and occasionally to play improvised solos.

1. Use standard rhythmic notation (using x and diamond-shaped noteheads) for drum parts.
2. Use the bass clef or percussion clef symbol.
3. Indicate the tempo, style, feel, dynamics, etc. at the beginning of the part. It's usually sufficient to write four quarter notes, with the tempo and rhythmic style (e.g., ♩ = 116, SWING or FUNK) written above the first measure, followed by repeat signs or slashes and "simile…."
4. Indicate where specific accents or fills are needed to support the horns by copying the precise syncopated rhythms played by the horns into the drum part. For fills, simply write the word *FILL—* above rhythmic slashes to indicate the duration of the fill.
5. There are some situations where it's necessary to write out a drum part exactly as it is to be played. In these situations it's common practice to put the bass drum (BD) on the bottom space, the snare drum (SD) on the third space, the hi-hat (HH), ride, and crash cymbals on the top space or the space above the top line of the staff, and the tom-toms anywhere in the middle of the staff. A "+" above a notehead indicates a closed HH, and an "o" above a notehead indicates an open HH.

6. It's generally acceptable to write only one drum line on the top space of the staff, with x noteheads indicating rhythmic hits (Ex. 13-1(4a)). Another option is to write rhythmic hits as cues above slashes or quarter notes, to indicate that the time continues under the hits (Ex. 13-1(4b)). Different levels of rhythmic intensity can also be indicated by adding a second drum line on the bottom space (Ex. 13-1(4c)) for extra emphasis. The second line also serves to display all the beats in a measure during a syncopated section.

7. Sometimes it can be helpful to write out one or two bars of a particular rhythm pattern or style at the beginning of a passage, followed by repeat signs and the term "simile…."

8. If the drummer is playing for a long stretch (e.g., behind an improvised solo), it can be useful periodically to indicate the number of elapsed bars by writing the number of bars in parentheses above a measure or with instructions such as "Play 16 bars" (Ex 13-1(4d)).

13-5 General Considerations

It's essential for any jazz arranger to understand how to notate rhythmic figures correctly in all the rhythm section instruments and how to notate chords and chord symbols correctly in the piano, guitar, and bass parts so that the chords played by the rhythm section instruments reflect those played by the rest of the ensemble. See Ex. 13-1 for illustrations of basic rhythm section notation.

Example 13-2 is the 12-bar blues from Chapter 12 (Ex. 12-2), with all the rhythm section parts notated correctly, illustrating these principles in a musical context. Notice in this example that not all syncopations in the horn parts are supported rhythmically by the rhythm section. It's often best if the rhythm section plays through some of the syncopated sections, since too much syncopation by the rhythm section can have the effect of breaking up the groove and making the music sound "square." It can also be effective to have part of the rhythm section support syncopated figures and part play through them (e.g., the drums, piano, and guitar playing the syncopation, with the bass walking through it).

The drums should generally support syncopated, full tutti sections, such as shout choruses, or any type of strong, rhythmic, melodic statement and should play fills in between the accented figures. There's no rule for when the bass should support syncopated figures in the rest of the band, although generally the bass should align rhythmically with the drums for shout choruses and other powerful sections. Listen and compare the difference between the two recorded versions, Ex. 13-2A, "Played with Rhythm Section Support," and Ex. 13-2B, "Played Without Rhythm Section Support."

Ex. 13-1

Rhythm Section Notation

168

Richard Sussman

Ex. 13-2A & B "I've Got The Articulations & Dynamics Blues"

13-6 **Rhythm Section Styles**

It's very important for any arranger to be familiar with the nature and function of specific parts played by the different rhythm section instruments in a variety of musical styles. For example, the bass, drums, and chordal instruments function very differently in a straight-ahead jazz groove compared to a funk groove. A thorough study of rhythm section styles and parts is beyond the scope of this book. Many excellent books are available on the subject. We particularly recommend *Essential Styles for the Drummer and Bassist*, Books 1 and 2, by Steve Houghton and Tom Warrington (Alfred Music) for those interested in gaining quick insight into the function of rhythm section instruments in the most common jazz and pop styles.

As with many aspects of the study of jazz music, if you're serious, the best way to learn any particular technique is to transcribe it. Pick a four- to eight-bar section of a recorded rhythm groove in any style, and transcribe the parts played by each rhythm section instrument onto separate staves of score paper or your notation software. For this exercise, use at least four to five staves for the drums. Put the kick and snare on the bottom staff, hi-hat on the next staff up, and ride and crash cymbals, toms, and any other percussion instruments (such as cowbell, triangle, shaker) on different staves. Write out the bass line exactly. Be sure to notate the precise rhythmic placement of piano and guitar chords with the chord changes. Don't worry if you can't hear every single note of the chord voicings. The rhythmic placement is more important.

When you've completed the transcription, record it into your sequencer, or input it into the notation program. For this type of exercise it's much easier and faster to get more musical results from MIDI playback with the sequencer, using the best drum, piano, guitar, and bass samples at your disposal. For more details on how to create satisfying playback of rhythm section parts in a notation program, consult the Software Tips for this chapter on the website. Be aware that it is *much* easier to create musically satisfying sequenced rhythm section grooves in a rock, funk, or even-eighths style than a straight-ahead jazz swing style.

◊ **Important:** *Never*, except in very specific situations, give a drummer a part with every detail notated! It will be impossible to read. The correct procedure is to provide an outline of the part to be played, with an indication of the general style and tempo, along with important, supportive rhythmic accents and fills, as described earlier. Any experienced jazz or rock drummer (including most college-level students) will be able to supply the rest of the part through improvisation.

Chapter Summary

In this chapter we described the functions and correct notation of the various rhythm section instruments and examined how the rhythm section, when properly notated, can effectively support rhythmic figures in the other parts. We examined important issues regarding the proper notation of chord symbols as well as some general considerations regarding writing for the rhythm section. Finally, we recommended transcription as the best way to learn the specific functions of each instrument in various rhythmic styles.

◊ **Software Tip:** It's often easiest simply to mute the bass and drum staves during MIDI playback in a notation program. On the other hand, it can be nice to hear some sort of basic drum and bass groove along with the other MIDI tracks. You can use a similar method to that used for creating piano parts to create bass and drum tracks in hidden layers, behind the written notation. Consult the Software Tips for this chapter on the website for more details.

Both Finale and Sibelius also now come supplied with various prerecorded generic drum grooves, which you can throw under the music to get a quick sense of what the piece will feel like with a rhythm section. However, this method is less than ideal, since you'll be missing the important accents and rhythm section support unique to whatever piece you're working on.

Exercises

Use techniques discussed in this chapter.

1. Listen to the recordings of Ex. 13-2A and 13-2B (the blues from the preceding chapter). Notice how the rhythm section parts, as properly notated, support the rhythmic figures in the horn parts.

2. Do several transcriptions of rhythm section grooves in different styles, as described in Section 13-6. Spend some time finessing the parts in your sequencer or notation program to get them to sound as musical as possible.

◊ 3. **Continue working on Arranging Project 1, the 3- to 4-horn arrangement of a standard tune.** Fill in the complete rhythm section parts for the piano, bass, drums, and guitar, taking care to adhere to principles discussed in this chapter.

Chapter 14

Completing the 3- to 4-Horn Arrangement

If you've been doing all the exercises labeled "Arranging Project 1," beginning with Chapter 8, your 3- to 4-horn arrangement of a standard tune should now be almost complete. The arrangement should consist of an intro, a head (arranged using a variety of techniques), a kicker, and one or more improvised solos with backgrounds. You should have proper dynamics and articulations indicated in the horn parts and properly notated rhythm section parts. All that remains for you to do is to add a recap and a short coda, make sure that you've created proper layouts and music spacing for the score and the parts, verified the transpositions for transposing instruments, and checked for any notational mistakes.

This chapter provides some basic principles regarding score and part layouts, music spacing, and printing the score and the parts. Detailed instructions on how to perform some of these functions in both Finale and Sibelius will be presented in the next chapter. If you're not familiar with these software functions, be sure to study the instructions in Chapter 15 before attempting to lay out and print the score and parts.

14-1 Adding a Recap and Ending

If you've just completed a solo section with backgrounds, you're probably ready for a recap of the tune or some other type of ending. Working out a conclusion for the chart can take several different paths. Here are a few possible directions:

1. Drop the level of intensity with a short transitional passage and proceed with a D.S. back to all or part of the original head, followed by a coda.

2. Maintain the intensity generated by the improvised solos, and recap all or part of the head with more powerful instrumentation, followed by a coda.

3. Have the last solo chorus lead directly to an ending/coda, foregoing a recap entirely.

4. Compose a *Through Composed* ending consisting of new material, or material derived from other sections of the tune or arrangement.

Refer to Chapter 11 for specific suggestions regarding endings and codas.

14-2 Score and Part Layouts and Music Spacing

Before proceeding with your score and part layouts, please take a few minutes to review Section 5-5, "Music Preparation Basics." Following these basic rules will ensure that your score and parts look professional and are easy to read, resulting in smooth and efficient rehearsals and performances of your music.

All of the notation programs seem to be getting better at creating automatic score and part layouts and music spacing, but there will still be times when you'll need to make adjustments manually. Study the detailed instructions in Chapter 15 to make sure you understand how to respace the music, adjust measure widths, adjust the distance between staves, and perform similar functions relating to the page layout of your score and parts in whichever notation program you're using.

If you haven't been entering articulations, dynamics, and full rhythm section parts, be sure to do that now. If you have been doing this, be sure to include, as part of the proofreading process, a thorough check of all articulations, dynamics, and rhythm section parts. It's especially important to take a little extra time to make sure that all chord symbols and rhythmic placement of chords in the piano, guitar, and bass parts correspond to the actual altered chord tones and rhythmic placement of chords played by the ensemble.

14-3 Proofreading and Part Transpositions

We can't stress enough how important it is to allow yourself adequate time to proofread both the score and the parts. There are two main reasons for this. First of all, human beings make mistakes. You can save yourself a lot of grief by catching as many mistakes as possible *before* you bring the chart to a rehearsal or recording session. Second, the intricacies of music notation programs sometimes results in odd note spellings, awkward rhythmic notation, missing courtesy accidentals, missing music expressions and articulations, etc.

Print out and proofread the score first. The best way to do this is to go to a piano or keyboard and play through the entire score to make sure you don't have any unintentional harmonic clashes or wrong notes, misspellings (e.g., an F♭ instead of an E natural), awkwardly notated rhythms (see Ex. 6-1), etc. Check the ranges and tessitura of all the parts. Check for parallel fifths, excessive repeated notes in an inner voice, unbalanced voicings, etc. Make sure all the dynamics, articulations, and courtesy accidentals are where they're supposed to be.

There is often a tendency to overwrite. Less is more! Use the proofreading process not only to correct mistakes but also to check for overly busy or cluttered sections, and take things out! *Do not trust MIDI playback as a substitute for thorough proofreading!* No matter how good your samples are, you're certain to miss things by relying solely on MIDI playback for proofreading.

Proofreading the score is generally easier with a concert score. However, we recommend switching to a transposed score *before* generating the parts. This makes proofreading the parts easier—and there's always the possibility that you'll wind up with some odd note spellings after having your software transpose the alto sax or trumpet part. So if you proof the concert score, it's a good idea to go quickly over the transposed parts one more time to check for note misspellings as well as music spacing and layout issues.

Obviously, it's essential that you now understand how to generate or extract the parts from the score with the correct transpositions. Both Finale and Sibelius now feature "Linked Parts," which retains the score and all parts as one file. This way, making a change to one part will be reflected in the score, and vice versa.

14-4 Printing the Parts and the Score

Understanding how to lay out and print the score and part pages is essential to continue with this method of working. Each software program has its own set of shortcuts and key commands that can speed up the process as well as certain features that may appear clumsy or frustrating. More detailed instructions and some software tips on how to perform these important functions in Finale and Sibelius are provided in Chapter 15. It's your responsibility to become familiar with these various features and to develop workarounds for problem areas.

For jazz and pop music, parts should always be printed on one side only, *never* on both sides of the page. Once you have the parts printed, they *must* be taped together "accordion style," with manageable page turns, as described in Section 5-5, "Music Preparation Basics." Score pages should be printed on *both* sides, in *landscape* orientation. Ideally, the score should be spiral or comb bound on the left side so that it opens like a book, with a clear plastic front cover and a solid black back cover. In a pinch you can get away with taping or clipping the left side.

14-5 Sample 4-Horn Arrangement and Analysis

"Bill Bossa" by Richard Sussman.

Tune Analysis

"Bill Bossa" is a medium-tempo bossa nova with an AABA form (labeled as ABCD on the lead sheet). However, the first "A" section is nine bars long, and the last "A" section is 14 bars, providing formal interest by means of asymmetrical phrase structure. The second "A" section and the "B" section are both eight bars long. Also, although there is an obvious melodic and harmonic relationship among the three "A" sections, the chord changes and melodic phrase structure are quite different in each version. It's also interesting to note that there are really just three melodic motives (a, b, and c), which are rearranged in different ways in the various sections of the tune. Unlike most AABA tunes, there is no distinctly separate melodic motive for the bridge, just a reharmonization of "c" from the first "A." The rhythmic motive from the intro, which recurs throughout the tune, is labeled "i."

Although the tune is basically diatonic in nature, it modulates in some unexpected ways, most notably the colorful modulation to D major in bar 7 (up a major third from the primary key of B♭ and with the root-motion skip of a tritone from the preceding chord of A♭ Maj). The use of the A♭ Maj9 ♭VII chord in the intro, bars 6, 15, 19, and 32, and the coda, although not diatonic in the key of B♭, is a typical progression commonly found in jazz and popular music and although analyzed as a quick modulation to A♭ in mm. 15-17, should not be viewed as a "true" modulation until the last "A" section (bars 32–35), where it makes sense to do so because the "A♭" key center is extended for four bars.

We've also indicated the use of *pivot chords* (circled), which are chords that can be analyzed as having different functions in different key centers, thereby facilitating a modulation. For example, the F Maj9 in bar 11 is also the V of B♭, with a change of chord quality. In bar 24, the G/A (V of IV in A major) leads us smoothly to the G13♭9 V of C major. Similarly, the B♭/C in bar 28 (V of V in B♭) could also be analyzed as V of IV in the key of C. In bar 29, note the V of V tritone substitution, with a change of chord quality to G♭ Maj7♭5. Also note that the "polytonal" sound of G♭/F can also be analyzed as F7 sus+5♭9. Similarly, in bar 13, B/F can be analyzed as F7 ♭5♭9. We'll be taking a closer look at some of these types of modern harmonies and chord voicings in Section 3.

Finally, in bar 31, A13♭9, V of iii in B♭, is also a V tritone substitution in the key of A♭, leading us naturally to that modulation. Notice how the modulation is supported by the chromatic walk-down from B♭ to G (mm. 30–33) and how this reharmonization differentiates and enhances the last "A" section of the tune. The Cm/D in bar 36, a somewhat unusual voicing with the ninth in the bass, is both iii in the key of A♭ and ii in the key of B♭. (No, it's *not* a D7sus♭9.)

Ex. 14-1

"Bill Bossa" by Richard Sussman Lead Sheet

"Bill Bossa"

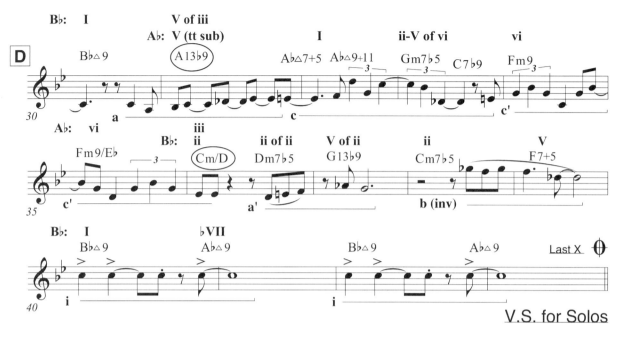

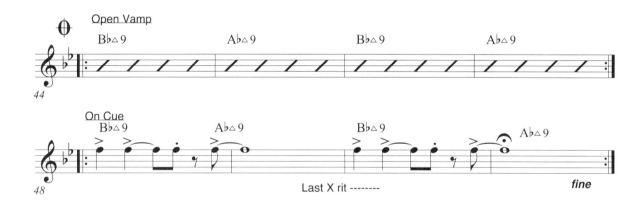

Legend

Form: A(9)A(8)B(8)A(14), indicated by: [A] [B] [C] [D]

Key Centers/Modulations indicated by: **B♭:**

Harmonic Analysis: Roman numerals indicate scale degrees of the Diatonic Scale of Key Tonal Center.
Upper case = Major, Dom., Aug. Lower case = minor, diminished, 1/2 diminished.
Melodic motives indicated loosely by: **a, b, c**
Intro rhythmic motive: **i**
XC = Chromatic Passing Chord
tt sub = tritone substitution
Pivot Chords indicated by: (**B♭/C**)

Ex. 14-2 "Bill Bossa" 4 Horn Arrangement

Transposed Score

by Richard Sussman

Medium Bossa (♩ = 152)

Ex. 14-2 "Bill Bossa" 4 Horn Arrangement - 2

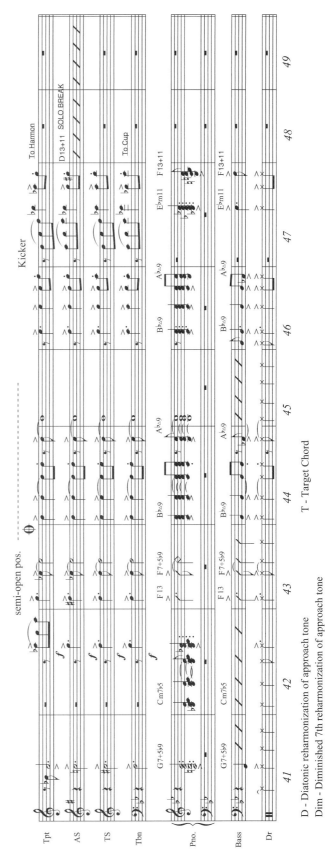

Ex. 14-2 "Bill Bossa" 4 Horn Arrangement - 3

D - Diatonic reharmonization of approach tone
Dim - Diminished 7th reharmonization of approach tone
T - Target Chord

179

Ex. 14-2 "Bill Bossa" 4 Horn Arrangement - 4

Ex. 14-2 "Bill Bossa" 4 Horn Arrangement - 5

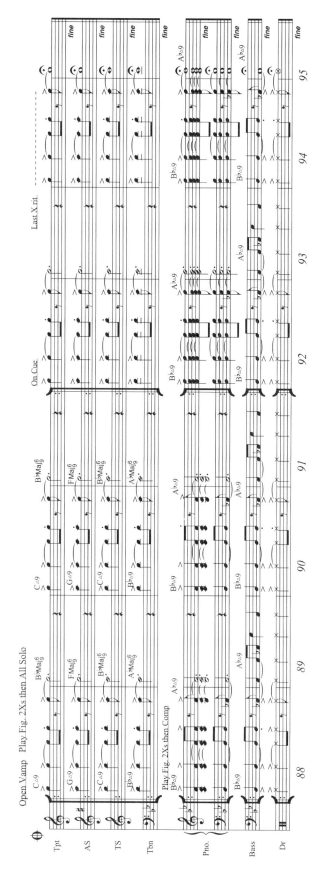

Ex. 14-2 "Bill Bossa" 4 Horn Arrangement - 6

4-Horn Arrangement Analysis

Possibly the most distinctive feature of the 4-horn arrangement of "Bill Bossa" is the use of contrasting types of instrumental textures and voicing techniques, as illustrated in Chapters 7, 8, and 11, and the use of counterpoint (Chapter 10). Because of the complex harmonic and melodic nature of the tune, it seemed that melodic alterations and reharmonization (including reharmonization of approach tones) were not as necessary for this arrangement.

The intro is a simple two-bar rhythmic motive played twice by the rhythm section and then echoed by the horns, first in close position and then semi-open in a higher register. This phrase provides a *rhythmic hook*, a unifying device, which recurs throughout the tune and arrangement. Note the rhythmic alteration of the last phrase.

The first "A" section begins with the melody played in unison by the trumpet and alto, expanding to a harmonized third on the last note of the phrase, emphasizing the modulation to D major. The trumpet/sax unison continues in bar 12, opening up to a two-part parallel harmonization at the end of m. 12, with the trombone entering in bar 13, playing a slow countermelody. The phrase continues, with the horns switching from unison to three-note chords when the melody ascends (voicing the lower-register melody notes wouldn't work because it would result in muddy-sounding voicings). The first "A" section ends with some more contrary motion, with the horns starting on a unison and expanding to a close position voicing as the melody rises. Notice the subtle color enhancement to the melody provided by switching from unison to three-part voicings and the use of contrary motion.

The second "A" section ("B" in the arrangement) begins with the three horns in octaves (building in intensity from the unison of the first section), opening up to a rich, open-fifth voicing of E♭m11 at the end of bar 20, followed by the entrance of the tenor sax playing a nice countermelody in bar 21. Bars 22–23 recap the close position, rhythmic hook figure from bars 5–6 of the intro. The melodic texture of bars 23–25 is trumpet melody over chords.

The bridge ("C") begins with the striking textural contrast of alto and piano in unison, with the tenor and trombone adding harmonic support at the end of the phrase. This is followed by a few bars of solo trumpet, with the alto and trombone entering in close position for the cadence in bars 32–33. The final "A" section ("D" in the arrangement) continues with all four horns voiced in close or semi-open position, depending on the register of the melody. Notice the contrary motion between the trumpet and the other horns at the beginning of bar 35.

The four horns are in rhythmic unison from m. 34 to m. 37. There are two approach-tone reharmonizations in bar 35, the first diatonic (altered chord tones of A7), the second a diminished seventh chord. In bars 38–42, the texture changes to trumpet melody over chords in the other horns. Bar 43 returns to

183

rhythmic unison with the cadence to the repeated "hook" figure from the intro, now voiced in semi-open position. Bar 47 is a one-bar kicker extension of the tune into the alto solo break.

At letter "E," the blowing section, notice first of all that the chord changes have been simplified and the harmonic rhythm evened out to make it easier for improvisation. The muted-brass backgrounds are meant to be played the second time only behind each solo, and will work behind both the alto and piano solos. A few different techniques are used in the background figures, starting with simple rhythmic comping, followed by a slow, then faster counter-melody, leading to the rhythmic hook in bars 62–64. Starting at bar 67 (the bridge), we leave some space for the soloist ("Less is more"). A few simple pads (bars 74–75, 77–78, and 82–83) lead again to the rhythmic hook figure from the intro.

The coda is basically just a repetition of the intro, with an extended open vamp for blowing and with the rhythmic figure returning on cue in the last four bars. Notice that the voicing has been changed slightly for the last four bars—raising the trombone up to an F, to double and support the trumpet melody. Finally notice that dynamics and articulations are clearly indicated in the horn parts, the rhythm section parts are properly notated, rehearsal letters and measure numbers are in place, and there are eight bars per system—and occasionally nine—so that double bar lines occur at the left and right margins. Be sure to listen to the recorded example on the companion website as you study the analysis.

◊ **Note:** We've printed the full score to "Bill Bossa" as a transposed score. We'll be showing full scores in transposed format so that you can get used to seeing the instruments displayed in their proper registers and transpositions, as they would appear in most professionally printed scores. If you have trouble with the transpositions, the MIDI files are available for download on the website. You can open them in Finale or Sibelius and choose to display the score in concert pitch. Also, on the recording, we only had time for one chorus of alto solo. The chart calls for two choruses of alto followed by two choruses of piano solo so that the alto player wouldn't have to jump on the melody immediately following his solo (see Section 3-1, item 5, and Section 3-2, item 6). This also explains why the backgrounds are played the first time on the alto solo chorus.

◊ **Special Bonus Score Available On Website!** For a great example of a hip 3-horn chart in a more contemporary funky jazz style, check out "Shanghigh" by the great jazz trumpeter and composer Randy Brecker.

The score is available for download as Ex. 14-3 on our website. As with other commercially available recordings examined in this book, we haven't provided a recording of this chart on the website. The recording is available on the album "34th N Lex" by Randy Brecker, Tone Center Records, 2003. We encourage you to support the great jazz musicians of our generation by purchasing the CD, or at least downloading the tune!

Chapter Summary

In this chapter, we've examined the steps necessary for completing the 3- to 4-horn chart, including creating a recap and coda, as well as a discussion of some basic principles relating to parts and score layout, and to printing, taping and binding the parts and score. We then discussed the importance of proofreading the score and the parts and made some recommendations in that regard. We also provided a sample 4 horn + rhythm arrangement, with a detailed analysis of the tune and arrangement. You should now be ready to call a rehearsal and enjoy the fruits of your labors!

◊ **Software Tip**: Make sure you understand how to work with "Linked Parts" in both Finale and Sibelius. It's an incredible time saver!

◊ **Software Tip**: It's important to understand how to assign certain expressions to specific staves in the score and the parts. This is especially useful with rehearsal marks and tempo indications, which are generally *not* placed on every staff of a score, to avoid clutter. There are shortcuts in both Finale and Sibelius for assigning text and symbol expressions to individual staves or groups of staves. Consult the website and your manuals or online Help for details.

Exercises

Use techniques discussed in this chapter and the following chapter.

1. Add a recap and ending to your 3- to 4-horn chart (Arranging Project 1).
2. Print out the parts and the score for **Arranging Project 1**. Call a rehearsal, and play through the chart several times. Record it.
3. Listen to the recording with the other musicians. Discuss which parts worked well and which didn't. Make any necessary changes (this usually means taking things out or revoicing sections that may be too thick or dissonant). Print everything out again, and play it again!

4. Pick a 3-horn arrangement from any Art Blakey and the Jazz Messengers or Art Farmer/Benny Golson Jazztet recordings. Listen to and transcribe the horn arrangement of the head and any backgrounds. Use a CD player, mp3 player, or sequencer with a repeat mode to loop a section you want to transcribe, and focus on one part at a time. Loop one, two, or four bars at a time, and then move on.

◊ **Software Tip:** When doing transcriptions, try slowing down the recording to half speed in your sequencer (the pitch will drop one octave), or use a program such as The Amazing Slow Downer or QuickTime Player (which *won't* change the pitch when you slow it down). Just open any audio file in QuickTime, go to Window > Show A/V Controls, and adjust the Playback Speed to 1/2x. It's not cheating! Anything that helps you to understand the music better is worthwhile.

Chapter 15

Notation Software: Generating Parts, Page Layout, and Printing

Generating parts, doing page layouts of the parts and the score, and printing out the parts and the score are crucial components in the process of completing your work using notation software. It is also an area where mistakes frequently occur. This chapter will present some more detailed instructions on how to perform these important tasks using Finale and Sibelius.

Both programs provide a multitude of various templates (referred to as "Manuscript Paper" in Sibelius) from which to choose when starting a new project. For the projects covered in this book—jazz lead sheets, small jazz ensembles of from three to six horns plus rhythm, and standard jazz big band (five reeds, eight brass, and four rhythm)—we recommend starting with one of the templates provided on our companion website, which have been adjusted for optimal spacing of staves and systems for our purposes.

Regardless of how well the templates are set up, you're still going to want to know how to customize and adjust them for specific projects. For example, you'll need to know how to add or delete staves without disturbing the appropriate spacing between staves (e.g., if you have a big band with five trumpets instead of four or only three trombones or no guitar). Also, there are subjective elements to the "look" of a score or parts that you should know how to control, such as which fonts to use and how to position measure numbers.

As we proceed through a more detailed examination of how certain specific functions are handled in Finale and Sibelius, it's important to appreciate one fundamental distinction between the two programs: There are significant differences in underlying concepts regarding how the user interfaces are designed. Finale has been developed with a "tools-based" interface, similar to a graphics program, with tools intended to perform specific tasks. For example, the Staff Tool is used for all functions regarding staves. Consequently, many menus in Finale are available only when the appropriate tool is selected (e.g., Staff Menu with Staff Tool, Text Menu with Text Tool). Sibelius, however, is essentially "menu-based" and "window-based" (more like a word processor); there are very few actual tools, and all menus are always available in the menu bar. However, each menu in Finale tends to be more focused on specific tasks, whereas many menus in Sibelius are more generalized (e.g., Create Menu, House Style Menu), requiring additional selections from submenus. It's unclear which system is actually more efficient or requires fewer mouse clicks.

Despite this fundamental difference in programming approaches, the actual experience of working in the two programs is more similar than you might expect. This is because so many of the most important functions in both programs can be accessed by keyboard/mouse shortcuts rather than by going to tools or menus. Finale, in particular, appears to have made a concerted effort in recent versions to overcome some of the inherent awkwardness of the tool-based approach. With "contextual menus" (drop-down menus accessed by control-clicking on a region) and other, similar enhancements, many functions can now be performed without the need to select a different tool or menu. Similarly, in Sibelius the abundance of shortcuts often makes it unnecessary to actually go to a menu to select something.

The most striking similarity between the two programs is the sheer complexity and number of functions that potentially need to be addressed while notating a musical score. There is also a somewhat more subjective difference in how some of the functions are organized within the two programs. For example, in Sibelius many different options are accessed through the House Styles menu and Engraving Rules, whereas in Finale similar functions may be spread out among several "tool-specific" dialogue boxes, such as Staff Attributes and Expression Selection.

In Section 5-3 we outlined some basic concepts relating to staves, page layout, music spacing, generating and editing linked parts, and printing the score and parts in Finale and Sibelius. The following sections present more details on how to perform these tasks in each program. Although the methods are not always completely analogous, both programs are capable of achieving comparable results.

Remember that one important consideration when laying out the parts pages is to make the page turns as easy as possible by having a few bars of rest before or after the page turn. This can usually be accomplished by laying out the music so that rests occur at the end of the last staff before a page turn or at the beginning of the first page after a page turn. Sometimes this means putting only five or six staves on a page (before a page turn) instead of eight or nine.

Finally, both programs give you a selection of several different music fonts and many text fonts to choose from. For example, you have a choice between Jazz Font (a more handwritten look) and Maestro (a more profession-ally engraved look) in Finale. In Sibelius the equivalent choices are Inkpen (handwritten look) and Opus (engraved look). This is really a subjective deci-sion, and any of the music fonts can produce professional-looking scores and parts.

◊ Because of the rapid pace of technological change and because both Finale and Sibelius seem to be coming out with major upgrades about once a year, we decided to put most of the specific instruction for the important tasks discussed in this chapter on the website only, where it can be easily updated as needed. Also, because of the importance of the material pre-sented in this chapter, we've chosen to include the entire text for Sections 15-1, 15-2, and 15-3 on the website as well, so that you can download and print out the complete text and have it available for quick reference. Please go to the website where indicated to download and study the complete, up-to-date text.

15-1 Finale

First of all, make sure you're in "Page View" (View Menu > Page View, or ⌘-E/Mac, ctrl-E/WIN), and start with one of the templates provided on the companion website. For the following examples, let's work with the "Jazz Big Band" template.

A. *Staves—the Staff Tool*

1. *Staff Tool Basics* (The Staff Tool's functionality was revamped in Finale 2011. In 2011, the Staff Attributes window opens when you double-click on a staff, but doesn't open when you click on a staff handle. In 2010 and prior, the Staff Attributes window opens by double-clicking on either the handle or the staff. As part of the Staff Tool's new func-tionality in 2011, you can add a new group for the entire score or only a region. The term "optimize" is no longer used when referring to groups or in the Page Layout Menu.)

   a. With the Staff Tool selected, double-click on any staff handle (2010 & earlier) or staff (2011) to access the Staff Attributes dialogue box. This is where you can edit the staff name, abbreviated staff name, initial clef, transposition, notation style, and items to display for any staff.

   b. It's a good idea to indicate any instrumental doubles in the staff name. For example, if Reed 1 will be playing alto sax and flute, the full staff name should be:

   Reed 1

   AS, Fl

189

If Trumpet 1 will also be playing flugelhorn, the staff name should be:

Trumpet 1

Tpt, Flugel

The abbreviated staff names should be AS 1 and Tpt 1. Those sections where the part switches to flute or flugelhorn will be indicated using "Staff Styles."

   c. To create a "Staff Group" that you want bracketed together (e.g., Reeds, Trumpets), drag over all the staff handles for a particular section. Go to Staff > Add Group and Bracket. Select a "Group Name" (we've chosen not to name the groups in this template), "Optimize (2010 & earlier) or Hide (2011) Normally," "Draw Bar Lines Through Staves," and select a "Bracket Type."

   d. The distance between staves can be adjusted manually simply by dragging a staff handle up or down (Finale 2010 & earlier), by dragging a staff handle up or down to apply to that system only (Finale 2011), or by double-clicking a handle and dragging to apply to the entire score. For greater precision go to Staff > Staff Usage. To change the spacing of all staves in a score globally, go to Staff > Respace Staves > Distance Between Staves (2010 & earlier) or Space Above Each System (2011), and select a percentage value.

   e. "Staff Styles" is a powerful function in Finale that allows you to indicate an instrumental doubling and transposition, alternate notation (slash, rhythmic, percussion, one or two bar repeats, etc.), and so on for a selected region. *Refer to the website for details.*

  2. *Resizing staves: Refer to the website for detailed instructions on resizing staves.*

  3. *Adding, deleting, and repositioning staves: Refer to the website for details.*

B. *Generating linked parts:* If you're creating a new score using the Setup Wizard, you have the option to generate linked parts automatically. If you're starting with a preexisting template, the linked parts will already be there. However, there are some situations where you may want to generate a new set of parts in order to quickly change music spacing settings or page formats for the parts. *Refer to the website for details on generating linked parts.*

◊ Once the parts have been generated, go to Document > Edit Score or Edit Part to select the score or a part to edit.

C. *Score and parts page layout—the Page Layout Tool:* Adjusting the page and system margins for the score and the parts in Finale can be a little confusing because many combinations of settings will produce similar results. We've provided one set of values in each of the relevant sections that will achieve the desired results.

1. *Adjusting page margins* (this is simple!): *Refer to the website for details.*

◊ Before adjusting the parts page margins, be sure to click on "Apply To Parts/Score" in the "Edit Page Margins" dialogue box to specify which parts will be affected. For this and the following procedures, you can save a lot of time by applying layout changes to sections or groups of instruments that will have similar layouts. Otherwise, you'll have to redo the layouts for each individual part.

2. *Adjusting system margins* (this is a little more complicated!): *Refer to the website for details.*
3. *Score system margins*: *Refer to the website for details.*
4. *Parts system margins*: *Refer to the website for details.*

◊ Adjusting the number of systems per page and the number of measures per system and editing the distance between systems are some of the most critical aspects to score and parts page layout. Before adjusting any of the page or system margins, be sure to click on "Apply To Parts/Score" in the "Edit System Margins" dialogue box to specify which parts or score will be affected.

5. *Adjusting score and parts page size/orientation*: *Refer to the website for details.*

◊ You must specify the page size and orientation in *both* the Page Layout menu *and* the File menu or it won't work! Alternatively, you can go to the Finale Menu > Preferences > Program Options > Save and Print and check the box labeled "Use Finale's Page Orientation Instead of the Printer's Page Orientation."

6. *Staff Optimization* (2010 & earlier) or *Hide Empty Staves* (2011): Staff optimization (or Hide Empty Staves), (Page Layout Menu > Optimize Staff Systems) removes empty staves on pages where there is no music contained in those staves. This can be useful in the case of orchestral scores with a large number of staves, but is generally *not* used for jazz scores. However, staff optimization may be used for jazz scores to hide empty staves on piano parts that sometimes require both treble clef and bass clef in grand staff and sometimes only single staves. *Refer to the website for details.*

7. *Page one file info—score and parts*: If you haven't created the score using the Setup Wizard or a preexisting template or if you need to change the title, the composer's name, etc., go to File > File Info and

enter the pertinent information, such as title, composer, arranger, copyright info, and score or part name. This information can then be added as text inserts on the score and parts where needed. *Refer to the website for details.*

8. *Subsequent pages file info/layout*: *Refer to the website for details.*

9. *Repositioning expressions, segnos, coda signs, and test blocks in parts*

   a. Most expressions in Finale are attached to notes or measures and will not require repositioning in the parts. However, occasionally it may be necessary to reposition certain expressions, such as rehearsal letters, coda signs, segnos, and other text blocks.

   b. With the Selection Tool, you can drag any text block or expression to reposition it. If items are very close together, it can be easier to select the Expression Tool, Repeat Tool, or Text Tool and then drag the handles to reposition any of these items.

10. *Measure numbers*: Finale has several methods for dealing with the necessary differences between the appearance of measure numbers on the score and on the parts. On a score for a small ensemble of 5–6 horns or less, measure numbers should be placed below every measure on the bottom-score staff in a large font size. For large ensembles, such as a big band or larger, measure numbers should also be placed every measure in the middle of the score (e.g., between the trombone and trumpet sections of a big band). For parts, measure numbers should be displayed only at the start of each system and in a much smaller font size. *Refer to the website for details.*

D. *Spacing the music—score and parts (the Selection Tool)*

1. *Adjusting the number of measures per system*: Go to Utilities > Fit Measures (⇧-⌘-M/Mac, ctrl-M/WIN) to specify the number of measures per system for a selected region or to lock a selected group of measures into one system.

◊ Generally, aim for eight measures per system for the score and four measures per system for parts. Wherever possible, try to have the beginnings of important sections, double bar lines, rehearsal letters, and repeat signs align with the left and right margins of score and parts pages.

Here's a useful shortcut to move individual measures from one system to another: Select the desired measure(s) to be moved, and press the up or down arrow key. With parts, pay special attention to multimeasure rests, musical phrasing, and the density of notes in any particular measures. If the music spacing seems to be too crowded, put three (instead of four) measures on those systems. For measures with fewer notes, it's easier to fit more measures onto a system. *Refer to the website for details.*

◊ When adjusting parts in the "Utilities Menu/Fit Music" dialogue box, be sure to click on "Change: 'Selected Parts/Score'" and "Select" to specify which parts or score will be affected.

2. *Spacing the music—score and parts (adjusting the note spacing)*: The normal default preferences in Finale are set to space the music automatically as you input it. Sometimes it can be useful to turn off this function so that you can space the music manually. When you're ready to do so, go to Finale Menu > Preferences > Program Options > Edit (Mac) or Edit Menu > Program Options > Edit (WIN), and uncheck "Automatic Update Layout" and "Automatic Music Spacing." *Refer to the website for details.*

3. *Adjusting measure widths*
   a. After you complete the page layouts and space the music, it may still be necessary to adjust some individual measure widths.
   b. Look over the entire score and all parts. If any measures seem too wide or too narrow, select the Measure Tool and simply drag the measure handles to the left or right. It's a good idea to do this *after* spacing the music and updating the layout, since these functions will undo manual measure-width positioning.

15-2 Sibelius

First of all, make sure you're in "Score View," and start with one of the manuscript papers provided on the companion website. For the following examples, let's work with the "Jazz Big Band" manuscript paper.

A. *Staves—adding/deleting/repositioning staves*
   1. Adding and deleting staves is accomplished in the Instruments dialogue box. The Instruments window allows you to add new staves/instruments, delete existing ones, and move staves up or down in the score. You can access all the built-in instruments in the Sibelius Essentials sound set, the General MIDI spec, and any third-party sounds you have installed. This is convenient because adding a staff or staff name and assigning an instrument sound and transposition are all accomplished in one step.
   2. *To respace staves*: Click in any empty part of any measure to drag staves up or down; however, doing so will adjust all staves on the entire page. To move an individual staff or group of staves, hold down the Shift key while dragging a staff. To select a group of staves, use Shift-click, then Shift-drag any of the selected staves to move the entire group.

   For greater precision, click on a staff and use Shift-Option-up/down arrow (Mac) or Shift-Alt-up/down arrow (Windows) to move a single staff or group of staves up or down.

193

3. *To create or modify an instrumental section ("Staff Group" in Finale):* Simply click on an existing bracket or brace to select it, and then drag the lower end up or down to add or delete staves from the group. To create a new bracket, select the top staff of a group of staves you want to bracket, and then go to Create > Other > Bracket or Brace and make your selection ("Brackets" have straight vertical lines; "Braces" are curved, suitable for a piano grand staff). Drag the lower end of the bracket or brace down to cover the staves you want included in the group.

4. Staff names in Sibelius are plain text. Instrument names on the first page of a score are separate elements from instrument names on page 2 to the end (which are typically abbreviated). Use the suggestion in Section 15-1A-1-b) for naming staves for Finale. *Refer to the website for details on adding, deleting, and repositioning staves in Sibelius.*

5. For staves with instrumental doubles, use the Instrument Change dialogue box. This functions in a similar manner to "Staff Styles" in Finale. *Refer to the website for details.*

6. There is no Resize Tool in Sibelius. Sibelius does a pretty good job of resizing the page and staves automatically when you add or delete staves. For greater precision, go to Layout > Document Setup > Page Size and Margins, and Staff Margins.

◊ **Generating Dynamic Parts:** Dynamic ("linked") parts are created automatically when you start a new score. New parts can be generated from the Parts window (Window Menu > Parts).

B. *Score and parts page layouts*

◊ Adjusting the number of systems per page and the number of measures per system and editing the distance between systems are some of the most critical aspects to score and parts page layout. *Refer to the website for details on adjusting score and parts page size and page and system margins, file info, and placement of measure numbers in Sibelius.*

1. *Repositioning expressions, segnos, coda signs, and text blocks*: All elements in parts are selectable and can simply be dragged around the score for repositioning purposes. When an element is moved, Sibelius will determine if the element needs to be repositioned in the score as you move it in the part.

2. *Measure numbers*: With a part open, click the Multiple Parts Appearance button in the Parts window. Choose the House Style tab to modify the frequency and placement of measure numbers in the part (or in multiple parts).

3. *Staff optimization (piano parts)*: Staff optimization in a piano part is achieved by going to Layout > Hide Empty Staves.

C. *Spacing the music—score and parts: Refer to the website for details on adjusting the number of measures per system and the number of systems per page and adjusting note spacing in Sibelius.*

◊ Generally, aim for eight measures per system for the score and four measures per system for parts. Wherever possible, try to have the beginnings of important sections, double bar lines, rehearsal letters, and repeat signs align with the left and right margins of score and parts pages.

15-3 Printing the Parts and the Score

When you've completed the score and parts layouts and the spacing of the music, it's easy to print everything out. In Finale, go to File > Print, and select which parts and/or score and how many copies of each you want to print. In Sibelius, go to File > Print or File > Print All Parts. Parts in Sibelius can also be printed from the Parts window. Adjust the number to the right of the part to indicate the number of copies of each part to be printed; then click the Print button at the bottom of the Parts window.

We recommend printing parts on at least a 24-lb-weight paper. For tabloid-size scores, if you don't have a tabloid-size printer, just e-mail a pdf file of the score to your local printer or copy shop. Remember, for jazz and pop music, parts should always be printed on one side only, *never* on both sides of the page. Once you have the parts printed, they *must* be taped together "accordion style" so that the player can flip two pages at a time while reading. Score pages should be printed on *both* sides, in landscape orientation. Ideally, the score should be spiral or comb bound on the left side so that it opens like a book, with a clear plastic front cover and a solid black back cover. In a pinch you can get away with taping or clipping the left side.

Chapter Summary

In this chapter we reviewed some basic principles of score and parts layouts and music spacing. Most of the detailed instructions on how to perform the most important score and parts layout functions in both Finale and Sibelius are provided on the website. Refer to Exs. 15-1, 15-2, and 15-3 on the website for illustrations of correct score and parts layout and spacing appearance, including correct placement of text, staff names, measure numbers, articulations and dynamics, and fully notated rhythm section parts, as well as for an example of staff optimization for a piano part (Ex. 15-3). As you can see in the alto sax part, it's OK if some rehearsal letters appear in the middle of a staff. Refer to Ex. 14-2, "Bill Bossa," for an example of a small ensemble score with two systems per page.

◊ **Software Tip:** Although much of the information provided in this chapter may appear tedious and time-consuming, in fact some of these steps need to be performed only once—when creating a template! You can save a lot of time by customizing templates carefully, saving them in a convenient location, and starting each new project from your custom templates ("manuscript paper" in Sibelius). If you find that you're adding custom text expressions, chord symbols, or other custom markings or commands, you can save them as a "Library" (File > Save Library) in Finale and then import the Library (File > Load Library) into your templates to keep them up to date. In Sibelius, you'll be making changes to the "Dictionary." Export the new Dictionary as a House Style (House Style > Export House Style), which you can then import into a template (House Style > Import House Style).

Exercises

Use techniques discussed in this chapter.

1. Open any of the score templates from the companion website. Experiment with adding and deleting staves and repositioning the staves.
2. Apply techniques discussed in this chapter to generating linked parts, doing score and part layouts, and spacing the music.

Chapter 16

Arranging for 5–6 Horns: Harmony and Chord Voicings

In this and the following several chapters, we'll be building and expanding on basic concepts regarding harmony, chord voicings, and instrumental texture that were presented in Chapters 7, 8, 9, and 10. The fundamental voicing principles still apply to the larger ensemble. In fact, in some ways it's actually easier to work out full, rich-sounding, and balanced chord voicings for 5–6 horns than for a smaller group. In addition, there are more possible instrumental combinations, providing a larger palette for more creative, contrasting color and textural options.

The basic concepts and rules presented in Sections 8-1, 8-2, and 8-3 regarding chords built by thirds, chord scales, vertical harmony, and horizontal harmony still apply. The principles of monophonic, homophonic, and polyphonic texture (Section 7-4) as well as of parallel, similar, oblique, and contrary melodic motion (Section 8-6) are equally important. Also, the definitions of standard jazz voicing positions presented in Section 8-4 are still relevant, although the practical application of these voicing principles becomes more expansive with the larger ensemble. It would be a good idea to review these sections now before proceeding.

We've chosen to use a 6-horn ensemble consisting of two trumpets, one trombone, and alto, tenor, and baritone saxophones as the basic instrumentation for presenting the principles and examples in this and the following chapters. This is a well-balanced ensemble that can function almost like a "small" big band. You can achieve a full chord voicing in either the brass or sax sections and play the two sections off against each other as you might in a full big band. Working with this instrumentation is therefore also good preparation for writing for the full jazz big band, which we'll examine in Section 3.

However, with this size ensemble, you'll find, more often than not, that the most effective voicing solutions will be achieved by intertwining the notes of the sax and brass sections to create colorful "cross-sectional" voicings. By eliminating one of the trumpets or the alto sax, you can achieve similar results with 5 horns, although you then lose the ability to create full three-note voicings in both the brass and sax sections.

16-1 Standard Chord Voicings for 5–6 Horns

Please review the basic principles of jazz chord voicings as well as the rules for close position, semi-open position, and open position voicings presented in Sections 8-2 and 8-4. In Example 16-1, we'll again use the first four bars of "I Could Write a Book" for musical illustrations of these principles as applied to 5–6 horns. Study the voicings in Exs. 16-1A and 16-1B and compare them with those for 3–4 horns in Exs. 8-4A and 8-4B.

The standard voicing positions can easily be achieved and demonstrated with 5 horns (or 6 horns, with the top two voices doubling the melody), as illustrated in Ex. 16-1A. In this example, for close position and drop-2, the melody is *always* doubled an octave below the lead.

In Ex. 16-1B, we transposed everything up a fourth, to the key of F, to create full voicings for all 6 horns. If we had kept the example in C, in the lower register we would have been forced below the standard low interval limits with the extra horn, resulting in muddy-sounding voicings. Taking everything up an octave could technically have worked, but in adhering to the strict rules for close position and drop-2, the voicings would have gotten too high and top-heavy (unbalanced). The logical solution is to modulate (transpose) to a different key, a standard arranging technique for achieving contrasts in texture and color.

Another important consideration in voicing for this size ensemble is how to position the various horns within the chord voicing. Some of the more obvious choices, going from top to bottom, would be Tpt 1, Tpt 2, AS, TS, Tbn, Bari; Tpt 1, Tpt 2, AS, Tbn, TS, Bari; Tpt 1, AS, Tpt 2, TS, Tbn, Bari; Tpt 1, AS, Tpt 2, TS, Bari, Tbn; AS, Tpt 1, Tpt 2, TS, Tbn, Bari, etc. Examples 16-1A and 16-1B are presented in piano grand staff, with suggested instrumentation on the left. We could change the instrumental color of a voicing by simply assigning different instruments to the various notes without changing the relative positions of the notes within the voicing.

Notice how, in Ex. 16-1A, the lead is doubled 8vb in close position and drop-2. In drop-2, the second voice from the top in close position drops down 8vb, providing a semi-open position voicing with more space. We've stuck to diatonic harmonization of approach tones in the first few examples and voiced the final C major chord in the close position example with the root in the second voice to avoid the interval of a major second between the top two voices. In number 5, Homophonic Texture, we used half-step planning in the second bar. In the following measure, the D7 chord is both a secondary dominant (V of V) and a diminished seventh passing chord (in the four lower voices).

Ex. 16-1A

Standard Jazz Voicing Positions—5 Horns: "I Could Write a Book" by Rodgers & Hart

Ex. 16-1B

Standard Jazz Voicing Positions—6 Horns: "I Could Write a Book" by Rodgers & Hart

---

* Indicates additional chord tones possible with 6 horns.

With 6 horns, strict close position already results in an 8vb doubling of the second voice along with the lead, so the drop-2 example actually results in "drop-2 and -3." Notice how we've taken advantage of the possibilities for adding additional chord tones and alterations with six horns to create 5- and even 6-note chords for extra richness (indicated by * in the examples). In the open position example, we've opted to continue the downward chromatic, contrary motion of the first three notes of the alto sax part to a C in the second bar (rather than moving to the major seventh E), in order to create smoother voice leading. The second chord, C7♭9+11, in the first bar of this example, provides a good illustration of the kind of harmonic richness available with 5 or 6 horns and not possible with a smaller ensemble.

◊ Remember: "The Rules" are presented here to help you build a foundation of knowledge and techniques that will enable you to make better musical choices while dealing with various arranging issues. However, in actual practice many more choices are available than those presented here as basic principles or rules. Ultimately your choices will be determined by what you hear and by your own creative instincts.

It's essential for the professional jazz arranger to understand the basic concepts of close position, drop-2, and open position voicings. However, you will probably discover that the most musical results are more likely to occur when switching from one technique to another, depending on the parameters of the particular musical situation at hand, or by employing the broader modal concepts of jazz chord voicings (Section 8-5) along with the basic principles of jazz chord voicings (Section 8-2).

Here are a few more voicing principles that are especially relevant to voicing for 5-6 horns.

1. Standard close position, drop-2, and open position voicings can be achieved with five horns. These principles may effectively be applied to the standard 5-piece sax section of a big band to achieve the typical *Block Voicing* sound, with the saxes voiced in close position, and the bari sax doubling the lead alto 8vb. Drop-2 can also be quite effective with the 5-piece sax section. In this case the lead alto will be doubled by the second tenor (see Chapter 23).

2. The sixth horn may be used to double any chord tone or to add an additional color tone.

3. Any note of the chord may be omitted or doubled.

4. With the 3 brass/3 sax ensemble, for the most part, chord voicings will be created by intertwining the notes of the sax and brass instruments,

although it's possible to create full, three-note voicings in either or both sections.

5. It can still be useful to view the saxes and brass as separate sections, as you would with a full big band. Then analyze the chord structure and *internal resonance* (relative degree of consonance or dissonance) created separately by the three-note groupings of saxes and brass instruments in any given chord voicing.

Example 16-1C illustrates this principle by separating each section, with the saxes placed above the brass in the score. For example, if we look at the second measure of Ex. 16-1C in close position, we see that for the F Maj9 chord, the two trumpets are playing C and A, with the trombone doubling the lead trumpet's C 8vb—all consonant intervals but not a complete chord. This voicing position continues from m. 1 through the end of m. 3, with the trombone doubling the lead trumpet an octave below, producing a clean, crisp sound, with the melody reinforced. The saxes are playing G, E, and A, a more complete chord structure for F Maj9, containing both the third and the seventh as well as the dissonant interval of a minor seventh formed by the A and the G. This produces a fuller, richer sound in the saxes.

In separating the saxes and brass, we notice hidden and parallel fifths created in the first three notes of the tenor and baritone saxes. Although in this case it's not really a problem, we've provided an example of how this could be avoided by changing some of the notes (the starred, corrected voicings are in parentheses). In the corrected version, the alto's first three notes are D-E-E, the tenor plays B♭-D♭-C (thus avoiding the parallel fifths), and the second trumpet plays the G (chord ninth) vacated by the alto. Please note that you will hear the corrected version in the audio recording of Example 16-1C-1.

In number 2, by switching the tenor sax and trombone parts so that the trombone is above the tenor and continuing that positioning through the end of m. 3, we wind up with full, three-note chords, with a little bit of dissonance in both the saxes and the brass. It's a subtle distinction but one worth exploring. In number 3, by eliminating the major second interval between the two trumpets on the third beat of m. 3, we've created a more interesting part, with some contrary motion for the second trumpet's last three notes. The new major second on m. 3 beat 4 is OK because of the improved voice leading and contrary motion in the second trumpet part. Because we just put trumpet 2 on F (the chord fourth), we need to get rid of the low E (chord third) in the saxes to avoid a minor ninth dissonance. By moving the tenor and bari sax both to F (momentarily on a unison), we not only avoid the unwanted dissonance, but also create more interesting lines with contrary motion. The possibilities are endless.

Ex. 16-1C

Brass and Sax Sections—6 Horns: "I Could Write a Book" by Rodgers & Hart

1. Close Position (Rhythmic Unison)

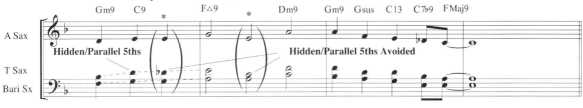

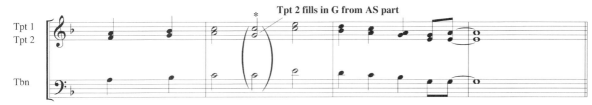

2. Tenor Sax & Trombone Parts Switched

3. Last Three Notes Changed to Improve Voice Leading in Tpt 2

203

* Indicates corrected voicing.

16-2 Reharmonization of Approach Tones for 5–6 Horns

The principles of reharmonization of approach tones, explained in Chapter 9, remain the same regardless of the size of the ensemble. Example 16-2 illustrates the same five basic techniques demonstrated in Ex. 9-1, now voiced for 6 horns. We've again used "My Romance" for our illustration. Play through and listen to the voicings in Ex. 16-2 and compare them with those for 4 horns in Ex. 9-2. Our voicing choices in both cases are determined by the principles of vertical harmony outlined in Section 8-2, such as balance, avoiding skips of more than a major sixth between any two adjacent notes, placing the third and the seventh in the low to mid-register, avoiding excessive repeated notes, following principles of good voice leading, and keeping the inner voices as musical as possible. We've put special emphasis on adding additional color tones and alterations in this example, indicated by * above the voicing. The bass line with stems pointing down represents a typical bass line, outlining the chord roots, which might be played by the bass. It's important to hear all of these examples referenced to the underlying harmony outlined by the chord roots.

Legend for Ex. 16-2
T = target note
P = parallel approach chord
D = diatonic approach chord
F = Free reharmonization
Dom = dominant approach chord
TT = tritone substitution
SD = secondary dominant
Alt = altered tones
Dim = diminished seventh passing chord

Ex. 16-2

Reharmonization Of Approach Tones—6 Horns: "My Romance" by Rodgers & Hart

1. Diatonic

2. Dominant

3. Diminished 7th

4. Parallel

5. Free Reharmonization

*Indicates additional color tones and alterations.

16-3 Repeated Notes, Static Harmony, and Voice Leading for 5–6 Horns

As in the case of approach tones, the methods for dealing with repeated notes in the inner voices, static harmony, and good voice leading remain the same regardless of the size of the ensemble. These principles are explained in detail in Chapters 8 and 9 and need not be repeated here (see Sections 8-6 and 9-1 and Exs. 8-6, 9-3, 9-4, and 9-5). As stated earlier at the end of Chapter 8, one of the most important things to remember about voice leading in general is the following principle: *The more interesting and musical the individual parts are for each player in an ensemble, the more musical and expressive the overall performance will be.*

16-4 Five and Six Note Close Position Voicings and Use of the Sus 4 and Natural or Augmented Eleventh

As illustrated in Sections 16-1 and 16-2, with 5–6 horns, it's possible to create close position or semi-open position voicings with five or six different chord tones by using more altered chord tones and dissonant intervals. This type of voicing will contain more tension, in contrast to the smoother, more traditional sounding voicings we've been looking at so far. It's OK to occasionally throw in this type of voicing to add color to a more consonant passage. It's also acceptable to occasionally use the fourth, eleventh, or augmented fourth or eleventh in a close position voicing in place of the third or fifth for variety. Examples of these types of voicings are provided by the starred voicings in Ex. 16-1B and 16-2. We'll take a closer look at some of these more "modern" sounding chords in Section 3.

◊ Example 16-3, "There Will Never Be Another You" provides an illustration of the application of these principles in a musical context voiced for 5 horns. The first 8 bars are voiced in close position, the second 8 in drop-2, the third 8 in a combination of close position and drop-2 (with some approach tone reharmonization), and the last 8 in open position, with some semi-open and close position thrown in to keep it musical. Use Ex. 16-3 as a model when doing Exercise 2 below.

In this example, we've made an effort to avoid excessive repeated notes through changing voicing positions, using altered chord tones and crossing the tenor and trombone lines in m. 30, while still staying within the guidelines of the exercise.

Ex. 16-3

Mixed Voicing Positions—5 Horns: "There Will Never Be Another You" by Harry Warren and Mack Gordon

1. Close Position

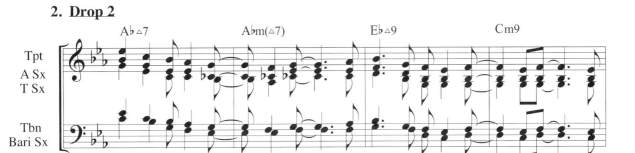

2. Drop 2

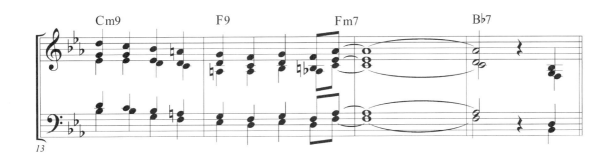

207

3. Combination w. Reharm

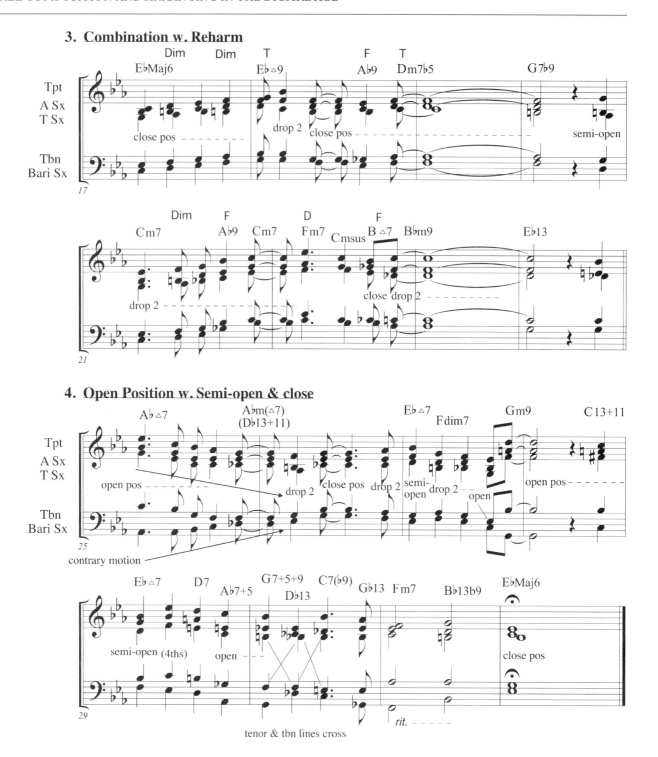

4. Open Position w. Semi-open & close

Chapter Summary

In this chapter we began to apply fundamental harmonic and voice-leading principles to a larger ensemble, consisting of 5–6 horns + rhythm section. We saw that many of the basic rhythmic, melodic, harmonic, and structural principles presented in Chapters 6–11 apply equally well to the larger ensemble. Topics covered include standard voicing positions, integrating the brass and saxes, homophonic and polyphonic textures, and the reharmonization of approach tones.

◊ **Software Tip:** When working in the piano sketch version of the following exercises, place the bottom notes of both the treble and bass clefs in Layer 2 in Finale (Voice 2 in Sibelius) so that the note stems of the bottom part in each staff point down. In Sibelius, if the stems of the notes in Voice 2 do not point down automatically, select them and press "X" to flip the stems down. Get into the habit of using this method whenever working with a piano reduction of a larger score, since it makes it much easier to read and understand. Use the Text Tool (Finale) or Create > Text (Sibelius) to indicate, to the left of each staff, which instruments are meant to be playing each line.

Exercises

1. Pick a tune you like of any 5- to 6-horn recording from the following Listening List. Listen to the recording in a focused way, and be able to describe what it is about the music that makes it sound great.

2. Voice "Out Of Nowhere" for 5 horns. Start with a piano sketch using the piano grand staff template. Put the top three voices in the treble clef and the bottom two in the bass clef.
   a. First eight bars—close position/diatonic.
   b. Second eight bars—"drop-2" position with some reharmonization.
   c. Third eight bars—close position or "drop-2" with more reharmonization/ passing chords.
   d. Last eight bars—open position (with some semi-open or close position as needed) with some contrary motion in the lower voice.

◊ **Important!** Use Ex. 16-3 as a model for this exercise.

3. Open the 5-6 Horns + Rhythm template. First change the key signature to G or the appropriate key. This template is provided as a Transposed Score. Change to "Display in concert pitch" if that makes it easier for you. Copy and paste the treble clef part from exercise 2 into the trumpet 1 staff of the 5-6 Horn template. Copy and paste the bass clef part into the Tenor Sax staff. Then use "Explode Music" in Finale or Sibelius (explained in the Chapter 9 Software Tip) to expand the voicings. Cut and paste the part in the Trombone staff into the Alto Sax staff. If you feel the need to cross any voices to avoid repeated notes, don't do that until *after* you've "exploded" the music.

4. Decided if you want your lowest voice to be the Bari Sax or Trombone, and cut & paste if necessary. Fill in the rhythm section parts, print out, and play.

5. Try the same exercise with a standard five-piece sax section (AS 1, AS 2, TS 1, TS 2, Bari).

Five- to Seven-Horn Ensemble Listening List

1. Miles Davis—"Birth of the Cool"—Capitol, 1949-50. Personnel: Miles Davis-tpt, Lee Konitz—as, Gerry Mulligan—bari sx, Junior Collins, Sandy Siegelstein, or Gunther Schuller—fh, Kai Winding or JJ Johnson—tbn, John Barber—tba, John Lewis or Al Haig—pno, Joe Shulman, Nelson Boyd, or Al McKibbon—bs, Max Roach or Kenny Clarke—dr.
   a. "Budo".
   b. "Boplicity".
   c. "Rocker".

2. Oliver Nelson—"Stolen Moments," Inner City, 1975. Personnel: Oliver Nelson—as, Bobby Bryant—tpt, Jerome Richardson—ss/fl/picc, Buddy Collette—ts/fl, Bobby Bryant, Jr.—ts/fl, Jack Nimitz—bari sx, Mike Wofford—pno/el pno, Chuck Domanico—el bs, Shelly Manne—dr.
   a. "Stolen Moments".

3. Oliver Nelson—"More Blues and the Abstract Truth," Impulse, 1964. Personnel: Thad Jones or Danny Moore—tpt, Phil Woods—as, Ben Webster or Phil Bodner—ts, Pepper Adams—bari sx, Roger Kellaway—pno, Richard Davis—bs, Grady Tate—dr.
   a. "Blues and the Abstract Truth".

4. Thelonious Monk—"The Thelonious Monk Orchestra at Town Hall"—Riverside, 1959. Personnel: Donald Byrd—tpt, Robert Northern—fh, Eddie Bert-tbn, Phil Woods—as, Charlie Rouse—ts, Pepper Adams—bari sx, Jay McAllister—tba, Thelonius Monk—pno, Sam Jones—bs, Art Taylor—dr.
   a. "Little Rootie Tootie".
   b. "Off Minor".

5. Charles Mingus—"The Black Saint & the Sinner Lady Impulse, 1964. Personnel: Rolf Ericson, Richard Williams—tpt, Quentin Jackson—tbn, Don Butterfield—tba, Jerome Richardson—ss/fl, Charlie Mariano—as, Dick Hafer—ts/fl, Jaki Byard—pno, Jay Berliner—gtr, Charles Mingus—bs, Dannie Richmond—dr.

6. Joe Lovano—"52nd St. Themes," Blue Note, 2000. Personnel: Tim Hagans—tpt, Conrad Herwig—tbn, Steve Slagle—as, Joe Lovano—ts, George Garzone—ts, Ralph Lalama—ts, Gary Smulyan—bari sx, John Hicks—pno, Dennis Irwin—bs, Lewis Nash—dr.
   a. "On a Misty Night".
   b. "Deal".
   c. "Tadd's Delight".

7. Joe Lovano—"On This Day At The Vanguard," Blue Note, 2003. Personnel: Barry Reis—tpt, Larry Farrell—tbn, Steve Slagle—as, Joe Lovano—ts, George Garzone—ts, Ralph Lalama—ts, Scott Robinson—bari sx, John Hicks—pno, Dennis Irwin—bs, Lewis Nash—dr.

8. Jim McNeely—"Group Therapy," OmniTone, 2001. Personnel: Billy Drewes—ss, as, ts, fl, cl, Dick Oatts—ss, as, fl, Scott Robinson—bari sx, bs cl, Greg Gisbert—tpt/flg hrn, Tony Kadleck—tpt/flg hrn, Scott Wendholt—tpt/flg hrn, Tom Varner—FH, Ed Neumeister—tbn, Jim McNeely—pn/cp/arr, Cameron Brown—bs, John Hollenbeck—dr.

9. George Robert Jazztet—"Remember the Sound (Homage to Michael Brecker)," TCB Music, 2010. Personnel: Jim McNeely—cp/arr; George Robert—as, Robert Bonisolo—ts, Matthieu Michel—tpt/flg hrn, Rene Mosele—tbn, Mathieu Schneider—fl, Laurent Wolf—ss, as, bari sx, Vinz Vonlanthen—gtr, Emil Spanyi—pno & kybds, Jean-Piere Schaller—el bs, Marcel Papaux—dr, Randy Brecker—tpt.

10. Shorty Rogers—"Shorty Rogers & His Giants," RCA, 1953. Personnel: Shorty Rogers—tpt, Milt Bernhard—tbn, Art Pepper—as, Jimmy Giuffre—ts, John Graas—fh, Gene Englund—tba, Hampton Hawes—pno, Joe Mondragon—bs, Shelly Manne—dr.

11. Lee Konitz—"Yes, Yes Nonet," Steeplechase, 1979. Personnel: Tom Harrell, John Eckert—tp, flg hrn, Jimmy Knepper—tbn, Sam Burtis—bstbn, Lee Konitz—as, ss, Ronnie Cuber—ss, bari sx, Harold Danko—pno, Buster Williams—bs, Billy Hart—dr.

12. Bill Kirchner—"Trance Dance," A-Records, 1990. Personnel: Bill Kirchner—ss, as, fl, picc, cl, bs cl, cp/arr, Ralph Lalama—ts, fl, cl, Michael Rabinowitz—bsn, bs, cl, Budd Burridge—tpt, flg hrn, Brian Lynch—tpt, flg hrn, Doug Purviance—bs, tbn, Carlton Holmes—pno, synth, Chip Jackson—bs, el bs, Ron Vincent—dr.

Please refer to Appendix B on the companion website, "Recommended Recordings for Further Study," for a more comprehensive listening list.

Chapter 17

Form and Planning the Arrangement (5–6 Horns)

In this chapter, as in Chapter 16, we'll continue to build on material presented in earlier chapters, in this case, primarily Chapter 11. The fundamental principles presented in Chapter 11 regarding form and planning the arrangement, including the basic elements of form, outlining and graphing the form, and instrumentation, still apply to the larger ensemble. Similarly, the techniques for creating Intros, Transitions or Kickers, Background Parts, and Codas or Endings can also be applied to the larger ensemble. The sections on Concept and Direction and Improvisation are equally relevant. It would be a good idea to review Chapter 11 now before proceeding.

17-1 Elements of Form (5–6 Horns)

As in Chapter 11, we are concerned here primarily with the overall, large form of an arrangement. For now we'll focus on the same formal elements examined earlier: intros, exposition (head), transitional passages (kickers and interludes), improvised solos, backgrounds, recap, and coda or ending. In the next chapter we'll add two additional formal building blocks commonly used by jazz arrangers: the soli and the shout chorus.

17-2 Woodwind and Brass Doubles and Muted Brass

In this section we'll continue to focus primarily on writing for trumpets, trombone, saxophones, and rhythm. However, if you have woodwind or brass doubles available, there's no reason you shouldn't experiment with using those colors.

Many professional alto and tenor saxophone players also double on flute, clarinet, and soprano sax. Some are woodwind "doublers"—specialists doubling on a variety of saxes, flutes, piccolo, clarinets, and sometimes even oboe and English horn. It's usually pretty safe to assume that at least the alto saxes can double on flutes and the tenor saxes can double on clarinets. Many baritone sax players also double on bass clarinet. Some also double on other saxophones, clarinet, and flute.

Most trumpet players also double on flugelhorn, but don't forget to ask them to bring the extra horn if you want to try that. It's also pretty safe to count on harmon and cup mutes for the trumpets and on cups, buckets, and plungers for the trombones. Just make sure you're familiar with the transpositions, descriptions, and recommended ranges for the doubles as described in Chapter 3 and with the section on brass mutes described in Chapter 12. We'll take a closer look at using woodwind and brass doubles and mutes in Section 3 in the context of the full jazz big band.

17-3 Instrumentation and Outlining the Form (5–6 Horns)

With 6 horns + rhythm, the list of possible instrumental color combinations is significantly greater than with 3–4 horns (Section 11-3). For example, it's now possible to state the melody with two instruments (e.g., trumpet and flute in unison or octaves) and still have four instruments left to provide a full, chordal backdrop (trumpet 2 or flugelhorn, tenor sax, trombone, and baritone sax). Following is a partial list of possible color combinations for 6 horns (two trumpets, each doubling on flugelhorn, trombone, alto sax doubling on flute, tenor sax doubling on clarinet, baritone sax doubling on bass clarinet).

1. Any horn playing solo with the rhythm section.
2. Any two horns playing in unison or octaves with the rhythm section.
3. Trumpet in harmon mute + flute 8va over chords played by flugelhorn, tenor and bari sax, and trombone.
4. Trumpet and alto sax voiced in thirds or sixths over rhythmic hits played by the other horns.
5. Two trumpets, alto, and tenor sax voiced in close position over a unison countermelody by the trombone and bari.
6. Flugelhorn melody over clarinet, alto sax, trombone, and bass clarinet chords.
7. All six horns voiced in rhythmic unison.

8. Any subset of the six horns playing in rhythmic unison.

9. Any two or three horns playing pads or counterpoint to any other two or three horns.

10. Piano and bass playing the melody, with rhythmic hits by the horns.

11. Piano or bass doubling the melody with any combination of horns.

It's obvious that the list of possible combinations is even more expansive than with the smaller group and we again recommend starting with just those combinations you think you may want to use for a given project. As with the 3- to 4-horn ensembles in Chapter 11, it can be useful to create a projected outline of the overall form of the arrangement. A sample outline of an arrangement for 6 horns and 3 rhythm of "My Romance" might look something like this:

Intro

    (4 bars) Six horns voiced in rhythmic unison with the trumpets on top playing a figure derived from the end of the tune.

    (4 bars) Piano and rhythm section echoing the horn figure to set up the entrance of the melody.

Head

    First "A" section (8 bars)—Trumpet melody above pads in saxes and trombone (homophonic).

    First "B" section (8 bars)—Tenor sax melody solo (Monophonic).

    Second "A" section (8 bars)—1 trumpet, alto sax, tenor sax, and trombone voiced in close or semi-open position, with trumpet on top (rhythmic unison—homophonic).

    Second "B" section (8 bars).

        First 4 bars—Alto sax and trombone melody in octaves.

        Second 4 bars—All six horns in rhythmic unison as in the intro.

Kicker (4 bars)—Continuation, building from previous 4 bars, with all six horns in rhythmic unison leading into the first solo.

Alto solo (1 chorus/32 bars)—Improvised solo + rhythm section.

Backgrounds (1 chorus/32 bars)—Alto solo continues, with background pads by muted brass.

Kicker (4 bars)—Same as first kicker to lead into the piano solo.

Piano solo (1 chorus/32 bars)—Improvised solo + rhythm section.

Backgrounds (1 chorus/32 bars)—Piano solo continues, with background pads by saxes; piano solo ends with a figure from the last 4 bars of the intro.

Recap—D.S. to second half of head.

    Second "A" section (8 bars)—1 trumpet, alto sax, tenor sax, and trombone voiced in close or semi-open position, with trumpet on top (rhythmic unison—homophonic).

Second "B" section (8 bars).

First 4 bars—Alto sax and trombone melody in octaves.

Second 4 bars—All six horns in rhythmic unison.

Coda (8 bars)—Four 2-bar phrases derived from the intro.

Trumpet, alto sax, tenor sax, and trombone (2 bars).

Alto sax and trombone (2 bars).

Rhythm section (2 bars).

Piano alone (2 bars).

Final chord—Brass in mutes, flute, clarinet, bass clarinet—*ppp*.

We've used contrasting instrumental colors and textures to create an arrangement that builds naturally, with peaks and valleys, and that winds down at the end with a recap and a coda. This outline could be displayed graphically in the same manner as in Chapter 11.

17-4 Intros, Transitions/Kickers, Background Parts, Codas/Endings

The same techniques described in Chapter 11 for creating intros, transitions, background parts, and endings can also be applied to a 5- to 6-horn ensemble. For intros, kickers, and endings, these include vamps and pedals, material derived from the tune, turnarounds, new material, and hooks. Techniques for creating background parts include pads, rhythmic comping, counter-melodies, and riffs. These various techniques are illustrated for the 6-horn ensemble in Examples 17-1, 17-2, and 17-3. All examples begin at bar 31 of the head.

Ex. 17-1

Intros—6 Horns: "Have You Met Miss Jones?" by Rodgers & Hart, arranged by R. Sussman

5. New Material

6. Hooks Latin ♩ = (*108*)

◊ Not everyone needs to be playing all the time! When orchestrating for larger ensembles, take advantage of the possible solo and subgroupings of instruments to create contrast and variety of instrumental colors throughout the arrangement.

Ex. 17-2

Kickers—6 Horns: "Have You Met Miss Jones?" by Rodgers & Hart, arranged by R. Sussman

Medium Up Swing ($\bullet$ = 176)

1. Derived From Tune

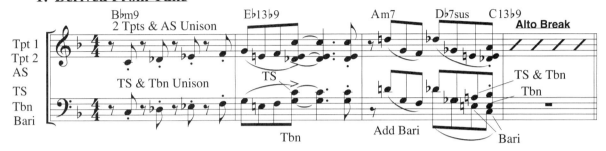

2. Derived From Tune (less obvious)

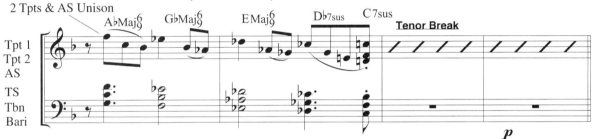

3. Derived From Intro (Pedal)

4. New Material

219

Ex. 17-3

Background Parts—6 Horns: "Have You Met Miss Jones?" by Rodgers & Hart, arranged by R. Sussman

Medium Up Swing ($\quad$ = 176)

1. Pads

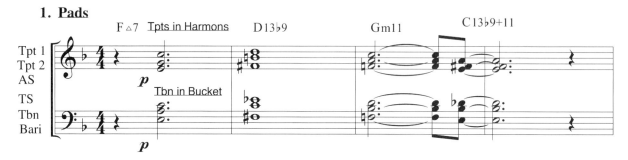

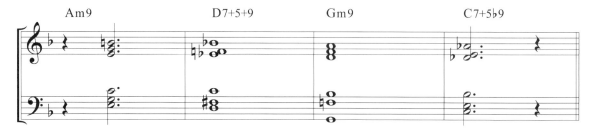

2. Rhythmic Comping

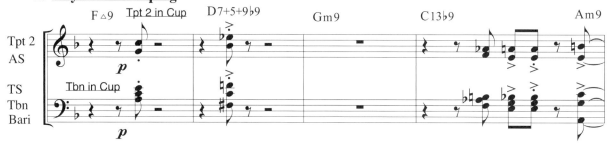

3. Counter Melody

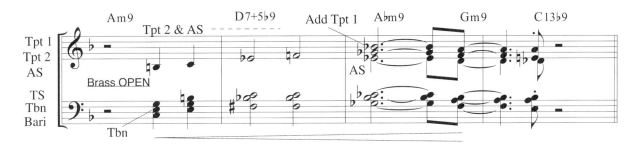

4. Riffs

17-5 Laying Out the Score: Workflow Concepts

When laying out the score for 5- to 6-horn arrangements or for larger ensembles, it's a good idea to first enter the chord changes and lead lines for any given section and then to go back and fill in the blanks. Here's an efficient workflow method for approaching any arrangement. Following this step-by-step method can not only save you a lot of time but also help you keep your musical perspective and focus throughout the writing process. For most jazz arrangements, we recommend starting with the head of the tune, then adding an intro, and then proceeding through subsequent sections (solos, backgrounds, soli, shout chorus, recap, coda, etc.).

We'll be working now with the 5–6 Horn + Rhythm Template, which uses the standard practice of placing the woodwinds above the brass. This can be a little confusing at first since it places low notes in the tenor and baritone saxes above the trumpets on the score page. However, with a little practice, this layout will come to feel completely natural, and separating the brass and woodwind sections in the score provides significant advantages.

1. Make a tentative outline of the arrangement, indicating instrumentation and textural changes for each section of the arrangement, as described in Section 17-3 (e.g., which instruments will be playing the melody, which sections will be solo, unison or octaves, voiced, homophonic, contrapuntal).

2. Enter the chord changes into the piano part using slash or rhythmic notation.

3. Enter the lead (melody) lines for each section indicated in your outline. Use the copy and paste functions for unison or octave doublings.

4. Go back and work out the chord voicings in those sections that call for it, and enter those parts. Use the "Explode Music" function described in Chapter 9 for sections where the horns are in rhythmic unison.

5. Make any necessary rhythmic and harmonic adjustments to the piano and guitar parts. Make sure that the chord symbols and rhythms in these parts accurately reflect and support what is being played by the horns.

6. Work out the bass and drum parts.

7. Check to make sure all dynamics and articulations are correctly in place.

8. Repeat steps 2–7 for each subsequent section of the chart.

Chapter Summary

In this chapter we reexamined some principles of musical form and how this relates to planning and outlining an arrangement for 6 horns + rhythm. We took a brief look at woodwind and brass doubles and also provided some specific examples of techniques for constructing intros, transitions/kickers, background parts, and codas/endings as applied to the 6-horn ensemble.

Finally we provided a sample workflow method for approaching any arrangement.

◊ **Software Tip:** It's important to become familiar with the *Edit Filter* for the *Selection Tool* in Finale and the Edit > Filter menu in Sibelius. This function allows you to determine what types of data (e.g., notes, articulations, expressions, chords) will be copied and pasted, and can be a big time saver. For example, in a voiced section in rhythmic unison, enter the articulations for the lead line. Then set the Edit Filter to select only articulations. You can now copy and paste the articulations into the other staves without affecting the notes.

In Sibelius, make sure you also understand the *Select More command* (Edit > Select > Select More), which allows you to filter text-based objects such as text expressions, chords, and lyrics. For example, you may need to reposition chord symbols in a guitar part for an entire line. First select the initial chord symbol in the line, and then use Select More to select the rest of the chord symbols in the line automatically. For non-text-based objects, use the *Simple Filter* (Edit > Filter) or the *Advanced Filter* (Edit > Filter > Advanced Filter). *Refer to the website for more details on using filters in Finale and Sibelius.*

Exercises

1. **Arranging Project 2:** Select a medium-tempo to medium up-tempo standard, jazz standard, or original tune to be arranged for 6 horns (two trumpets, trombone, alto, tenor, and baritone sax) + rhythm. Pick one from the following list of recommended tunes, or choose one of your own liking. Stick to a straight-ahead or Latin jazz feel for this project. Avoid choosing a ballad, because that opens up a whole set of issues which we haven't dealt with yet. We also recommend sticking to 4/4, 3/4, or 6/4 meter and avoiding tunes with complex meter changes, because that can cause you to lose focus on the basic arranging principles covered so far. Start by arranging just the head of the tune using voicing and workflow techniques discussed in this chapter and the previous chapter. Focus on contrasting textural and instrumental colors to provide contrast and variety. Use the 6 Horn + Rhythm Concert Score Template.

2. Add a four- to eight-bar intro and a kicker into the first solo.

3. Add solo sections and background parts.

4. Fill in the rhythm section parts, and add articulations and dynamics. Print out the score and parts. Be sure to observe correct transpositions for the horn parts. Play and analyze the results.

◊ **Important Note:** If this book is being used as a classroom textbook, these exercises should be spread out over two to three weeks.

Recommended Standards and Jazz Standards

1. "Out of Nowhere"
2. "Just Friends"
3. "You and the Night and the Music"
4. "Alone Together"
5. "Speak Low"
6. "Have You Met Miss Jones?"
7. "In Your Own Sweet Way"
8. "Woody 'n You"
9. "Voyage" (Kenny Barron)
10. "Nica's Dream"
11. "Whisper Not"
12. "In Walked Bud"
13. "Nardis"
14. "Fee-Fi-Fo-Fum"
15. "Dolphin Dance"
16. "The Way You Look Tonight"

Chapter 18

The Soli and Shout Chorus

In this chapter we'll examine two additional formal building blocks commonly used by jazz arrangers: the *soli* and the *shout chorus*. Both the soli and shout chorus are part of the larger, development section of an arrangement. Unlike the improvised solo sections with backgrounds, where the arranger's job is naturally to highlight and support the efforts of individual soloists, the soli and shout chorus can be thought of as "the arranger's chorus." These are the sections of an arrangement that typically allow the arranger the greatest degree of creative freedom.

It's important to recognize that in modern jazz writing the distinction between soli and shout chorus may be blurred and that a modern ensemble section of an arrangement may combine elements of both. However, it's still valuable to study techniques for constructing solis and shout choruses in the traditional sense as they evolved out of jazz big band writing of the swing era.

18-1 The Soli Section

1. A *soli section* can be defined as two or more instruments, featured, playing simultaneous written (*not* improvised) lines.
2. The soli is "composed" and is generally written to sound like an "improvised" solo line.
3. Apply the basic principles for constructing a good melody described in Chapter 7:
   a. Interesting melodic shape, with change of direction within the melodic phrase

    b. Contrasting melodic motion (scalar or skips of larger intervals)

    c. Use of standard techniques of motivic development

    d. Asymmetrical melodic phrase structure (relative to the harmonic rhythm)

4. Reharmonization of the original chord structure is an option.

5. The soli can be written in unison or octaves, or it may be harmonized in a variety of textures, the most common being close position or drop 2, or a combination of the two. It may also be part unison/octaves and part harmonized.

6. When harmonizing a soli section, use the principles of reharmonization of approach tones from Chapter 9.

7. Solis are usually written with the various parts in rhythmic unison; however, melodic or rhythmic counterpoint is also an option.

8. In traditional big band writing, the soli is usually voiced for one section (e.g., saxes, trumpets, or trombones) in unison, octaves, or close position. However, a soli can be written for a mixed (cross-sectional) combination of instruments, which is probably a better option when writing for 6 horns.

When writing a soli section, start with a single melodic line, and then decide whether or not you want to harmonize it. At this stage, we recommend keeping it simple—rhythmic unison and all parts in unison or octaves. If you're a jazz improviser, try to imagine how you might want a solo to sound on the tune you're arranging, and then write it down. Always be careful to respect the ranges and technical limitations of the instruments for which you've chosen to write. For example, if you're a sax player writing for brass, be careful to avoid writing soli lines that may be easy to play on saxophones but difficult or impossible to execute on brass instruments. Likewise, if you're a rhythm section player, be sure to leave space for the horn players to breathe. Example 18-1A illustrates the first eight bars of a possible soli line, in unison and octaves, for an arrangement of the tune "Analycity" (see Ex. 8-3). Example 18-1B is the same line harmonized in close position. Refer to the Listening List later in this chapter for some examples of classic solis.

Legendfor Ex. 18-1B

T = target note

P = parallel approach chord

D = diatonic approach chord

F = free reharmonization

Dom = dominant approach chord

TT = tritone substitution

SD = secondary dominant

Alt = altered tones

Dim = diminished seventh passing chord

Ex 18-1A "Analycity" Soli - Unison/Octaves

Richard Sussman

Ex 18-1B "Analycity" Soli - Voiced

Richard Sussman

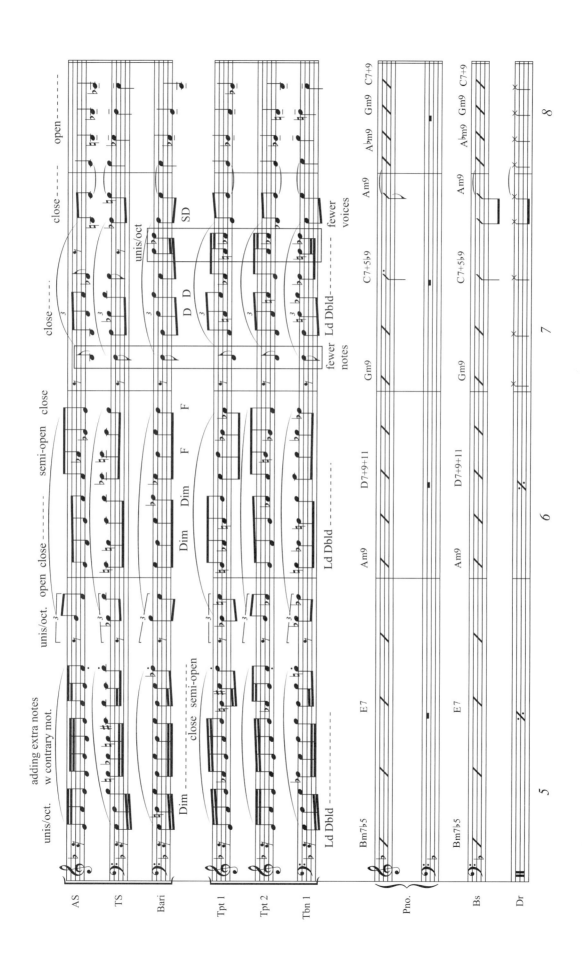

18-2 Analysis of Soli Examples 18-1A and 18-1B

We created these examples by following the steps outlined earlier, beginning with composing a single melodic line over the changes to the tune. Care was taken to give the line an interesting shape with changes in direction and contrasting types of melodic motion and note values. Notice how all of the melodic phrases are asymmetrical—crossing over the bar lines and overlapping the harmonic rhythm—until the last two-bar phrase.

In the first measure of Ex. 18-1B, we start with only 4 horns in octaves, because of the initial low register of the melody, gradually expanding to the full 6-horn ensemble by the end of m. 1, with some contrary motion and diminished seventh passing chords as the melody ascends in register. Various techniques for reharmonization of approach tones have been used and are labeled in the example. Occasionally we return to unison/octaves for some of the triplet figures, the faster sixteenth-note runs, when the melody descends into the lower register, and for the ornamental figure in m. 7. This provides contrast as well as maintaining lightness and mobility, preventing the line from becoming too thick and heavy-sounding in faster sections. The first measure begins with the alto sax as the second voice, creating a more interesting color for the opening. When the second trumpet enters at the end of m. 1, it is below the alto, and remains in that position until m. 3 beat 1. Also notice that the entrance of trumpet 2 imitates the opening melodic motive, creating some unexpected contrapuntal interest. Measure 3 features semi-open position voicings, with the bari sax descending down to the root for an open position chord on the A7+5+9. The lead trumpet is doubled intermittently (though not always), most frequently by the trombone but occasionally by the tenor sax. Priority is given instead to maintaining the melodic quality of each voice, good voice leading, and the internal resonance within each section. Any chord tone may be doubled or omitted to this end. Play through each part and each section separately to get a sense of this.

Bar 4 provides a good example of straight close position voicings, as does the beginning of m. 6. The passage ends forcefully, with descending, chromatic quarter notes in full open position in the last bar. As we pointed out at the end of Section 16-1, the most musical results are more likely to occur when switching from one technique to another. In other words, it's more effective to use your ear and creative instincts to make voicing decisions rather than attempting to voice an entire passage all with one particular technique. *There are no formulas for writing good music!* Study Exs. 18-1A and 18-1B carefully, and listen to the recorded examples for tips on how to create and voice a soli passage.

18-3 The Shout Chorus

1. The shout chorus is generally more rhythmic and syncopated and less lyrical than the soli.
2. It is often voiced full tutti for the entire ensemble in rhythmic unison.

3. There is generally full rhythm section support for rhythmic figures played by the horns. In other words, the piano, bass, drums, and guitar may also play in rhythmic unison with the brass and saxes, often with drum fills occurring in the spaces between the rhythmic phrases played by the ensemble.

4. The shout chorus is usually more intense and powerful than the soli.

5. It is generally a climactic section, usually at or near the end of an arrangement. It often occurs just before the recapitulation, or it may replace the recap with new material to end the arrangement.

6. Shout chorus characteristics may also include:
   a. Percussive lead lines
   b. Repeating riffs
   c. High lead trumpet register
   d. Loud dynamic level
   e. Extensive reharmonization and/or melodic development
   f. Call and response between sections (including the rhythm section and drum fills)
   g. Special effects in the brass (e.g., shakes, falls, rips)
   h. Contrapuntal texture
   i. Dense voicings, with lots of altered tones
   j. Wide, spread, open position voicings

As with the soli, when writing a shout chorus, begin by writing the lead line first, which in the case of shout choruses will always be the lead trumpet. Then fill in the voicings for the other horns using a combination of close position, drop-2, and open position. For now, keep everybody in rhythmic unison. Then fill in the rhythm section parts, with the piano, bass, and drums all supporting the rhythmic unison figures played by the horns.

Make sure that any altered tones or reharmonizations played by the horns are reflected in the rhythm section parts. If the chord symbols become too complicated, sometimes it's necessary to write out exact voicings for the chordal instruments. In fact, there are some situations, especially with a full big band, where it's best to have the piano/guitar lay out completely during a shout chorus. A big band shout chorus in full tutti, fortissimo, will easily overpower a piano; if the passage is exceptionally dense harmonically and rhythmically, the piano/guitar may actually detract from the overall power of the brass and saxes.

Make sure that all important syncopations in the horns are supported by all the rhythm section instruments, and that drum fills are clearly indicated. We recommend using x notehead notation with accents to indicate the rhythmic figures in the drums and slash notation with the word "Fill" above to indicate fills. Finally, it's essential to enter all articulations and dynamics precisely for all the parts. All parts should have identical articulations so that the attacks and durations of all notes will be in sync. Example 18-2 illustrates the first eight bars of a possible shout chorus for "Analycity." Refer to the Listening List later in this chapter for examples of some classic shout choruses.

231

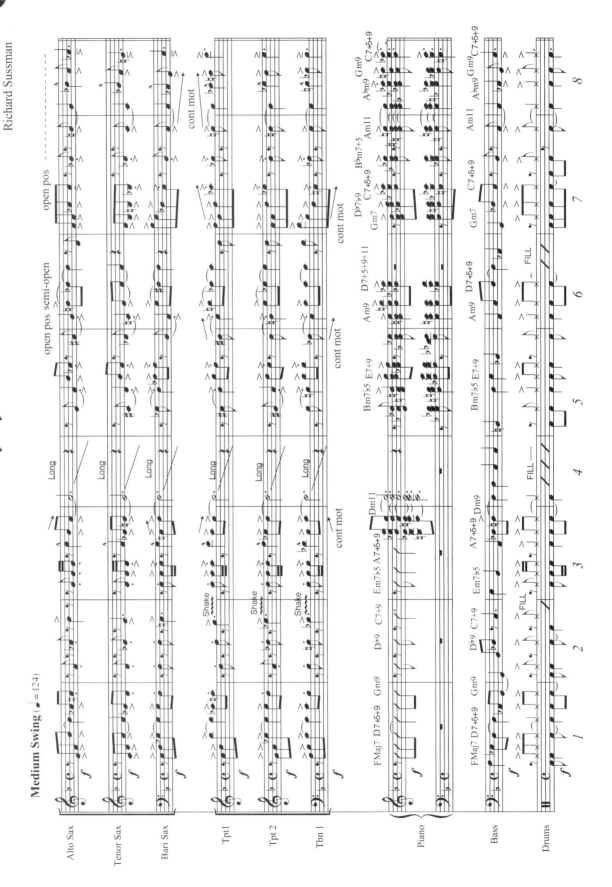

18-4 Analysis of Shout Chorus Example 18-2

The sample shout chorus follows the most important guidelines listed earlier: all 6 horns in rhythmic unison, rhythmic syncopation with spaces for drum fills, powerful and intense high lead trumpet, dense voicings, brass effects, full support from the rhythm section, and all articulations clearly indicated and identical for each part.

The basic melodic motive is derived from the tune (see Ex. 8-3). Most of the horn voicings are semi-open, with a few open position for greater power. There's some contrary motion to keep things interesting. The altered chord tones played by the horns are clearly labeled in the piano part, with the voicings written out in the last four bars. Study Ex. 18-2 carefully, and listen to the recorded example of the shout chorus. Notice in this example that we chose to voice the 6 horns as a single unit, placing more emphasis on full, fat voicings with lots of color tones. The lead trumpet is easily able to carry the melody in this register with this size ensemble.

18-5 Recorded Examples of Solis and Shout Choruses for 5–7 Horns

Many of the available recordings of this size ensemble are really, conceptually, vehicles for improvised solos and don't feature written solis and shout choruses in the same way that has become a standard trademark of much of the classic big band repertoire. Still, there are some great recordings worthy of study, including the classic *Birth of the Cool* by Miles Davis, the complete scores of which are now available on Hal Leonard. Here are a few listening suggestions.

Listening List
1. Miles Davis—*Birth of the Cool*—Capitol, 1949/50:
   a. "Budo"—Soli, voiced, after the trombone solo.
   b. "Godchild"—Shout chorus, after the baritone sax solo.
   c. "Rocker"—Shout chorus, after the alto sax solo.
2. Thelonius Monk—*Live at Town Hall* - Riverside, 1959:
   a. "Little Rootie Tootie"—Soli, at the end of the chart—actually Hall Overton's transcription and brilliant orchestration of Monk's solo on this tune from an earlier recording. The soli begins all in unison/octaves and builds to some voiced chords with rhythmic counterpoint. Notice how the long descending line at the end is distributed among the various instruments as it descends and leads into the recap of the tune.
3. Joe Lovano Nonet—*52nd Street Themes* - Blue Note, 2000:
   a. "On a Misty Night"—Soli—first half unison/octaves, second half voiced with some characteristics of a shout chorus. Check out the complete score at the end of Chapter 19.

b. "Tadd's Delight"—Soli, unison/octaves, with occasional voicings.

c. "Deal"—The four-bar figure played by the band before 8s with the drums sounds like a classic Basie-style shout chorus.

To get a better sense of what we mean by a soli and a shout chorus, it would be useful to listen to some classic big band tracks at this point. For some great Count Basie–style shout choruses, check out Neal Hefti's charts on "Splanky" and "Fantail" from *The Complete Atomic Basie*. For some more great examples of soli and shout chorus writing, on the classic Basie recording *Chairman of the Board* there's Frank Foster's "TV Time," featuring brass riffs playing off against a sax soli and leading to a tremendous shout chorus. Also on the same recording is Foster's "Who, Me?," with a more relaxed sax soli and shout chorus.

Some classic examples by Thad Jones include the incredible sax soli and shout chorus on "Three and One" and some great ensemble writing on "Little Pixie" and "Don't Get Sassy," all available on *The Complete Roulette Studio Recordings of Thad Jones and Mel Lewis*. We'll examine some more examples of solis and shout choruses in greater detail in Section 3 of this book.

Chapter Summary

In this chapter we examined techniques for creating solis and shout choruses and provided some musical examples of these techniques for the 6-horn ensemble. We've also included analyses of a sample soli and shout chorus as well as some recommended listening in this area.

◊ **Software Tip:** The soli (if harmonized) and especially the shout chorus are both great places to experiment with the Explode Music technique described in earlier chapters. The shout chorus also provides an excellent opportunity for using the Edit Filter techniques described in Chapter 17. Enter all articulations into the lead trumpet line, set the Edit Filter to copy only articulations, and copy and paste them into the other parts.

◊ **Software Tip:** When writing for the rhythm section, it's essential to be familiar with your software program's method of dealing with alternate notation. That means slash and rhythmic notation for piano, bass, and guitar and alternate notehead notation (usually x and ◊-shaped noteheads) as well as slash and rhythmic notation for the drums. Refer to the software tip in the Chapter 13 section of the website for General MIDI playback of drum parts. Both Finale and Sibelius have developed very intuitive and user-friendly methods in this area over the past few years. We've come a long way since Finale 2.5! *Refer to the website for more details on creating percussion parts in Finale and Sibelius.*

Exercises

1. Listen to and analyze recordings of solis and shout choruses from this chapter's Listening List (earlier in the chapter).

2. Pick one example of a shout chorus, and transcribe the rhythm figures played by the band. Transcribe the notes, too!

3. **Arranging Project 2:** Write 16 bars of a soli (first half of the tune) for your 6-horn arrangement using techniques discussed in this chapter.

4. Write a 16-bar shout chorus (second half of the tune) using techniques discussed in this chapter.

5. Fill in the rhythm section parts, and add articulations and dynamics. Print out the score and parts. Be sure to observe correct transpositions for the horn parts. Play and analyze the results.

◊ Important Note: If this book is being used as a classroom textbook, this assignment should be spread out over two weeks.

Chapter 19

Completing the 6-Horn Arrangement

If you've been following all the exercises labeled *Arranging Project 2*, beginning with Chapter 17 your 6-horn arrangement should now be nearly complete. The arrangement should consist of an intro, a head (arranged using a variety of techniques), a kicker, one or more improvised solos with backgrounds, a 16-bar soli, and a 16-bar shout chorus. You should have proper dynamics and articulations indicated in the horn parts and properly notated rhythm section parts. All that remains is to add a recap and a short coda, make sure you've created proper layouts and music spacing for the score and parts, verify the transpositions for transposing instruments, and proofread everything.

19-1 Adding a Recap and an Ending

If you've just completed a shout chorus, you're probably at the climax of the arrangement. Working out a conclusion for the chart can take several different paths. Here are a few possible directions.

1. Drop the level of intensity with a short transitional passage, and proceed with a D.S. back to all or part of the original head, followed by a coda.
2. Maintain the intensity generated by the shout chorus, and recap all or part of the head with more powerful orchestration to match that of the shout chorus, followed by a coda.
3. Have the shout chorus lead directly to an ending/coda, foregoing a recap entirely.
4. Compose a *through-composed* ending consisting of new material or material derived from other sections of the tune or arrangement.

Refer to Chapter 11 for specific suggestions regarding endings and codas. As always, try to let your musical instincts and inner ear guide your decisions. Remember, music has a life of its own. Learn to develop a sensitivity to this by stepping back from the music periodically to maintain your perspective; the music will show you which path to take. Never try to force the music in a particular direction just because it seems to make sense intellectually. Music is *always* more about emotions and feelings than about intellect; if it doesn't *feel* right, it's not going to work.

19-2 Score and Part Layouts/Transpositions/Proofreading/Printing

All of the guidelines regarding laying out the score and parts, parts transposition, proofreading, and printing the score and parts presented in Chapters 14 and 15 apply to larger ensembles of any size as well. We recommend reviewing the material in Chapters 14 and 15 before proceeding. Following these basic procedures regarding the layout and printing of the score and parts will ensure smooth and efficient rehearsals and performances of your music.

◊ Once again, remember to allow yourself adequate time to proofread both the score and the parts. *Do not trust MIDI playback as a substitute for thorough proofreading!*

19-3 Six-Horn Arrangement and Analysis: "On a Misty Night" (Tadd Dameron/arr. Willie Smith)

"On a Misty Night," by Tadd Dameron, was arranged by Willie Smith for Joe Lovano's nonet recording *52nd Street Themes* (Blue Note, 2000). This arrangement provides a great example for study, illustrating some of the more traditional, "inside," techniques we've been discussing as applied to a 6-horn ensemble. The instrumentation, although for only one trumpet and two tenor saxes, is otherwise the same as that of the 6-horn ensemble with which we've been working. Study the score, with reductions, of the head and ensemble sections (Exs. 19-1A and 19-1B) and the following analyses. We haven't provided a recording of this one because we want to encourage you to support one of the great jazz musicians of our generation by purchasing the CD or at least downloading the tune. It's well worth the investment!

The intro begins with five horns in close position, with all diatonic passing chords, over a B♭ pedal played by the bass and bari sax. Despite the relatively traditional chord voicings and harmonies, one very striking feature of this arrangement is the unusual placement of the trombone in its high register, above the two tenors throughout most of the chart. This provides a little more intensity for the brass, helping to balance the two brass instruments against the four saxes and producing an unusual sonority. Also, the second tenor is frequently placed above the first.

The emphasis is on keeping the lines interesting and independent rather than on internal resonance. In fact, if you study the reduction, you'll see that there's actually quite a few dissonant parallel seconds between the two tenors. However, if you look at the vertical harmonies as a whole, they fall into very traditional close position, drop-2, and open position voicings, and the harmonies sound smooth and consonant. Willie Smith seems to be treating the ensemble as a single unit rather than thinking in terms of brass and saxes.

The intro builds in mm. 5–8 by expanding to semi-open position and finally to full open position voicings, with some diminished seventh and dominant/tritone-sub passing chords. We've used the same symbols to indicate the different types of approach tone reharmonizations as in previous examples: **D** = diatonic, **Dim** = diminished seventh chord, **P** = parallel approach (half-step or whole-step planing), **Dom** or **SD** = secondary dominant, **TT** = tritone substitution, and **F** = free reharmonization. Notice the contrary motion between the upper and lower voices in m. 7. This type of contrary motion is used quite effectively throughout the chart and is indicated on the reduction by arrows.

At letter **A**, we return to straight close position, alternating with open position, for the first eight bars. Parallel and dominant approach tones as well as contrary motion are used throughout this section. At the second ending, the phrase begins in unison/octaves, for contrast, and ends with some nice fat, open-position chords by fourths, descending chromatically. This produces a more modern sound, in contrast with the more traditional sound of the first 16 bars.

The bridge (**B**) provides a dramatic change in texture, with the tenor sax solo melody answered by the other horns in open position. Letter **C** (m. 28) begins with a recap of **A** (m. 9) but quickly expands to full open position voicings at m. 31. Once again, notice the use of contrary motion as well as parallel and dominant/tritone-sub approach tones in mm. 32–35.

The soli section (**G**) begins with a classic bebop-style line played in unison and octaves by everybody for the first eight bars. At m. 70 we return to close position and then semi-open and open position, moving to another line in unison/octaves and ending with some full open position chords and a parallel resolution down to the final E♭ Maj7 chord. Again, check out the interesting placement of the trombone above the two tenors (for contrasting color) and the huge spread between the bari and other horns in mm. 73–74 (breaking one of our main voicing rules!). Also pay attention to the very specific and clearly indicated dynamics and articulations in mm. 70–75.

Ex. 19-1A "On a Misty Night" Intro/Head with Piano Reduction

by Tadd Dameron
arr. by Willie Smith

240

Ex. 19-1A "On a Misty Night" Intro/Head - 2

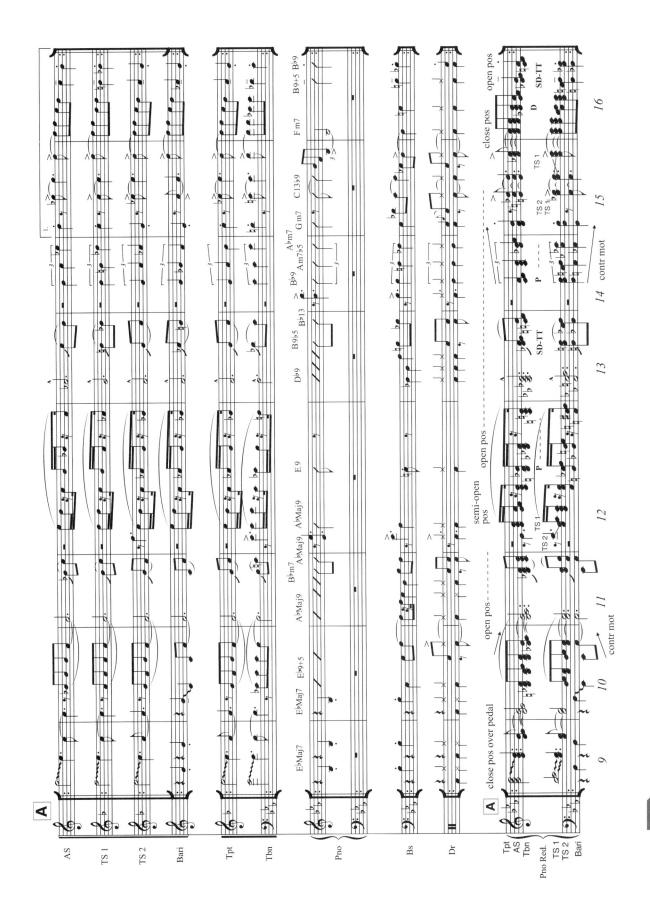

Ex. 19-1A "On a Misty Night" Intro/Head - 3

Ex. 19-1A "On a Misty Night" Intro/Head - 4

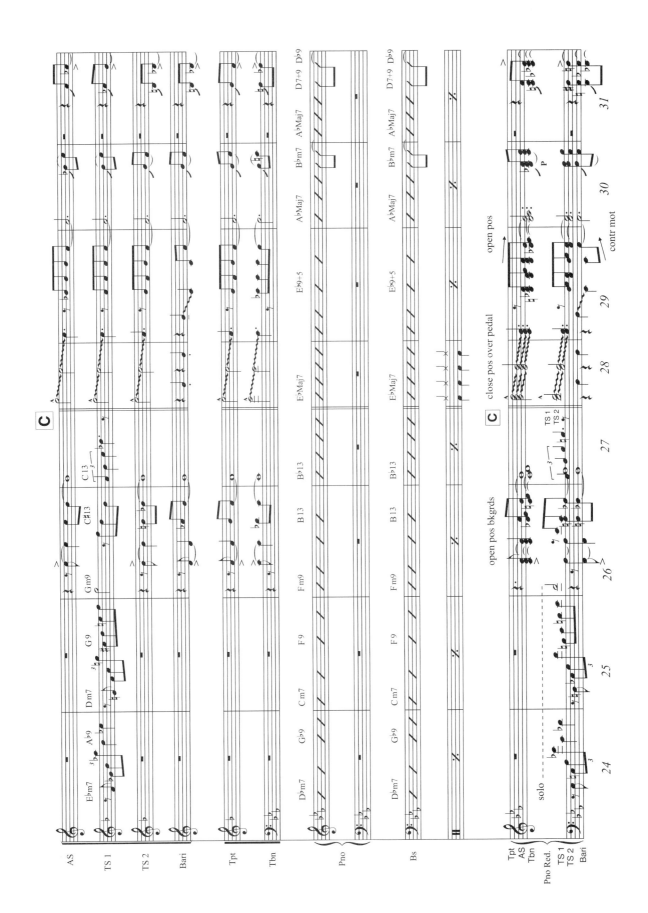

243

Ex. 19-1A "On a Misty Night" Intro/Head - 5

Ex. 19-1B "On a Misty Night" Soli with Piano Reduction

by Tadd Dameron
arr. by Willie Smith

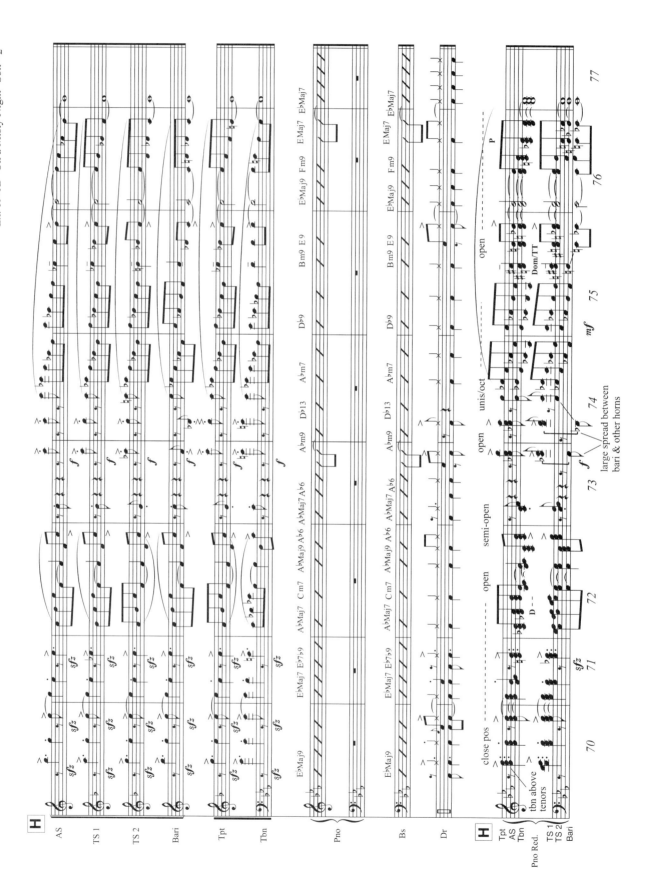

Ex. 19-1B "On a Misty Night" Soli - 2

19-4 Six-Horn Arrangement and Analysis: "Minor Infraction" (Michael Abene)

"Minor Infraction" is an original tune by Michael Abene, written and arranged for 6 horns for this book. It provides a great example of a more modern, edgy approach to scoring for this size ensemble, with modern, dissonant harmonies, non-diatonic chord progression, interesting contrapuntal sections, and unexpected formal twists. Study the score, with reductions, of the head and ensemble sections (Exs. 19-2A and 19-2B) and the following analyses, and listen to the recordings on the companion website. The complete score is also available for download on the website. As with "On a Misty Night," notice the complete rhythm section notation and clearly indicated articulations and dynamics on the score. One effective device used by Michael in this arrangement is the creation of *Instrumental Subdivisions* within the ensemble, or groupings of instruments for color purposes, which we've labeled on the score. We'll re-examine this technique in greater detail in Chapters 24 and 33.

The intro begins with a rhythmic motive played by everyone except trumpet 2 (Subdivision 1), which is being saved for the entrance of the melody at m. 9. The horn voicings are low and close, with a modern edge due to the use of Maj7 ♭5 chords and chords built by fourths (Cm sus4 in m. 3). Notice that the lowest note in the horn voicing is the fifth, not the root, as might be expected with this type of figure. The root is handled by the bass and piano (playing open fifths in the left hand). This figure returns as a unifying device throughout the chart. In Section 3 of the book we'll take a closer look at chords by fourths and some of the other modern voicing techniques used in this chart, such as m9(Δ7) chords, polytonal sounds, and non-diatonic chord progressions.

The tonality of the tune is established as F minor at the beginning of the head (**A**) with the progression Fm-D♭Maj7♭5-Cmsus4 (i-VI-v) in mm. 9–14. However, from m. 15 to m. 30, there is really no functional harmony at all, with the chord roots moving by half-steps and major or minor thirds. Yet the tune seems to maintain its F minor tonality, through the repeated Gm7♭5 (ii) (mm. 18 and 20) and the F#m9Δ7-Fm9Δ7 (mm. 21–22), a kind of twisted V(tritone sub)-i.

247

The melody enters at m. 9 (**A**), with trumpet 2 and the alto sax in unison (Subdivision 2) playing a figure based on an F melodic minor scale, answered by the tenor, bari, trombone, and rhythm section (Subdivision 3) playing the voiced rhythmic figure from the intro. The following phrase (mm. 13–14) is built on a C locrian mode, and contains the striking dissonance of G♭ above the perfect fifth C-G in the piano left hand and bari sax. In mm. 15–16, the answering figure breaks the rule of "no seconds between the top two voices." It works because the biting minor second dissonance between the trumpet and tenor sax is exactly the kind of tension that fits here, proving once again that rules are made to be broken (provided that the result sounds good and you know what you're doing!).

The tension continues to build in mm. 17–23 with the unison call-and-response counterpoint between the two instrumental groupings. The chords themselves are inherently dissonant, and there are some striking dissonances in the horns, most notably the concert D♭ over C in m. 20 and the E over F in m. 21. The faster harmonic rhythm (one chord every bar instead of one chord every two bars) also helps to build the intensity. The harmonic tension is finally released at the end of m. 22 with the progression Em11-E♭m11-D♭m9-E♭/D♭. The voicings are consonant but modern, using fourths and modal concepts in close position. Check out the first chords of m. 24—the dissonant D♭m9Δ7 (an A♭ major triad over A♭ augmented) to the pure E♭ major triad over D♭!

Harmonic tension returns immediately through some pretty dissonant polytonal sounds in mm. 25–30, with the horns voiced in close position and clusters. Letter **B** finally brings us some release, with a return to the rhythmic figure from the intro, reharmonized, and with the slower harmonic rhythm (one chord every two bars). The minor 11 fourth voicings sound quite consonant now. The progression D♭m11-Em11-D♭m11-Fm11 serves as a kind of cadence back to F minor. **B** appears to be the end of the head, but it is also a transitional section because the trumpet solo starts to sneak in at m. 33. The solo changes at **C** are derived from the structure of the tune, but simplified for easier blowing. Although the feeling of F minor tonality is maintained throughout the blowing section, there is very little functional harmony, with the chord roots moving primarily by major/minor thirds and half-steps. The repeated two-bar phrases in mm. 63–71 help to stabilize things. Notice the interesting relationship between the chord progression at **B** and the last four bars of **C** (mm. 73–77), the harmonic rhythm now condensed.

Backgrounds enter at **D** (m. 77) with a unison countermelody in the tenor sax and trombone. This builds to five-part close position dissonant voicings in mm. 85–95 ("D9"). There's a striking color change and release of tension at **E** (m. 95), with lighter, more consonant voicings, sustained chords, staggered rhythmic entries, and an interesting extension of every second chord to two bars duration (compare to mm. 63–71). All of this serves to give the soloist more space and freedom at the end of the solo section.

Letter **F** begins the ensemble soli section (see Ex.19-2B) with a return to the instrumental grouping from **A** (Tpt 1/AS and TS/Bari/Tbn), all in rhythmic unison, first in a unison call-and-response for two bars and then with everyone voiced with some contrary motion for two bars, with rhythmic breaks by the rhythm section. As in the head, trumpet 2 lays out here, this time to give him a chance to catch his breath after the solo. Then follows **G**, with everyone in rhythmic unison playing an unusual unison/octave quarter-note triplet figure alternating with dissonant six-part chords. The end of mm. 126–135 functions as a sort of climactic shout chorus, with everyone playing dense, dissonant, close position chords in rhythmic unison, with rhythmic support and breaks in the rhythm section.

There's one more formal twist. If you compare mm. 129–135 to mm. 63–71 (the corresponding spot in the blowing section), you'll find that the two-bar phrases don't repeat here, so the end of the shout chorus is more concise and to the point. Letter **H**, a transition before the D.S., is simply the last four bars of **C** repeated. This is followed by a recap (D.S.) of **A**. The coda is actually just the first three bars of **B**! Please note – the audio file Ex. 19-2 on the website is the entire chart of "Minor Infraction", including both Ex. 19-2A and 19-2B. The full score to "Minor Infraction", including both examples, is also available for download from the companion website.

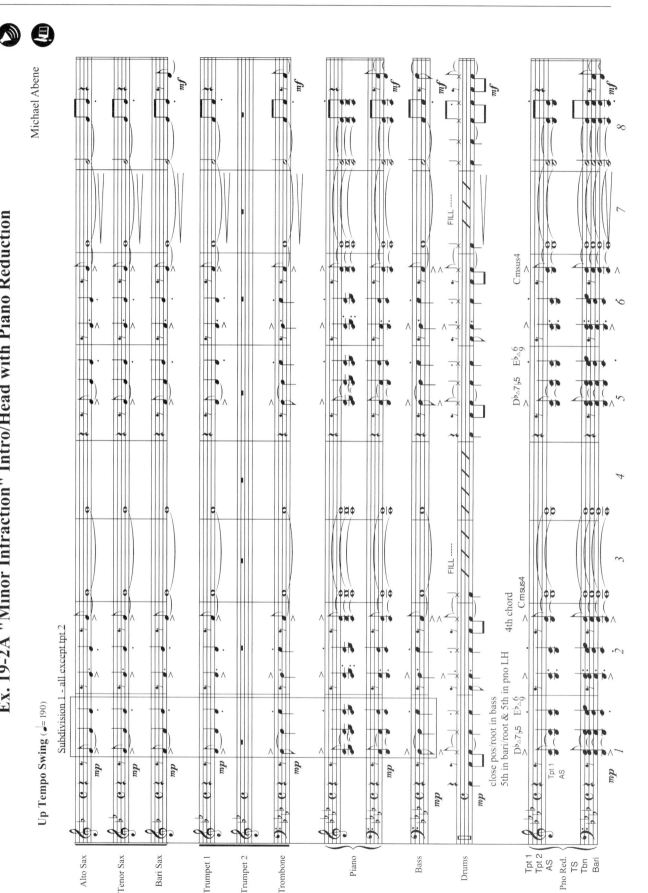

Ex. 19-2A "Minor Infraction" Intro/Head with Piano Reduction

Michael Abene

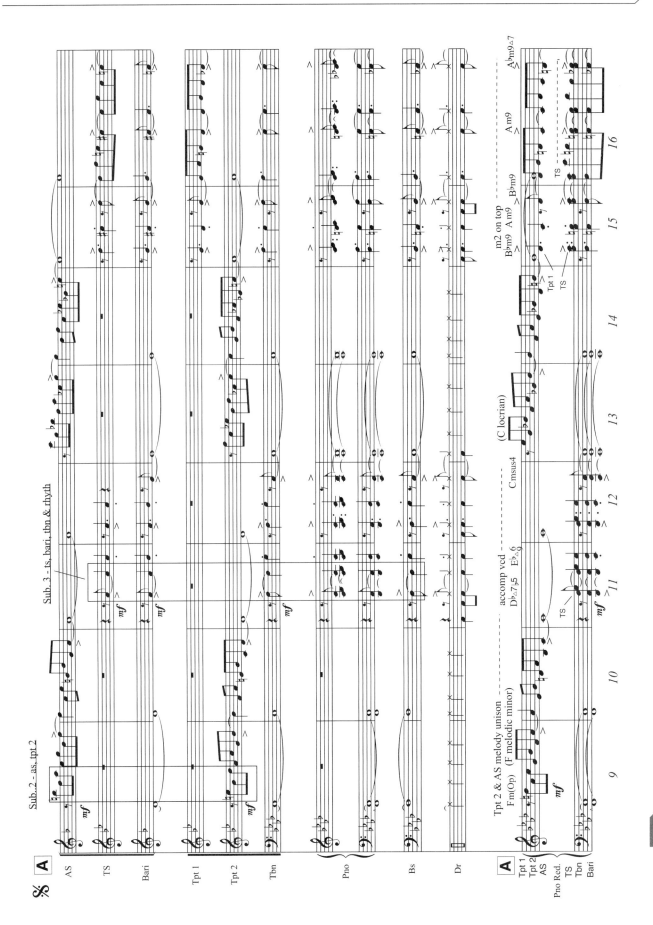

Ex. 19-2A "Minor Infraction" Intro/Head - 2

Ex. 19-2A "Minor Infraction" Intro/Head - 3

Ex. 19-2A "Minor Infraction" Intro/Head - 4

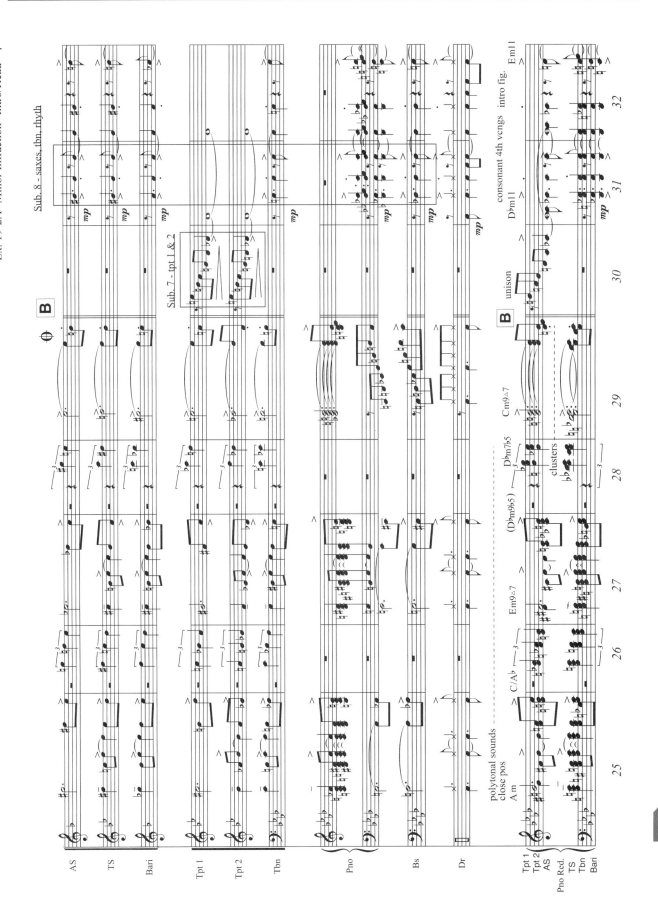

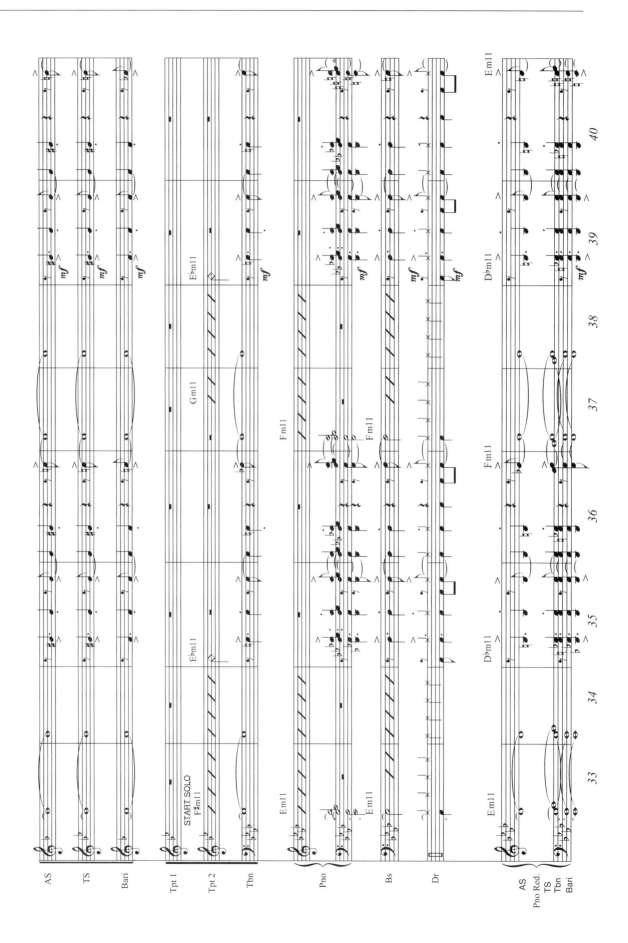

Ex. 19-2A "Minor Infraction" Intro/Head - 5

Ex. 19-2A "Minor Infraction" Intro/Head - 6

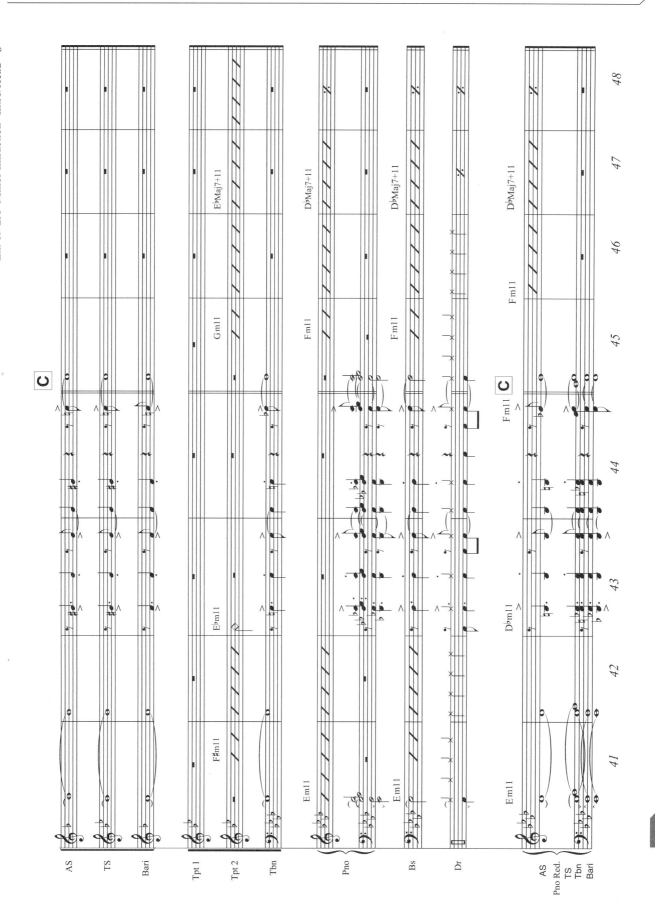

Ex. 19-2B "Minor Infraction" Ensemble Section with Piano Reduction

Michael Abene

Ex. 19-2B "Minor Infraction" Ensemble Section - 2

Ex. 19-2B "Minor Infraction" Ensemble Section - 3

◊ **Special Bonus Score Available On Website!** For another great example of a hip 6-horn chart in a more contemporary jazz style, check out "Burn" by the great jazz pianist and composer/arranger Jim McNeely. The score to the head and some ensemble sections of the chart is available for download as Example 19-3 on our website. As with other commercially available recordings examined in this book, we haven't provided a recording of this chart. The recording is available on the album "Remember the Sound" by the George Robert Jazztet on TCB Music, 2008. We once again encourage you to support the great jazz musicians of our generation by purchasing the CD, or at least downloading the tune.

Chapter Summary

In this chapter we reviewed the steps necessary for completing the 6-horn chart, including adding a recap and coda, parts and score layout, and proofreading. We've also provided two examples of 6 horn + rhythm arrangements, complete with detailed analyses. You should now be ready to call a rehearsal and have a reading of your own 6-horn arrangement!

This completes our study of the most important melodic, harmonic, textural, and formal principles essential to the art of arranging for both small and large jazz ensembles. For a reference guide to these principles, please refer to Appendix C, "Summary of Basic Arranging and Voicing Principles," available for download and printing from the companion website.

Many of these same fundamentals can be applied directly to the process of arranging for the jazz big band. We recommend that you print out Appendix C and keep it handy for future reference, since we'll be referring to this information frequently in Section 3 of the book.

◊ **Software Tip:** Even for the most seasoned arrangers, it can sometimes be useful to have a piano reduction of a complex section of a score. There are several methods for creating piano reductions in both programs like those used in Exs. 19-1A, 19-1B, 19-2A, and 19-2B. *Consult the website for details.*

Exercises

Use techniques discussed in this chapter.

1. Add a recap and ending to your 6-horn chart (Arranging Project 2).

2. Print out the parts and score for Arranging Project 2. Call a rehearsal, and play through the chart several times. Record it.

3. Listen to the recording with the other musicians. Discuss which parts worked well and which didn't. Make any necessary changes (this usually means taking things out or revoicing sections that may be too thick or too dissonant). Print everything out again, and play it again!

4. Take a well-deserved break!

Arranging for Large Jazz Ensemble (8 Brass, 5 Reeds, and Rhythm)

Chapter 20

Overview of Large Ensemble Writing

20-1 Overview and Historical Perspective

We now turn our attention to composing and arranging for the classic 17-piece jazz big band configuration of four trumpets (all doubling on flugelhorn), four trombones (three tenor trombones and one bass), five reeds, and four rhythm. The reeds consist of the basic five-piece saxophone section (two altos, two tenors, and one baritone), with possible flute, clarinet, bass clarinet, and soprano sax doubles. The rhythm section consists of piano (or electric piano), electric guitar, bass (acoustic or electric), and drums.

Granted, over the years there have been many other configurations of large jazz ensembles, from smaller groups consisting of three trumpets, two trombones, three to four saxes, and three rhythm (11–12 pieces), to larger groups with five trumpets, five trombones, French horns, extra woodwinds, and additional percussion (20+ pieces), and just about every imaginable possible combination of instruments in between. A little historical perspective could prove useful at this point.

In the early 1920s, Fletcher Henderson, sometimes credited with creating the jazz big band sound, began working in New York with 9- and 10-piece groups consisting of two trumpets, one trombone, three reeds, and three to four rhythm (similar to our six horns + rhythm configuration). By 1927 his band had evolved to 12 pieces, consisting of three trumpets, two trombones, three saxes, and four rhythm. Henderson, along with arranger Don Redman, was one of the first to conceive of the band in terms of three contrasting sections: brass, woodwinds, and rhythm. Henderson later became a frequent arranger for

Benny Goodman in the 1930s, achieving great success and recognition for his arrangements, which played off the brass and sax sections against each other.

A few years later, Duke Ellington began his career as a leader, with a small group that had evolved to nine pieces by 1926. By 1932, Duke had settled on a configuration of four reeds (one alto, two tenors, and one bari, with clarinet doubles), three trumpets, three trombones, and four rhythm. This was a typical configuration throughout much of the 1930s. Benny Goodman, Glenn Miller, and Count Basie all led and recorded with groups comprising four saxes, three trumpets, two or three trombones, and four rhythm during this period.

It's interesting to note that the typical jazz rhythm section of the 1920s (and even into the early 1930s) consisted of piano, banjo, tuba, and drums. It wasn't until the 1930s that the tuba and banjo were replaced by string bass and guitar. It's also interesting to note that the clarinet was much more prominently featured in the reed sections of jazz bands in the 1920s and '30s than in modern times and that almost all jazz saxophone players of that period doubled on or were featured on clarinet.

In fact, it wasn't until the 1940s that the jazz big band instrumentation began to coalesce into its standard modern configuration of five saxes, four trumpets, three to four trombones, and three to four rhythm instruments. Ellington's famous 1943 Carnegie Hall concert recording featured a 5 (reeds), 4 (trumpets), 3 (trombones), and 4 (rhythm) configuration. Basie first recorded with this instrumentation in 1941, and by the 1950s this had become firmly established as the "Basie sound," with such classic recordings as *Atomic Basie* (1957) and *Chairman of the Board* (1958). Duke eventually dropped the guitar and settled on a 5, 4, 3, 3 grouping.

Also in the 1940s, some band leaders, most notably trombonists Glenn Miller and Tommy Dorsey, began expanding the number of trombones to four (including the leader). During the 1940s, '50s, and '60s, the brass section was often expanded to include five trumpets and, less frequently, five trombones. Some band leaders and arrangers, such as Claude Thornhill and Gil Evans, experimented with adding French horns, tuba, and additional woodwinds. In the 1950s, Stan Kenton featured a band consisting of five reeds, five trumpets, five trombones, and four rhythm.

The innovative, initial recordings by the Thad Jones–Mel Lewis Orchestra (1966–68) undoubtedly played a major role in the final standardization of the jazz big band instrumentation to its modern configuration of five saxes, four trumpets, four trombones, and three to four rhythm instruments. The guitar was eventually dropped, but most of those original Thad and Mel recordings included guitar in the rhythm section.

Of course there still continues to be experimentation and variations of instrumentation, most commonly by adding a fifth trumpet or by dropping one of the trombones (for a three-piece trombone section) and occasionally by adding French horns, tuba, and extra woodwinds. However, 5, 4, 4, 3–4 (the guitar being optional) continues to the present day to be by far the most common instrumental configuration of jazz big bands, both for professional as well as student ensembles.

20-2 Basic Principles and Considerations

In the following chapters, as with Chapters 16–18, we will continue to build on the harmonic, melodic, rhythmic, timbral, and formal concepts presented in Chapters 7–11. Most of these basic musical principles apply equally well to the larger ensemble. The fundamental difference lies in the expanded sound palette and dynamic range provided by the big band. The possible instrumental textural and color combinations increases exponentially with the larger ensemble. The arranger can now create full chord voicings in both the sax and brass section, and play the two sections off against each other in a dramatic fashion. There are also now a multitude of cross-sectional instrumental combinations, capable of producing much richer and more complex chord voicings.

In a sense, the jazz big band is the "symphony orchestra" of jazz, providing the jazz arranger with the greatest number of creative options. We don't mean to discount the importance of the so-called jazz studio orchestra or jazz philharmonic (jazz big band augmented by strings and classical woodwinds), but the sheer size of these ensembles (usually at least 35–40 musicians or more) tends to make them not very viable economically, thus limiting the number of possible venues and available performance opportunities. On the other hand, the 16- to 17-piece jazz big band seems to be flourishing all across the country (and around the world), with virtually every city (and even many small towns) as well as most high schools and colleges with jazz programs supporting at least one such ensemble. The musicians may not be getting rich, but the jazz big band is definitely *not* dead!

20-3 The Expanded Sound Palette

In the standard professional jazz big band, usually all four trumpets double on flugelhorn, there is at least one and sometimes two bass trombones in the trombone section, and one can generally count on at least two flutes, two clarinets, bass clarinet, and soprano sax doubles in the reed section (very often there may even be four to five flutes and clarinets available).

Following is a partial list of possible color combinations for big band, similar to that provided in Chapter 16 for six horns:

1. Any horn playing solo with the rhythm section.
2. Any two or more horns playing in unison or octaves with the rhythm section.
3. Trumpet in Harmon mute + flute 8va over chords played by flugelhorn, tenor and bari sax, and trombone.

4. Trumpet and alto sax voiced in thirds or sixths over rhythmic hits played by the other horns.

5. Two trumpets and alto, tenor, and bari saxes voiced in close position over a unison countermelody by the trombone section.

6. Four flugelhorns playing the melody in unison or voiced over two clarinets, alto sax, tenor sax, two trombones, and bass clarinet chords.

7. Two trumpets, one trombone, and three saxes voiced in rhythmic unison.

8. Three trumpets, two trombones, and four saxes voiced in rhythmic unison.

9. Any subset of all the horns playing in rhythmic unison.

10. The full brass and sax sections playing in rhythmic unison with full rhythm section support (the shout chorus).

11. Three trumpets in a variety of mutes, flugelhorn, three trombones in mutes, two flutes, two clarinets, and bass clarinet playing rich, cross-sectional voicings.

12. Four flutes playing the melody in unison over muted brass and bass clarinet.

13. Flugelhorn, one trumpet in harmon mute, and one trombone in cup mute playing a melody in octaves over chordal accompaniment played by flute, soprano sax, clarinet, tenor sax, and bass clarinet.

14. Any two to five horns playing pads or counterpoint to any other two to five horns playing the melody.

15. Piano and bass playing the melody, with rhythmic hits by the horns.

16. Piano or bass doubling the melody with any combination of horns.

As you can see, the list of possible instrumental color combinations is virtually endless and is significantly greater than with six horns (Section 17-3). We'll return to this variety of color combinations in Chapter 25, "Form and Planning the Arrangement."

20-4 Laying Out the Score

We'll now be working with the Jazz Big Band Template, available for download from the companion website. As with the Six Horn + Rhythm Template used in Chapter 17, the big band template follows the standard practice of placing the woodwinds above the brass. In addition, we'll now be displaying full-score examples, primarily in *transposed score* format, with all the instruments appearing in their appropriate transpositions, just as they would in the printed parts. (We'll still provide concert-score reductions where appropriate.)

We recommend that you also begin working in transposed score, for the reasons stated in Section 5-5. "The chief disadvantage of a concert score is that it forces us to put the low saxophones in the bass clef or to use many ledger lines, which can be very confusing to a conductor reading the score. It can also lead us to make mistakes regarding the actual ranges of the instruments and the relative tessitura of the parts."

Although, as we pointed out in Chapter 5, analyzing the vertical harmonies can at first seem more difficult with a transposed score, this has become a moot point, since any notation program provides the capability to switch easily back and forth between concert and transposed views. However, we still believe that the advantages of working in a transposed score ultimately outweigh the disadvantages and that the transposed score will enable any aspiring arranger to maintain a more accurate sense of instrument ranges and tessitura while working.

20-5 Selecting a Tune for a Big Band Arrangement

Not all tunes necessarily lend themselves equally well to being easily arranged for big band. There are certain qualities of tunes and thematic material that seem better suited for the larger ensemble. This is all fairly subjective. The following suggestions are meant to help steer the less experienced reader toward selecting an appropriate tune for the first arranging project. For example, "It Could Happen to You" and "Whisper Not" would probably lend themselves more readily to a first big band arrangement than "Donna Lee" or "The Sorcerer." Of course, in experienced and capable hands, almost anything can be made to work.

Suggestions for Tune Qualities Suitable for a First Big Band Arrangement

1. Simplified melodic density (not a lot of notes), with space to breathe.
2. Contrast of melodic shape and motion, but with a greater percentage of scalar material.
3. Use of blues/funk jazz tune characteristics:
    a. Simple major-, minor-, and blues-scale melodic material.
    b. Use of vamps, rhythmic breaks, pedal points, riffs, etc.
    c. Use of simple, blues-based harmonies.
4. Use of irregular melodic phrase structures, syncopation, and other techniques of melodic development.
5. Use of diatonic/functional (ii-V) harmonies with minor third and tritone substitutions.
6. Use of some nonfunctional root motion (chord roots moving by major and minor thirds, half steps, and whole steps).
7. More regular than irregular harmonic rhythm.
8. More regular than irregular form and structure.
9. Some use of dissonant and complex chord qualities.
10. Use of simplified blowing changes where appropriate.

20-6 Recommended Listening

There's an incredible wealth of recorded examples of big band jazz, from the early Fletcher Henderson and Duke Ellington records of the 1920s to the most recent recordings by such modern jazz composers as Bob Brookmeyer, Jim McNeely, Bob Mintzer, Maria Schneider, John Clayton, and numerous others. Following is a partial Listening List of some of our favorites to get you started. As always, listen to as much and as great a variety as possible.

Large Ensemble Listening List

1. Duke Ellington—"The Blanton-Webster Band," RCA, 1940–42; "Such Sweet Thunder," Columbia, 1956–57; "The Great Paris Concert," Atlantic, 1963; "Live at Newport," Columbia, 1963.

2. Count Basie—"The Best of Count Basie," MCA, 1937–38 (reissued as "The Best of Early Basie"); "The Atomic Basie," Roulette, 1957; "Chairman of the Board," Roulette, 1958; "Echoes of an Era", Roulette, 1958–61 (many of these recordings available on "The Complete Roulette Studio Count Basie" Mosaic box set); "Basie Straight Ahead," Dot, 1968.

3. Fletcher Henderson—"Swing's the Thing," MCA, 1931–34.

4. Benny Goodman—"Arrangements by Fletcher Henderson & Eddie Sauter," Collectables, 1935–53.

5. Woody Herman—"Keeper of the Flame," Capitol, 1947; "Verve Jazz Masters #54," 1962–64.

6. Stan Kenton—"New Concepts of Artistry In Rhythm," Capitol, 1952; "Contemporary Concepts," Capitol, 1955.

7. Smithsonian—"Big Band Box Set" (various artists 1920s–50s).

8. Gil Evans with Miles Davis—"Miles Ahead," Columbia, 1957; "Porgy and Bess," Columbia, 1958: "The Complete Pacific Jazz Sessions," Blue Note (reissue), 1958–59.

9. George Russell—"New York, NY," MCA, 1958; Jazz In the Space Age," MCA, 1958.

10. Terry Gibbs—"Dream Band," Contemporary, 1959 (reissued on Fantasy, 1986).

11. Quincy Jones—"The Quintessence," Impulse, 1961.

12. Oliver Nelson—"Full Nelson," Verve, 1962; "Swiss Suite," Flying Dutchman, 1971; "Verve Jazz Masters #48" (1962–67).

13. Thad Jones/Mel Lewis—"Presenting Thad Jones/Mel Lewis & The Jazz Orchestra," Solid State, 1966; "Live at the Village Vanguard," Solid State, 1967; "Monday Night," Solid State, 1968 (many of these recordings available on "The Complete Solid State Recordings of the Thad Jones/Mel Lewis Orchestra" Mosaic box set), "Consummation," Solid State/Blue Note, 1970.

14. Mel Lewis—"Bob Brookmeyer—Composer/Arranger," Gryphon, 1980.

15. Vanguard Orchestra—"Lickety Split" (Jim McNeely cp/arr). New World Records, 1997.

16. Bob Mintzer—"The Art of the Big Band," DMP, 1991.

17. Maria Schneider—"Concert In the Garden," Artistshare, 2004.

Please refer to Appendix B on the companion website, "Recommended Recordings for Further Study," for a more comprehensive listening list.

Chapter Summary

This chapter introduced the study of arranging for jazz big band with a brief historical overview. We then examined some basic concepts and some of the enhanced textural possibilities made available by the expanded instrumental palette of the larger ensemble. We also discussed issues relating to laying out the score and offered some recommendations for selecting a suitable tune for the next arranging project. Finally, we provided a suggested Listening List for a wide variety of jazz big band recordings.

◊ **Software Tip**: In order to take full advantage of your notation software's MIDI playback capabilities, this would be a good time to become thoroughly acquainted with the instrumental libraries included with the program as well as to explore any third-party sample libraries that may be available as an option. You can do this by taking a little extra time to play through and listen to the various sampled options for each instrument available in your system before you actually begin writing. Then create a custom Instrument or MIDI Setup and Instrument List (Finale), or Playback Configuration/Sound Set (Sibelius).

It's also especially important that you understand how the software deals with articulations and dynamics, such as basic dynamic markings (*p, mp, f, ff*, etc.), accents and other articulations, crescendos and decrescendos, tempo changes, and swing feel. Very often the default settings for these features will need to be adjusted in order to produce musically satisfying results. Refer to the Software Tips for Chapter 12 and the "Additional Software Tips" in Chapter 34 for more details on how to fine-tune playback of expressions and articulations in Finale.

In Sibelius, when writing for a large ensemble, you actually may want first to try using the standard MIDI sounds generated by your computer's internal synthesizer, since this allows the program to run at its fastest pace. Although these sounds are not the most realistic, you'll appreciate the speed with which you can work. For more realistic playback once you've

269

completed a large section of the score, switch to the sampled sound set called Sibelius Essentials included with the software. *Refer to the website for more details on controlling MIDI playback of expressions in Sibelius.*

Exercises

1. Pick a tune you like from any big band recording on the preceding Listening List. Listen to the recording in a focused way, and be able to describe what it is about the music that makes it sound great.

2. Pick another recording and analyze the instrumentation of the arrangement. Get a hold of a copy of the score if possible. List, in outline form, the various instrumental combinations used in each section of the arrangement.

3. Select a suitable standard tune, jazz standard, or original composition to be used for your first big band arrangement (Arranging Project 3). Refer to the list of "Recommended Standards and Jazz Standards" at the end of Chapter 17 for ideas.

Chapter 21

Unison and Octave Writing/Monophonic Texture

We'll begin our study of jazz big band arranging by examining the process of scoring a melodic line with different instruments in either unison or octaves. This seemingly simple technique is actually a very powerful and important component of the arranger's palette, providing the ability to state a melody with a clarity and directness not possible if the line is harmonized. It also provides a comfortable starting point for focusing on and becoming familiar with the sounds of the available instruments and the multitude of instrumental combinations possible within the big band.

A unison or octave line, by definition, means at least two or more players on a line. It's still considered to be a monophonic texture, but one distinctly different from a single instrument playing a solo written or improvised part.

21-1 Melodic Considerations

Whether the melodic line is going to be in unison, in octaves, or voiced, one of the arranger's first tasks is to instill some character and expressiveness into the melody through the application of rhythmic alteration, ornamentation, and other techniques of melodic development. All the principles regarding melodic shape, motion, and development presented in Chapter 7 apply equally well here and to ensembles of any size. We recommend that you take a moment to review these sections now before proceeding.

21-2 Combining the Instruments: Considerations of Timbre, Register, and Tessitura

When considering how to combine the various instruments of the band to create contrasting colors, there are two approaches that can prove useful for organizing your thoughts. First, consider the register, or pitch range (high, mid, and low), of an instrument. Then consider the instrument's timbre, or tone color (bright—a lot of overtones, or dark—fewer overtones). Let's (somewhat arbitrarily) define the low register as extending from C1* (or below) to G2, the mid-range from C2 to C4, and the high register from G3 on up. Obviously, a trumpet or flute would fall into the high register, a clarinet or alto sax could overlap the mid- to high register, a tenor sax would fit pretty squarely in the mid-register (with a few notes extending into the low), a tenor trombone overlaps the low to mid-range, and a baritone sax and bass trombone would normally fit into the low register.

The categories of timbre may not be quite as obvious, but they are equally important. It's possible to measure precisely the exact overtone structure of any sound, but it's not necessary to study the physics of sound to be able to identify the differences in timbre between the different families of instruments. The human ear is a truly remarkable and sensitive organ.

As we pointed out in Chapter 3, all brass instruments, by virtue of the nature of their method of tone production and the material from which they are constructed, contain more overtones than woodwinds, although flugelhorns and French horns are somewhat darker in timbre than trumpets and trombones. Within the woodwind family, saxophones have more overtones (are brighter sounding) than clarinets, which in turn are brighter sounding than flutes and recorders. This can seem a little confusing at first, but it's actually true that a bass clarinet has more prominent overtones than a flute and is therefore brighter in timbre, despite the difference in register. From the perspective of the physics of sound, pitch and timbre are independent of each other. An instrument can be high in register but dark in timbre and with less prominent overtones (flute), or it can be low in register and bright in timbre and with more prominent overtones (bass clarinet or trombone).

Sticking to instruments of one section creates a homogeneous sound. For example, combining two or more trumpets in unison will achieve a bright, direct, agile, and homogeneous quality. Adding a trombone or two an octave below will result in a more powerful and homogeneous sound with slightly less agility. A slightly mellower but still direct and homogeneous sound will result from two alto saxophones in unison, with greater power being achieved by adding the tenor saxes or baritone sax at the octave. Now, granted, there are big differences in the sounds produced by individual players on different instruments, but whether you're listening to Paul Desmond or David Sanborn, you can still tell the difference between an alto sax and a trumpet.

---

* C3 = middle C (Chapter 3, footnote 2).

Everything becomes much more interesting and creative when we start combining instruments from different families with different overtone structures as well as different registers. For example, a trumpet and an alto sax playing in unison sound quite different than two trumpets or two alto saxes. Two trumpets and one tenor sax and trombone in octaves sound different than one trumpet, clarinet, and an alto sax over two trombones and a baritone sax in octaves.

The weighting of the different instruments at their various registers and timbre has a big impact as well. Basically, the more instruments of a particular register or timbre you have playing, the louder that particular sound quality will be in the overall mix. For example, if you have three trumpets and two trombones mixed with one alto sax and one tenor sax, the timbral impact of the saxes will be fairly subtle in relation to the powerful sound of the brass. Conversely, in a combination of five saxes with one trumpet and one trombone, the overall timbral quality would be predominantly that of the saxophones, colored slightly by the brass.

Finally, when combining various instruments, it's important to consider the *tessitura*, or relative position of each instrument in relation to its overall range. As we pointed out at the end of Section 7-5 all acoustic instruments sound brighter and more intense in their upper registers. This is especially the case with wind instruments, where the greater force needed to produce a tone in the upper register creates additional overtones as well as increased volume (see Ex. 7-6). To repeat our mantra from Don Sebesky, "the intensity of the lower instruments should never exceed that of the higher."* Example 21-1 demonstrates some simple but effective octave and unison instrumental combinations available to the big band arranger. Listen to the recordings on the companion website as you study the written examples. Please note that we're sticking to open brass and saxophones here. We'll get into woodwind doubles and brass mutes in the following chapters.

A. **High Unison**

   1. 2 trumpets

   2. 2 altos

   3. 1 tpt/1 alto

---

* Sebesky, *ibid.*

274

B. **Low Unison**

    1. 2 trombones

    2. 2 tenors

    3. 1 tbn/1 tnr

    4. 1 tbn/1 bari

C. **Octaves**

1. 1 tpt/1 tbn	7. 2 tpts/1 tnr/bari
2. 1 alto/1 tnr	8. 2 altos/2 tbns
3. 1 tpt/1 tnr	9. 2 altos/2 tnrs
4. 1 tpt/1 bari	10. 1 tpt and 1 alto/1 tnr and 1 tbn
5. 1 alto/1 tbn	11. 2 tpts and 1 alto/1 tbn, 1 tnr, and 1 bari
6. 2 tpts/2 tbns	

21-3 Melodic Phrase Structure

When orchestrating a melodic line for any jazz ensemble, it's important to be aware of the melodic phrase structure of the line, which typically will tend to fall into one-, two-, or four-bar phrases. When changing the instrumentation of a line, the most natural approach is to do so at or around the phrase breaks rather than in the middle of a phrase (although there's no rule that says you can't do that). The arranger can choose any number of various possible melodic subdivisions when changing instrumentation. However, if the phrase structure of the tune is symmetrical (two- or four-bar phrases), changing instrumental color right at the phrase breaks can have the effect of reinforcing the regularity of the phrasing, making the instrumentation sound too predictable.

One way of overcoming this problem is to overlap, or "dovetail," the instrumental entrances and exits so that the next instrument enters while the previous one is still playing. However, it's important to use a little musical common sense when applying this technique. For example, entrances at the beginning of a phrase should include any pickup notes, and an instrument shouldn't stop playing abruptly in the middle of a phrase. There are usually obvious places within a phrase that will work, or you can use dynamics (e.g., a slight decrescendo as an instrument drops out) to help ease the transitions.

Example 21-3 illustrates these principles with the tune "Unithology" (Lead Sheet—Ex. 21-2), composed for the occasion (note the unusual six-bar bridge). The example is written in piano sketch format, using only unison and octave scoring, with the intended instrumentation indicated for each musical phrase. Notice the contrast between one-, two-, and four-bar melodic subdivisions and overlapping phrases where indicated. Also note the slight alterations to the melody (compare to the lead sheet) in mm. 9, 17, 18, 19, and 23. Notice how the crescendos and diminuendos at the beginnings and ends of phrases help to smooth out the transitions from one grouping to another.

Ex. 21-2

"Unithology" by Richard Sussman (Lead Sheet)

Ex. 21-3

Unison and Octave Scoring: "Unithology," composed and arranged by Richard Sussman

Ex. 21-3

"Unithology" Unison & Octave Scoring

Ex. 21-3

"Unithology" Unison & Octave Scoring

Chapter Summary

In this chapter we examined the technique of scoring the horns in unison and octaves. We focused on some principles relating to the multitude of timbral combinations available in the big band. We also examined ways in which the melodic phrase structure can influence scoring decisions.

◊ **Software Tip**: Sometimes it's necessary to enter chord symbols into empty staves, as in Example 21-3 or Exercise 21-2. In Finale 2009 and earlier it was necessary to attach chords to notes or rests, which created a problem, since the default whole rest that Finale inserts automatically into blank measures is not a "true" rest. This situation was corrected in Finale 2010. *Consult the website for details on how to accomplish this in Finale 2009 or earlier.* This is not an issue in Sibelius because chord symbols are generally entered as plain text.

Ex. 21-2

"Whisper Not" Unison & Octave Scoring

A | Cm7 | Cm7/B♭ | Am7♭5 | D7♭9 | Gm7 | Gm7/F | Em7♭5 | A7♭9 |

Saxes

Tpts

Tbns

| Dm7 | Bm7♭5 | Em7♭5 | A7♭9 | Dm7 | Em7 | Fm7 | G7♭9 |

Saxes

Tpts

Tbns

5

| Cm7 | Cm7/B♭ | Am7♭5 | D7♭9 | Gm7 | Gm7/F | Em7♭5 | A7♭9 |

Saxes

Tpts

Tbns

9

Exercises

1. Pick a few tracks from the Listening List, and identify some sections where the horns are playing in unison or octaves. Try to identify which horns, and how many of each, are playing.

2. Using techniques discussed in this chapter, arrange the head of "Whisper Not" (or any 32-bar AABA standard or jazz standard) for 8 brass and 5 saxes. Use only unison or octave doublings. Change the color every four bars for the first "A," every two bars for the second "A," and every two or four bars for the bridge and last "A." Include two to four instruments in each melodic subdivision, and list them over each line's entrance, as in Example 21-3. Use the four-stave concert sketch template provided here as Exercise 21-2 or available for download in Finale, Sibelius, or General MIDI format on the website. Use both sectional and mixed-family combinations. Use some overlapping of phrases, as discussed in Section 21-3. If you want to try a different tune, just replace the chord changes above the top staff.

3. Start planning the instrumentation for the head of your big band chart. Pick a spot that might sound good in unison or octaves, and enter the notes. Use the Jazz Big Band Template.

Chapter 22

Concerted Writing for Brass

22-1 Overview of Concerted Writing for Brass

As we'll see throughout Section 3, many instrumental textures are available to the arranger when orchestrating a given passage for jazz big band. For example, the unison and octave techniques examined in the preceding chapter, a solo instrument playing the melody over a chordal bed played by contrasting instruments, and creating smaller subdivisions within the band (e.g., 2 trumpets, 3 saxes, 1 trombone) are all viable choices. In other words, not everyone has to be playing all the time, and not all passages need to be voiced for all instruments.

As obvious as this point may seem to some, it is often overlooked by the young or inexperienced arranger. There is frequently a tendency to overwrite, even on the part of those with some experience. Very often "less is more." We'll keep coming back to this point in subsequent chapters. Yet there is obviously something uniquely exciting and intriguing about those passages where the whole band is playing together voiced in full tutti, and it's essential for any jazz arranger to have a mastery of the techniques for attaining that sound. This may also appear to be the most daunting task facing an arranger when first approaching the jazz big band, and it can be an easy place to "lose sight of the forest for the trees."

We'll begin our study of concerted big band writing with some simple techniques and guidelines for writing for 8 brass. In the next chapter, we'll examine techniques for arranging the sax section and for combining the brass and saxes.

22-2 Review of Basic Harmonic and Voicing Principles (Vertical Harmony)

Most of the fundamental harmonic and voice-leading principles presented in Section 2 can easily be applied to voicing for the larger ensemble. Please review the earlier chapters on harmony (Chapters 8, 9, 10, and 16), and refer to Appendix A, "Summary of Basic Arranging and Voicing Principles," on the companion website. It's important to have a firm grasp of all of these principles before proceeding. Pay special attention to Section 8-4, "Standard Jazz Voicing Positions," since we'll now be applying those principles to voicing the brass and sax sections.

22-3 Application of Basic Voicing Principles to 8 Brass

Let's now take a look at how our definitions of close position, drop-2, and open position voicings would apply to the jazz big band 8-piece brass section. Example 22-1 illustrates how Exs. 8-4A, 8-4B, 16-1A, and 16-1B could be adapted for 4 trumpets and 4 trombones. In the first example (close position), we have the trombones doubling the trumpets exactly an octave lower. We chose to include the root (instead of the ninth) in the voicing for the last C Maj chord in order to avoid the major second interval between the top two voices.

In number 2, drop-2 position, observe that we keep the trumpets in close position and put only the trombones in a drop-2 configuration. This way we avoid having the fourth trumpet overlap the lead trombone, which would sound muddy and confusing. It also keeps both sections in better registers, with the trumpets in their bright, upper mid-register and the trombones voiced a little lower than in the first case, creating a more balanced voicing. In number 3, open position, we've once again reharmonized the second pickup note with the V7 tritone substitution (Db7) to create contrary motion between the lead trumpet melody and the fourth trombone bass line.

As in Exs. 16-1A and 16-1B, with close position and drop-2 the melody is *always* doubled an octave below the lead. We've also provided additional examples of homophonic and polyphonic textures (as in Exs. 8-4 and 16-1), again indicating the possibilities for adding additional chord tones with more instruments (*). It wasn't necessary to transpose this example, as we did in Ex. 16-1B, because there are now enough instruments to fill in notes in the low mid-register to balance and support the high-register trumpets. Play through Ex. 22-1 at a keyboard and compare to Exs. 8-4 and 16-1.

We will continue to apply these basic harmonic and voicing principles in the following chapters. But, as we've said before, "The Rules" are there to help you make voicing decisions quickly that will have stylistic integrity. Following "The Rules" while doing the exercises in this book will help you to build a foundation of knowledge and techniques that should enable you to make better

Ex. 22-1

Standard Jazz Voicing Positions—8 Brass: "I Could Write a Book" by Rodgers & Hart

285

musical choices. However, in the creative arts, "Rules are made to be broken," and ultimately your voicing choices should be determined by what you hear and by your own creative instincts!

22-4 Reharmonization of Approach Tones, Repeated Notes, and Voice Leading for 8 Brass

The principles of reharmonization of approach tones explained in Chapter 9 remain the same regardless of the size of the ensemble. The same five basic techniques demonstrated in Exs. 9-1, 9-2, and 16-2 still apply to 8 brass. Please refer to Chapters 9 and 16, and Appendix A, to review these techniques.

As in the case of approach tones, the methods for dealing with repeated notes in the inner voices, static harmony, and good voice leading also remain the same regardless of the size of the ensemble. These principles are explained in detail in Sections 8-6 and 9-2 and Exs. 8-6, 9-3, 9-4, and 9-5. As always, the most important thing to remember about voice leading in general is that *the more interesting and musical the individual parts are for each player in an ensemble, the more musical and expressive the overall performance will be.*

22-5 Voicing Considerations If the Melody Is in the Low Mid-Register *(8 Brass)*

If the lead line is in the lower to low mid-register of the trumpet, it's impossible to create standard close or open position voicings with eight individual notes without sounding muddy, unless you're going for a more dissonant sound using "cluster voicings," which we'll examine in Chapter 26. Following are some basic guidelines for creating "consonant"-sounding voicings in this type of situation (see Ex. 22-2a).

1. Use various techniques of unison, octaves, homophonic texture (unison or octave melody over chords), or "cross-sectional" applications of close, semi-open, or open position voicings (e.g., 2 trumpets/3 trombones).
2. Allocate instruments according to register and desired color effects.
3. You can double or omit any chord tone.
4. You may introduce additional chord tones as the melody ascends, and vice versa.
5. Not all instruments need to be playing all of the time.

Ex. 22-2

Brass Voicing Examples—8 Brass: "Dancing on the Ceiling" by Rodgers & Hart, arranged by R. Sussman

a. Low Register Melody

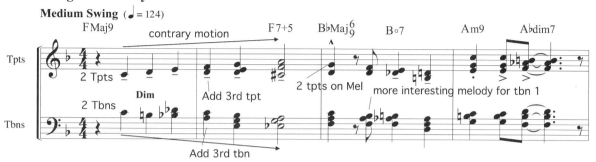

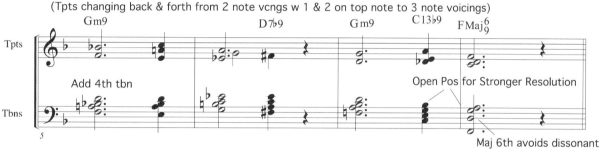

b. "The Basie Sound"

---

*In m. 10, there's a momentary break in the exact doubling of the trumpets by the trombones in order to create a more complex voicing with more dissonance. Trumpet 4 doubles the lead 8vb for one chord as trombone 1 moves to the chord ninth.

**In m. 11, trombone 1 again doubles the lead trumpet 8vb.

† B♭ lydian mode.

22-6 Voicing Considerations If the Melody Is in the Mid-Upper Register (8 Brass): "The Basie Sound"

We'll conclude our study of brass voicing techniques with a look at one of the most common and easily attainable of big band textures. "The Basie Sound," associated with the classic Count Basie bands of the 1950s and '60s, was first developed by arrangers such as Benny Carter, Frank Foster, Frank Wess, Neal Hefti, and Sammy Nestico, and is designed to produce maximum clarity, power, and mobility. However, in order for this technique to be effective, the lead line must be in the mid- to upper register of the trumpet (approximately from concert B♭ above middle C on up). If the lead line gets too low, you'll wind up with weak-sounding trumpet voicings and muddy trombone voicings, since they'll get pushed below the standard "low-interval limits."

There are two basic methods for achieving this sound.

1. *Style 1*—Voice the trumpets in close position, with trombone 1 doubling trumpet 1 8vb.
   a. Keep all chord tones (of each section) within one octave.
   b. The most common note choices will be the third, the fifth, the seventh, and the ninth, and occasionally the eleventh.
   c. The root will usually not be contained in the chord voicing of *Target Chords*, unless it is the melody note, or to avoid the interval of a second between the top 2 voices, or to create better voice leading in the inner voices by avoiding repeated notes or awkward skips. The root may be included in the chord voicings of *Approach Tones* when using any of the techniques for reharmonization of approach tones.
   d. Voice the trombones in close position, doubling the trumpets exactly one octave lower. The lead trombone will double the lead trumpet 8vb.
   e. *Don't overlap the trumpets and trombones.*

◊ Style 1 works best with a lead trumpet register from B♭ above middle C to B♭ above the staff, concert. If the melody gets much lower than that, both the trumpets and trombones will get pushed into weak and muddy registers, and the trombones will get pushed below the low interval limits established in Chapter 8. In this case it's best to use techniques described in Section 22-5. If the melody gets much higher than indicated, both trumpets and (especially) trombones will get pushed into their extreme upper register, and the sound will become overly intense and shrill. In this case it's best to use Style 2 described next.

2. *Style 2*—Voice the trumpets in semi-open position, with trumpet 4 doubling trumpet 1 8vb

a. The trumpet voicings will be primarily triads.

b. The most common note choices will be the third, the fifth, the seventh, the ninth, the thirteenth, and occasionally the eleventh.

c. The root will usually *not* be contained in the chord voicings of *Target Chords*, but may be used in voicings of *Approach Tones*, as described in Style 1 item c.

d. Voice the trombones in close, semi-open, or open position, supporting the trumpets using parallel, similar, oblique, or contrary motion.

e. The trombones will tend to be in the lower mid- to mid-register, often playing standard "piano left hand" voicings containing the third and the seventh of the chord.

f. Trombone 1 may occasionally double trumpet 4 in this voicing style, but the trumpets and trombones should *not* overlap, as in Style 1.

◊ Style 2 works best when the lead trumpet ascends into the upper register from D an octave above middle C to C above the staff and higher, concert. If the melody gets much lower than that, both the trumpets and trombones will get pushed into weak and muddy registers, and the trombones will get pushed below the low interval limits established in Chapter 8. In this case it's best to use Style 1 above or the techniques described in Section 22-5. With the lead trumpet reaching into its upper register, the trumpet section will sound more balanced, powerful, and less shrill voiced in triads rather than close position. Voicing the trombones a little lower, in semi-open position, will help balance the overall range of the entire brass section. If the lead trumpet goes into the extreme upper register (E above the staff or higher), it's best to voice the trumpets in drop-2, leaving a little more space between trumpets 1 and 2, to avoid an overly shrill and piercing sound. In this case, the lead would be doubled by trumpet 3.

◊ Important! It's critical to understand the distinction between *Target Notes* and *Approach Tones*, defined in Chapter 9, when harmonizing a line. The definition is repeated here for clarity: "Target notes tend to be longer or emphasized notes, usually the ones underneath chord symbols on a lead sheet, or at the end of a phrase, which can be harmonized directly by primary chord tones or tensions derived from the chord symbol. Approach tones, often referred to as *Passing Tones* in classical music theory, are the notes in between, often of shorter duration, leading to the target notes." The last note of a phrase should also usually be treated as a *Target Tone*, and harmonized with primary chord tones or alterations derived from the chord symbol.

Exs 22-2b, 22-3A, and 22-3B illustrate these two techniques. It's no accident that in Ex. 22-2b we switched to Technique 2 in measure 4. As explained above, it's almost always a good idea to open up your voicings as the lead trumpet ascends into the upper register. This is necessary to maintain balanced voicings. Consider what would happen if we continued with Style 1 in bars 4 and 5 of the example, keeping everything in close position. The trombones would be forced into their extreme upper register, and the resulting brass voicing would sound thin and top heavy. Ex. 22-3X illustrates some common mistakes made by students writing for big band for the first time. Listen to the recorded example on the companion website to hear what it sounds like when you don't follow some of the basic principles. Ex. 22-4, Dear Old Stockholm, provides another example of voicing 8 brass in both the low-mid and upper registers.

Ex. 22-3A

Brass Voicing Examples—8 Brass: "12-Bar Blues" Style 1, composed and arranged by Richard Sussman

Momentary break in style to get full F13 voicing

Momentary dissonance between tpt D nat. &
tbn Db OK for better tbn 1 voice leading

Ex. 22-3B

Brass Voicing Examples— 8 Brass: "12-Bar Blues" Style 2, composed and arranged by Richard Sussman

* Bb mixolydian +4

Ex. 22-3X

Brass Voicings Common Mistakes: "12-Bar Blues," composed and arranged by Richard Sussman

1) Tbns Too Low/Tpts & Tbns Too Far Apart

2) Tbns In Better Register/Tpts & Tbns Still Too Far Apart

3) Tbns Overlapping & Too High Relative to Tpts

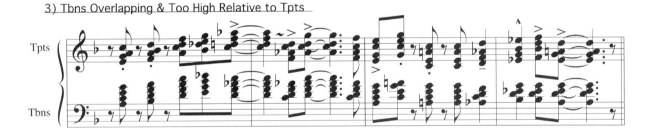

Ex. 22-4

Brass Voicing Examples — 8 Brass: "Dear Old Stockholm," traditional, arranged by Richard Sussman

* We broke one of our rules about not overlapping the trumpets & trombones here in order to avoid the dissonant major 2nd intervals between the trumpets & top 2 trombones.

22-7 When To Use Open Position Voicings

Because they will generally be spread out over a range of several octaves, as well as frequently having either the bass trombone or bari sax playing chord roots in the low register (below C2), open position voicings will tend to be both more powerful, as well as weightier than close and semi-open position voicings.

They will therefore generally work best in powerful sections such as shout choruses or kickers, or at slower tempos with notes of longer duration. Close and semi-open position voicings will tend to be lighter with greater mobility, and more suited for faster moving, syncopated lines, consisting of quarter notes, eighth and sixteenth notes, and triplets. That doesn't mean you can't occasionally throw in an open position voicing in a moving line, for extra emphasis, enhanced voice leading, or at the end of a phrase for extra emphasis at a cadence.

It's also perfectly OK to have a tightly voiced line moving over chord roots or other pedal tones of longer duration in the low register. (A good example of this kind of writing is mm. 9–11 of Ex.19-1A, Willie Smith's arrangement of "On a Misty Night," as well as the intro, vamps, and coda to Ex, 22-4, "Dear Old Stockholm." "On a Misty Night" also provides a good example of moving effectively from close to semi-open to open position and back throughout the entire chart.) It's only when all voices are moving in rhythmic unison at medium to fast tempos that open position can become cumbersome and heavy-handed.

22-8 Software Considerations

By this point you should be fairly familiar with most basic functions in Finale or Sibelius or both. You should have some templates established and tailored to your individual system, enabling you to play back your scores using synthesizer and/or sampled sounds. This provides a quick and easy way to check your voicings to see if everything's working or not. However, it can also lead you into some dangerous traps.

Sampled sounds (even from the best libraries) don't sound exactly like the real acoustic instruments for which you're writing. The overtone structures are different, and some voicings that sound good with samples won't sound the same with acoustic instruments, and vice versa.

It's often a good idea to try playing your voicings on a good acoustic piano. The natural overtones produced by an acoustic piano will often provide a more realistic sense of what your brass and sax voicings will sound like than your sample libraries. Of course, whenever possible, print out the parts and have the music played by live players.

Here's a good way to illustrate this point using the tools provided in this book: Download the MIDI files for Ex. 22-3A, or Ex. 22-3B from the companion website and copy the trumpet voicings from one of them into the trumpet 1 staff of your Big Band Template. Then "explode" the music downward so that you wind up with four separate trumpet parts, one per staff. Do the same thing with the trombones. Then use your playback controls to play back the music using the best trumpet and trombone samples at your disposal. Compare that with the sound of real instruments on the companion website's recording of the same example.

The computer is also capable of easily playing parts that would be technically impossible on an acoustic instrument. Always take the time to make sure your parts are technically playable by the real instruments for which you're writing. Make sure you leave space for wind players to breathe. Playing the trumpet or trombone in the upper registers for long periods of time can be physically exhausting. Be kind to your brass players! There are technical limitations to the slide trombone that make certain passages extremely difficult or unplayable. Example 22-5 provides a rather extreme and somewhat humorous illustration of this. Download the MIDI file for this example, and play it back using your best trumpet sample. Sounds pretty hip. Now give it to a real trumpet player to play, and see what kind of reaction you get.

Refer to the basic information on the practical ranges and technical limitations of the instruments in Chapter 3. In Sibelius you can turn on colors in the score, which causes notes out of the practical range of an instrument to appear in red. In Finale you can use the "Check Range" plug-in under Plug-ins > Scoring and Arranging > Check Range. We still recommend that any aspiring arranger be thoroughly familiar with the ranges, transpositions, and technical limitations of all instruments for which you will be writing.

The best way to learn this is to talk with other instrumentalists about technical issues relating to their instruments. Have them demonstrate the sound of their instruments in various registers and with different articulations and mutes. Always make sure that the musical choices you make are based on the sounds that you hear from within, not your computer's playback capabilities. Following is a Listening List of tracks that illustrate some of the techniques described in this chapter. For a more extensive listening list refer to Appendix B on the companion website.

Ex. 22-5

Unplayable

Big Band Listening List

1. Count Basie—*Chairman of the Board*, Roulette, 1958.
   a. "TV Time" (Frank Foster).
   b. "Half Moon Street" (Frank Wess).
   c. "Kansas City Shout" (Ernie Wilkins).
2. Count Basie—*Echoes of an Era*, Roulette, 1958–1961.
   a. "The Trot" (Benny Carter).
   b. "The Swizzle" (Benny Carter).
   c. "Rat Race" (Quincy Jones).
   d. "Mutt and Jeff" (Thad Jones).
3. Count Basie—*The Atomic Basie*, Roulette, 1957.
   a. "The Kid from Red Bank" (Neil Hefti).
   b. "Splanky" (Neil Hefti).
4. Duke Ellington—*The Great Paris Concert*, Atlantic, 1963.
   a. "Kinda Dukish"/"Rockin' in Rhythm".
   b. "Perdido".
   c. "Happy Go Lucky Local".

Chapter Summary

In this chapter we reviewed some basic harmonic and voicing principles as applied to writing for 8 brass in rhythmic unison. We examined how various techniques may be employed depending on the register of the lead line. We also described two distinct methods for achieving the classic "Basie sound" for 8 brass. Finally, we provided a suggested Listening List specific to topics discussed in this chapter.

Exercises

◊ Listen to as much big band jazz as possible. Get the sound of those instruments in your "inner ear." Refer to the preceding Listening List and the one near the end of Chapter 20, or in Appendix B on the website.

Use "Speedy Entry" in Finale or "Note Input" in Sibelius to do the following.

1. Do Brass Voicing Exercise 22-1, "12-Bar Blues." (Use the Piano Grand Staff Template.)
   a. Voice for 8 brass using Style 1 (trombones doubling trumpets 8vb).
   b. Voice for 8 brass using Style 2 (trumpet 4 doubling trumpet 1 8vb).

Exercise 22-1

12 Bar Blues

 For best results, please do the exercises yourself first, before referring to the solutions on the website! When you've tried it yourself, compare to Solutions 22-1A and B

2. Download Solutions # 22-1A and B "12-Bar Blues" from the website. Print out your solutions to the exercises and compare to the sample solutions on the website.

3. Voice (for 8 brass) "Somebody Loves Me" or any standard that ascends by step-wise motion in the low mid-register such as "Dancing On the Ceiling" or "Dear Old Stockholm." Use these two examples as models for your solution. Hint: not all instruments need to playing at the same time. Use a combination of appropriate voicing techniques based on the register of the lead line. (Use the Piano Grand Staff Template.)

4. If you have access to a large jazz ensemble, copy your solutions into the Jazz Big Band Template using the "Explode Music" technique described at the end of Chapters 9 and 18. Copy and paste the treble clef trumpet voicings from the piano sketch of Exercise 22-1 or 22-3 into the trumpet 1 staff of the Big Band Template. Then use "Explode Music" to separate the chords into the four individual trumpet parts. Copy and paste the bass clef trombone voicings into the trombone 1 staff and do the same thing. Then generate and print out the parts, and have the exercises played by the brass section. Note that "Explode Music" will work best on Exercise 22-1, where you'll have four distinct notes for each chord. With Exercise 22-3 you may have to do a little additional copying and pasting to make the individual parts complete.

Chapter 23

Concerted Writing for Saxes/Combining Brass and Saxes

As we direct our attention to the task of voicing for the standard five-piece saxophone section, we find that many of the same principles used in the preceding chapter for voicing for 8 brass also apply to the saxophone section. The main differences are that the timbre of the saxophones is mellower and not as bright as that of brass instruments and that there are fewer instruments in the section (5 saxes compared to 7 or 8 brass).

As stated in Chapter 20, the standard modern big band saxophone section consists of two altos, two tenors, and one baritone. Occasionally the lead alto may be replaced by a clarinet (a sound made famous by Glenn Miller, Benny Goodman, and other swing band leaders in the 1930s and 1940s) or a soprano sax. Most contemporary reed players are proficient on a number of doubles, such as clarinets and flutes in addition to various saxophones, and a tremendous number of woodwind colors are generally available to the present-day jazz arranger. However, the standard five-piece sax section described here is so prevalent that we believe it's important to first focus on writing for this particular instrumentation. We'll return to the woodwind doubles, in detail, in Chapter 28.

23-1 Standard Voicing Techniques for Saxes

Our first concern is to create homogeneous and balanced chord voicings for the sax section, in close, semi-open, and open position, as we did for the brass section in the preceding chapter. In fact, we've already done this in Chapter 16 (Exs. 16-1A and 16-3)! We demonstrated there that the standard voicing positions can be fully realized with five instruments. If we take Ex. 16-1A and simply change the instrument assignments, replacing the brass instruments with saxophones, we have a perfect illustration of standard voicings for the sax section (see Ex. 23-1). All of the other basic voicing principles and rules from Chapters 8 and 16 also apply to writing for the sax section.

Ex. 23-1

Standard Jazz Voicing Positions—5 Saxes: "I Could Write a Book by Rodgers & Hart"

It should thus come as no surprise that the principles for dealing with reharmonization of approach tones, repeated notes, static harmony, and good voice leading in general also apply to saxophones. The same is true for the techniques of dealing with low mid-register lead lines described in Section 22-5.

23-2 Combining Brass and Saxes: Constant and Variable Coupling

Our next goal is to add the full sax section to the eight-piece brass section voicings we arrived at in the preceding chapter. Specifically, we want to flesh out the "Basie Sound" by adding five saxes to the brass section in order to create a powerful, vibrant, full tutti passage in rhythmic unison for the full big band. If you can master the principles outlined in this and the previous chapter, you'll have a solid foundation for working out big band voicings in any style.

There are several important concepts underlying this procedure. First of all, for this particular voicing style we'll be *adding* the saxes to the brass, *not* integrating the two sections (you'll have plenty of opportunities to do that later on). Second, we want each section, brass and saxes, to sound complete within itself. That means that most of the time each section, brass or saxes, will form chord voicings on *destination tones,* or *target tones,* containing the chord third and seventh and at least one other chord tone. Sax voicings of passing chords should also contain at least three separate chord tones in order to sound complete.

Using this method, the chord voicings are first worked out for the brass section. Then the saxes are added to the brass by doubling notes in the brass section, generally without adding any new notes not played by the brass. The result is a lean and dynamic voicing, relatively simple harmonically (typically with only four notes per chord), and with each note of the chord being doubled at least twice, for maximum power and mobility. It doesn't matter whether you use "Basie Sound" Style 1 or Style 2 from Chapter 22 or whether there are three or four trombones in the trombone section. The method for voicing the saxophones will remain the same.

The key to this method is first to work out the lead alto line. There are two main options.

1. *Constant Coupling*: The lead alto doubles one of the trumpet lines exactly, note for note. The other sax parts may be filled in using close, semi-open, or open position techniques or simply by copying the lines from the corresponding brass parts. The decision as to which trumpet part the lead alto should double is a function of the trumpet section register. If the lead trumpet stays in the mid-register (within the staff), the lead alto can double the lead trumpet for maximum power. However, if the lead trumpet rises above the staff, which is often the case, the alto would be forced into its highest register (or out of its range entirely), resulting

in a shrill and unbalanced sound. The most logical choices are for the lead alto to double either the second, third, or fourth trumpet (and occasionally the lead trombone), filling in the notes of the rest of the saxes, as described earlier (see Ex. 23-2A). In any case, in this style the saxes generally move in parallel motion with the brass.

Ex. 23-2A

Combining Brass and Saxes: Constant Coupling; composed and arranged by Richard Sussman

1. Voice the melody for the brass section using primarily close and semi-open position voicings.

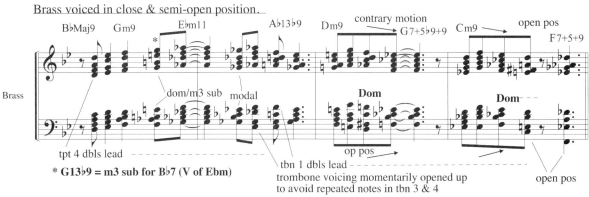

2. Create the lead alto part by choosing one of the trumpet parts to double. In this case the lead alto doubles the second trumpet.

3. Voice the rest of the sax section below the lead alto, using primarily close and semi-open position voicings.

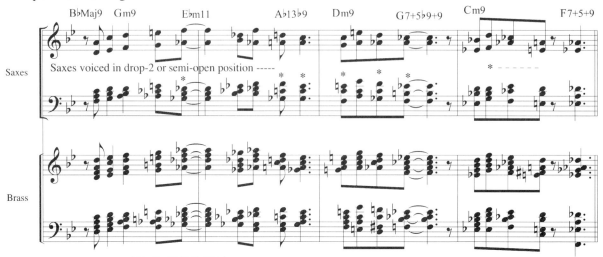

*In mm 1, 2, and 3, the saxes momentarily spread out to include the third and seventh for a more complete voicing.

*In m. 4, the change of position in the saxes is to improve the melodic lines of the inner voices.

2. *Variable Coupling*: The lead alto part is constructed by extracting notes from the various trumpet parts, in a linear fashion, creating a more interesting melody. The choice of which trumpet notes to double will be a function of the creative instincts and skill of the arranger with regard to the principles for constructing a good melody discussed in Chapter 7. Occasionally notes not found in the brass voicing may be used to create a more satisfying lead alto melody. The other sax parts are filled in as previously by using techniques of close, semi-open, or open position voicings. In this case the sax section may move in similar, oblique, or contrary as well as parallel motion to the brass. Variable coupling gives the arranger more creative freedom. See Ex. 23-2B for an illustration of this technique.

Ex. 23-2B

Combining Brass and Saxes: Variable Coupling; composed and arranged by Richard Sussman

1. Voice the melody for the brass section using primarily close and semi-open position voicings.

2. Create the lead alto part by choosing notes from various trumpet parts to create a more interesting melody moving in contrary motion to the lead trumpet.

3. Voice the rest of the sax section below the lead alto, using primarily close and semi-open position voicings.

In this example, care was taken to ensure interesting melodic lines in the inner voices, rather than simply filling in the notes by mechanically applying close position or drop-2.

*Indicates sax voicing contains notes not duplicated exactly from brass voicing.

◊ We've provided two mixes of Exs. 23-2A and 23-2B. First, a full mix with brass and saxes and then a mix with saxes and rhythm only. Listen to the mix with just saxes a few times; then go back to the full mix and see if you can hear how the saxes are working in relation to the brass. Ex. 23-3 is our close position 12-bar blues brass voicing Ex. 22-3A from the last chapter, with the saxes now added using the technique of variable coupling. Notice how the lead alto part jumps around quite a bit from one trumpet part to another, to create a more interesting melody, descends to double the lead trombone part in mm. 9–10 to balance the high register brass voicings, and expands to full open position, moving in contrary motion for the half-step, tritone sub resolution on the last two chords. Notice also how the sax voicing descends below the trombones to balance the high brass register in the first two bars. The saxes play only notes contained in the brass voicings throughout the entire example, although sometimes in different registers, except for two notes in m. 10 (marked *), the A (chordal thirteenth) on beat 3, and the low G♭ (V tritone sub) on beat 4.

◊ It's possible to voice the saxes in this style using only notes actually found in the various trumpet and trombone parts. In fact, we recommend this as a good way for the beginning arranger to approach the following exercises. However, in some situations it's acceptable, and in fact desirable, to bend these rules a little. First of all, if a chord tone (say, the 13th) is played by the trumpets but not the trombones (or vice versa), it's OK for a saxophone to play that chord tone in the lower (or higher) register. Second, if the entire brass section ascends to the upper register (not uncommon), it can be effective to voice the saxes below the brass, to balance the overall chord voicing.

Finally, there are many occasions when using chord tones in the saxes not played by the brass is fine, provided that unwanted dissonances are not produced by doing so and if it creates better voice leading in the saxes and a more satisfying musical result overall. In Solutions 23-1, 23-2, and 23-3 we've taken liberties with the rules in this regard, making our priority the best possible musical solution rather than strict adherence to the rules!

Ex. 23-3

Combining Brass and Saxes: "12-Bar Blues, composed and arranged by Richard Sussman"

305

* indicates sax notes not contained in the brass voicings.

Ex. 23-4 is our brass voicing Ex. 22-4, "Dear Old Stockholm," from the last chapter, with the saxes now added using a variety of techniques. Notice that we've taken some creative liberties in how the saxes are utilized in this arrangement, again illustrating that the most musical results are often not achieved by following mechanical formulas. In the four bar intro, the bari replaces the bass trombone for contrast. In m. 5 the altos and tenors essentially double the brass voicings, but in mm 6–7 jump to an octave doubling to reinforce the melody, expanding to some nice fat open position voicings at the end of m. 7. In mm. 9–16, the saxes support the trombones in open position. They continue to support the trombones in the first ending, and support the entire brass section in the second ending. Finally, in mm. 21–24 we use some constant coupling, with the lead alto doubling trumpet 4 for most of the passage, although with quite a few notes not contained in the brass voicings thrown in for color by the rest of the sax section. In the coda, the saxes first harmonize the unison trumpet melody, then reinforce the low trombone hit in m. 28, and finally utilize a constant coupling technique, with the lead alto doubling the lead trumpet 8vb, in the last three measures (until the last two notes).

Ex. 23-4

Combining Brass and Saxes: "Dear Old Stackholm," traditional, arranged by Richard Sussman

* indicates sax notes not contained in the brass voicings.

Here the saxes reinforce the low tbn hits.

Here the saxes are used differently - to harmonize the unison trumpet melody.

** here there is no F present in the brass voicing, so this is an added note, but one that makes sense if you interpret the chord as G13♭9+11/C.

23-3 Summary of Basic Principles of Combining Brass and Saxes: "The Basie Sound"

Following are some basic principles and guidelines for combining brass and saxes to achieve the "Basie Sound" for jazz big band:

1. The simpler the harmonic content, the more vibrant the overall sound (e.g., with four note chords and thirteen instruments, each note will be doubled/reinforced several times).

2. Voice each section so that it forms a complete chord (ideally containing at least the third, the seventh, and one additional chord tone) within itself.

3. Voice the brass section first, using close, semi-open, or open position.

4. Add sax voicings to the brass using the techniques of constant or variable coupling, with close, semi-open, or open position voicings.

5. The saxes should be added to the brass, voiced as a separate entity (complete within itself), not integrated with the brass but supporting them where appropriate, based on register. Saxes will mainly be doubling notes contained in the brass voicings. There are some situations where it's OK for the saxes to play notes not contained in the brass voicing, to add extra color to the chord, or create better voice leading for the saxes.

6. Always be conscious of the principle of internal resonance and the relative degree of consonance or dissonance in the voicings within each section.

7. Use logical voice leading to create continuity of the melodic lines and melodic interest for the inner voices. Each part should be as melodically interesting as possible. Generally this means inner voices moving by step or thirds. No inner voice should skip by a third more than the lead line.

8. It's not necessary to adhere strictly to any one technique within a particular passage (e.g., contrast techniques of constant and variable coupling with other techniques, such as unison, octaves, counterpoint, and melody over sustained chords).

9. Strive for contrast in texture and register.

10. Things to avoid:

    a. Avoid voicing the saxes too low (refer to low-interval limits in Section 8-2).

    b. Avoid too many roots in the baritone sax. The bari sax and bass trombone should generally be playing roots only in the most powerful, open position sections or in spread voicings (discussed in Chapter 26) for ballads and slower tempos.

    c. Avoid too many isolated sax notes (not contained in the brass voicing).

    d. Avoid excessive chordal fifths (unless going for a light and airy sound) - ninths, elevenths, and thirteenths will be more colorful).

    e. Avoid excessive repeated notes in inner voices (see Chapter 9).

    f. Avoid awkward skips (always) or crossing voices within inner voices, except to avoid excessive repeated notes (see number 7 above).

    g. Don't double the bari sax and bass trombone, especially in the low register, except for special effects.

11. *Observe all other previously discussed principles of good chord voicings and voice leading.*

The choices as to which chord tones should be doubled or omitted are subjective and should be based on the relative degree of consonance or dissonance desired in a given passage.

23-4 Reharmonization of Approach Tones, Repeated Notes, and Voice Leading for 5 Saxes

All the techniques for dealing with reharmonization of approach tones, repeated notes, and voice leading presented in Chapters 8, 9, and 16 are applicable to writing for the sax section. Please refer to those chapters as well as to Appendix A, "Summary of Basic Arranging and Voicing Principles," on the website.

At this point, decisions regarding which type of voicing position to use (e.g., close, drop-2, open) for the brass or saxes should be based primarily on register and on considerations of intensity, density, and balance. As the melody rises into the upper register, close position voicings will naturally start to sound more intense. This can be balanced by opening up the sax and trombone voicings to semi-open or open position. Close position voicings and clusters (discussed in Chapter 26) will sound denser. Chords will generally sound more balanced with larger intervals on the bottom, with the third and seventh of the chord in the low mid-register, and with upper-structure chord tones and smaller intervals in the upper register.

The decision as to when and how to reharmonize approach tones is also subjective; it depends essentially on how colorful you want a harmonized line to sound (see Chapter 9).

Chapter Summary

In this chapter we continued the study of concerted (full tutti) writing begun in the previous chapter. We then examined methods for combining the brass and saxophone sections using the techniques of constant or variable coupling and reviewed some general principles regarding voicings and voice leading.

◊ **Software Tip**: It's possible to make audio mixes of your scores in both Finale and Sibelius. This can be especially convenient if you want to listen to the score or play it for someone away from your computer. You can print out a copy of the score and play it as an mp3 or a CD.

Both programs have mixing boards (in Finale, ⌘-option-M/Mac or Control-Shift-M/WIN, or "M" in Sibelius), which allow you to record and control the volume of each instrument with greater precision. You can also add reverb and other effects through whichever AU or VST virtual instruments and plug-ins you have available. It's definitely worth spending a little extra time with this before converting your mix to an audio file. When you're ready, simply go to File > Export to Audio File in Finale to export as a standard audio file or mp3, or File > Export > Audio in Sibelius.

Exercises

◊ Listen to as much big band jazz as possible. Get the sound of those instruments in your "inner ear." Refer to the Listening Lists near the end of Chapters 20 and 22, and in Appendix B on the website.

Use your note entry method of choice in Finale or Sibelius for the following exercises. For best results, please do the exercises yourself first *before* referring to the solutions on the companion website!

Exercise 23-1

Combining Brass and Saxes

1. Constant Coupling - Voice the Brass using close or semi-open position. Then, using constant coupling, voice the saxes in close or semi-open position. The last few chords can be open position.

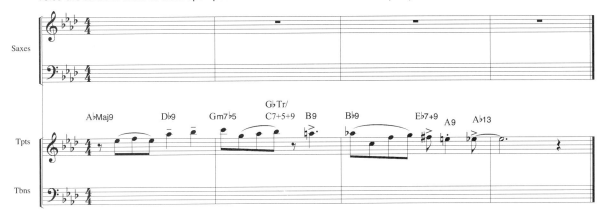

2. Variable Coupling - Voice the Brass using close or semi-open position. Then, using variable coupling, voice the saxes in close or semi-open position. The last few chords can be open position.

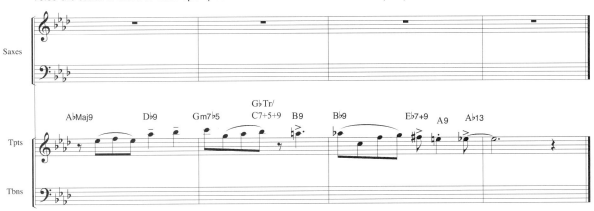

3. Constant and Variable Coupling - Voice the Brass using close or semi-open position. Then, using a combination of constant and variable coupling, voice the saxes in close or semi-open position. The last few chords can be open position.

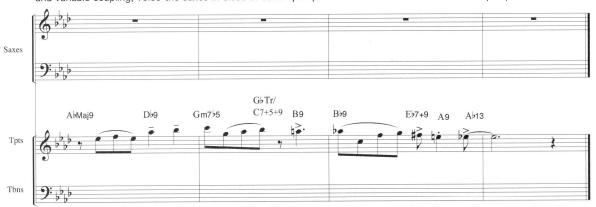

1. Do Exercise 23-1, "Combining Brass and Saxes." You can download the file from the website or use the 4-Stave Brass/Saxes Template.
   a. First voice the brass section using mainly close or semi-open position.
   b. Voice the sax section using the technique of constant coupling.
   c. Voice the sax section using the technique of variable coupling.
   d. Voice the sax section combining the techniques of constant and variable coupling.

2. Pick one of your solutions to brass voicing Exercise 22-1, "12-Bar Blues." Add five saxes using techniques of constant and/or variable coupling. Use the 4-Stave Brass/Saxes Template. Start by copying and pasting your brass voicings from Exercise 22-1 into the brass staves of the new 4-stave template; then add the saxes. Use Ex. 23-3, "12-Bar Blues," as a model for this exercise.

3. Add saxophones to your brass solution of Exercise 22-3. Use Ex. 22-4, "Dear Old Stockholm," as a model for this exercise. Use the same methods as in Exercise 23-2. *Hint:* Not all instruments need to be playing all the time. Use the 4-Stave Brass/ Saxes Template.

4. Print out your solutions to Exercises 23-1 and 23-2 and compare to the sample solutions and recordings on the companion website (Solutions 23-1A, B, and C, and 23-2, "12-Bar Blues").

5. If you have access to a large jazz ensemble, copy your solutions into the Jazz Big Band Template using the "Explode Music" technique described at the end of the last chapter. Then generate and print out the parts and have the exercises played by the full band. Note that "Explode Music" will work best with Exercises 1 and 2. With Exercise 23-3, you may have to do a little extra copying and pasting to make the individual parts complete.

◊ Listen to the recordings of the solutions to Exercises 23-1 on the companion website. We've provided two mixes of all the solutions to Exercise 23-1, first a full mix with brass and saxes and then a mix with saxes and rhythm only. Listen to the mix with just saxes a few times; then go back to the full mix and see if you can hear how the saxes are working in relation to the brass.

Go to the website to download and listen to the solutions to Exercises 23-1A, B, & C (Exercise 23-1, "Sxs & Br" Solutions).

Go to the website to download the solution to Ex. 23-2 (Solution 23-2) (Exercise 23-2 "12-Bar Blues" Solution).

Chapter 24

Big Band Instrumental Subdivisions

In the preceding two chapters we treated the brass and saxes as separate entities, each voiced complete unto itself, starting with the brass section and then adding the saxes to the brass. The emphasis was on concerted, full tutti writing, with everyone in rhythmic unison—the most powerful of big band timbres, suitable for shout choruses and peak sections of the head, intro, or ending. We also examined the techniques of unison and octave writing in Chapter 21. Before plunging into our first full-scale big band arrangement, it's important to consider some other scoring possibilities for brass and saxes.

24-1 Contrasting the Brass and Sax Sections

One of the most time-honored jazz big band techniques, going all the way back to Fletcher Henderson and Don Redman's early charts of the 1920s and used effectively over and over again throughout the swing period of the 1930s and 1940s, is that of contrasting and playing the brass and sax sections off against each other. In its most basic form, this can be in "call and response" format, using blues-based riffs or other relatively simple melodic material with the full brass and sax sections or smaller subdivisions of each. For example, you can contrast all eight brass against all five saxes or treat the trumpets, trombones, and saxes as three distinct sections. Or you could create smaller subsections within the band, such as three trumpets and two trombones contrasting with three saxes or two trumpets and one trombone against two tenors.

    One of the reasons this type of orchestration is so effective is that there is such a distinct difference in timbre between brass and saxophones, so the contrast can be direct, obvious, and dramatic. One section plays a short melodic phrase, usually one to four bars long, answered by the other section. In its simplest form, the phrases are distinct and don't overlap. The level of complexity can be increased by having the phrases overlap and repeat, forming a kind of rhythmic and melodic counterpoint where the various parts fit together like pieces of a puzzle.

For a great early example of this sound, listen to "Every Tub" or "Doggin' Around" from the 1938 Count Basie Decca recordings. The effect is mesmerizing, rhythmically infectious, and very "danceable," similar to modern-day R&B recordings of the 1960s, '70s, and '80s. Compare these early Basie (and other swing band) recordings to anything by the Temptations, James Brown, or other Motown and R&B artists. The main difference, along with the feel of the rhythm section groove, is that in R&B the riffs are being played by guitars and keyboards (and sometimes horns) or sung, rather than being played by brass and saxes.

In this type of writing, the sections are typically voiced in close or semi-open position or scored in unison or octaves. Some additional examples of this type of sectional writing would include a melody played in unison/octaves or voiced by one section with rhythmic hits by the contrasting section, a melody played over any type of chordal accompaniment played by the other section, or the brass and sax sections playing independent, contrapuntal lines.

Example 24-1, the 12-bar blues "Riffology," is an illustration of basic riff-type scoring, which builds from simple to more complex writing throughout the 12-bar chorus. The first two bars consist of a simple one-bar ascending bluesy line played in octaves by the saxes, answered by a one-bar descending riff played in octaves by the brass. In mm. 3–4, the last note of each phrase is harmonized. In mm. 5–8, the saxes stay in octaves, but the brass begin to play their line in parallel sixths, first by the trumpets (m. 6) and then joined by the trombones (mm. 7–8). The entrance of the brass riff also begins to overlap the saxes, first by one beat (m. 6) and then by three beats (mm. 7–8), creating some interesting, bluesy counterpoint as well as increasingly dissonant chord voicings. The texture changes dramatically in m. 9, with the saxes playing a simple three-note figure in drop-2, answered by forceful rhythmic hits in open position by the brass. The two sections come together in full tutti for the final phrase in m. 11. The gradual increase of harmonic and contrapuntal complexity creates a natural build of intensity from the beginning to the end of the passage.

Example 24-2 is the intro and first eight bars of the head to "Fletcher," a chart by Richard Sussman commissioned by Dean Pratt in the 1980s. This chart, written after many hours spent listening to and studying Fletcher's scores, provides a good example of some of the different variations of sectional writing we've been discussing. We'll analyze this chart in more detail in Chapter 33, and sections of the full chart are available for download on the companion website. (Please note: Audio Ex. 24-2 contains the entire head to "Fletcher". Refer to Ex. 33-1A in the text for a reduction, or Ex. 33-1A on the website for a full score of the complete passage.)

Ex. 24-1

"Riffology," composed and arranged by Richard Sussman

Ex 24-2 "Fletcher" Intro-Head

Richard Sussman

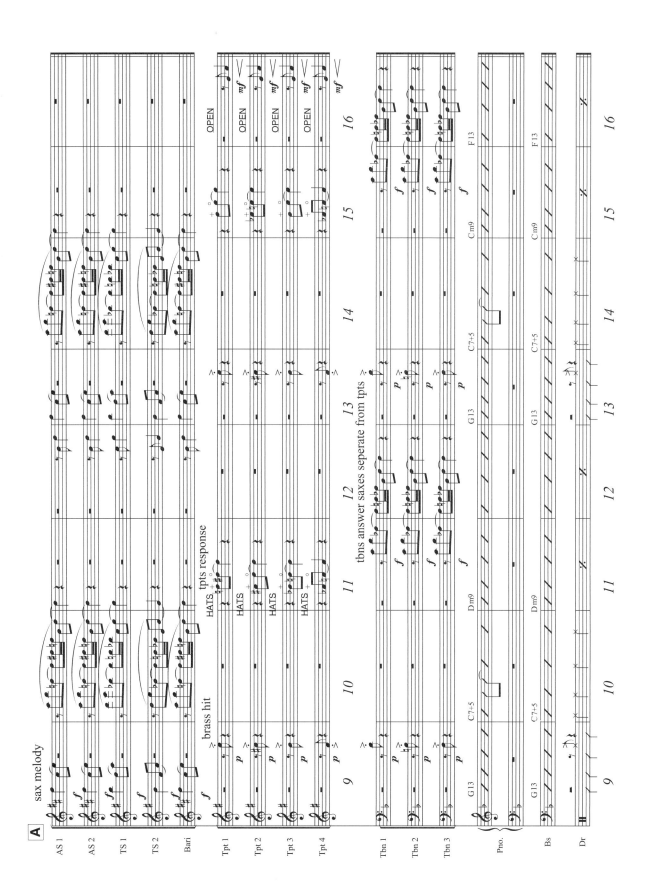

Ex 24-2 "Fletcher" - 2

24-2 Cross-Sectional Instrumental Subdivisions

It's possible to create a wide array of *cross-sectional* instrumental combinations and subdivisions within the big band. This is an effective and musical way of providing a variety of timbres and instrumental textures, in contrast to the homogeneous sound of the separate brass and sax sections we've examined up to this point. Cross-sectional groupings can be used in unison/octaves or harmonized settings. The same principles we've applied to the brass and sax sections regarding chord voicings, voice leading, melodic motion, and texture are equally relevant to cross-sectional groupings.

For example, instead of having the melody played by the trumpets, with a sax section chordal accompaniment and rhythmic hits by the trombones, we could create three cross-sectional groupings within the band and assign different functions to each. Let's create one grouping consisting of two trumpets, one tenor sax, and one trombone (group A). The second grouping will consist of one alto sax, baritone sax, one trumpet in Harmon mute, one trombone in bucket mute, piano in octaves, and guitar (group B). The third grouping will consist of one flugelhorn, one alto sax and one tenor sax, one tenor trombone, and one bass trombone (group C). Now we'll give groups A and B each a contrasting melodic line and assign chord voicings in semi-open or open position to group C.

Example 24-3A, "Cross Section" Sketch, is our initial sketch of this idea. As you can see, we anticipated having the three groups come together in full tutti at the end of the eight-bar phrase. In Example 24-3B we've fleshed out the score for the big band. Notice how, as we got into the scoring process, the natural flow of the musical phrases began to suggest other scoring possibilities. We wound up bringing groups A and B together for a full chord voicing in bar 5 as group C switches to an octave melodic figure—a kind of role reversal of the groupings that provides an unexpected timbral twist. We'll take a closer look at the process of how we arrived at the final version of "Cross Section" in the next chapter.

Another option for cross-section scoring is to combine a homogeneous section sound with a heterogeneous cross-sectional sound. For example, we could have a melody played by four trumpets in unison over chords played by a grouping of three saxes and three trombones. Ex. 24-4 illustrates an example of this type of scoring with the tune "Unithology" from Chapter 21.

The possibilities are endless, and we encourage you to experiment with any possible cross-sectional combinations you can imagine, including the use of the rhythm section to play melodic lines.

Ex. 24-3A

"Cross-Section" Sketch, composed and arranged by Richard Sussman

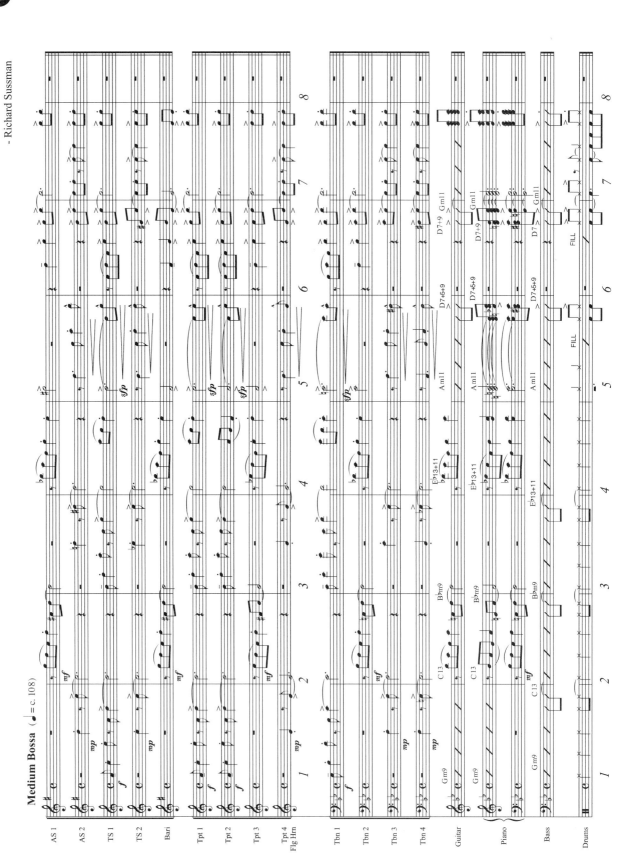

Ex 24-3B "Cross-Section" Score

- Richard Sussman

Ex 24-4 Cross-Sectional "Unithology"

- Richard Sussman

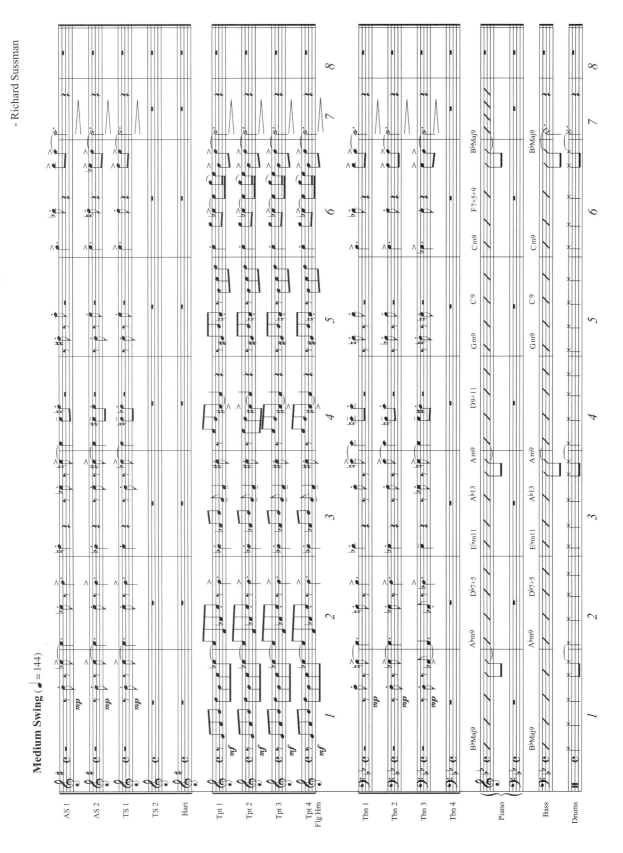

Chapter Summary

In this chapter we examined different ways of grouping the instruments of the band in order to provide the arranger with a variety of contrasting instrumental timbres. First we looked at the technique of assigning contrasting functions to the full brass and sax sections. We then examined the possibilities of creating cross-sectional groupings and smaller instrumental subdivisions within the band. We'll return to this concept in Chapter 28 when we reexamine the use of woodwind doubles and brass mutes for the big band.

◊ **Software Tip**: It's important for anyone working with a notation program such as Finale or Sibelius to be familiar with the basic MIDI concepts outlined in Chapter 5. Although it is possible to input music in both Finale and Sibelius using only the computer keyboard and mouse, it's much more common, and probably more musical, to use a MIDI keyboard to input notes. *MIDI Patch Thru* or *Instrument Assign* is the function available in most sequencers and notation programs that enables you to determine how the MIDI keyboard will interact with the synths and sampled sounds (whether hardware or virtual) available to the particular program and MIDI configuration. This allows you to route the outgoing Note On/Off and other MIDI messages coming from the keyboard to the appropriate sound sources.

The default settings in Finale, Sibelius, and most sequencers enable you to hear the sound assigned to whichever track or staff you have selected while playing the MIDI keyboard, which is logical, since this setting allows you automatically to hear a saxophone sound when a sax staff is selected and a trumpet sound when that staff is selected, etc. However, there are some situations where it can be useful to override this setting so that you can hear a piano or some other sound regardless of which track or staff is selected. Please refer to the website for more details on this technique.

◊ **Software Tip**: MIDI *stuck notes* (when the MIDI Note Off message gets somehow lost or deleted), common in the early days of MIDI, have resurfaced as an annoyance with the advent of virtual instruments. Most MIDI software provides the ability to send a MIDI *All Notes Off message*. Be sure you know how to access this function (MIDI/Audio > All Notes Off in Finale and Play > All Notes Off in Sibelius).

Exercises

◊ Continue listening to as much big band jazz as possible. Get the sound of those instruments in your "inner ear." Refer to the Listening Lists near the end of Chapters 20 and 22, and in Appendix B on the website.

Use "Speedy Note Entry" in Finale or "Note Input" in Sibelius for the following exercises.

1. Compose a riff-type 12-bar blues similar to "Riffology." Orchestrate it for the brass and sax sections as in Example 24-1, using one- or two-bar phrases for each section. Use the 4-Stave Brass/Saxes Template.

2. Create two or three cross-sectional subdivisions within the big band. Using the eight-bar melody provided in Exercise 24-2. Assign the melody to one subdivision, and create a chordal accompaniment and/or contrapuntal line for the other subdivision(s). Use the Jazz Big Band Template. Try downloading the file Exercise 24-2 from the website; then copy and paste the melody and other parts into appropriate staves in the template.

3. If possible, extract and print out the parts (as described at the end of Chapters 22 and 23) and have them played.

Exercise 24-2

Cross-Sectional

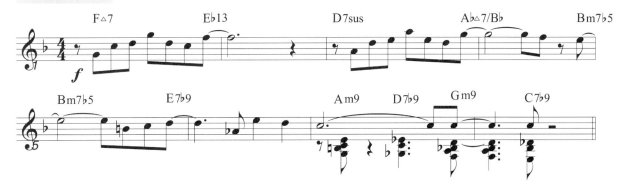

Chapter 25

Form and Planning the Arrangement

Having a game plan and some type of rough outline for an arrangement before you start writing is just as important, or even more so, for the big band as for smaller ensembles. All of the basic concepts presented in Chapters 11 and 17 regarding the elements of the form, outlining and graphing the form, instrumentation, and having a clear concept and direction for an arrangement are applicable to writing for the full big band. Similarly, the techniques for creating intros, transitions or kickers, background parts, and codas or endings can also be applied to the larger ensemble. It would be a good idea to review Chapters 11 and 17 now before proceeding. We also suggest that you keep the Summary of Basic Arranging and Voicing Principles (Appendix A) handy for reference regarding any of the fundamental arranging principles covered so far.

25-1 Elements of Form

As in Chapters 11 and 17, we are concerned here primarily with the overall large form of an arrangement, including the intro, the exposition (head), transitional passages (kickers and interludes), improvised solos, backgrounds, the soli section, the shout chorus, the recap, and the coda or ending. Refer to Exs. 17-1, 17-2, and 17-3 for illustrations of various techniques for writing intros, transitions, backgrounds, and endings. These techniques are just as effective with ensembles of any size.

25-2 Instrumentation and Outlining the Form (Big Band)

Many of the workflow methods suggested in Chapters 11 and 17 for smaller groups are also relevant when working with the full big band. We strongly recommend creating and writing down a tentative outline of the arrangement and listing possible instrumentations for the various sections of the chart before actually beginning to score the music. In Chapter 20 we examined some features of the expanded sound palette and possible instrumental color combinations available with the full jazz big band.

One point we want to emphasize here is that there's no secret formula or one distinct method for approaching a big band arrangement (or a musical composition of any type). Different musical situations will call forth different approaches and methods of working. As we said in Chapter 1, once you break the ice and begin writing, the music has a way of taking on a life of its own and leading you in directions not anticipated at the outset. The process of musical composition can be a journey of exploration and discovery, full of surprises and unexpected twists and challenges along the way!

However, one thing we both definitely agree on is that in any writing situation, it's important from the beginning to have an outline or sense of direction as to the overall musical structure. As Michael puts it, "Even if I don't write it down, there's still an outline in my head. And, yes—for beginners—write it down! Who's the soloist? How are you going to get into the chart? Which instruments will play the melody on the head? Will there be a soli or shout chorus, etc.?" Nothing's written in stone, and your outline is very likely to change as you proceed, but it's important to have a plan and a sense of direction from the outset.

Following are some important considerations to keep in mind when outlining and planning the arrangement.

1. Who or what is the arrangement for? Is it for a specific band or artist, performance, recording session, or commission? If it's for a specific artist or ensemble, it may be useful to do a little homework and listen to some existing recordings to get familiar with the artist's or ensemble's style and musical preferences.

2. Were any specific requests made (or anything you believe should be considered) regarding musical style, instrumentation, tempo, meter, groove, key, etc.?

3. List available instrumental combinations and textures you may want to use. (See Sections 11-5, 17-3 and 20-3.)

4. Make sure you've thoroughly analyzed and understand the musical aspects of the tune to be arranged, even if it's an original tune.

5. Consider whether you might need any melodic alteration or reharmonization of the tune.

6. Write down a tentative outline of how you might orchestrate the different sections of the chart, paying special attention to the ebb and flow of intensity, tension and release, and the overall development of the form. (See Sections 11-5 and 17-3.)

7. Consider how you might want to contrast various instrumental textures, such as monophonic, homophonic, and polyphonic.

8. Consider what type of harmonic treatment and chord voicings are called for, including close, semi-open, and open position voicings, clusters, chords by fourths, and other techniques, as well as the relative degree of consonance and dissonance.

9. Consider possible cross-sectional instrumental groupings, the use of woodwind doubles and brass mutes, and the melodic use of rhythm section instruments.

10. Which instruments will play improvised solos, and what type of background parts are called for?

11. Will there be transitions, soli sections, a shout chorus, etc.?

12. What type of intro can be used to get into the piece, and how will the piece end?

13. What is the overall length of the piece, in measures and duration?

Following is a sample outline of a jazz big band arrangement for a standard AABA tune.

Sample Outline of Arrangement

1. *Intro*—4 Bars, full tutti, derived from the tune.
2. *Head*
   a. First "A"—2–5 saxes playing the melody in unison or octaves.
   b. Second "A"—2–3 trumpets (open or in mutes) playing the melody in unison or lightly voiced over mixed saxes and trombones playing sustained or rhythmic chords (homophonic texture).
   c. "B"—5 saxes voiced in close position or semi-open position. Add a slow, unison trombone countermelody and/or some brass hits. Build to the last "A."
   d. Last "A"—full tutti brass + saxes in rhythmic unison (lead trumpet melody doubled 8vb).
3. *Transition*—4-bar kicker overlapping the last two bars of the melody (derived from the intro) into the first solo.
4. *Improvised solo*—(trumpet 4) on the form of the tune.
5. *Backgrounds*—2nd X, add sax backgrounds—pads or a slow countermelody building to rhythmic hits and a kicker into the next solo—trumpets and trombones join saxes for the kicker.
6. *Repeat Steps 4–5 for the next solo*—piano solo with backgrounds.
7. *Sax soli*—16 bars voiced in close or semi-open position. Add brass hits and build to the shout chorus.

8. *Shout chorus*—16 bars of full tutti brass + saxes in rhythmic unison.

9. *D.S.*—recap of the head (on the entire form of the tune).

10. *Coda*—4 bars, full tutti, based on the intro.

25-3 Laying Out the Score and Workflow Concepts

When laying out the score for your first big band arrangement, we recommend following the workflow method described in Chapter 17. Although, as we said earlier, there's no one set way of approaching a musical arrangement, we both agree on the value of a few key points for beginners. This includes writing down an outline, starting with the head or body of the chart, then proceeding through subsequent sections (solos, backgrounds, soli, shout chorus, recap, coda, etc.), and at some point going back to fill in the intro. With more experience, you may find yourself starting with the intro or even with some ideas for middle sections of the arrangement. Ultimately, follow your musical and creative instincts, and go with whatever leads you to the desired result!

We'll be working now with the Jazz Big Band Template. We also recommend that you attempt to work with a transposed score, which gives you the advantage of seeing all the parts in their proper registers and transpositions, as they would appear on the parts. Of course, as we mentioned earlier, both Finale and Sibelius give you the option to switch easily between transposed and concert score views. Following is a review of the workflow method presented in Chapter 17.

1. Make a tentative outline of the arrangement, indicating instrumentation and textural changes for each section of the arrangement as described in Section 17-3 (e.g., which instruments will be playing the melody, which sections will be solo, unison or octaves, voiced, homophonic, contrapuntal).

2. Enter the chord changes into the piano part using slash or rhythmic notation. Michael confides that often he doesn't do this, because, while working on the horn parts, he may not know what the vertical harmonies or chord changes will be until after completing a section. Of course, in his head he knows what the underlying harmonies are—and you can always go back and change the chord symbols in the piano part if the horn parts dictate it.

3. Enter the lead (melody) lines for each section indicated in your outline. Use copy and paste functions for unison or octave doublings.

4. Go back and work out the chord voicings in those sections that call for it, and enter those parts. For harmonically complex or tutti sections, it's OK to work things out in a piano sketch or to use the "Explode Music" function described in Chapter 9.

5. Make any necessary rhythmic or harmonic adjustments to the piano part.

6. Work out the bass and drum parts.

7. Check to make sure all dynamics and articulations are correctly in place. (Michael definitely recommends doing this as you go along, rather than coming back to it after the fact, so that you're hearing the sounds of the actual instruments, with their articulations, in your head as you work.)

8. Repeat steps 2–7 for each subsequent section of the chart.

25-4 Observations on the Creative Process

One of the challenges in writing a book like this or in teaching music composition and arranging in general is finding the proper balance between presenting principles, rules, or guidelines and pointing the way toward freedom of creative expression on the highest level. We've had many discussions about this during the course of writing this book. The essential issue boils down to this: Although we both agree completely on the principles, rules, and workflow methods we're recommending, we also both admit that we don't always adhere to these methods while working. For example, we may not follow these rules religiously for more than two or three bars in any chart. Yet, if we didn't have those principles thoroughly ingrained in our subconscious, we wouldn't be able to work.

In any discipline, the creative process combines specific elements of craft—techniques and principles that can easily be defined—with a very nebulous, instinctive, mental and emotional process that is very difficult to describe. When you're really creating, whether performing an improvised solo, composing a tune or an arrangement, or working in any other art form, you enter an intense, focused, almost mystical state, where you're not "thinking" in the intellectual sense. You're "in the zone," and the music is flowing through you.

At the same time (if you're really there), you're intensely focused on the technical considerations and details of the music as it appears, and you're drawing on the totality of your musical experience and training. A seemingly infinite array of technical issues and problems might need to be solved and decisions made as you proceed. Sometimes you may have two, three, or more different ideas for a section and need to choose one or to combine several ideas into one. During the process of working out a harmonized section, unwanted dissonances, clashes, repeated notes, parallel fifths, registration issues, and other problems that need to be fixed will most certainly arise. Sometimes you may have nine or ten different ideas for how to approach a tune, and you may procrastinate for days or weeks because you can't decide which way to go. The important thing is just to take the plunge, choose a direction, and trust your instincts.

How do you get into this "zone"? How will you know when you're really there? Well, many books have been written on the subject. Many attempts to define methods for attaining this state have been made, some more effective than others. Sometimes meditation or following a spiritual path can help; sometimes just sheer will power and determination will do the trick. There's no one way to accomplish this.

Suffice it to say that with experience, you will definitely know when you're there and when you're not. The more you listen, play, study, and compose, the easier it gets. Also, you have to be motivated! You must truly desire, in your heart, to create the best possible music that you're capable of producing. And you may not always be able to get there! You can expect to be dissatisfied with your efforts more often than not, especially at the beginning, but this is a good thing. It means that you're seriously critiquing your work and are likely to make the necessary effort to improve your work. Here's a relevant quote by the French philosopher Voltaire seen years ago on the walls of the Juilliard School of Music: "Dissatisfaction is the first sign of progress."

What if you have a bad day or "writer's block"? One of the things that separates true professionals from students and amateurs is the ability to produce music of consistently good quality regardless of your mental state. This is where a solid foundation in the basic principles comes into play. The more secure you are with this basic foundation, which comes through study, practice, and experience, the more likely you will be able to realize your creative goals consistently.

25-5 Workflow Analysis of "Cross Section"

We thought it would be a good idea at this point to demonstrate some of the process that went into creating Ex. 24-3B, "Cross Section," from the last chapter, as a way of illustrating some of the points just mentioned. Study the following notes, and compare Example 25-1, "Cross Section," First Draft (based on the original sketch, Ex. 24-3A) with the final version in Ex. 24-3B and reprinted here as Ex. 25-2 for easy reference. The changes did not take place in numerical order but, rather, became apparent as better choices as the music evolved. Each of the following numbered comments is clearly indicated in both versions of the score. Listen to the recording of Ex. 25-1 (the first draft), and compare it to the final version, Ex. 25-2 (identical to Ex. 24-3B with annotations).

1. The first version of the group A melody was OK, but when we added the group C chords with the dotted quarter–eighth rhythm, it seemed rhythmically clumsy, with too much emphasis on the upbeat of beat 4. By changing the syncopation and articulation slightly so that the third notes of the phrase are short and the fourth note falls on beat 4, the line becomes crisper, creating some interesting rhythmic counterpoint with the chordal part on the "and" of beat 4.

2. Our first version of the C chordal accompaniment part seemed to make things muddy with the sustained chords and was boring melodically with all the repeated notes. By making the first note in mm. 1 and 3 short, we leave space for the A melody to cut through. We also provided melodic interest by creating a melodic contour in the second alto sax part, which now ascends continuously from concert F to D over the first five bars. We provided some textural variety by changing the first measure to semi-open position, saving the open position voicing for m. 3. The group C part now builds gradually from m. 1 to the break at m. 6.

3. The first version of the answering group B melody has a parallel melodic shape and phrase structure in mm. 2 and 4. We changed the melodic shape slightly in both measures to provide some contrast.

4. In m. 3, the first version of the repetition of A was boring and predictable, with the melodic phrase starting on the chord root (B♭), as it did in m. 1 (with the chord root G). Starting the phrase a whole step higher on concert C is not only unexpected but also creates harmonic interest by introducing the chord ninth in mm. 3 and 4. We also created a little contrary motion, and harmonic interest, in the second trumpet part by descending to the concert C at the end of the measure. This also prepares trumpet 2 for the drop in register in m. 4.

5. We continue the ascending melodic motion of C begun in m. 1 and provide harmonic interest by introducing the augmented 11th (A natural).

6. Looking ahead to bar 5, beat 1, we realized there was a hidden (exposed) fifth between the lead trumpet and the lead alto. The revised melodic phrase for group B not only gets rid of the hidden fifth but also provides greater harmonic interest by expanding to a full, open position Am11 chord on the downbeat of m. 5 (the chord root is in the baritone sax).

7. We avoid the hidden fifth and provide some contrary motion within the B group.

8. We're gradually building intensity by beginning to harmonize some of the unison/octave figures. The original A group voicing of (concert) D-B-E-C (from top to bottom) on the downbeat of m. 5 sounded good, but it created an awkward melodic skip from E♭ to B natural in the second trumpet part. Dropping the second trumpet an octave and giving it a (concert) G on the downbeat of m. 5 solves the problem. To compensate, we decided to open up the group "B" voicing so that the chord ninth is now covered by alto sax 1 (group B).

9. We see that on m. 5, beat 1, both of our melodic groupings (A and B) have expanded to four-note sustained chords. If we brought in another chord with group C here, it would sound too thick. Eureka! Let's do a little role reversal and give group C a melodic line to play, leading to the break at m. 6. While we're at it, that break on the downbeat of m. 6 seems a little stiff, so let's move everything up a half beat so that the break happens on the "and" of beat 4.

10. Initially we thought it would sound cool to voice the trumpets in fourths on the last chord. For some reason, it also sounded good to end with the trombones up, in close position with trombone 4 on the root, and the sax section opened up, providing the bottom end with the low root (concert) G played by the bari sax. Ultimately, we decided that there were now too many chord roots (G) and that it felt stronger to have trumpet 4 double the lead and wind up on the concert A. Notice also that we chose to have trombones 3 and 4 double the C on m. 6, beat 4, providing some internal contrary motion and avoiding repeating the B♭ (the most logical other note choice) in the third trombone part.

11. Almost as an afterthought, we decided to bring back the rhythmic component of group C in m. 7 and to give everybody a little sting on the "and" of beat 4—a stronger ending. Notice that on the final resolution, we've actually abandoned our initial three subdivisions and voiced the brass and saxes as sections, which helps to make the ending more powerful.

All of this took a lot longer to explain than it did to write the music. The point is to illustrate just how much thought and attention to detail can go into scoring even a seemingly simple eight-bar musical phrase.

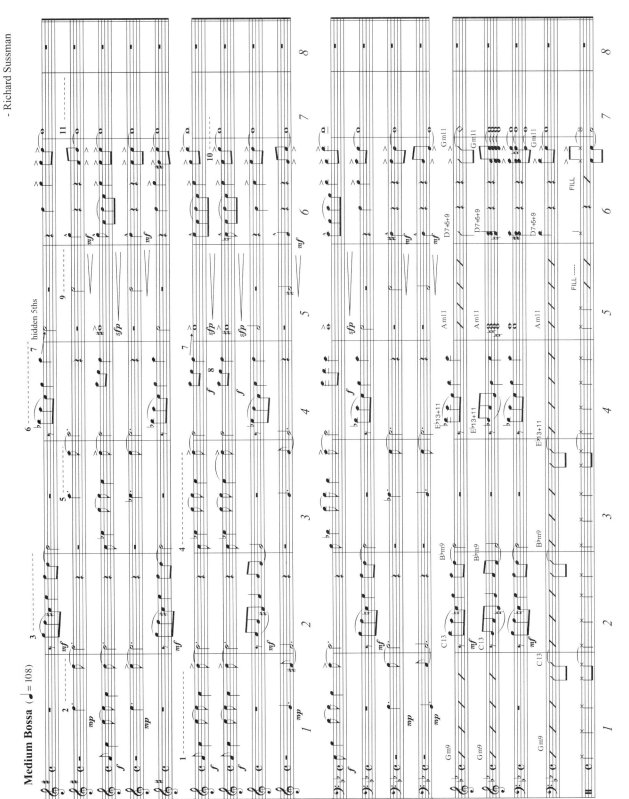

335

Ex 25-2 "Cross-Section" Final Score Reference

- Richard Sussman

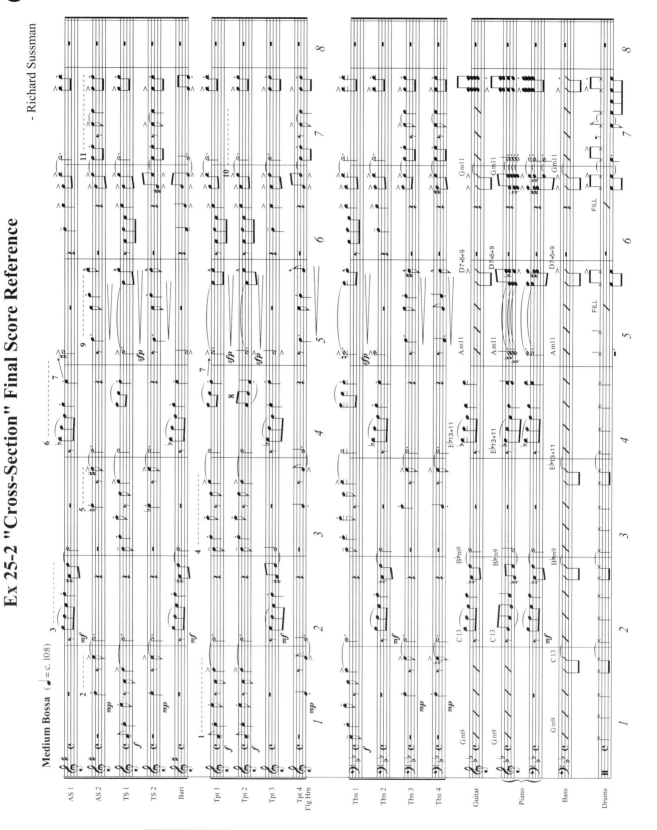

Ex.25-2 is identical to Ex.24-3B and is reprinted here for easy reference. Please listen to the audio track for Ex. 24-3B on the website.

Chapter Summary

In this chapter we examined the elements of form and instrumentation and provided suggestions regarding the process of outlining a jazz big band arrangement. We provided a sample outline of a big band arrangement. We reviewed the steps for laying out the score and a recommended workflow procedure from Chapter 17. We then offered some observations on the creative process. Finally, we provided an example of the kind of focus and attention to detail necessary for mastering the art of composing and arranging for the jazz big band.

◊ **Software Tip**: By now you should be quite familiar with your chosen software platform. Make a concerted effort not to think about the software at all for the next week! This is your score pad and pencil. Its sole function is to facilitate and assist you in the creative process. Take a step back to make sure you're setting the right priorities. For now, your attention and energy should be focused completely on creating the music.

◊ **Important**: Review the suggested workflow procedure in Section 25-3. We strongly recommend that you add all articulations, dynamics, and full rhythm section parts as you work and complete each section of an arrangement. Try applying this workflow principle to the full big band arrangement "Arranging Project 3," which we'll be focusing on for the remaining chapters of this book. Refer to Chapters 12 and 13 for detailed information on articulations, dynamics, and rhythm section notation.

Exercises

1. **Arranging Project 3:** Select a medium-tempo to medium up-tempo standard, jazz standard, or original tune to be arranged for jazz big band: eight brass, five reeds, and three or four rhythm. Refer to the list of Recommended Standards and Jazz Standards at the end of Chapter 17. Refer to Section 20-5 for suggestions on how to select a suitable tune. Stick to a straight-ahead or Latin jazz feel for this project. For this project, as with Arranging Project 2, we recommend using 4/4, 3/4, or 6/4 meters, avoiding tunes with complex meter changes, and not choosing a ballad.

2. Start planning the overall form of the arrangement. Write down a projected outline.

3. Arrange the head of the tune using scoring and workflow techniques discussed in this chapter and the preceding chapters. Focus on using different textural and instrumental colors to provide contrast and variety, so that the music develops and builds naturally as you proceed. Use the Jazz Big Band Template. Add dynamics, articulations, and rhythm section parts as you go along.

337

◊ **Recommended:** Use the following outline from Section 25-2 (for an AABA tune) or a similar outline (utilizing a variety of contrasting timbres for the different sections of the tune).

 a. First "A"—2–5 saxes playing the melody in unison or octaves.

 b. Second "A"—2–3 trumpets (open or in mutes) playing the melody in unison or lightly voiced, over mixed saxes and trombones playing sustained or rhythmic chords.

 c. "B"—5 saxes voiced in close position or semi-open position. Add a slow unison trombone countermelody and/or some brass hits. Build to the last "A."

 d. Last "A"—full tutti brass + saxes in rhythmic unison (lead trumpet melody doubled 8vb).

4. If necessary, do a concert sketch (two or four staves) of the tutti sections.

5. If possible, print out the score and parts, and play and analyze the results. Be sure to observe correct transpositions for the horn parts.

Chapter 26

Modern Harmonic Concepts and Voicing Techniques

Modern harmony is a vast topic that could easily fill an entire book (and has—*Twentieth Century Harmony* by Vincent Persichetti, *A Chromatic Approach to Jazz Harmony* by Dave Liebman, *Contemporary Harmony* by Ludmilla Ulehla, *The Lydian Chromatic Concept of Tonal Organization* by George Russell, to name a few). In this chapter we'll attempt to uncover the tip of the iceberg.

The harmonic language of jazz has developed from the 1920s to the present in much the same way that Western European classical music evolved from the Baroque to the mid-20th century. Both traditions began as dance music relying on relatively consonant tonal structures based on dominant harmony (V-I). Over time, composers began to push the limits of tonality by emphasizing upper-structure chord tones and shifting tonal centers (modulations) and through the use of increased dissonance (Beethoven through the late Romantics to the early 20th century and jazz of the 1940s and '50s).

Experiments were made at abandoning tonality and dominant harmony while still keeping the music relatively consonant and accessible (the Impressionists and modal jazz of the 1950s). Finally, tonality was thrown out altogether (serialism and atonal jazz of the 1960s). Eventually, some stylistic barriers seemed to relax, leaving composers in both worlds with a variety of harmonic approaches from which to choose, including tonal with dominant harmony, modal, polytonal, atonal, and even microtonal, all with varying degrees of consonance and dissonance.

So far in this book we've focused primarily on dominant harmony and chords built by thirds, starting with triads and seventh chords and working our way up to ninths, elevenths, and thirteenths (Chapter 8). Several important and distinct modern harmonic techniques are also available to the contemporary jazz arranger.

26-1 Chords by Fourths

Building chords based on the interval of a perfect fourth is a simple technique for creating hip, modern-sounding voicings, in contrast to the more traditional chords built by thirds. Because the third is often missing from the chord voicing, chords built by fourths tend to have an ambiguous quality, neither major nor minor and suggesting *modal* rather than dominant harmony.

If you consider the modes of the major scale commonly used by jazz musicians in this context—Dorian, Phrygian, Lydian, Mixolydian, Aeolian, and Locrian—you'll discover that none of the "V" chords associated with these modes contains the half-step leading tone. Only the V chord of the Ionian mode (major scale) as well as the harmonic minor scale have this unique and decisive characteristic, which also produces the tritone interval contained within the dominant seventh chord built on the fifth scale degree, the principal defining feature of dominant harmony (V-I).

Chords built by fourths were used effectively by 20th-century classical composers such as Hindemith and Bartok and by jazz musicians such as Oliver Nelson, Joe Henderson, McCoy Tyner, and Chick Corea. There are several ways of constructing chords by fourths in a jazz arrangement. See Ex. 26-1, "Modern Voicing Techniques," for illustrations of the following techniques.

1. To create a basic *fourth chord structure*, place successive perfect fourths, either descending from the lead line or ascending from the lowest note of the voicing (which is not necessarily the chord root). The most common fourth chord structure is a three-note chord consisting only of intervals of a perfect fourth. Building a three-note fourth chord on F would result in F, B♭ (P4), and E♭ (m7). Adding another note a perfect fourth above the top note would create a four-note voicing containing the minor third (in this case A♭), though without the distinct "minorness" of a minor triad or seventh chord (Ex. 26-1a). You can drop the A♭ down an octave or add the perfect fifth (C) without destroying the "fourths" quality of the chord. Typically this chord would be labeled Fsus4, Fm7sus4, or F7sus4, depending on how it's used within the chord progression. The term "suspended fourth" (sus4) comes from classical theory, where the fourth was considered to be suspended above the third. However, in the Baroque and Classical periods, the suspended fourth almost always resolved downward to a major or minor third, which is not the case in jazz harmony (Ex. 26-1a).

2. A distinctive and useful variation on the standard fourth chord voicing can be obtained either by adding a major third above the top note of a standard three-note fourth chord, for example, (from bottom to top)

F, B♭, E♭, G (check out the tune "Peresina" by McCoy Tyner on *Expansions* for an example of the use of this voicing), or by separating two three-note fourth chords by an interval of a major third, for example (from bottom to top), F, B♭, E♭, G, C, F (Ex. 26-1b, c, & d). Notice in the third and fourth examples (Ex. 26-1c & d) that the lowest and highest notes of the chords are the same. Another useful variation is to build a chord based on two perfect fourth intervals separated by a major second (e.g., F, B♭, C, F, from bottom to top), used effectively in Ex. 26-2.

3. Once a basic fourth chord structure is in place, you can fill in other chord tones derived from the appropriate mode, such as Dorian or Phrygian, using modal concepts of chord voicings (see Section 8-5) (Ex. 26-1a and e).

4. The interval of an augmented fourth may also be used, either between the bottom or the top two notes of a three-note structure or between any two notes of a more complex structure, especially with the Lydian or Mixolydian modes (Ex. 26-1e).

5. Two three-note fourth chords, with or without the augmented fourth, can be combined, separated by any interval, to create a fourth chords harmonic texture. In this case it is the presence of fourth chord structures, rather than a chord progression (or functional harmony), that becomes the unifying and defining characteristic of the harmonic style (Ex. 26-1e).

Bob Mintzer and Jim McNeely are two contemporary jazz arrangers who make frequent use of fourth chords in their music. For some musical illustrations of the use of fourth chords, please see either Ex. 26-2, the brass + rhythm from the intro to "Ivories Tower" by Richard, or our analysis of Bob Mintzer's *The Art of the Big Band* in Chapter 33.

341

Ex. 26-1

Modern Voicing Techniques

1. Chords by 4ths

2. Upper Structure Triads

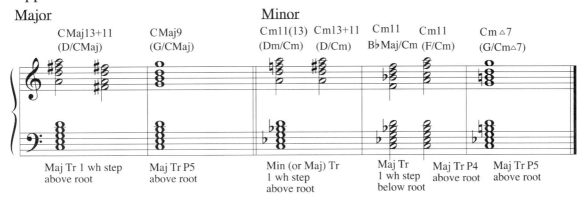

Major
CMaj13+11 (D/CMaj)   **CMaj9** (G/CMaj)

Maj Tr 1 wh step above root   Maj Tr P5 above root

Minor
Cm11(13) (Dm/Cm)   **Cm13+11** (D/Cm)   **Cm11** Bb Maj/Cm   **Cm11** (F/Cm)   **Cm △7** (G/Cm△7)

Min (or Maj) Tr 1 wh step above root   Maj Tr 1 wh step below root   Maj Tr P4 above root   Maj Tr P5 above root

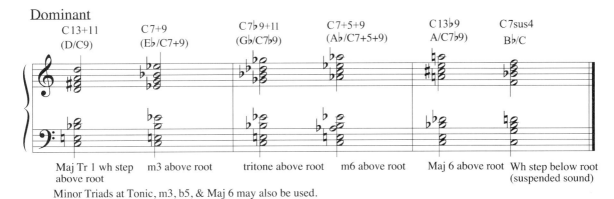

Dominant
C13+11 (D/C9)   **C7+9** (Eb/C7+9)   **C7b9+11** (Gb/C7b9)   **C7+5+9** (Ab/C7+5+9)   **C13b9** A/C7b9   **C7sus4** Bb/C

Maj Tr 1 wh step above root   m3 above root   tritone above root   m6 above root   Maj 6 above root   Wh step below root (suspended sound)

Minor Triads at Tonic, m3, b5, & Maj 6 may also be used.

3. Polytonal Sounds

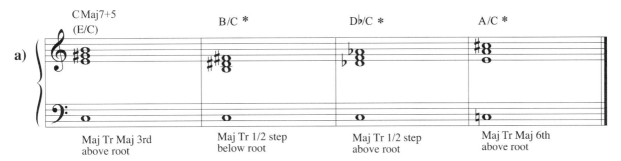

a)   **CMaj7+5** (E/C)   **B/C** *   **Db/C** *   **A/C** *

Maj Tr Maj 3rd above root   Maj Tr 1/2 step below root   Maj Tr 1/2 step above root   Maj Tr Maj 6th above root

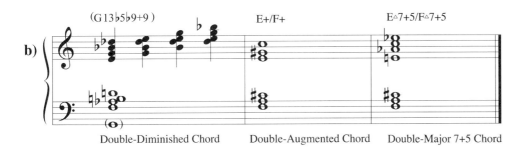

b)   **(G13b5b9+9)**   **E+/F+**   **E△7+5/F△7+5**

Double-Diminished Chord   Double-Augmented Chord   Double-Major 7+5 Chord

* These chords are always represented as "slash" chords since it makes no sense to analyze them using traditional tonal harmony.

343

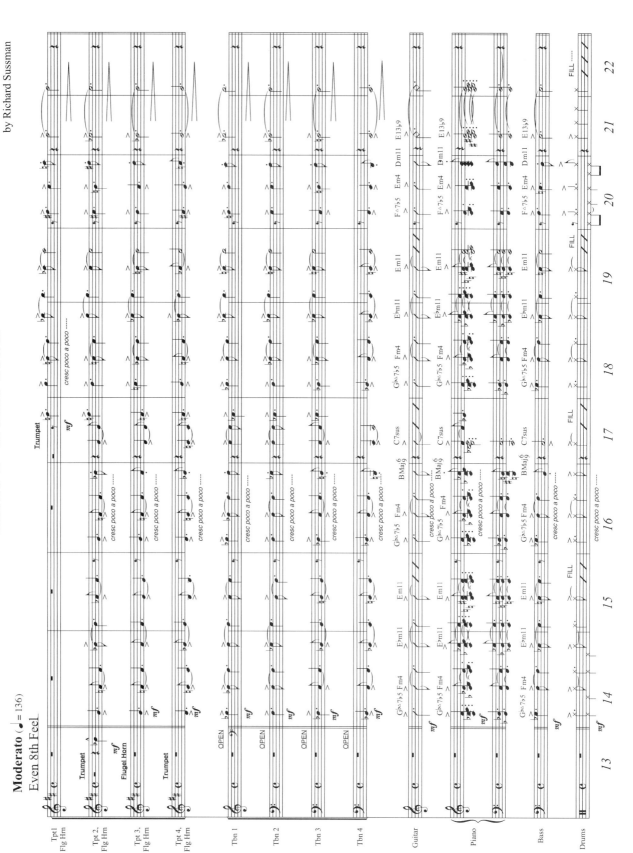

26-2 Upper-Structure Triads

Voicing the brass and/or saxes using *upper-structure triads* can be an extremely effective way of achieving a powerful and modern harmonic sound for the big band. This technique is especially effective with the full brass section. Essentially, the way this works is to give the trombones a typical piano left hand voicing of a ninth or thirteenth chord, containing the third and the seventh of the chord in the low mid-register. Then voice the trumpets above that in triads, playing the ninths, elevenths, and thirteenths of the chord or their possible alterations (♭9, +9, +11, ♭13). In this style, the lead trumpet will normally be doubled by the fourth trumpet an octave below.

For each chord quality—major, minor, or dominant—several possible triads are available. Following are examples of some of the most commonly used upper-structure triad voicings, illustrated in Ex. 26-1-2.

1. *Major*
   a. A major triad a whole step above the root (Maj13+11).
   b. A major triad a perfect fifth above the root (Maj9).

2. *Minor*
   a. A major triad a whole step above the root (m13+11).
   b. A minor triad a whole step above the root (m11/13).
   c. A major triad a perfect fourth above the root (m11/13).
   d. A major triad a whole step below the root (m11 or m7sus4).
   e. A major triad a perfect fifth above the root (m∆7).

3. *Dominant*
   a. A major triad a whole step above the root (dom13+11).
   b. A major triad a minor third above the root (dom7+9).
   c. A major triad a tritone above the root (dom7♭9+11).
   d. A major triad a minor sixth above the root (dom7+5+9).
   e. A major triad a major sixth above the root (dom13♭9).
   f. A major triad a whole step below the root (dom7sus4).
   g. Minor triads built on the tonic, m2nd, m3, ♭5, & Maj6 may also be used.

◊ Note that upper structure triads provide another situation where it's OK to include the chord root in the voicing, while still sounding "modern." This is because the notes of the upper structure part of the voicing (e.g., an A♭ major triad over C7) tend to become more relevant to each other as a structure, rather than in relation to the chord root. The ear is more conscious of the overall dissonant effect created by the A♭ major triad over C7, rather than the fact that the A♭ triad happens to contain the C chord root. Any upper structure triad may be used in any inversion to create better voice leading, or to achieve variety in the overall spacing of the chord. Upper structure triads can be used effectively on target notes, as well as for approach tone reharmonization with moving lines.

Upper-structure triad voicings can be quite dissonant, with a lot of edge, but they always rest solidly on top of conventional seventh and ninth chords and can always be analyzed as variations of chords built by thirds. They generally function diatonically in the same manner as the major, minor, and dominant chords on which they're built. Most of the Basie alumni and the post-Basie writers of the 1960s and 70s, including Neal Hefti, Bill Holman, Thad Jones, Don Sebesky, Nelson Riddle, and many others, made frequent use of upper-structure triads. Example 26-3 is a sketch of how a typical, modern, "Basie style" shout chorus could be voiced for eight brass and five saxes using upper-structure triads (m. 5, beat 3, to m. 7, beat 4, is meant to be played by the sax section only).

Ex. 26-3

"Upper-Structure Triads," composed and arranged by Richard Sussman

347

26-3 Polytonal Sounds

Polytonality (literally "many tonalities") refers to the superimposition of two or more chords or melodic lines with distinctly different tonal centers. In jazz, this usually means either combining two or more different triads or seventh chords with tonal centers that are foreign to each other or simply placing a triad or seventh chord above a dissonant bass note from a different tonality. In order for the sound to be truly polytonal, each element has to contain an identifiable tonal center, and the resultant combination of notes cannot easily lend itself to a functional, tonal analysis, as in the case of upper-structure triads. It's *not* just a bunch of dissonant intervals thrown together.

Following are examples of some of the most common polytonal sounds used in jazz today, formed by superimposing a major triad over a dissonant root from a different tonality.

1. A major triad a major third above the root (e.g., E/C or C Maj7+5).
2. A major triad a half step below the root (e.g., B/C).
3. A major triad a half step above the root (e.g., D♭/C).
4. A major triad a major sixth above the root (e.g., A/C).

The innovative and influential jazz pianist Richie Beirach has made frequent use of the first three of the listed chords, both in his original compositions and in the reharmonization of standards. He was also fond of demonstrating that there are many similar structures in the music of Schoenberg, Webern, and other 20th-century classical composers. There are also examples of Maj7+5, dom13, m11, and other so-called jazz chords in the piano music of Debussy and Ravel. A great instance is the solo piano piece "Forlane" from "Le Tombeau de Couperin," composed by Ravel in 1918. It's obvious that Chick Corea (as well as many other jazz musicians) was heavily influenced by Ravel (Chick Corea, *Piano Improvisations* Vols. 1 and 2, ECM). See Ex. 26-1-3a, for examples of polytonal sounds.

26-4 Other Types of Modern Chord Structures

Two other important modern jazz chords formed by superimposing simpler structures bear mentioning here. The *double-diminished chord* is formed by superimposing two diminished seventh chords separated by the interval of a major seventh and then playing any inversions of either chord (Ex. 26-1-3b). When collapsed into the same octave, the two diminished seventh chords form the *diminished scale*, commonly used by modern jazz improvisers (Herbie Hancock, Chick Corea, and just about everybody since the late 1960s) and contemporary classical composers, most notably Béla Bartok. The double diminished chord can be analyzed tonally as a dense and dissonant alteration of a dominant seventh chord; it was used frequently in this manner by the great

Thad Jones in his arrangements. Check out Ex. 26-3, mm. 1, 8, and 10, for examples of the use of double diminished chords in the brass voicings. The root of the chord will generally be a major third below any note of the lower diminished seventh chord (see Section 8-1, Ex. 8-2).

Another fascinating (and much more polytonal) sound is created by superimposing two augmented triads a major seventh apart (e.g., C augmented and B augmented). When collapsed into the same octave, these two chords form the so-called double augmented scale favored by jazz improvisers like John Abercrombie and Andy Laverne in the 1970s and '80s. If you extend this structure further (C Aug, B Aug, B♭ Aug, A Aug), you wind up with a 12-tone row! Another variation on the same sound is to superimpose two major 7+5 chords a major seventh apart (e.g., CMaj7+5 and BMaj7+5—from bottom to top C, E, G♯, B, E♭, G, B♭) (see Ex. 26-1-3b).

◊ Interesting facts (**Believe it or not!**):
1. There are only *three* diminished scales and *three* diminished seventh chords. Each diminished scale contains *two* diminished seventh chords.
2. There are only *two* whole-tone scales and *four* augmented triads. Each whole-tone scale contains *two* augmented triads.

26-5 Clusters and Spread Voicings

Cluster voicings are formed by creating chords containing two or more intervals of a major or minor second, usually contained within one octave. Cluster chords can be tonal (if created using modal concepts of chord voicings) or atonal. Cluster voicings generally produce a dissonant and abrasive effect, but, unlike *cluster bombs*, they are generally not fatal when used. Gil Evans, Charles Mingus, Bob Brookmeyer, and Jim McNeely have made frequent use of cluster voicings in their music.

Spread voicings are chords containing five or more different chord tones spread out over two or more octaves, often in root or open position. Spread voicings can have varying degrees of consonance or dissonance. Although often associated with modern jazz composers, they should not, strictly speaking, be limited to the category of "modern" jazz harmony, because they've been used by jazz composers since the 1920s. Spread voicings are most effective when serving as sustained pads supporting a melody or improvised solo, especially for ballads or slower tempos. Duke Ellington, Gil Evans, Thad Jones, and Bob Brookmeyer are among the many jazz arrangers who have made effective use of spread voicings in their writing. Example 26-4 illustrates the use of clusters in muted brass under a woodwind melody. Example 26-5 uses the same theme, this time scored with spread voicings in the brass. Listen to the two recorded examples, and compare how the change in voicings affects the overall color of the passage.

Notice that in Ex. 26-4, we momentarily suspend our rule about not over-lapping the trumpets and trombones. The use of the mutes and flugel horns creates a unique sonority making it acceptable in this case. We also wanted to preserve the more consonant internal resonance within each section resulting from keeping the trumpets in triads through the first 8 bars.

Ex. 26-4

"Clusters," composed and arranged by Richard Sussman

Ex. 26-5

"Spreads," composed and arranged by Richard Sussman

Chapter Summary

In this chapter we examined several techniques for creating chords associated with modern jazz harmony. The techniques include chords by fourths, upper-structure triads, polytonal sounds, clusters, and spread voicings.

◊ **Software Tip**: It's important to understand the theoretical concepts behind the proper, or "enharmonic," spelling of accidentals (e.g., A♭ vs. G♯) and how to control this in your notation program. Generally, if you're raising a note (augmented), it should be spelled with a sharp or a natural; if you're lowering a note (minor or diminished), it should be spelled with a flat. Double sharps and flats are rarely used in jazz notation, even if that would be the theoretically correct marking.

Similarly, it's important to understand when and how to use courtesy accidentals. Here's the general rule: If there's an accidental in a measure (e.g., A♭) and the same note without the accidental (A natural) occurs in the measure immediately following, use a courtesy accidental, even though, technically, bar lines cancel the accidental. Very often it will be useful to insert courtesy accidentals even two or three bars after the fact, especially when following a section with many accidentals. If you're not sure, it's usually better to err on the side of too many rather than too few.

Finale and Sibelius both provide easy tools for changing the spelling of an accidental, for inserting courtesy accidentals, and for setting preferences to "weight" accidentals toward sharps or flats within a given section. In Finale, while in Speedy Entry, select a note to which you want to assign the courtesy accidental, and then press the * key on the computer's numeric keypad. To toggle between a sharp or flat enharmonic note spelling, press "9" on the numeric keypad while in Speedy Entry. In Sibelius, choose the note in question, and, in the (fifth) keypad window, press the parentheses button to add a courtesy accidental. To toggle between enharmonic spellings, simply select a note and press the Return key.

Exercises

1. Voice Exercise 26-1 for five saxes using a variety of techniques for building fourth chords. First harmonize the line and add chord symbols according to your taste. The phrase begins and ends in E minor, but the harmonization has been left blank on purpose, and there's plenty of room for interpretation throughout. Use the 2-Stave Concert Sketch Template.

2. Voice Exercise 26-2 for eight brass using upper-structure triads. Start with the written chord changes, but feel free to reharmonize approach tones and destination tones as you hear it. Use the 4-Stave Brass/Saxes Template.

3. Voice Exercise 26-3 for eight brass and five saxes using spread voicings and clusters with the brass in mixed mutes accompanying the saxes playing the melody in unison and octaves (as in Exs. 26-4 and 26-5). Use the 4-Stave Brass/Saxes Template.

4. **Arranging Project 3:** Add a four- to eight-bar intro and a kicker into the first solo of your chart. Include articulations, dynamics, and full rhythm section parts.

5. Experiment with applying modern voicing techniques discussed in this chapter to the head, the intro, and the kicker of your big band arrangement.

Exercises 26-1, 26-2, and 26-3 are all available as downloads in Finale, Sibelius, or Standard MIDI File format on the companion website.

Exercise 26-1

"Fourths"

Medium Swing (♩ = 116)

Exercise 26-2

"Upper-Structure Triads"

Medium Up Swing (♩ = 144)

Exercise 26-3

"Clusters and Spreads"

Moderate Ballad (♩ = 80)

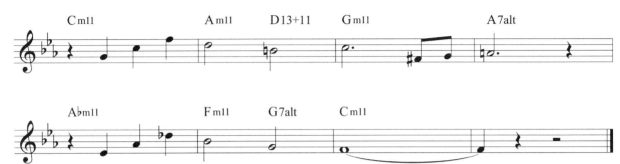

354

◊ In Exercise 26-3, we purposely used the dominant 7 alt chord symbol to allow the reader greater freedom in choosing any of the many altered tones possible in this example.

Chapter 27

More on Modern Harmony and Melodic Reharmonization

When applying modern harmonic concepts to jazz big band voicings, whether you're using chords built by thirds, fourths, upper-structure triads, or some other technique, the most important considerations are likely to be the following.

1. The relative degree of consonance or dissonance present in the chord voicing.
2. The overall spread of the voicing, that is, the distance between the lowest note and the highest note.
3. The number of different chord tones present in a voicing, and how many and which chord tones are doubled or omitted.
4. The overall register and tessitura of the instruments assigned to the notes of the chord.
5. The actual instrumentation (assignment of instruments) of the various notes of the chord.
6. How you choose to reharmonize approach tones, and whether or not you choose to reharmonize the underlying harmony of the basic chord progression.

◊ **Important!** At this point, harmony becomes a textural element in the arrangement, not just a set of chord changes supporting a melody and providing structure for the tune. You can increase the tension and density by adding chord tones and dissonance, using upper-structure triads or polytonal sounds, or increasing the overall spread of the voicings. You can release tension and decrease harmonic density by introducing more consonance or by using chords built by thirds in the more traditional close, semi-open, and open positions. Whether or not and how you choose to reharmonize a melody will have a tremendous effect on the emotional impact of the music.

Many of the specific guidelines presented in Chapters 8 and 16 regarding chords built by thirds and standard voicing positions can now be seen as methods for achieving a particular harmonic texture rather than as ironclad rules that must always be obeyed. Still, certain principles presented in earlier chapters are relevant in any harmonic context.

1. Observe standard low-interval limits (see Section 8-2 and Appendix A).
2. Keep the chord voicings balanced. In general, avoid having a gap of more than a major sixth between any two adjacent voices, except for the bottom two voices, which can be separated by a seventh, an octave, or a tenth unless going for a special effect.
3. Always be aware of the relative tessitura of the instruments and the basic principle that the intensity of the lower parts should normally not exceed that of the higher ones.
4. Major and minor thirds and sixths and perfect intervals are still considered to be consonant. Major and minor seconds and sevenths and the tritone are still considered to be dissonant.

The extensive degree of subtle and not-so-subtle harmonic shadings along with the vast array of possible instrumental color combinations are some of the most important creative and expressive tools available to the jazz arranger. Our advice is to immerse yourself in the study and exploration of jazz harmony. The more solid your harmonic foundation, the more expansive your palette and expressive options will be while composing.

Following are some more techniques for achieving modern-sounding chord voicings.

27-1 Constant Structures

Creating a chord structure, such as the fourth chord voicing in Ex. 26-1d, and "hanging" it from a melodic line in parallel motion is another way of achieving a modern harmonic texture. There are really no rules about which intervals to use, aside from the consideration of how much consonance or dissonance you want in the sound. Example 27-1A illustrates the application of this technique to the melody of the first four bars of "I'll Remember April." Additional examples of the use of constant structures can be found in Ex. 27-1B, the shout chorus to Michael Abene's "Uncertainty" (Ex. 31-3), and at the beginning of and throughout the head to Bob Mintzer's "Art of the Big Band" (Ex. 33-3).

Another variation of this technique is to combine two dominant 7+9 voicings derived from the same diminished scale and move them in parallel motion

Ex. 27-1A

Constant Structures: "I'll Remember April" by Raye and DePaul

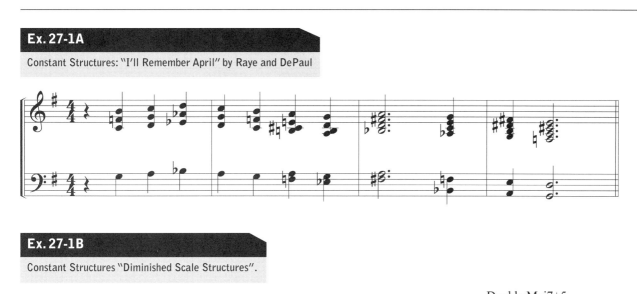

Ex. 27-1B

Constant Structures "Diminished Scale Structures".

Double Maj7+5

(illustrated in Ex. 27-1B). There's a seemingly endless array of harmonic structures that can be derived from the diminished scale.

27-2 Parallel Five-Voice Structures

We've seen in earlier chapters that doubling the lead line is an effective and powerful way of projecting a melody with clarity and mobility (the "Basie" sound). However, sometimes that's not the desired effect. Sometimes you may actually want to obscure the melody to create a mysterious effect, or you may want to add edginess with increased dissonance. One way of accomplishing this is to return to the standard close or drop-2 positions, but *without* doubling the lead (see Ex. 27-2). In this situation, the primary concern is simply the degree of consonance or dissonance desired in any particular voicing.

Ex. 27-2

Parallel Five-Note Close Position and Drop-2: "I'll Remember April" by Raye and DePaul

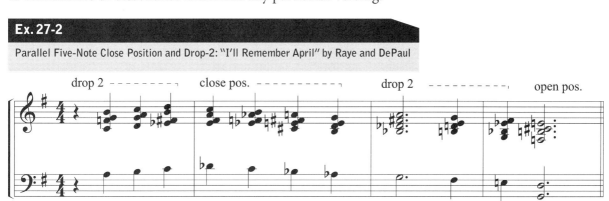

27-3 Modern Techniques of Melodic Reharmonization

We can now revisit Section 10-1, "Techniques of Melodic Reharmonization," with the tools for understanding the additional numbers 13–17 in the list of reharmonization techniques.

"Techniques of Modern Reharmonization, Revisited"

13. Polytonal sounds (slash chords).
14. Nonfunctional harmony—arbitrary root motion or root motion by:
    a. Step/half step.
    b. Maj/min third/tritone.
15. Constant structures.
16. Free reharmonization: Any melody note can be harmonized by any chord root as:
    a. Chord tone.
    b. Altered chord tone or upper structure.
    c. Nonchord tone.
17. Atonal sounds.

We covered polytonal sounds in the preceding chapter and constant structures in Section 27-1. Nonfunctional (nondiatonic) chord progressions occur in a given musical passage when the chord root motion creates chords that fall outside of the diatonic scale–derived chords or their secondary dominants (Sections 8-1 and 8-3). Nonfunctional chord progressions can often be achieved when the chord roots move by major or minor seconds or thirds. For this principle to apply, however, it's important to understand that the resultant chords cannot be scale-derived chords. For example, if we're in the key of F major and the root moves by a major third from F to A, forming the progression FMaj7 to Am7, it's diatonic, because Am7 is a scale-derived chord in the key of F. However, if the progression is FMaj7 to AMaj7, we have a more colorful, nonfunctional progression. Similarly, in the key of F minor, the progression Fm7 to AbMaj7 is diatonic and the progression Fm7 to Abm7 is not.

Jazz musicians especially from the 1960s on, such as Joe Henderson, Wayne Shorter, Herbie Hancock, and Chick Corea, as well as classical composers, including Ravel, Debussy, and some of the late Romantic composers, such as Mahler, Strauss, and Bruckner, all used this type of nonfunctional harmony to produce colorful and unexpected harmonies. Virtually all 20th-century classical composers (Stravinsky, Copland, Bartok, Adams, etc.) not using strict serial techniques made use of these harmonic principles, as did Schoenberg in his "pre-serial" works. It's also interesting to note that these types of progressions have worked their way into the standard harmonic vocabulary of many of the top film and TV composers.

"Free reharmonization," number 16 in the preceding list, works like this. Suppose the melody note is G. It can be harmonized by any note of the chromatic scale as follows:

Key of G: tonic
Key of A♭:   Maj 7th
Key of A: m 7th
Key of B♭:   Maj 6th
Key of B: m 6th (or +5)
Key of C: P 5th
Key of D♭:   Aug 4th (or 11th)
Key of D: 11th (or sus 4)
Key of E♭:   Maj 3rd
Key of E: m 3rd (or +9)
Key of F: 9th
Key of G♭:   ♭9th

How you choose to voice the resultant chords is simply a function of the relative degree of consonance or dissonance desired.

Number 17, "Atonal sounds," simply means harmonizing a melody by combining notes in such a way as to consciously avoid any reference to traditional, diatonic harmony. Play through the illustrations of these techniques in Ex. 27-3 at a keyboard. Notice how the techniques of nonfunctional harmony and free reharmonization often produce more striking results when the chords are more consonant than dissonant. The difference between the two techniques is that anything is permissible with free reharmonization, including dominant or functional root motion. In the atonal example, we took some liberties with the melody, but it still sounds like "Autumn Leaves."

◊   Be sure to refer back to Ex. 10-2B, which illustrates the application of some of these techniques to a modern reharmonization of "Autumn Leaves."

Ex. 27-3

Modern Techniques of Melodic Reharmonization: "Autumn Leaves" by Kosma, Mercer, and Prevert

13. Polytonal Sounds

Ex. 27-3-13 illustrates superimposing a triad, seventh chord, or some other type of tonal structure over a dissonant root from a different tonality, or combining two or more tonally derived chords with different tonal centers (described in Section 26-3).

14. Non-Functional Harmony

Example 27-3-14 shows that when the chord roots move by major or minor seconds or thirds, it's possible to create chord progressions that are nondiatonic, with no reference to dominant harmony.

15. Constant Structures

In Example 27-3-15 we see chord structures moving in parallel motion, as described in Section 27-1.

16. Free Reharmonization

Example 27-3-16 illustrates how any melody note can be harmonized by any note of the chromatic scale.

17. Atonal Sounds

Example 27-3-17 illustrates combinations of notes constructed in such a manner as to consciously avoid any similarity or reference to tonality or dominant harmony.

27-4 Independent Countermelodies and Polyphony with Modern Harmonies

All of the principles regarding melodic motion and voice leading presented in Section 10-2 still apply to counterpoint using modern harmonic concepts, even if the harmonies are completely atonal, *except* for the reference to landing on consonant intervals at key destination points. However, it's still important to be aware of the degree of consonance or dissonance formed by the vertical harmonies resulting from contrapuntal lines. This is something that should be controlled by the composer/arranger, not a random element.

On the other hand, if you happen to improvise two atonal lines that produce great-sounding vertical harmonies, by all means use it! It's your choice. It's the end result that counts, and any means to that end is valid, *as long as you're really hearing what you write or play*. Refer to the list of contrapuntal principles in Section 10-2, which are still valid for counterpoint using modern harmonies, with the one modification listed earlier. Example 27-4 illustrates the use of counterpoint in an atonal treatment of "Autumn Leaves."

In Ex. 27-4, the goal was to write interesting counterpoint with no obvious tonal harmonies while still preserving some point of reference to the original melody and form of "Autumn Leaves" (an extremely tonal composition). The first four melody notes, 'a,' are identical to the original but reharmonized with the polytonal B/C chord on the downbeat of m. 1. The next step was to fill in the spaces in the original phrase structure with an atonal-sounding countermelody

Ex. 27-4

Modern Counterpoint: "Autumn Leaves," composed by Kosma, Mercer, and Prevert, arranged by Richard Sussman

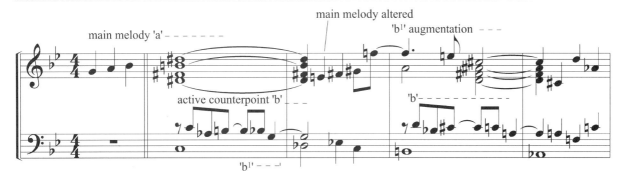

with a contrasting melodic shape, 'b,' always ending on dissonant, atonal-sounding chords at destination points. The main melody was altered in m. 2 to avoid any tonal reference or suggestion of dominant harmony. A suggestion of a passing, nonfunctional harmonic progression is provided by the bottom line in m. 2; however, if you check the vertical relationships, you'll see that they're all consonant intervals!

The answering phrase in m. 3 is a repetition of 'b' from m. 1, transposed up a half step (providing unity) while the bass note moves down by a half step. Notice that the lead melody line in m. 3 is a rhythmic augmentation of the last three notes of 'b' (labeled 'b¹,' a descending half step–m3), ending on a nice, juicy D Maj7+5 chord, followed by the very dissonant C♮-A♮-A♭ (a retrograde inversion of 'b¹') in the bass clef. Aside from being three quarter notes, all reference to the original melody is abandoned in m. 4, again harmonized in a nonfunctional manner with consonant intervals. (Consonance and atonality are *not* mutually exclusive!)

Measure 5 is really another development of 'b¹,' accompanied by some nice, dissonant fourth structures and ending on A♭ Maj7+5. A reference to the 'a' melody of "Autumn Leaves" now appears in the left hand, toying with a reference to G minor and ending on the G♭/G chord, followed by yet another reference to 'b¹.'

Chapter Summary

In this chapter we completed our study of modern jazz harmony as it relates to arranging for the big band. We revisited and filled in the blanks in our study of modern techniques of melodic reharmonization begun in Chapter 10. Finally, we took a look at creating contrapuntal textures within the context of modern harmonies and atonal sounds.

◊ **Software Tip**: In Chapter 26 we discussed the importance of the proper spelling of accidentals and courtesy accidentals. Understanding the methods for respelling accidentals and inserting courtesy accidentals is especially important when notating a musical composition or section that utilizes modern, atonal, or polytonal harmonies. If you're writing a concert score, there's no problem. Just use a key signature of C major, and manually write in all the correct accidentals. However, with a transposed score, the notation software will try to use default algorithms for calculating accidentals for the transposing instruments, based on the given key signature of the piece. However, when using polytonal sounds or if the piece or section doesn't really have a key signature (which is often the case with more modern jazz and classical harmonies), these default accidentals are likely to be totally erroneous and will most likely need to be corrected manually (e.g., C major will become D major for B♭ instruments, and all Fs and Cs will become F♯ and C♯, even if you hide the key signature). Finale and Sibelius have simple techniques for handling this type of situation. Please consult the website for details. Be sure to pay close attention to all note spellings when proofreading this type of music!

Exercises

1. Pick a standard tune, and reharmonize it using any or all of the techniques for creating modern harmonies discussed in this and the previous chapter. Use the Piano Grand Staff Template.
2. Arrange your reharmonized standard for jazz big band (just the head). Use the Jazz Big Band Template.
3. **Arranging Project 3:** Add a solo section and backgrounds to your big band arrangement. Include articulations, dynamics, and full rhythm section parts.
4. Experiment with applying the techniques of modern melodic reharmonization, voicings, and counterpoint discussed in this chapter to the head of your big band arrangement.

Chapter 28

Woodwind and Brass Doubles and Mutes

There's a seemingly infinite number of possible subdivisions and combinations of the instruments of a jazz big band, especially when factoring in possible woodwind doubles and muted brass. Before proceeding, make sure you're thoroughly familiar with the range, transpositions, technical limitations, and sound of the various woodwind instruments and brass mutes as described in Chapters 3 and 12. Listen to as much music as possible that incorporates these sounds. The scores of Duke Ellington, Gil Evans, Thad Jones, and Bob Brookmeyer, among many others, provide numerous examples of various mixes of flutes, clarinets, saxophones, and muted or unmuted brass. Study the scores, and listen to the recordings of classical composers such as Brahms, Mahler, Ravel, Debussy, and Stravinsky. Most importantly, get together with individual players, and have them demonstrate the sounds of the various woodwind instruments and brass mutes.

28-1 Woodwind and Brass Doubles

The most common woodwind doubles for a jazz big band sax section, typical for many dance bands and college jazz bands, are altos 1 and 2 doubling on flutes, tenors 1 and 2 doubling on clarinets, and baritone sax doubling on bass clarinet. In most professional jazz big bands, all trumpets double on flugelhorn, and you can usually count on at least one bass trombone in the trombone section. Before beginning an arrangement for any ensemble, it's essential to have a list of the specific woodwind and brass doubles available for that ensemble. It's equally essential to request that the players bring their doubles if you're planning to use them!

The possible doubles for different bands are certain to be slightly different, depending on the doubling skills of the individual musicians. For example, take a look at some of the incredible and unusual combinations available with the WDR band: five flutes, five alto flutes, three clarinets and two bass clarinets, five soprano saxes, etc. The Maria Schneider Orchestra also has an impressive array of woodwind doubles, especially with the oboe and English horn options in reed 2, several alto flutes, bass flute, etc. Following are the available woodwind and brass doubles for some of the top professional jazz ensembles.

The Village Vanguard Orchestra

Reed 1—alto sax, soprano sax, flute
Reed 2—alto sax, soprano sax, flute, clarinet
Reed 3—tenor sax, flute, clarinet
Reed 4—tenor sax, flute, clarinet
Reed 5—baritone sax, bass clarinet
Four trumpets, all doubling flugelhorns, with all mutes
Three tenor trombones and one bass trombone, with all mutes

The Maria Schneider Orchestra

Reed 1—alto sax, soprano sax, flute, alto flute, bass flute, clarinet
Reed 2—alto sax, soprano sax, flute, alto flute, piccolo, clarinet, oboe, English horn
Reed 3—tenor sax, flute
Reed 4—tenor sax, soprano sax, flute, clarinet
Reed 5—baritone sax, clarinet, bass clarinet, contra bass clarinet, alto flute
Four trumpets, all doubling flugelhorns, with all mutes
Three tenor trombones and one bass trombone, with all mutes

West German Radio Band (WDR Band—Cologne)

Reed 1— alto sax, soprano sax, flute, alto flute, piccolo, clarinet
Reed 2—alto sax, soprano sax, flute, alto flute, piccolo, clarinet
Reed 3—tenor sax, soprano sax, flute, alto flute, piccolo, clarinet
Reed 4—tenor sax, soprano sax, flute, alto flute, clarinet, bass clarinet
Reed 5—baritone sax, soprano sax, clarinet, flute, alto flute, piccolo, bass and contrabass clarinet, bass sax
Five trumpets, all doubling flugelhorns, with all mutes
Three tenor trombones, also doubling on euphoniums, and one bass trombone, doubling tuba, with all mutes

The Metropole Orchestra (Holland)

Alto sax 1—soprano sax, clarinet, bass clarinet
Alto sax 2—soprano sax, clarinet, bass clarinet
Tenor sax 1—soprano sax, clarinet, flute

Tenor sax 2—soprano sax, clarinet, bass clarinet, flute

Baritone sax—bass and contrabass clarinet, clarinet, flute

Additional woodwinds:

    Flute 1—piccolo, alto flute

    Flute 2—piccolo, alto flute

    Oboe—English horn

Four trumpets, all doubling flugelhorns, with all mutes

Three tenor trombones and one bass trombone, with all mutes

Also: French horn, full string section, harp, timpani, and orchestral percussion

When writing for woodwind or brass doubles, as when writing for brass mutes (described in Section 12-3), it's important to give the players ample time to switch from one instrument to another (e.g., alto sax to flute, tenor sax to clarinet, or trumpet to flugelhorn). Usually at least four to eight bars of rests at a medium tempo is necessary. It's equally important to prepare the players for the upcoming change of instrument in the part (and in the score for the conductor). To indicate the change to a different instrument, simply write on the part or score "To Flute," "To Clarinet," etc. at least four to eight bars before the switch, and then write "Flute," "Clarinet," etc. at the beginning of the new passage to be played on that instrument.

Be sure to indicate any change of transposition (e.g., from alto sax in E♭ to flute in C) in both the parts and the score. If a key change due to change of transposition is needed, put the key change either at the first measure to be played by the new instrument or, if there are measures of rests before the new part begins, at the first measure of a particular section (letter **A**, letter **B**, etc.). When you want reed 1 to switch from flute back to alto sax, follow the same procedure in reverse (e.g., "To Alto," then "Alto").

28-2 Woodwind Doubles, Dynamics, and Balance

Probably the most important consideration when writing for flutes and clarinets, as well as for muted brass, is to be conscious of the limited volume and projection of these instruments as compared to saxophones or open brass. In general, flutes and clarinets will blend well with muted brass or flugelhorns but will be easily overpowered by open brass, unless the brass are playing extremely softly or in the stands. Similarly, muted trumpets could be overpowered by open trombones, or vice versa.

It's important for the skilled arranger to have a sense of the relative power of the different instruments. With the proper dynamic markings, a workable balance can be achieved for many different instrumental combinations. We don't believe, as has been postulated in some orchestration books, that there's a simple formula that always applies, such as two flutes equal one clarinet or two clarinets equal one saxophone (in volume). We prefer to take a more

367

commonsense approach. Flutes are soft, alto flutes are even softer, clarinets are a little louder, becoming brilliant in the upper register, saxophones are louder still, and open brass are the most powerful. Yet one piccolo has the ability to cut through an entire orchestra!

All wind instruments tend to be louder in the upper registers and softer and mellower in the lower registers. In any performance situation, it's important for flutes, clarinets, and muted brass to be properly miked in order to be heard in the correct relation to open brass and saxes. It takes a skilled sound-mixing engineer to adjust the balance of various instruments carefully during the course of any performance. In fact, it's almost as important to have a good sound mixer as it is to maintain the quality of the individual musicians in a band. A bad house mix can ruin an otherwise great performance just as effectively as a bad drummer or conductor!

28-3 Woodwind and Brass Doubles and Mutes: Homogeneous Combinations

Flutes sound good as a section in unison or voiced, reinforced with piccolo at the octave, or as a mix of flutes, alto flutes, and piccolo. Clarinets also sound good as a section in unison, octaves, or voiced, with bass clarinet on the bottom. Flutes and clarinets in almost any conceivable combination will blend well and enable the jazz arranger to simulate a classical woodwind section. The typical combination of two flutes, two clarinets, and bass clarinet is capable of producing a beautiful, lush, and well-balanced orchestral timbre.

A section of four flugelhorns provides a rich, warm, and mellow contrast to the bright and brassy sound of four trumpets. Flugelhorns alone or in combination with open or muted trombones can be used to simulate the warmth and spread of French horns, providing the jazz arranger with an orchestral brass timbre. The various brass mutes, in conjunction with flugelhorns or playing in the stands, can be used in many different combinations, either homogeneously (e.g., four trumpets in harmons or cups) or mixed (e.g., one trumpet in harmon, one in cup, one in straight mute, one flugelhorn, two trombones in cups, one in bucket mute, one in the stand). When mixing mutes within a brass section, take care to use appropriate dynamic markings in order to maintain a dynamic balance within the section, since different mutes will sound at different dynamic levels. Please refer to Chapter 12 for detailed information on the various brass mutes.

Examples 28-1, 28-2, and 28-3 provide illustrations of some homogeneous combinations of woodwind and brass doubles as well as a few examples of some of the many possible brass mute configurations. Note that Ex. 28-2 features the trumpets and trombones, each separately as a section, with the rhythm section. In Ex. 28-3 the trumpets and trombones play together as a section with rhythm.

Concert Score

Ex 28-1 - "Woodwind Doubles"

Richard Sussman

A. Four Flutes, One Alto Flute

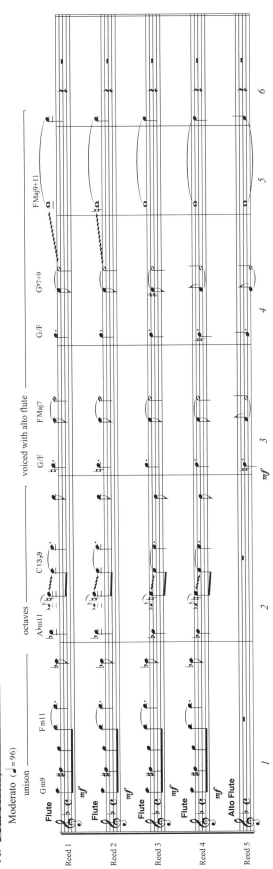

B. Four Clarinets, One Bass Clarinet

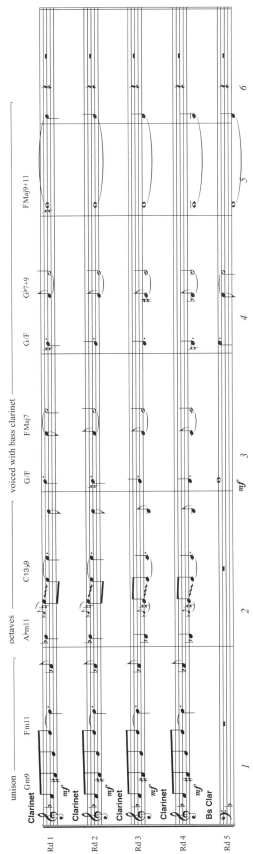

369

Ex 28-1 - "Woodwind Doubles" - 2

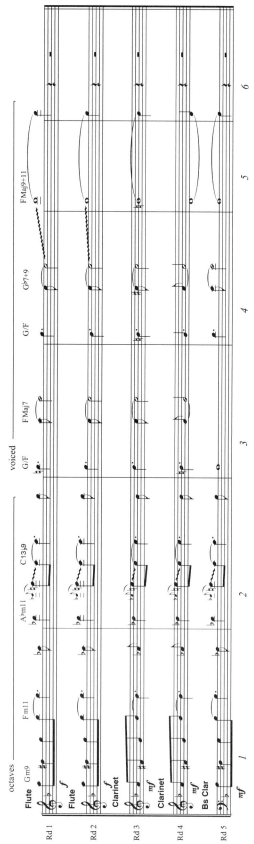

C. Two Flutes, Two Clarinets, One Bass Clarinet

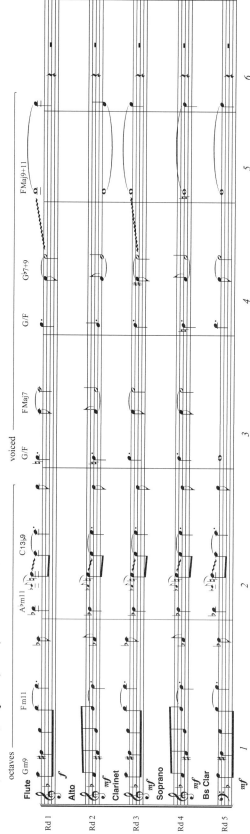

D. Flute, Clarinet, Soprano, Alto, Bass Clarinet

Notice the subtle difference between Ex. 28-1C and Ex. 28-1D. Replacing one flute and clarinet with the soprano and alto saxes adds body and richness to the timbre without negating the orchestral feel provided by the other flute, clarinet, and bass clarinet. The alto sax part is given to reed 2, and the clarinet and soprano parts are given to reeds 3 and 4, because tenor saxophonists (reeds 3 and 4) rarely double on alto sax. This would be the standard way of distributing these particular doubles among the reed section.

Ex. 28-2

"Brass Colors" 1: composed and arranged by Richard Sussman

Concert Score

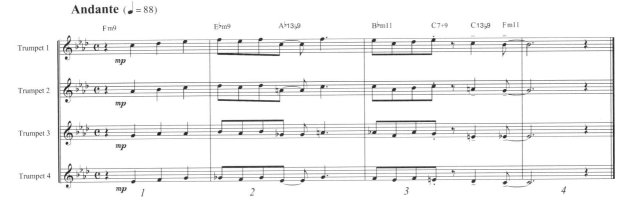

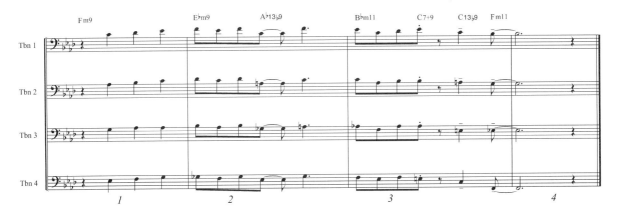

[Brass Mute Comparisons—Trumpet and Trombone Sections Separate]

a. Four flugelhorns
b. Four trumpets
c. Four trumpets in harmons
d. Four trumpets in cups
e. Four trumpets in straight mutes
f. Four trombones
g. Four trombones in buckets
h. Four trombones in cups
i. Four trombones in straight mutes

Ex. 28-3

"Brass Colors" 2: composed and arranged by Richard Sussman

Concert Score

[Brass Mute Comparisons—Trumpet and Trombone Sections Combined]

    a. Four flugelhorns + four trombones in buckets

    b. Four trumpets in cups + four trombones in cups

    c. Four trumpets and four trombones in straight mutes

    d. Two trumpets in harmons, one cup, one flugelhorn

       Two trombones in cups, one bucket, bass trombone in stand

28-4 Woodwind and Brass Doubles and Mutes: Mixed Combinations

Unison or octave combinations of woodwinds and/or muted brass can impart a distinctive color to a melody. A simple and classic device is doubling a trumpet in the mid-range with a flute an octave higher. In "Ivories Tower," an original composition by Richard Sussman commissioned as a tribute to Hank Jones, the melody is stated in this fashion at letter **B** (Ex. 28-4A).

Ex 28-4A & B "Ivories Tower" Letter "B"

by Richard Sussman

With the flute an octave above the trumpet, it projects well, although the trumpet is still the predominant timbre, with the flute sounding almost like another overtone reinforcing and coloring the sound of the trumpet. It's still a good idea to mark the flute *forte* and the trumpet *mf* or *mp* to achieve the proper balance. If the flute were an octave lower, in unison with the open trumpet, it would not be heard. Putting a Harmon mute in the trumpet in unison or octaves with the flute produces an upbeat, pixie-like quality, which has become a trademark of the great arranger/producer Quincy Jones. Example 28-4B illustrates this technique, with the same melody now played by the flute, with trumpet in Harmon mute.

Doubling two, three, or four flutes in unison can be an effective way of overcoming the flute's limited ability to project. Example 28-5A illustrates four flutes in unison playing a melody over mixed muted brass and bass clarinet. In the recorded example, Ex. 28-5A has the flutes playing with the rhythm section only. In Ex. 28-5B, a piccolo is added 8va for extra brilliance; in Ex. 28-5C, the muted brass and bass clarinet are added.

The extended lower register of the alto flute enables us to create a flute section consisting of two C flutes and two alto flutes. Example 28-6, "Exercise in Flutility," uses this technique, coupled with bass clarinet, muted brass, a flugelhorn melody, and modal harmonies, to create a haunting, ethereal piece reminiscent of Gil Evans.

Ex. 28-5

"Analycity": composed and arranged by Richard Sussman
28-5A—Four Flutes in Unison
28-5B—Three Flutes in Unison with Piccolo 8va
28-5C—Four Flutes + Bs Clar & Muted Brass

Moderate Jazz Swing (♩ = 116)

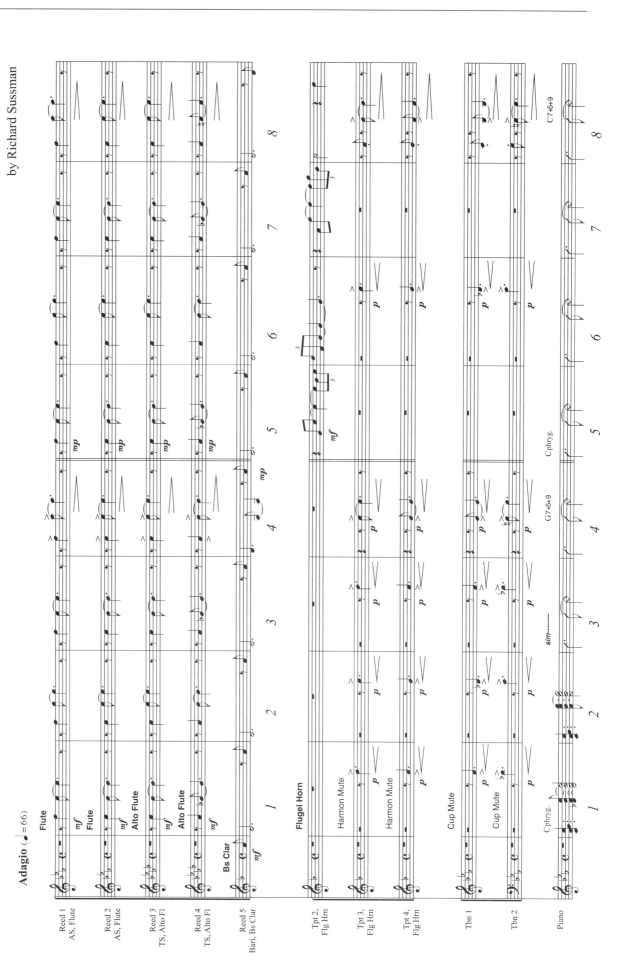

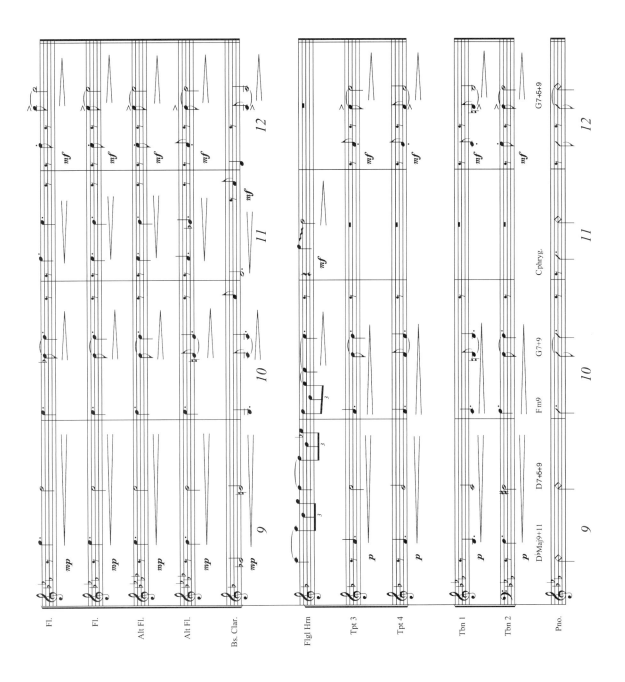

Ex 28-7 "Ivories Tower" Intro

by Richard Sussman

28-5 Orchestral Colors Within the Big Band

Flutes and clarinets can be used to impart an orchestral feel to the big band. In the absence of French horns, flugelhorns and trombones in mutes or in the stands may be used to simulate that color. A blend of flutes, clarinets, flugelhorns, and muted trombones can create a warm, lush, orchestral timbre, in stark contrast to the typical bright and brassy sound of the jazz band. Substituting a soprano sax or alto sax for one of the clarinets adds a little more body and fullness without detracting from the overall orchestral color. Listen to the lush, orchestral sound of Ex. 28-7, the intro to "Ivories Tower," scored for two flutes, clarinet, soprano sax, bass clarinet, four flugelhorns, and four trombones in stands. Notice the mellow warmth of the sound of the four flugels, a completely different timbre from anything possible with four trumpets. Incidentally, the trombones would have sounded great in buckets except that they have to be open right at m. 10, which would have given them no time to remove the mutes.

28-6 More Instrumental Subdivisions and Color Combinations

Two classic variations on the standard five-piece sax section, with alto sax lead, is to substitute a clarinet or soprano sax for the lead alto. In both cases, the extended upper range of the soprano sax and clarinet makes it possible to voice the entire sax section a little higher than is possible with alto lead. With soprano lead, the result is a slightly brighter timbre while maintaining the homogeneous quality of the sax section. With clarinet lead, the distinctive tone quality of the clarinet results in a very different timbral color for the whole section. This is the classic Glenn Miller or Benny Goodman sound popularized in the 1930s and '40s but still valid in a contemporary setting. Soprano or clarinet leads can be especially effective as an alternative color for a sax soli. Example 28-8, the sax soli from "Ivories Tower" illustrates these contrasting sounds, Ex. 28-8A with soprano lead (the original version), 28-8B with alto lead, and 28-8C with clarinet lead. Notice how the sound gets a little shrill in Ex. 28-8B because the lead alto is forced into its highest register. That's why the soprano (or clarinet) is usually a better choice if the lead line goes above the staff (concert).

Ex 28-8A, B, & C "Ivories Tower" Soli

by Richard Sussman

Chapter Summary

In this chapter we examined some of the many possible instrumental colors available to the arranger through utilizing woodwind and brass doubles and mutes. We began with a look at the most common woodwind doubles and then listed the available doubles for some of the top professional jazz orchestras. We discussed the importance of dynamics and balance when using doubles and mutes. We then examined various homogeneous and mixed (cross-sectional) combinations of these instruments.

◊ **Software Tip**: This seems like a good place to review and elaborate on some information presented in Chapter 15. To achieve satisfying MIDI playback of sections using doubles and mutes, it's important to understand how your software deals with *MIDI bank and program changes* or *key switching*. In both Finale and Sibelius, inserting an expression indicating a change to a double or mute sends a bank and program change or key switch, to call up the appropriate sound. If you stick to the default factory sound libraries (Garritan in Finale and Sibelius Essentials in Sibelius), the default settings work well. However, if you want to enhance your palette with some third-party libraries (highly recommended), you may have to do a little extra work setting up the expressions so that they send the appropriate *Bank* and *Program Changes* to the correct instruments.

If you do use third-party plug-ins for sound libraries, such as Kontakt, EWQL, or the VSL Ensemble, you will also need to be familiar with how those instruments handle program changes and dynamics. Each one is a little different in its MIDI implementation, and you will probably need to do a little tweaking on that end to ensure musically satisfying MIDI playback in your notation software.

It's also important, when working in a transposed score, to be able to manage the inevitable changes of key signature that result within a wood-wind part when changing from one instrument to another of a different transposition. For example, if reed 1 begins on alto sax (E♭), changes to flute (C), then to soprano sax (B♭), and back to alto (E♭), it will be necessary to change key signatures three times within the part, even though the actual key of the piece is not changing. Refer to the website for details on how to manage doubles and transposition changes on a staff in Finale or Sibelius.

Exercises

1. Listen to recorded examples by the composers mentioned at the beginning of this chapter. If possible, get hold of the scores, or try to identify the various doubles and mutes by ear.

2. Reorchestrate your reharmonized standard from Exercise 27-2, making use of the woodwind and brass colors discussed in this chapter. Use the Jazz Big Band Template.

3. **Arranging Project 3:** Experiment with reorchestrating sections of your big band project using the woodwind and brass colors discussed in this chapter. Do this especially in the background sections behind improvised solos.

Chapter 29

Line Writing and Polyphony

Polyphony refers to the musical texture consisting of two or more independent melodic lines. Polyphony, or counterpoint, has been a major component of the vocabulary of Western European music since the Middle Ages. The use of polyphony provides the jazz arranger with a powerful tool for adding a level of depth and complexity to the music not possible with monophonic or homophonic textures. No study of jazz arranging would be complete without a look at the specific technique for achieving independent, polyphonic lines known as *line writing*.

In all of the harmonic arranging and voicing techniques examined up to this point, the emphasis has been predominantly on considerations relating to the vertical harmonies created by combining two or more parts and the manner in which those harmonies relate to the underlying chord progression of the music. We've discussed the importance of making the inner voices as melodic as possible, but generally (with the exception of our prior, brief discussions of polyphony and countermelodies in Chapters 10 and 27) as a secondary issue to the vertical harmonies.

29-1 Basic Principles of Line Writing

The technique of line writing places the emphasis first on the melodic content of each voice, with the resultant vertical harmonies being of secondary importance. Because the priority is the melodic contour of each part, the vertical harmonies produced can tend to be more dissonant, ambiguous, and less functional than those produced by more traditional voicing techniques. For this reason, the technique of line writing is generally more effective at faster tempos, where the passing vertical harmonies produced are less noticeable.

The first step in the line-writing procedure is to analyze the harmonic content of the primary, lead melody and to designate target notes within it. These target notes will generally be of longer duration at the beginning or end of a phrase and frequently coincide with a chord change in the primary harmony. In other words, a target note will usually coincide with a chord symbol. This is similar to the first step in the various techniques for the reharmonization of approach tones. However, this is where the similarity ends. With line writing, the next step is to select a suitable chord scale based on the chord symbol harmonizing the notes in between target points. Then you simply construct independent melodies derived from the appropriate chord scale for each of the remaining voices.

All previously examined principles for constructing good melodies and good voice leading are relevant to this process. For example, each line should have an interesting melodic shape, with a balance between scalar motion and skips of larger intervals. Generally, no inner voice should skip by an interval larger than the lead melody. Avoid gaps larger than a major sixth between any two adjacent voices except the bottom two, avoid excessive repeated notes in any given part, and basically just strive to make each part as melodically interesting as possible. Contrary motion, especially between the outer two voices, is always effective. After completing a section, go back and carefully analyze the vertical harmonies and correct any voicing or voice leading problems that may have occurred, such as unwanted dissonances or doublings, parallel fifths, and parallel seconds between the top two voices.

29-2 Line-Writing Procedure

Example 29-1 illustrates the application of line-writing techniques using the following procedure.

1. Analyze the primary melody, and designate target notes.
2. Voice the vertical harmonies at the target points, based on the designated chord symbol and using any of the harmonic techniques examined thus far for chord voicings, such as close position, semi-open, drop-2, open position, chords by fourths, clusters, and modal techniques.
3. Based on the designated chord symbols assigned to target notes, determine the appropriate chord scales for notes in between the target points.

4. Create melodic lines connecting the target notes for each part using notes from the appropriate chord scales. Observe all applicable principles for melodic construction and good voice leading. If there are chromatic passing tones in the lead melody line, the chord scales used by the under voices should be adjusted accordingly (e.g., up or down a half step), or you can reharmonize those notes using approach tone reharmonization techniques.

5. Analyze the resultant vertical harmonies, and correct any voicing or voice-leading problems, such as unintended dissonances or doublings, parallel fifths, or parallel seconds between the top two voices.

6. In general, try to preserve the same positioning of voices as in other voicing solutions; however, it's OK occasionally to land on unisons or to cross voices to prioritize the melodic integrity of each part.

7. Strive for contrary motion whenever possible, especially between the outer two voices.

Example 29-1A shows the original melody ("Linealogy"—a variation of "Unithology" from Chapter 21) with chord changes. In Example 29-1B we indicate the target notes and chords. Example 29-1C displays the target chords voiced in sketch format. Example 29-1D shows the target chords voiced in score format. Example 29-1E illustrates our first pass at a line-writing solution, with the chord scales (derived from the target chords) written above the lead alto part. Finally, Ex. 29-1F illustrates a revised line-writing solution, with some unwanted dissonances and voice-leading problems corrected and with chromatic passing tones reharmonized in an appropriate manner.

Our primary concern here is to preserve the integrity of each line and to observe principles of good voice leading rather than focusing on the vertical harmonies, as we would when using approach tone harmonization techniques (except where there are chromatic passing tones in the melody, as pointed out in number 4 in the preceding list). However, if we can find other places to work in a secondary dominant, parallel approach or a diminished chord, that would only be a plus. Study carefully and compare the differences between Exs. 29-1E and 29-1F at a keyboard and while listening to the recordings. Play through each part in Ex. 29-1E separately. Notice that each part has an interesting melodic shape of its own. The melodic strength of all the voices results in a passage that sounds musical in spite of some voice leading problems and unwanted dissonances because they go by so quickly. Our ear is drawn to the melodic, lyrical quality of all the inner voices. However, the revisions in Ex. 29-1F result in a much smoother and more satisfying solution.

Ex. 29-1

"Linealogy," composed and arranged by Richard Sussman.

A. Original Melody & Changes

B. Melody with target points indicated by "x"

C. Melody with target points voiced

D. Melody with target points voiced in score

Ex. 29-1D "Linealogy"

Richard Sussman

E. First pass at line writing solution

Ex. 29-1E "Linealogy"

F. Revised line writing solution

Ex. 29-1E "Linealogy"

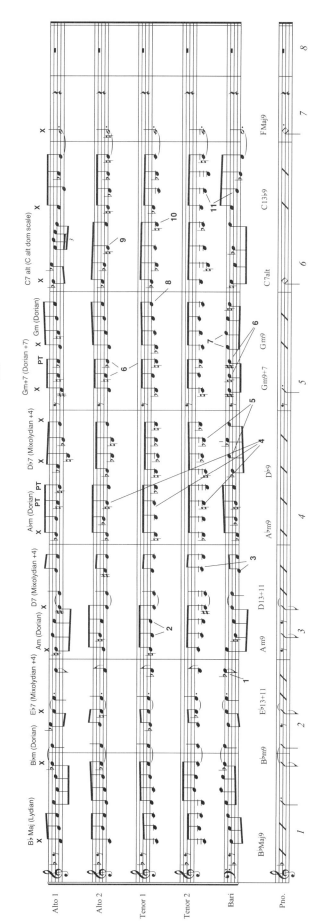

1. Avoids too many B♭s on the last note of m. 2.
2. Avoids a m7 gap between TS 1 and 2, avoids hidden fifths between AS 2 and TS 1 and between TS1 & 2, and creates more interesting counterpoint with contrary motion.
3. Avoids a "too consonant" B minor triad on beat 4 and a hidden fifth between TS 2 and the bari, and provides more contrary motion between AS 1 and the bari.
4. Avoids an unwanted dissonance between the A natural in the lead and the A♭ in TS 2 on m.3 beat 2. A smoother sound is achieved by harmonizing the A and G natural chromatic passing tones in AS 1 as Am7 and C9.
5. Avoids crossing TS 2 and the bari.
6. Reharmonizing both passing tones creates more interesting harmonic motion on beat 2 and eliminates unwanted dissonance on the and of beat 2. It also avoids TS1 crossing under TS2. Melodic shape and contrary motion are preserved in the bari part.
7. A more musical line for the bari after the other changes.
8. Avoids a "too consonant" F Maj triad.
9. Keeps a chord third in the voicing.
10. Creates a full D♭13 voicing, by keeping the chord seventh in the voicing, for a stronger secondary dominant (tritone sub) pull to the following C13 chord.
11. Avoids doubling A by the two tenors, and creates a better melodic line for the second tenor. We opted *not* to give TS 1 the concert B♭ here, which would have been a stronger choice harmonically, in favor of creating a more interesting melodic line with contrary motion to the bari.

Line writing is most commonly used when all voices within a section are moving in rhythmic unison. However, the same techniques can be applied to rhythmically independent voices (Ex. 29-2A) or to a subset of instruments within a larger ensemble. In Ex. 29-2B we added harmonized rhythmic hits and a countermelody in the brass to the sax section line writing passage. (It was necessary to modify a couple of spots in the sax parts to avoid clashes with the brass.)

Concert Score

Ex. 29-2A "Linealogy" - Rhythmically Independant Lines

Richard Sussman

Medium Swing (♩ = 132)

Ex. 29-2B "Linealogy" Line Writing in Sax Section with Brass Added

Medium Swing (♩ = 132)

- Richard Sussman

29-3 Increasing or Decreasing the Number of Harmonized Voices: "Lineaology"

It can be musically expressive and dramatic to increase or decrease the number of voices harmonizing a line within a melodic phrase. For example, if a melodic line is ascending, you can begin the phrase in unison or octaves, adding additional harmonizing notes as the line ascends, or vice versa. Line-writing techniques can be effectively applied to this process (Ex. 29-3). Study Ex. 29-3 and listen to the recording on the companion website. Notice how the line expands from unison/octave to a thick five-note voicing in mm. 1–2 and 5–6. If the new parts are added at regular intervals (e.g., every two or four beats), using melodic imitation from the top down or the bottom up) a cascading or pyramid effect can be produced (Ex. 29-4).

1. Starts in unison/octaves and expands to three voices by the end of bar 1.
2. Continues to expand to five voices on the E♭13+11 chord.
3. Stays around four to five voices.
4. Four voices contract to three.
5. Stays with three or four voices through bar 4.
6. Back to unison/octaves.
7. Expanding to four voices.
8. Back to five voices. Stays with 4 or 5 voices until the end.

Ex. 29-3 "Linealogy" Increasing/Decreasing Voices

Richard Sussman

Concert Score

Medium Swing (♩ = 132)

Ex. 29-4

Cascade Effect: "Linealogy," composed and arranged by Richard Sussman

Concert Score

29-4 Additional Examples of Polyphonic Big Band Writing

The number of ways to apply polyphonic techniques to jazz writing is almost unlimited. One method that's relatively straightforward and effective is to have two sections playing independent polyphonic lines, either with both sections in unison/octaves or with one section in unison/octaves and the other section voiced. All of the basic principles regarding polyphonic writing, first presented in Section 10-2, still apply. It's especially important to give the two (or more) polyphonic lines contrasting melodic shapes that complement each other, keeping the individual lines distinct from one another. Following are several simple techniques for accomplishing this.

1. Contrary motion (one line ascends while the other descends).
2. Contrast of melodic density (less active—longer note values in one line—vs. more active—shorter notes values in the other).
3. Contrast of melodic shape and motion (one line skips around while the other plays more scalar motion).

All of these techniques can be switched from one line to another at any point to create more interesting textural contrast and variety. A great example of this kind of contrapuntal writing is the end of the head to Bob Mintzer's chart "Art of the Big Band." (See Ex. 33-3 for this example and a more detailed analysis of this chart.) Notice how the simple, lyrical unison trumpet line contrasts beautifully with the more active unison/octaves sax section line. The entire passage is supported harmonically and rhythmically by the trombone section playing syncopated chordal hits. The passage develops into a shout chorus, with the brass voiced in rhythmic unison and the sax section continuing the more active linear counterpoint from the preceding section. We'll examine "Art of the Big Band" in greater detail in Chapter 33.

Another approach to polyphony in jazz writing is to borrow concepts from classical music, such as imitative and fugal techniques. In Ex. 29-5A, "One for Thad," Richard's tribute to Thad Jones, check out the initial theme at letter **A** and the contrapuntal interplay between the voiced brass and the unison saxes. This becomes the thematic material at letter "J" for a short three-voice fugue, scored for two trombones, two saxes, and two trumpets (Ex. 29-5B).

Ex. 29-5A "One For Thad" Head

Richard Sussman

397

Ex. 29-5A "One For Thad" Head - 2

Ex. 29-5B "One For Thad" Fugue

Richard Sussman

Up Tempo Swing (♩ =180)

Ex. 29-5B "One For Thad" Fugue - 2

Ex. 29-5B "One For Thad" Fugue - 3

There is a wealth of examples of polyphonic writing in the music of most modern jazz writers, including Thad Jones, Bob Brookmeyer, Bill Holman, Jim McNeely, Bob Mintzer, and, of course, Michael Abene.

Chapter Summary

In this chapter we examined the important jazz-arranging technique known as *line writing*. We provided a step-by-step procedure for achieving this effect and reviewed some basic principles of good melodic construction and voice leading. We illustrated techniques for creating cascading (pyramid) effects within a phrase. We also provided several additional examples of the effective use of polyphony in jazz big band writing.

◊ **Important**: As with other elements of the music, the most effective use of polyphony will generally be achieved by drawing on a variety of techniques, such as line writing in combination with reharmonization of approach tones. Concepts of counterpoint drawn from classical theory, such as rhythmic independence of the contrapuntal lines (Ex. 29-2A), can be applied with good effect to jazz writing. In fact, we highly recommend that any serious aspiring jazz writer undertake a thorough study of classical species counterpoint, just as any aspiring classical composer would. Although the strict rules of species counterpoint (no parallel or hidden fifths, etc.) need not be applied in a strict manner to jazz writing, we find that when these principles are considered, it invariably leads to better and more musical voicing choices.

◊ **Software Tip**: It's important to understand how to manage *layers* (Finale) and *voices* (Sibelius), especially when working with polyphonic parts that you may want to reduce down to one or two staves for a piano reduction or a piano part. Refer to the website for details on how to manage layers and voices in Finale or Sibelius.

Exercises

1. Listen to any recorded examples by the arranger Bill Holman. If possible, get hold of the scores. Try to identify sections where he employs line-writing techniques. Analyze how the use of polyphony adds depth and complexity to the music.

2. Voice the following melody (Exercise 29-2, available for download from the companion website) for five saxes using the line-writing techniques discussed in this chapter. Copy and paste into the 5-6 Horn + Rhythm Template. Adjust the staff names and transpositions using the Staff Tool (Finale), or by using Create > Other > Instrument Change (Sibelius).

3. Copy and paste your solution to Exercise 29-2 into the Jazz Big Band Template. Add chordal hits and/or countermelodies in the brass section.

4. **Arranging Project 3:** Experiment with reorchestrating sections of your big band project using line-writing techniques.

Exercise 29-2

Line Writing

Medium Swing (♩ = 124)

Chapter 30

The Soli Section (Big Band)

The soli section and the shout chorus of a big band arrangement are those segments of the chart that allow the arranger the greatest degree of creative freedom. Unlike improvised solo sections with backgrounds, where the arranger's job is naturally to highlight and support the efforts of individual soloists, the soli and shout chorus are actually composed by the arranger.

It's important to understand that the strict differentiation between the soli and shout chorus (described in the next chapter) stems from classic forms that evolved during the swing era of the 1930s and '40s, culminating in the work of arrangers such as Duke Ellington, Frank Foster, Frank Wess, Benny Carter, and Thad Jones in the 1950s and '60s and beyond.

However, among more modern jazz arrangers, the distinction between soli and shout chorus can often become blurred, resulting in what could be better referred to as an "ensemble" section. For example, a sax soli may be punctuated with brass hits that become more active, eventually evolving into more of a shout chorus. Similarly, a rhythmic shout chorus in the brass may be accompanied by more active counterpoint in the saxes rather than keeping the saxes in rhythmic unison with the brass (as in a classic "Frank Foster/Basie" type of shout).

Nevertheless, it's beneficial to approach each of these two elements of the arrangement separately, since there are still many situations where you may be called on to write a classic sax soli or shout chorus. With experience, it's easy to make the jump to combining the various elements into a more free-flowing ensemble section.

30-1 Basic Principles and Method for Creating the Soli Section

The basic considerations for constructing a soli section are presented in Section 18-1. Before proceeding, please take a few minutes to review that material, which may be applied to ensembles of any size. Big band solis can be spiced up in a number of other ways, including switching the line from one section or group of instruments to another, introducing polyphonic countermelodies, and supporting the melodic line with chordal and rhythmic parts played by other instruments.

When writing a soli section for any size ensemble, always start with a single, strong melodic line; then decide whether or not to harmonize it. If you're a jazz improviser, try to imagine how you might want a solo to sound on the tune you're arranging, and then write it down. Always be careful to respect the ranges and technical limitations of the instruments you've chosen to write for. For example, if you're a sax player writing for brass, be careful to avoid writing soli lines that may be easily playable on saxophones but difficult or impossible to execute by brass instruments; if you're a rhythm section player, please remember to leave space for the horn players to breathe!

Once you've got the primary melodic line, if you're going to harmonize it, it's important to give the line a strong and distinctive harmonization, using the various techniques for harmonizing a melody and reharmonization of approach tones. It's equally important to pay close attention to the voice leading and melodic shapes of all the inner voices, avoiding excessive repeated notes, awkward melodic skips, and boring melodic shapes. A strong melodic line supported by a weak harmonization and poor inner voice writing will sound weak. Conversely, a weaker primary melody supported by a strong harmonization and good inner voice writing may sound stronger.

If you do decide to harmonize the line, it's not always necessary to maintain the same number of chord tones in each voicing. For example, if writing a five-part sax soli, you may start with the saxes in unison and octaves, then move to four-note close position chords, with the melody doubled 8vb in the bari, then drop down to two- or three-note chords (*not* by dropping out instruments but by having more chord tones doubled), and then move back to four- or five-note chords, similar to the technique demonstrated in Ex. 29-3. Remember, any chord tones may be doubled or omitted. The determining factors are the desired amount of consonance or dissonance, the chord density, and whether or not to double the melody.

Contrary motion is almost always a good thing. Although parallel motion is easier and more obvious, contrary motion will make the passage more interesting. The solution may not always be apparent. It can be time-consuming, even for the most seasoned professionals, but it is time well spent! Also, a unison line with a three- or four-octave spread can sometimes sound thicker and more powerful than a weakly harmonized line.

Example 30-1 A presents a melody for the first eight bars of a possible soli line on the tune "Analycity," borrowed from Ex. 18-1. This will now be scored as a traditional sax soli within the big band arrangement. Example 30-1B shows the line scored for the sax section in unison and octaves. Example 30-1C is the same line harmonized primarily in close and semi-open position, making use of a variety of approach tone reharmonization techniques (indicated in the score), with some brass hits and a trombone countermelody thrown in for spice. For a reduction of Ex. 30-1C please refer to Ex. 30-1D on the website." Listen to the recorded example, study the score, and compare this example to the earlier version, Ex. 18-1 for six horns.

Refer to the Listening List at the end of this chapter for more examples of classic big band solis.

Ex. 30-1A

"Analycity" Soli Line Melody, by Richard Sussman

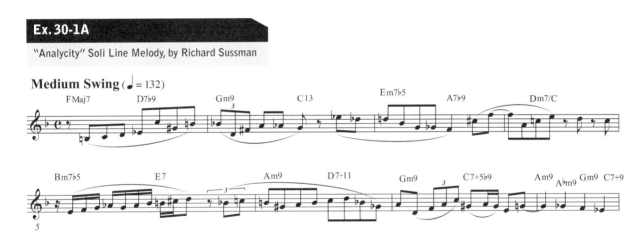

Ex. 30-1B

"Analycity" Sax Soli Unison/Octaves, composed and arranged by Richard Sussman

Medium Swing ($\bullet$ = 132)

Concert Score

Ex 30-1C "Analycity" Sax Soli Voiced

Medium Swing (♩ = 132)

— Richard Sussman

Ex. 30-1C Legend for Reharmonization of Approach Tones

T = target note
D = diatonic
P = parallel
SD = secondary dominant
Alt = altered chord tones
F = free reharmonization

30-2 Analysis of "Analycity" Soli Example 30-1A, B, and C

We created this example by following the steps outlined earlier, beginning with composing a single melodic line over the changes to the tune. Care was taken to give the line an interesting melodic shape, with lots of changes in direction and contrasting types of melodic motion and note values, bop-style chromatic passing tones, and asymmetrical phrase structure overlapping the bar lines and harmonic rhythm.

In Ex. 30-1B we scored the line in unison and octaves, starting with the first tenor doubling the altos and the second tenor doubling the bari 8vb. Notice on the last beat of m. 3 that we dropped TS 1 down an octave, because the high G would have put it out of the instrument's range. We moved the part back up in m. 5, dropping it down again at the end of the bar because it seemed to feel more relaxed and less shrill to do so. On the last measure we decided to expand the saxes to an open position voicing, just because it seemed logical and felt right.

In Ex. 30-1C we voiced the line for five saxes and added some brass hits and a trombone countermelody in mm. 5–6. The saxes were voiced first, using a combination of techniques, including reharmonization of approach tones, line writing, contrasting voicing positions, and contrary motion. The emphasis was really on maintaining melodic interest in all of the inner voices, so in a sense this was more an exercise in line writing. However, a great deal of care was also given to maintaining a strong and interesting harmonization of the melody, especially with regard to approach tones, so more attention was given to vertical harmonies than in line writing in the strictest sense.

The voicings change freely from close position to semi-open to drop-2 and back, with a few unisons thrown in for good measure, finally winding up in open position on the last bar, as in Ex. 30-1B. Occasionally the two tenor parts cross to provide more melodic interest through contrary motion (mm. 1 and 4). The various types of approach tone reharmonization and voicing positions are indicated above the top staff (see the accompanying legend). Note the effectiveness of successive diminished seventh chords for harmonizing the sixteenth-note run in m. 5. We left out some of the slurs and articulations to keep things legible and uncluttered.

Finally, the brass hits and trombone countermelody were added to the saxes. There are a few real dissonant crunches between the brass and saxes (m. 3, first chord, and the trombone countermelody in m. 5), which don't seem to matter because of the strong melodic content of the brass parts and the fast eighth-note motion of the saxes.

30-3 Analysis of "Swangalang" Sax Soli by Bob Mintzer

The sax soli in Bob Mintzer's "Swangalang," a 12-bar blues in B♭, is a great example of a fairly straight-ahead yet modern-sounding soli, based on a strong, simple, bluesy melody (see the reduction with analysis in Ex. 30-2). The full score of the soli is also available for download from the website. The voicing positions move freely between close position, semi-open position, fourth chords, and open position. The passage begins in traditional close position for the first 2½ bars, complete with some classic half-step planing at the beginning of m. 2. By the middle of m. 3 we're ready for some contrary motion, as the voicings open up to drop-2, and drop-2 and -4.

Bar 5 begins with an example of Mintzer's fondness for fourth chords, instantly lending a more modern sound to the harmonies. However, the voicings immediately begin moving away from the fourths sonority in m. 6, winding up back in close position in mm. 7 and 8. Notice how the tasteful use of contrary motion and the consequent expansion of the voicings adds interest and spice to the passage. Above all, when studying the individual lines closely, we get the feeling that a key underlying priority was maintaining the melodic interest and integrity of each of the parts.

The second chorus begins with a simple Basie-ish rhythmic figure on the tonic B♭, but voiced solidly with fourths. The half-step planing down provides a hip reharmonization of the IV chord in m. 14, which quickly resolves upward with a stock chromatic figure to B♭13 in the following measure. Fourth chords heavily color the next three bars. Notice the textural contrast provided by the quick alternation between fourths and open position for the two-note repeated rhythmic figure in mm. 17–18. In measures 19–20 we return to a more inside drop-2 feel, with a couple of fourth chords thrown in.

Measures 21–22 are notable for the use of parallel *constant structures* (a series of chords that maintains constant intervallic relationships between the various inner voices—see Section 27-1), in this case triads in the top three voices over perfect fourths in the bottom two. Notice the unexpected rhythmic twist and asymmetrical phrase structure given to a familiar blues lick in mm. 22–23. The drop down to the low G in the bari at the end of m. 23 provides contrary motion to the downbeat of m. 24. The constant-structure fourths in the bottom two voices return in m. 24. A quick descent in the bari for a contrasting open position voicing on the dominant F prepares us for a stronger resolution to the last, fat, dissonant B♭7+9 (13) chord. As with Joe Lovano's "On a Misty Night" and also the later example of Bob's "Art of the Big Band," we haven't provided a recording. Please support these great artists and buy the CDs or download the music!

411

Ex. 30-2

Sax Soli Reduction of "Swangalang," composed and arranged by Bob Mintzer

412

30-4 Analysis of "Memories of Lives Past" Mixed-Section Soli by Michael Abene

The beautiful, lyrical soli section to Michael Abene's gorgeous original tune "Memories of Lives Past," written for Dick Oatts, provides a striking contrast to the more traditional sax solis examined in the previous two examples. First of all, it's scored for a cross-sectional ensemble consisting of two flutes, three B♭ clarinets, three flugelhorns, two trumpets in harmons, three euphoniums, bass trombone, guitar, and rhythm. A euphonium is a conical-bore, tenor-range brass instrument, similar to a tuba, commonly found in brass bands but unusual in a jazz context. Its range is similar to that of the tenor trombone, but its conical bore results in a softer, mellower timbre.

The passage begins in unison/octaves with two flutes, two clarinets, one trumpet in harmon mute, and one flugelhorn. This light, unison timbre provides an ethereal sound perfectly suited to the lush harmonies of the tune. Although the underlying tonality is definitely E, the long F pedal, overlaid with a nonfunctional, modulating chord progression, creates a polytonal, impressionistic mood, which resolves only in the last four bars of the section. One striking feature of the melodic line is the use of groups of four quarter notes against the underlying 3/4 meter. Combined with triplet syncopation, this creates a free-flowing, lyrical melody that seems somehow to float across the bar lines. Abene builds the soli in m. 11 by adding more instruments and by introducing a parallel m3/Maj 6 harmonization of the melody in some parts.

The intensity builds again in mm. 19–21 with the introduction of the euphoniums, bass trombone, and guitar. Notice the subtle use of contrary motion in the entrance of the first five notes of euphoniums 1 and 2—accomplished without adding any additional chord tones! In fact, the two-note parallel m3/Maj 6 harmonization is maintained until the introduction of the low E in the trombones and guitar in m. 25. We finally hear a full, four-note jazz voicing with the B7♭9 chord in m. 28. The passage ends with some lush four- to six-note clusters in the last three bars. Study the reduction (Ex. 30-3) as you listen to the recording. The complete score of the soli is available on the website.

413

414

Ex 30-3 "Memories Of Lives Past" Soli Reduction

- Michael Abene

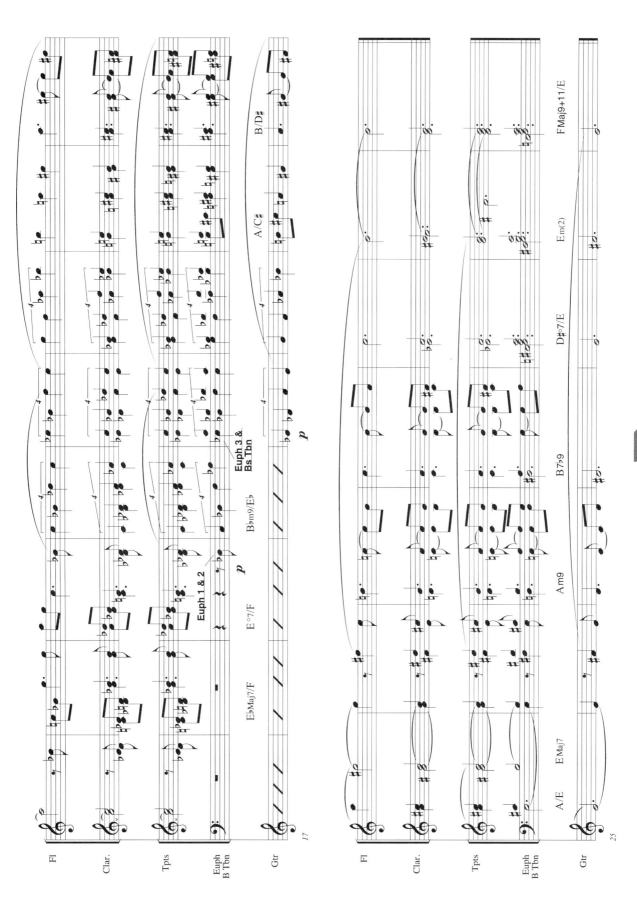

Ex 30-3 "Memories Of Lives Past" Soli Reduction - 2

415

Chapter Summary

In this chapter we examined the process of constructing a soli section for the big band. We reviewed some material from Chapter 18 and determined that the soli can be scored in unison/octaves or voiced, or a combination of the two, and can be written for one section or for cross-sectional combinations. We then analyzed three contrasting soli sections from different arrangements.

◊ **Software Tip**: Occasionally it's necessary to manually adjust the position of an accidental, rest, or notehead, or adjust the length of a stem, position of a beam, or other symbols, in order to keep the music looking clean and legible. Repositioning expressions, dynamic markings, and articulations are easily handled in both Finale and Sibelius. Please refer to the website for details.

Exercises

1. Listen to any recorded examples of solis by Duke Ellington, Frank Foster, Thad Jones, and others from the following Listening List. If possible, get hold of the scores. Try to identify whether the soli is unison/octaves or voiced and what types of voicing positions are used. Analyze what the rest of the ensemble is doing to support or enhance the soli.

2. **Arranging Project 3:** Add a 16- to 32-bar soli to your big band arrangement. It can be all unison/octaves, all voiced, or any combination of the two. Use techniques discussed in this chapter. Include articulations, dynamics, and full rhythm section parts.

Listening List of Some Classic Big Band Solis
1. Duke Ellington—"Perdido" (The Great Paris Concert)
2. Frank Foster (Basie)—"TV Time," "Who Me?" (Chairman Of the Board)
3. Benny Carter (Basie)—"Easy Money" (Echoes Of an Era)
4. Thad Jones—"Three And One," "Cherry Juice," "Little Pixie"

Refer to Appendix B on the companion website for a more extensive list of big band solis.

Chapter 31

The Shout Chorus (Big Band)

The shout chorus is traditionally the most powerful and climactic section of a big band arrangement, generally occurring near the end of the chart, just before the recapitulation, and occasionally replacing the recap entirely to end the arrangement. Like the soli, it is an ensemble section composed by the arranger, often based on material derived from the tune or earlier sections of the arrangement but sometimes containing entirely new material. However, unlike the soli, the classic shout chorus is often written for the entire ensemble playing in rhythmic unison or for the brass section in rhythmic unison accompanied by counterpoint or riffs in the saxes. It is generally more powerful, more rhythmic, and less lyrical than the soli.

As we pointed out in the preceding chapter, in contemporary jazz big band writing the distinction between soli and shout chorus is not always as clear-cut as it was in the 1940s, '50s, and '60s. Shout-like rhythmic figures may be combined with more linear, soli-type melodies in an ensemble section. There may be more than one shout chorus and several solis interspersed throughout an arrangement. There's really no formula for composing either a soli or a shout chorus, and the composer/arranger has a great deal of flexibility in terms of where to place these elements within the overall structure of an arrangement.

31-1 Basic Characteristics of the Shout Chorus

The basic considerations for constructing a shout chorus are presented in Section 18-3, as well as in Appendix A. Before proceeding, please take a few minutes to review that material, which may be applied to ensembles of any size. As with the soli, we recommend beginning with a single, strong lead line, which in the case of a shout chorus will always be played by the lead trumpet, often in its upper register. For the shout chorus, it can be best to start with a strong rhythmic idea and then to fill in the notes of the melodic contour. The actual melodies may be fairly simple, blues-oriented, and riff-like, with the emphasis being more on the rhythmic than the melodic content of the lead line.

In contrast to the soli, which may be in unison/octaves, harmonized, or a combination of the two, the shout chorus is almost always harmonized. A good way to achieve a lean and powerful harmonization for a shout chorus is to start with the four-note chord voicings associated with the "Basie Sound," described in Section 22-6. Use either Style 1, with the trumpets voiced in close position and trombones doubling the trumpets 8vb, or Style 2, with the trumpets voiced in triads, trumpet 4 doubling the lead, and the trombones supporting the trumpets in semi-open or open position. However, since the lead trumpet will often reach into the upper register during a shout, Style 2 will generally be the most likely choice.

Work out the brass voicings first, and then add the saxes to the brass using one of the coupling techniques described in Chapter 23. By keeping the harmonic content relatively simple (four-note chords), a more powerful and vibrant overall sound will be achieved (e.g., with four-note chords and 13 instruments, each note will be doubled/reinforced several times). Because the shout chorus is more powerful and climactic, generally with simpler melodic content than the head, it can be very effective to expand the voicings to open position, with chord roots in the lowest part. In this case, contrary motion between the top and bottom voices or between the sax and brass sections (through the technique of variable coupling) can effectively increase the impact and musical interest of the shout chorus.

In general, it's a good idea to voice the brass and sax sections so that each sounds complete harmonically, as described in Chapter 23. However, sometimes the baritone sax may replace the bass trombone as the lowest voice of the ensemble, putting the bari more with the brass than with the saxes. It's usually not a good idea to have both the bari and bass bone doubling the chord roots, because this can cause the ensemble to sound bottom heavy and sluggish.

More complex, dense chord voicings, containing five or more notes, may also be used to create a powerful sound for the shout chorus, provided that the melodic content is simple and rhythmically strong. The powerful rhythmic unison sections may also be combined with linear or rhythmic counterpoint played by another instrumental color, to increase the musical complexity and intensity of the passage (e.g., powerful, rhythmic material voiced for the full brass section accompanied by a more active countermelody played by the saxes in unison/octaves). Refer to the Listening List at the end of this chapter for more examples of classic big band shout choruses.

31-2 Analysis of "Unithology" Shout Chorus

We created a sample shout chorus on the last eight bars of "Unithology" (Ex. 21-2) by following the steps outlined earlier, beginning with the composition of a simple rhythm figure suitable for a shout (Ex. 31-1A). Then we created a lead trumpet melody based on our rhythm sketch and the changes to the tune (Ex. 31-1B).

We reached into the upper register of the lead trumpet for extra power and also made some reference to the original melody of the tune (mm. 4 and 6). Some characteristic brass effects were added: a rip up to the high G in m. 4, a long fall in m. 7, and a shake in m. 8. We ended the melody with a characteristic blues-based figure in the last three bars. Some liberties were taken with the original harmonization of the tune in order to create a more powerful, direct, and bluesier reharmonization to support our lead line.

Then we voiced the brass section in a "Basie Sound" style, with trumpet 4 doubling the lead most of the time and with liberal use of open position voicings in the trombones for extra strength. An effort was made to create contrary motion between the lead and the bass trombone part wherever possible. Approach tones were reharmonized, and some of the original harmonization from the sketch got changed as a result. Notice how we opened up the trumpet voicings on the last beat of m. 4 through beat 3 of m. 6 so that trumpet 3 (instead of trumpet 4) is doubling the lead. This was done to avoid having the entire trumpet section become too high and screechy as the lead rises into the upper register. *Listen to the recording of Ex. 31-1C, "Unithology" Shout Chorus and study the reduction in Ex. 31-1D for more detailed illustrations of the following analysis. It would also be a good idea to print out the lead sheet (Ex. 21-2—go to the Chapter 21 section on the website) or to turn to that page in the book while following the harmonic analysis.*

Ex. 31-1A

"Unithology" Shout Rhythmic Sketch

Medium Swing (♩ = 144)

Ex. 31-1B

"Unithology" Shout Lead Trumpet Line

Medium Swing (♩ = 144)

Ex. 31-1C "Unithology" Shout Chorus

- Richard Sussman

Ex. 31-1D

"Unithology" — Shout Chorus Reduction, composed and arranged by Richard Sussman

Legend for Ex. 31-1D

Alt = altered tones   Dis = displaced harmony

SD = secondary dominant   RHrm = melodic reharmonization

TT = tritone substitution   Over Dom Ped = over dominant pedal

The B♭ Maj 7 in m. 1 was changed to B♭13+11, and the second bar was given an E♭13+11, preceded by an altered D7 chord to lend a bluesier feel to the opening of the shout chorus. The A♭m9-D♭7+5 and E♭m11-A♭13 from mm. 2–3 of the original tune were preserved, but they were displaced rhythmically to support the syncopated rhythms of the shout. Also, the E♭m11 and A♭13+11 are each approached by reharmonized approach tones. The A♭ on the "and" of beat 2 of m. 4 (originally harmonized by D9+11) is reharmonized as G13♭9, the secondary dominant of the next chord, Gm7/C (C7sus), an alteration and rhythmically displaced version of the ii chord from m. 6 of the original tune.

The bluesy figure in mm. 5–6 of the shout is harmonized by secondary dominants over a dominant pedal. The resolution to B♭ in m. 6 is accomplished with a tritone substitution to B7+9, and once again the B♭ Maj 7 is replaced by B♭13+11 for a bluesier feel more characteristic of the shout chorus. The final F7+5+9 is approached by a series of secondary dominants moving in contrary motion to the lead.

The saxes were voiced using a variable coupling technique, with the lead alto frequently in contrary motion to the lead trumpet for added musical interest. The saxes, trombones 3 and 4, bass, and piano left hand hit a low F pedal in bar 5 for contrast. Finally we filled in the rhythm section parts. The brass voicings are written out for the piano, to avoid clashes, and the guitar part is given only the lead trumpet melody to double, for the same reason. The brass rhythms are indicated in the bass and drum parts, and drum fills were added in the spaces between melodic phrases.

In m. 1, the bass trombone drops down to the low B♭ to create contrary motion with the lead, and the baritone doubles the B♭ root 8va to fill in the resulting large gap between trombones 3 and 4. The bass bone jumps up an octave in m. 2, beat 3, to prepare for the higher semi-open position trombone voicing in the following measure. We decided to keep the bari on the low F in m. 6, reinforcing the bass and creating a little rhythmic counterpoint with the rest of the band.

31-3 Analysis of "Get a Handel on It" Shout Chorus by Richard Sussman

"Get a Handel on It" is an arrangement by Richard written for the WDR big band in Cologne, Germany, for a concert featuring jazz interpretations of the music of George Frederic Handel. The chart is based on a tune derived from a march from Handel's "Water Music Suite," which somehow seemed to develop naturally into a romping shout chorus. The shout chorus (Ex. 31-2) grows out of a mixed-section soli scored for flute, alto sax, clarinet, tenor sax, bass clarinet, two muted trumpets, and two flugelhorns. The trombones enter toward the end of the soli, and the trumpet section switches to five open trumpets for the two-bar pickup into the shout at letter **H**.

This shout chorus differs from the preceding example in that the "Unithology" shout chorus features the brass and saxes predominantly in rhythmic unison, whereas here the brass and saxes are played off against each other in a series of overlapping riff-like phrases. The shout begins at m. 185, with four measures of the brass section voiced in a classic, tight "Basie Sound" style. The addition of the fifth trumpet gives us some more options, with the 8vb lead double shifting between trumpets 4 and 5, the second trumpet also occasionally doubling the lead, and the trombones supporting the trumpets in semi-open or open position. The voicings consist of four- or five-note voicings, with lots of upper-structure triads in the trumpets.

At m. 189, the saxes enter with a two-bar response to the brass voiced in unison and octaves. Then follows a quick call and response between the brass and saxes of a two-bar bluesy riff derived from the brass melody at mm. 187–188. The phrases overlap, creating some interesting yet simple counterpoint, with the two sections finally joining together in rhythmic unison in the last two measures.

Notice the full rhythm section support of all the horn figures, including the written-out piano part (without chord symbols) and the guitar tacet (to avoid harmonic clashes with the horns and the piano). The original score and piano part do not contain chord symbols in this section; they are provided here only to facilitate analysis of the chord voicings. Notice also the rhythmic anchor provided by the unison/octave trombones, piano left hand, and bass in mm. 191–193.

The fundamentally rhythmic and bluesy nature of the passage provides a good example of traditional, classic shout chorus writing. Note the contrary motion between the trumpets and the bass trombone in the open position voicings of mm.187 and 194. Finally, pay attention to the meticulous articulations notated for the entire ensemble.

423

Ex 31-2 Get a Handel On It Shout Chorus

arr by Richard Sussman

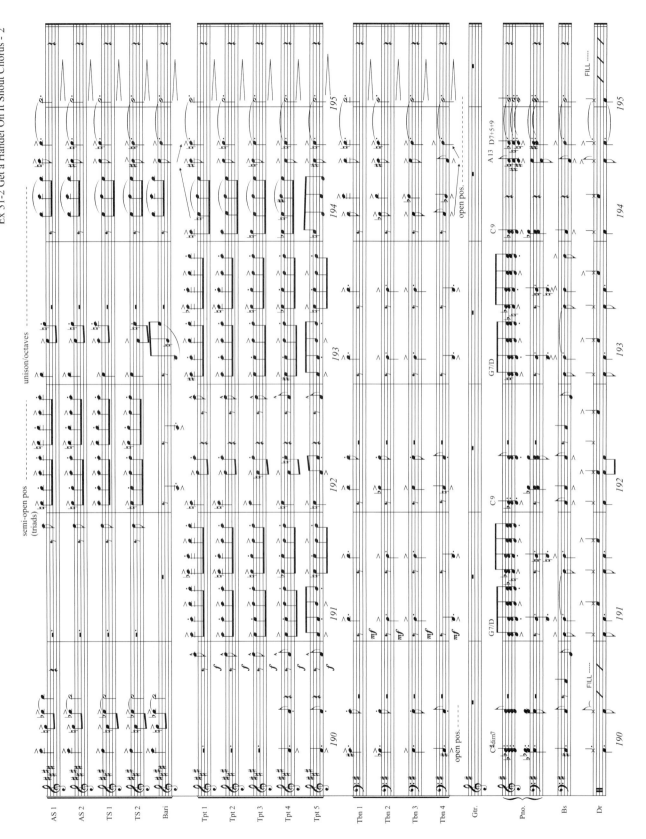

Ex 31-2 Get a Handel On It Shout Chorus - 2

31-4 Analysis of "Uncertainty" Shout Chorus by Michael Abene

With "Uncertainty" (Ex. 31-3), we have an example of a much more modern-sounding, less traditional shout chorus, but a shout chorus nonetheless. Immediately following a very modern-sounding soli section, the shout begins with some typical shout-like rhythms played by the brass section, offset by rhythmic hits in the rhythm section, baritone sax, and bass trombone. True to form and appropriate for a shout chorus, Michael's first priority seems to be to establish a series of rhythmic motives and to develop them through rhythmic displacement, augmentation, and extension. Listen to the recording and study the analysis in the reduction. The full score of this passage is also available for download from the website.

In m. 1, rhythmic motive 1 (R1) is first stated on the "and" of beat 2, in bar 2 on the "and" of beat 1, and in bar 3 again on the "and" of beat 2, but now extended and developed into a more linear phrase. Rhythmic motive 2 (R2) is simply two eighth notes placed on different beats over measures 8–10. Melodic motive 'a' (mm. 10–14) is a longer (two-bar), more linear phrase, stated twice and possibly derived from the extension of R1 in mm 3–4. What's interesting about these two phrases is the subtle differences in syncopation between m. 11 and m. 13. The phrase builds with additional instruments in mm. 13–14 and continues with the cascading effect in mm. 15–16 (again making use of rhythmic displacement). This brings us to the more forceful quarter-note motive, R3, combined with melodic motive 'b,' which is then developed by rhythmic displacement and extension to the climax at m. 23. Notice the intricate rhythmic counterpoint created between the horns and rhythm section (plus bari and bass bone) during the first ten bars of the section.

The predominantly modern, dissonant harmonies are formed by a series of constant-structure modal clusters, frequently using fourth chords, which contribute to the modernistic sound of the voicings. If we analyze the very first brass voicing (Ex. 31-3, Voicing #1) intervallically from the top note down, we find that the chord consists of A, E♭, D, and B♭ in the trumpets over an F major triad in trombones 1–3, all notes of a C Dorian mode. This produces a structure consisting of a tritone, minor second, major third, minor second, major third, and perfect fourth (from top to bottom). In spite of all the dissonant intervals, if you play this chord by itself at a keyboard it will sound consonant (like a Cm 13), because all the notes are derived from C Dorian.

The entire first four bars consist of this same voicing moving rhythmically as a constant structure over the C-G pedal played by the piano, bass, bari, and bass trombone. Although the C-G pedal provides us with a sense of C Dorian, Abene really seems more concerned with preserving the dissonant quality caused by the constant-structure voicings than with any real sense of tonality or chord changes. In fact the dissonant constant structures moving over the pedal produce a sense of polytonality that heightens the hip, modern quality of the passage. The real emphasis throughout this whole section is on the rhythmic syncopation and preservation of the dissonant, polytonal harmonies.

In m. 5, the first chord continues the preceding constant structures, now over a D♭ pedal, so it could be analyzed as D♭ Dorian. However, the voicing structure changes in the middle of the measure to a much more consonant D♭ Maj 7/E♭ min triad (E♭ Dorian). This voicing moves up a half step and then jumps, with some contrary motion between trumpets and trombones, to a C♯m7 fourth voicing (Aeolian mode).

Any momentary sense of tonality, however, is immediately abandoned for another four bars of dissonant, modal, constant-structure voicings moving over pedal points. Looking at the first voicing in m. 7 (Ex. 31-3, Voicing #2), we find (again from top to bottom) A♯, F♯, E, B, G♯, D♯, A♯ (major third, major second, perfect fourth, minor third, and two perfect fourths), all notes of an E Lydian mode, over an E-B pedal. The dissonant intervals now include a tritone (E-B♭), major second (E-F♯), major seventh (B♮-B♭), minor seventh (G♯-F♯ and A♯-G♯), and minor ninth (B♭-B♮). The whole chord sits on top of a standard fourth chord played by the trombones.

This voicing now becomes the predominant constant structure through m. 10, with the low pedals now being abandoned in favor of a series of modulating perfect fifths. Again, the emphasis is on the syncopated rhythms and preservation of dissonant, polytonal sounds through the use of constant-structure voicings. One interesting feature of all of these harmonies is that despite the overall dissonant and polytonal feel, if you analyze each chord vertically you discover that each chord consists entirely of the notes of a standard major scale mode, such as Dorian or Lydian (refer to Chapter 8 and Ex. 8-5 for modal concepts of chord voicings).

In mm. 11–16 we switch to a more linear texture. The dissonance and polytonality is preserved through a descending three-note motive (melodic motive 'a'—half step–major third), sequencing downward by major seconds, played over a simple descending chromatic scale. The resulting random dissonance created by this effect is heightened by the sustained B and E naturals played by various instruments. This whole idea is extended further in mm. 15–16, now using a perfect fourth–half step development of the melodic motive in a downward cascading effect.

In mm.16–23 we return to the dissonant, modal, constant-structure, polytonal voicings and rhythmic character of the first ten bars. Now the brass and saxes are together in true shout chorus rhythmic unison. The constant-structure voicings are Lydian in nature (Ex. 31-3, Voicing #3). Notice that mm. 17–21 consist entirely of one motive (melodic motive 'b'), repeated twice with rhythmic displacement and then developed to an ascending figure in mm. 22–23.

427

Ex. 31-3

"Uncertainty" — Shout Chorus Reduction, composed and arranged by Michael Abene

428

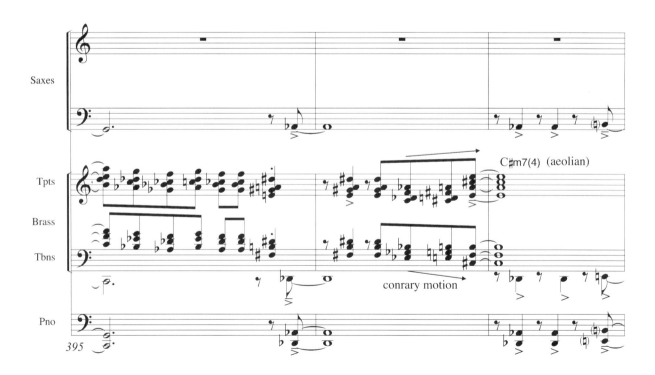

Although not really a typical shout chorus, we decided that the following 24 measures should also be included as part of this musical example (in the recording—*not* included in the reduction). The rationale is that the traditional shout chorus is generally the climax of the arrangement immediately preceding the recap of the head. In this case the intensity of the shout chorus is sustained through the section of free blowing by the entire ensemble within rhythmic hits by the rhythm section. There is a brief return to the shout chorus ensemble rhythmic unison figures in the last few bars, which then leads immediately to the recapitulation.

Chapter Summary

In this chapter we examined the process of constructing a shout chorus for the big band. We again reviewed some material from Chapter 18 and proceeded through a step-by-step composition and analysis of a shout chorus on the tune "Unithology." We then analyzed two additional contrasting shout choruses from existing arrangements.

◊ **Software Tip:** The shout chorus, as with any passage where the brass and sax sections are playing in rhythmic unison, is a great place to use the Explode Music function in Finale or the Arrange function in Sibelius. Refer to the Software Tip at the end of Chapter 9 for more information on these functions.

◊ **Software Tip:** It's important to know how to manage music and text fonts in a notation program. In Finale, make sure you know how to select your default music font properly (Document > Set Default Music Font).

Typically this will be Maestro 24 or the Jazz font. It's also sometimes necessary to make specific adjustments to other fonts. Go to Document Options > Fonts to make any global adjustments to default fonts for text blocks, lyrics, and any music notation symbols, including noteheads, measure numbers, expressions, articulations, and chord symbols. Font changes to individual elements can be made in the menus of various tools, such as the Expression, Text, Chord, and Lyrics tools.

In Sibelius, use the House Style Menu > Edit All Fonts, Edit Text Styles, or Engraving Rules to make global changes to fonts and text styles. The default music font will typically be Opus or Inkpen. You can also change individual elements using the Properties window. Select any element, and go to Window > Properties > Text to make changes to font, size, and style.

Exercises

1. Listen to any recorded examples of shout choruses by Duke Ellington, Frank Foster, Thad Jones, Bill Holman, and others from the following Listening List. If possible, get hold of the scores. Try transcribing just the brass rhythms; then compose several alternate lead melodies based on the same rhythm patterns. Take an eight-bar passage and voice for 8 brass and 5 saxes in a classic "Basie Sound" style, as described in this chapter.

2. **Arranging Project 3:** Add a 16- to 32-bar shout chorus to your big band arrangement. Place it so that it builds from the soli into the climax of the chart and then leads back to a recap of the tune. Use techniques discussed in this chapter. Include articulations, dynamics, and rhythm section parts. Be sure to provide full rhythm section support for the horns, notate all chord alterations in the chord symbols for the rhythm section, leave space for drum fills, and indicate clearly where the drum fills should occur.

Listening List of Some Classic Big Band Shout Choruses

1. Duke Ellington—"Rockin' in Rhythm" (*The Great Paris Concert*).
2. Frank Foster (Basie)—"TV Time," "Who, Me?" (*Chairman Of the Board*).
3. Frank Wess (Basie)—"Half Moon Street" (*Chairman Of the Board*).
4. Neil Hefti (Basie)—"Splanky," "Fantail" (*The Atomic Basie*).
5. Thad Jones—"Tiptoe," "Fingers," "Cherry Juice," "Little Pixie".
6. Bob Brookmeyer (Terry Gibbs, Dream Band)—"Don't Be That Way".
7. Bill Holman (Terry Gibbs, Dream Band)—"After You've Gone".

Refer to Appendix B on the companion website for a more extensive list of big band shout choruses.

Chapter 32

Arranging for Vocalists and Instrumental Soloists

No textbook on jazz arranging would be complete without a chapter on arranging for vocalists and instrumental soloists. In fact, understanding how to write an arrangement to accompany a featured artist, whether vocal or instrumental, is perhaps one of the most important skills for an aspiring arranger to learn, since this is likely to be one of the more frequent requests made of any professional arranger.

As Michael puts it, "One thing about being able to function and survive as an arranger is to be able to work with and support an artist and yet still maintain your own creativity within those restrictions. You're working with an artist and you're still writing your own thing." Some of the best arrangers, such as Nelson Riddle, Billy May, Johnny Mandel, John Clayton, Gil Evans, and Manny Albam, understood this and have written some great charts for vocalists and instrumental soloists. Whether it's for the lead singer with the local dance band or a recording session for a Grammy-winning jazz or pop star, many of the considerations will be the same.

32-1 Basic Principles for Accompanying a Soloist

Certain aspects of writing for a featured artist are similar to principles for writing background parts behind a jazz soloist, as outlined in Chapters 11 and 17. The real creative challenge when writing for featured artists is to keep things simple enough so as not to get in their way or interfere with their phrasing and yet still be able to interject a creative stimulus to spur them on and give them something to bounce off of.

All of the melodic, harmonic, rhythmic, voicing, textural, and expressive techniques examined thus far can be applied to this process. It can also be useful to list some of the possible textures and styles for accompanying a soloist, as we did in the sections on form and planning the arrangement (Chapters 11, 17, and 25). Here's a list of some of the possibilities.

1. Vocalist/soloist + rhythm section only.
2. Vocalist/soloist + pads (brass and/or reeds).
3. Vocalist/soloist + rhythmic accompaniment or rhythmic hits (brass and/or reeds).
4. Vocalist/soloist + countermelodies or fills (brass and/or reeds).
5. Vocalist/soloist + improvised obligato lines/fills (any instrument).

Ensemble parts can be written for any conceivable arrangement of available instrumental colors from the brass or woodwind section, including the use of woodwind doubles and brass doubles and mutes. Accompanying figures can be played by solo instruments, instrumental subdivisions, the sax or brass section, or the full tutti ensemble. These arrangements can also contain improvised solo sections (in addition to those for the featured artist), solis, shout choruses, intros, kickers, and transitions.

It can be especially useful when arranging a standard tune for a featured artist to come up with some original twist, such as a unique rhythmic or melodic accompanying hook, a striking reharmonization, or an unexpected rhythmic feel. As with any musical composition, whatever specific musical techniques are employed, the arrangement should build naturally and tell a story. Most importantly, in this situation the arrangement should support and focus attention on the featured artist's strengths and creativity. The arrangement should be a frame within which the artist can shine. Some specific musical considerations include:

1. Know the vocalist's range (or range of instrumental soloist).
2. Avoid thick harmonized background pads or overly active counter lines in the soloist's register while they're singing (or playing). Try to stay above or below their primary register—or keep the parts relatively thinly voiced, or moving at a slower pace rhythmically than that of the main melody.
3. Place more active counterpoint or rhythmic punctuations by the ensemble during breaks in the soloist's melodic phrases.
4. Be conscious of how the soloist plans to phrase the melody, and don't "step on" their entrances or phrase endings (e.g., if you know the soloist

tends to end a phrase on the & of 4, don't put a rhythmic hit there—wait a beat or two!).

5. Be sure the soloist is aware of, and comfortable with, any planned chord alterations or reharmonizations of the melody.

6. *All of this is to ensure that the soloist has space, rhythmically and harmonically, to express themselves freely, without feeling "boxed in" by the arrangement.*

Example 32-1 illustrates the use of some of these devices, including countermelodies, pads, fills, woodwind and brass doubles and mutes, rhythmic comping, and reharmonization, in a sketch for a vocal chart on "Autumn Leaves."

32-2 Principles Specific to Vocalists/ The Importance of the Lyric

According to Michael, the first priority with vocalists is to find their range and then to find the best key possible for the tune at hand. "Don't go with what they say! Get together with them and record. Ask them their key, then try taking it up or down, just in case. If you want to modulate, how far up or down can you go?"

Many of the best ideas may come from improvising instinctively with the artist to see what works best in terms of direction, tempo, and accompaniment. Ideally, this type of arrangement should be a true collaboration between artist and arranger. In this case, there may be some advantage to being a pianist, but it's not essential. In fact, even for a pianist, getting together with a singer or soloist can be a great opportunity to experiment with different colors and feels using a MIDI sequencer.

With vocalists, it's also essential for the arranger to understand the content and phrasing of the lyrics. The lyrics are important in one sense because it helps the arranger to know when the singer is going to breathe and, therefore, how to arrange accompanying melodic and rhythmic figures. Knowing the content of the lyric is also very important because often that will suggest choices for musical accompaniment and colors, usually supporting the lyric but sometimes (with the artist's permission) working against it—not in an overt, heavy-handed manner but with the same subtlety and artistry you would bring to any musical challenge.

Understanding the lyric content of a standard may be almost as important when arranging for an instrumental soloist. Many of the greatest jazz soloists, from Lester Young to Dizzy Gillespie, Miles Davis and beyond, have attested to the importance of knowing the lyrics of a tune in order to truly interpret and improvise on it.

435

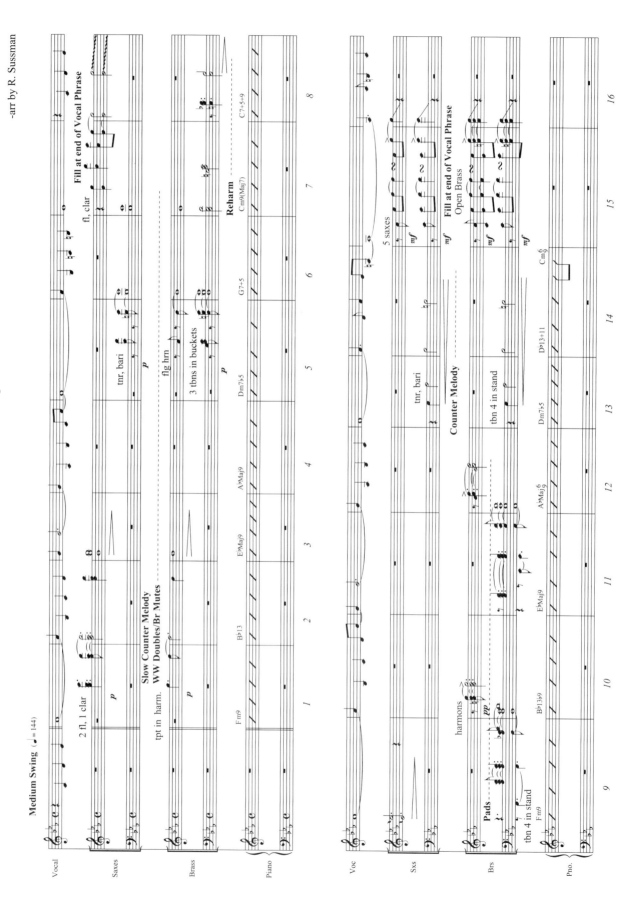

Ex 32-1 "Autumn Leaves" Sample Vocal Chart

-arr by R. Sussman

Ex 32-1 "Autumn Leaves" Sample Vocal Chart - 2

437

* Melody notes changed to fit reharmonization. Must be done only with artist's permission.

32-3 Analysis of "Who Cares?" by Michael Abene

Michael Abene's wonderful arrangement of Gershwin's "Who Cares?" is a highlight of *Avant Gershwin*, Patti Austin's 2008 Grammy-winning CD (for best jazz vocal album), with arrangements by Michael Abene and recorded by the Cologne WDR jazz big band. This chart provides a great illustration of a successful jazz big band vocal arrangement. Study the score reduction of the intro and head in Ex. 32-3, and, if possible, get hold of the original recording with Patti Austin and the WDR band. Example 32-2 provides a lead sheet comparing Michael's reharmonization of the tune with the original changes. The full score of the head is also available for download on the companion website.

The first unexpected twist comes right at m. 1, with the rhythm section playing a samba feel, in stark contrast to the medium up-tempo swing feel typically given this tune. Michael immediately grabs our attention in the intro with an unusual five-bar melodic figure, with melody and harmony loosely derived from the verse of the tune, played by trumpet and baritone sax in octaves over the chord progression's chromatic descent from E♭ major to B major, with the rhythm section playing over an E♭ pedal.

The melodic phrase is answered by the trombone section playing sustained chords with the rhythm section to repeat the five-bar chord progression. The entire five-bar phrase is repeated again, with the trumpet/bari melody now played over the trombone section pad. Finally, the chord progression is repeated once more, this time by the full ensemble, ending on a nice, fat E♭7 (V7 of A♭) altered chord (instead of B major). In addition to ending the intro on the dominant E♭, the addition of an extra bar, extending the five-bar phrase to six bars, helps to set up the entrance of the vocal at m. 22. This is because the tension of the asymmetrical five-bar phrase is released a bit by the addition of the extra measure (m. 21), providing a little more space for the vocal entrance. Notice also how the entire intro builds in intensity through the addition of instruments on each repetition of the five-bar phrase.

Patti enters with the verse at m. 22, accompanied only by the rhythm section playing the descending progression over the E♭ pedal from the intro. If you check out the lead sheet (Ex. 32-2), it now becomes more apparent that the intro progression is really a reharmonization of the original changes to the verse. Abene pulls the changes a bit closer to the original to support the vocal by landing on the E♭7 sus dominant chord in m. 25. The four-bar vocal phrase is answered by a two-bar phrase in the trombones, continuing the reharmonization and avoiding the original resolution to the tonic.

Further examination of the lead sheet reveals that George Gershwin's original phrase structure for the verse was asymmetrical in its own right, consisting of two six-bar phrases followed by an eight-bar phrase and two four-bar phrases. It now seems that the five-bar intro phrase is actually a truncation of Gershwin's original six-bar verse phrase!

At m. 28, the verse continues to develop in a manner similar to the intro, with the trombones adding their sonority to the chords and the answering two-bar phrase (mm. 32–33) now played by the full ensemble. At m. 34, the arrangement continues to build with the addition of a descending countermelody in the saxes and trombones. Here the chart moves a little closer to the original chord changes, while at the same time preserving Gershwin's phrase structure for the verse, keeping things comfortable for the vocalist. The slower, half note motion of the counter line outlines the harmony, forming consonant intervals with the melody, and doesn't conflict with the vocal even though it passes through her register.

Michael throws us a little curve in mm. 40–41 by reharmonizing the expected V chord (Eb7) with an E Maj6/9+11 accompanied by a high rhythmic fill played in unison by all five trumpets. The horns drop out for the final two four-bar vocal phrases of the verse, reentering at m. 48 with an exciting four-bar pyramid, which ascends upward from the trombones and low reeds to the trumpets and sopranos and functions as a kicker into the entrance of the more familiar vocal chorus of the tune at m. 52.

Now it's just Patti and the rhythm section again for contrast, with a direct and comfortable entrance of the familiar melody to the chorus. The rhythm section comps on the original changes to the tune (with a slight reharmonization) for the first eight-bar "A" section (mm. 52–59), landing on an EMaj7/Gb reharm of the V chord in m. 59, with a trumpet/sax fill at the end of the vocal phrase, which was apparently cut for the recording session. Also, on the recording the pianist does not play the figures written in the score, instead just comping on the changes!

In the next eight-bar phrase (mm. 60–67—the form of the chorus is ABAC, so this would be "B") the vocal continues with the rhythm section comping on the original chord changes, with some slight reharmonization (see the lead sheet, Ex.32-2). At m. 68, the arrangement builds for the second "A" section by introducing a light fill by the tenors plus two trombones playing in the vocal holes. The fills become a supportive countermelody at mm. 72–74, returning to fills for the final "C" section of the tune (mm. 76–82).

The entire first statement of the chorus, for 30 bars, is pretty straightforward and unassuming. However, we're in for a real surprise at m. 82, with a deceptive cadence to a four-bar tag extension of the tune based on a samba-like rhythmic figure in F minor played by the trombones and rhythm and then echoed by the entire band in full tutti. Check out the great sound of the bass trombone part on the roots in this section. Abene keeps the intensity going here with yet another surprise—an unexpected return to the vocal verse, now stated as a four-bar phrase in F minor and answered by the entire ensemble playing the rhythmic figure from mm. 86–89, with Patti occasionally joining in and scatting along with the band.

439

This section repeats for the second phrase of the verse. Then it's just Patti and the rhythm section again and a slight drop in intensity as the verse continues, with a two-bar tutti fill by the band at the end of the phrase (mm. 112–113). The vocal concludes with the last two phrases of the verse, followed by a dovetailing tag derived from the fill at mm. 48–51, now syncopated, rhythmically displaced, and extended to seven bars as a kicker into the ensemble soli on the chorus at **D**. (Only the Intro and Head of the chart are displayed in Ex. 32-3.) A few interesting orchestrational choices are worth noting. Throughout much of the chart, the bari is voiced more with the trombones than with the other saxes (mm. 26–27 and mm. 82–114). Also, notice the unusual sax section configuration of four sopranos and bari from mm. 82–114.

After the joyful soli chorus, the chart continues with jazz guitar and trumpet solos. The trumpet solo continues with an extension into the first half of the verse, à la letter **C**. Patti picks it up for the second half of the verse. Then follows an instrumental statement of the first eight bars of the chorus, with some nice instrumental counterpoint. Patti finishes the recap of the chorus to continue with a wonderful extension of the tag from letter **C**, with the vocals scatting around the verse melody and lyrics, accompanied by the rhythmic figure in the full band, now reharmonized in fourths as E/F♯ –D/E, with the rhythm slightly altered. The chart ends with the surprise two words "Who Cares?" followed by a dissonant, diminished scale chord in the brass.

Ex. 32-2

"Who Cares?" — Lead Sheet, by George and Ira Gershwin

Verse

441

(E7)
F7+5
F7
B♭m9
D♭m9
E△9/G♭
E♭7
33
A♭Maj7
B♭m7/A♭
C m7/F
F m7
A♭dim7
B♭m9
B♭m7
E♭13
E♭7
37
A♭Maj7
B♭m7/A♭
C m7/F
F m7
A♭dim7
B m9
E 9
E 13
E♭7+5
E♭13
E♭7
41
A♭Maj7
G7+5
C7+5♭9
45
F m7
(Fm7/E♭)
Dm7♭5
B♭9
D♭m9(△7)
49
A♭Maj7
A♭Maj
B♭m7/A♭
A♭dim
A♭Maj7
B♭m7
F7♭9.
E♭7
F 7
53
B♭m7
B♭m7/E♭
E♭7
Fm Tag
A♭Maj
57

The full score of the head is also available for download on the companion website.

Ex 32-3 "Who Cares" Head Reduction

George & Ira Gershwin
arr. by Michael Abene

443

Ex 32-3 "Who Cares" Head Reduction - 2

Ex 32-3 "Who Cares" Head Reduction - 3

Ex 32-3 "Who Cares" Head Reduction - 4

Ex 32-3 "Who Cares" Head Reduction - 5

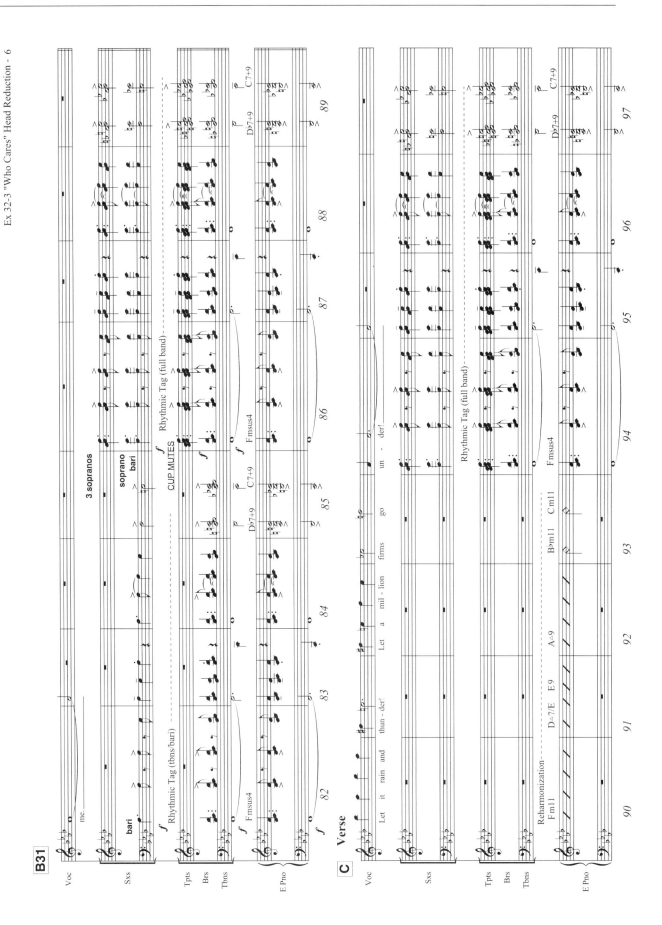

Ex 32-3 "Who Cares" Head Reduction - 6

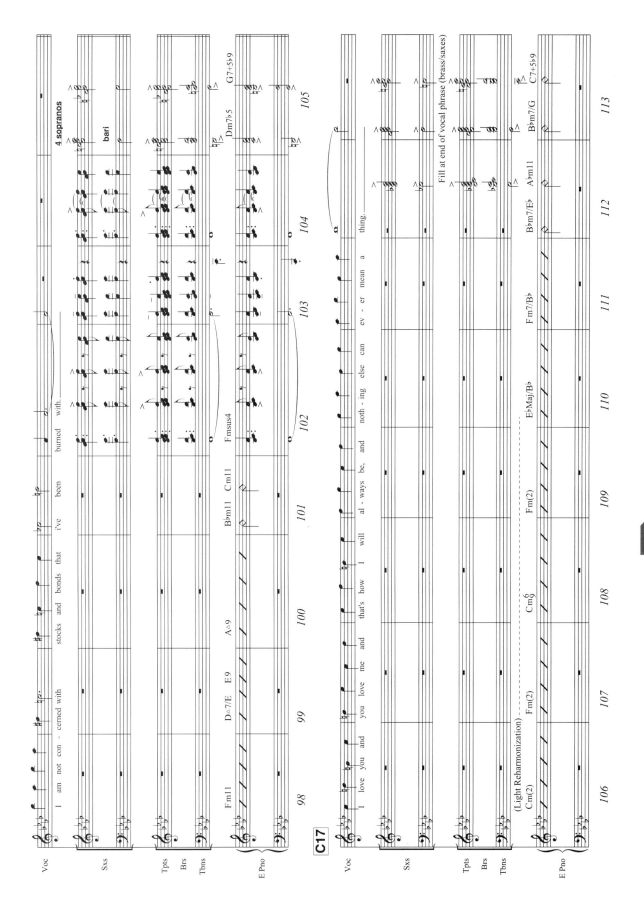

Ex 32-3 "Who Cares" Head Reduction - 7

449

Ex 32-3 "Who Cares" Head Reduction - 8

Chapter Summary

In this chapter we examined some of the concepts and tools for writing a big band arrangement for a vocalist or featured instrumental soloist. We provided examples of some applicable techniques and a sketch of a sample vocal chart for "Autumn Leaves." Then we examined some issues specific to writing for vocalists, including the importance of the lyrics. Finally, we analyzed Michael Abene's arrangement of Gershwin's "Who Cares?" for Patti Austin.

◊ **Software Tip**: Make sure you know how to enter, edit, and position lyrics on a vocal staff in your notation program. In Finale, go to the Lyric Tool > Type Into Score. Click on the note where you wish to add lyrics. Type the lyrics into the score using a hyphen to separate the syllables and press the space bar to separate words. In Sibelius, select a note; then go to Create > Text > Lyrics and type the lyrics into the score.

◊ **Software Tip**: Whenever you work on a MIDI mockup of a score, be sure to keep in mind all the caveats provided throughout the book regarding working with sampled sounds. On the other hand, the more extensive your expressive sequencing skills, the more effective this method of working will be. This can come in handy if you need to provide a demo for a singer to rehearse with or for a producer to approve. In this situation, it's definitely advisable to work with the sequencer rather than the notation program. For more detailed suggestions on using a sequencer in conjunction with notation software, see Section 34-4.

Exercises

1. Listen to any recorded examples of vocal or featured soloist arrangements from the Listening List that follows. If possible, get hold of the scores. Listen in a focused way, and be able to describe how certain arranging devices support and enhance the soloist without getting in the way.

2. If possible, get together with a vocalist. Select a standard tune, and work through some of the steps described in this chapter, including finding the best key, reharmonizing part of the melody, coming up with a distinctive twist or hook for the arrangement, and working out some appropriate fills and accompanying figures for the horns. Arrange the head of the tune, with an intro and coda, for vocalist and big band.

3. Try using a sequencer program such as Digital Performer, Logic, or Cubase to create a MIDI mockup of an arrangement for a vocalist or instrumental soloist. Use the best samples at your disposal, and try to make the sequence as musical as possible through the use of expressive

sequencing techniques. The demo can serve as a means of working out musical ideas with the soloist and as something which they can practice with. Export the sequence as a standard MIDI file, and open it in your notation program. Then do whatever's necessary to clean up the score and generate parts.

Listening List of Some Classic Big Band Vocal and Instrumental Solo Arrangements

1. Duke Ellington—"On the Sunny Side of the Street" (Johnny Hodges).
2. Nelson Riddle—Anything with Sinatra!
3. Billy May—Anything with Ella Fitzgerald, Nancy Wilson, Mel Tormé, Peggy Lee, Anita O'Day.
4. Johnny Mandel—Natalie Cole ("Unforgettable"), anything with Sarah Vaughan, Tony Bennett, Mel Tormé.
5. Gil Evans—Anything from *Sketches of Spain*, *Porgy and Bess*, or *Miles Ahead* (Miles Davis).

Refer to Appendix B on the companion website for a more extensive list of big band vocal and instrumental solo arrangements.

Chapter 33

Completing the Big Band Arrangement

If you've been doing all of the exercises labeled *Arranging Project 3*, beginning with Chapter 25, your big band arrangement should now be nearly complete. The arrangement should consist of an intro, a head (arranged using a variety of techniques), a kicker, one or more improvised solos with backgrounds, a soli chorus, and a 16- to 32-bar shout chorus. You should have proper dynamics and articulations indicated in the horn parts and properly notated rhythm section parts. All that remains is to add a recap and a short coda, make sure that you've created proper layouts and music spacing for the score and the parts, verify the transpositions for transposing instruments, and proofread everything.

33-1 Adding a Recap and an Ending

If you've just completed a shout chorus, you're probably at the climax of the arrangement. The information regarding completing the arrangement provided at the beginning of Chapter 19 is equally applicable to the larger ensemble. We recommend that you review that material before proceeding. You should also refer to Chapter 11 for specific suggestions regarding endings and codas. We think the following paragraph from Chapter 19 is worth repeating here.

> As always, try to let your musical instincts and inner ear guide your decisions. Remember, music has a life of its own. Learn to develop a sensitivity to this by stepping back from the music periodically to maintain your perspective; the music will show you which path to take. Never try to force the music in a particular direction just because it seems to make sense intellectually. Music is *always* more about emotions and feelings than about intellect; if it doesn't *feel* right, it's not going to work.

33-2 Score and Part Layouts/Transpositions/Proofreading/Printing

All of the guidelines presented in Chapters 14 and 15 regarding laying out the score and the parts, parts transposition, proofreading, music preparation, and printing the score and the parts still apply to larger ensembles of any size. Again, we recommend reviewing the material in those chapters at this point before proceeding. Following the basic procedures regarding the layout and printing of the score and parts will ensure smooth and efficient rehearsals and performances of your music.

If you haven't been entering articulations, dynamics, and full rhythm section parts, be sure to do that now. If you *have* been doing this, be sure to include, as part of the proofreading process, a thorough check of all articulations, dynamics, and rhythm section parts. It's especially important to take a little extra time to make sure that all chord symbols and rhythmic placement of chords in the piano, guitar, and bass parts correspond to the actual altered chord tones and rhythmic placement of chords played by the ensemble.

◊ Once again, remember to allow yourself adequate time to proofread both the score and parts. *Do not trust MIDI playback as a substitute for thorough proofreading!*

33-3 Analysis of "Fletcher" by Richard Sussman

"Fletcher" is an arrangement of an original tune by Richard, originally commissioned by trumpeter Dean Pratt in 1983 for a program honoring the work of legendary arranger Fletcher Henderson. Most of the program consisted of transcriptions of old Fletcher Henderson charts, but Dean wanted to include a modern piece that would pay homage to Fletcher's accomplishments. Consequently, there's a lot of typical Henderson devices, such as contrasting the brass and sax sections and the use of riffs, but with a more modern harmonic flavor. It seems appropriate to now analyze parts of this chart, since it illustrates some of the more straight-ahead principles examined throughout the book. The form of the tune is ABAC.

A reduction of the intro and the head (we looked at the first 16 bars of this chart in Ex. 24-2) is provided in Ex. 33-1A. The eight-bar intro starts things off in classic swing style, with the saxes echoing one-bar riff-like phrases played by the brass section. Starting with a single whole note on the tonic in m. 1, the melodic motive grows with each repetition, finally extending to two bars played by the saxes in mm. 6-7. The brass is voiced in a tight, "Basie Sound" style, with the four trumpets in close position and the three-piece trombone section supporting them in close, semi-open, or open position, typically with the third and seventh of the chord contained in the trombone voicing. Note the standard, upper-structure triad trumpets over the open position trombones brass voicing on the G♭13+11 chord in m. 8.

Here and throughout the chart, the lead trumpet is most frequently doubled 8vb by trumpet 4 (mm. 1, 8, 26–31), partly because the smaller, three-piece trombone section places some limitations on voicing possibilities for the brass. Occasionally the lead is doubled by trombone 1 (mm. 5, 25, 38–41) and sometimes not doubled at all (mm. 3, 11, 15, 17, 19, etc.). The saxes are in close position (m. 1), a tight cluster (m. 4), opening up to drop-2 with the contrary motion in m. 6, and in octaves for the final melodic phrase of the intro. The important thing to note here is that use was made of various voicing techniques, not in a formulaic way but, rather, by switching freely from one technique to another, following the ebb and flow of the music, and to create musical interest and contrast. Also important to notice is that an effort was made to voice each section complete unto itself, each playing a full chord (unless playing the melody in unison/octaves).

The riff-like head of the tune (**A**) begins at m. 9 with the saxes in octaves, interspersed with tightly voiced rhythmic hits by the brass and answered by the trombones in unison. At m. 17 (**B**), the roles reverse, now with the brass playing the melody in close position or octaves, answered by unison hits in the saxes. The saxes pick up the melody again in octaves in mm. 21–22, with the brass reentering in close position in mm. 23–24, here with trombone 1 doubling the lead. Notice the open-position sax voicings moving in contrary motion to the brass for extra fullness and musical interest (mm. 23–24).

At m. 25 (**A1**), the brass section takes the melody, in full "Basie Sound" style, with trombone 1 doubling the lead at m. 25, and trumpet 4 from mm. 26–30, with the saxes lending chordal support. Notice the subtle yet refreshing fourth-chord voicing in m. 26. Alto 1 is intentionally left out of the voicings in m. 26 to highlight its solo answering phrase in mm. 27–28. The saxes complete this phrase with five-note semi-open position voicings in mm. 31–32. Notice the contrary motion between the outer two voices as well as alto 2 crossing tenor 1 to avoid playing repeated notes on beat 4 of m. 32.

The trombones, in unison, pick up the melody at m. 33 (**C**) for contrast. At m. 37, we return to the call-and-response sound of the intro, with the two sections finally coming together melodically at m. 41 and harmonically on the last chord (mm. 42–43). The final G♭13+11 voicing is exactly the same in the brass as that at m. 8, only this time joined by the saxes using a standard coupling technique (the lead alto doubling trumpet 2). Note how the repetition of the call and response between the brass and saxes here winds up extending the last eight-bar section of the tune (**C**) to eleven bars.

Some of the salient points to pay attention to in this analysis include the characteristic playing off of the brass and sax sections against each other, typical "Basie Sound" brass voicings, with the lead trumpet usually doubled by either trumpet 4 or trombone 1, placement of the chord third and seventh in the low mid-register trombones, voicing of the brass and sax sections so that they each sound complete within themselves, contrasting of unison/octaves with voiced sections, and the frequent use of contrary motion between outer voices or between the brass and sax sections.

The full scores of all examples in this chapter are also available for download on the companion website.

Ex 33-1A "Fletcher" Intro/Head - 2

Ex 33-1A "Fletcher" Intro/Head - 3

Example 33-1B illustrates a typical big band kicker that grows out of the background figures behind the tenor solo and then extends across the double bar line four measures into the beginning of the next chorus to kick into the short piano solo. The horns are voiced in rhythmic unison with the brass in a tight "Basie Sound" style, and the saxes added to the brass using a variable coupling technique. What's most interesting here and in the earlier transition from the trumpet solo into the tenor solo (mm. 88–96) is that the kicker comes in the middle of the chorus. The trumpet and tenor both play an extra 16 bars into the next chorus, so the next solo starts in the middle of the chorus rather than at the beginning.

Example 33-1C is a recap of the head out. The first eight bars at **K** (mm. 212–220) are the same as mm. 9–17, transposed up to A♭. However, from m. 220 to the end, what we really have is a shout chorus based on the changes to the last eight bars of the head (transposed to A♭). The brass is once again voiced in "Basie Sound" upper-structure triads, with the trombones in close or open position. At m. 223, the saxes begin a series of melodic phrases answering the rhythmic brass figures, recalling the call-and-response style of the intro and the opening head. The two sections come together at mm. 230–231 and again for the final two bars, with the saxes playing some contrary motion to the brass. Also indicated on the score are several examples of the bass trombone playing in contrary motion to the lead (mm. 221, 222, 226, 231, 233, and 237).

◊ Be sure to listen to the recorded examples on the companion website as you study this analysis and the following analyses. The full scores for all the examples in this chapter are also available for download on the website.

459

Ex. 33-1B

"Fletcher" Kicker Reduction, composed and arranged by Richard Sussman

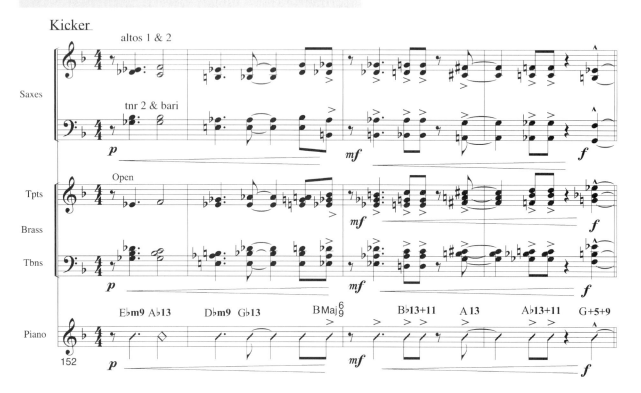

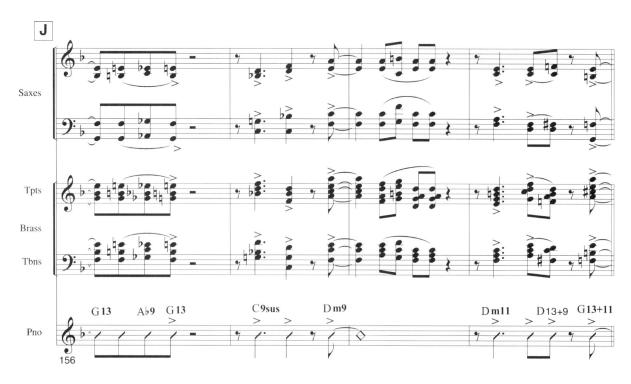

Ex 33-1C "Fletcher" Head Out

Comp/Arr. Richard Sussman

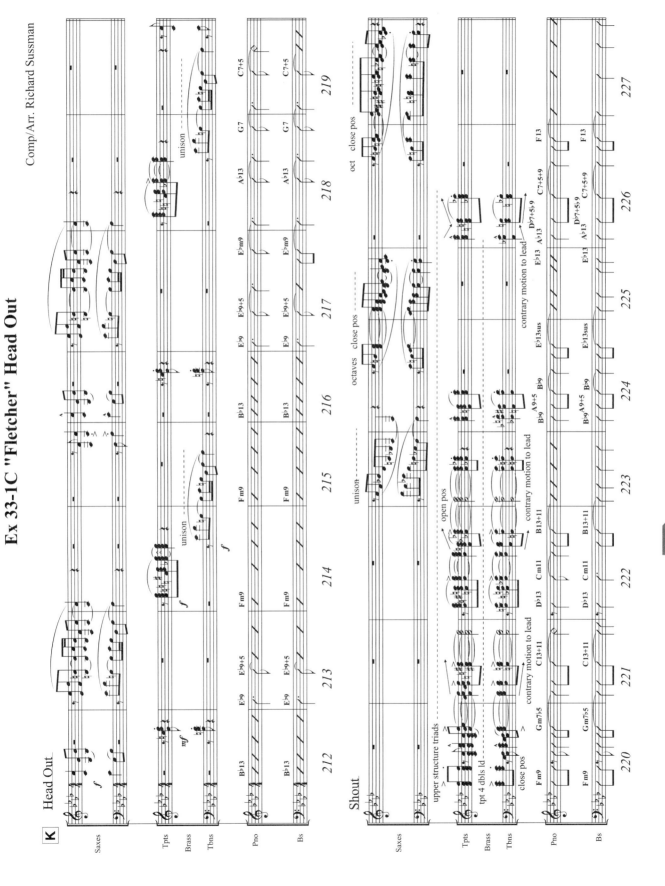

Ex 33-1C "Fletcher" Head Out - 2

33-4 Analysis of "Uncertainty" by Michael Abene

Michael Abene's arrangement of his original tune "Uncertainty" provides us with an exciting and high-energy example of some more modern arranging techniques. The harmonies are modal, nondiatonic, and dissonant, with lots of fourth chords and parallel-structure voicings. An abundance of irregular phrase lengths are interspersed with hip, syncopated rhythmic hits. Unlike "Fletcher," where the brass and sax sections are clearly defined and function in traditional roles, "Uncertainty" employs a variety of unusual cross-sectional subdivisions within the band, producing colorful and contrasting instrumental textures. A reduction of the head is provided in Ex. 33-2.

The modal, fourth-chord quality is established right at the first bar of the intro, with the characteristic F-Bb-Eb-G voicing (three perfect fourths with a major third on top) played by the saxes. The brass plays essentially the same chord, but with the addition of a few extra notes, to create a slightly more dissonant, cluster voicing. The entire ensemble, with the exception of the bari, bass bone, piano left hand, bass, and drums (which play rhythmic hits on a low C pedal—rhythmic motives "R1" and "R2"), moves in parallel motion and rhythmic unison in ascending perfect fourths to state the opening motive, labeled "i."

The first three chords could be described modally as C Dorian, Phrygian, and Locrian. Both the initial voicings as well as the first melodic motive, "i" (G-C-F), are quartal in nature. Another immediately striking, modernistic feature of the intro is the one-bar extension of the first phrase to five bars (mm. 1–5). This phrase is then repeated verbatim (mm. 6–10).

At m. 11 we have a signature Abene dissonant, rhythmic phrase, again for five bars. The defining fourth-chord structure is once more outlined in the sax section and filled in as a cluster in the brass. Comparing the first chord in m. 11 to the first chord of the piece, we see that by moving the top note of the chord up a whole step (from G to A), the voicing becomes much more dissonant (from bottom to top F-Bb-Eb-A), now with a tritone between the top two notes as well as the major seventh between the top note and the third note.

This dissonant voicing then ascends as a parallel constant structure, following a simple chromatic scale (motive "j"), again interspersed with rhythmic hits by the bari, bass bone, and rhythm section. The chord voicings change at m. 15 (looking at the full brass section voicing) to a simple m11(13), again ascending by a chromatic scale, but now over a *descending* chromatic scale in the bari, providing contrary motion as well as random dissonances, and continuing to build in intensity through the end of m. 15.

Tension is released at m. 16, with a return to the more consonant fourth-chord voicings of the first 10 bars (with the major third, instead of the tritone, above the perfect fourths) as well as a more predictable, standard rhythmic figure (motive "k"/rhythmic motive "R2"). The phrase is again extended to five bars and then echoed by the trombone section, to wind down the intro and set up the entrance of the main melodic motive at **A** (m. 26).

463

Despite all the fourth chords and dissonance, the primary musical interest of the intro is provided by the constantly shifting and evocative rhythmic figures as well as by the asymmetrical five-bar phrases. Two simple rhythmic motives, which recur throughout the piece as a unifying device, are stated in the first few bars of the intro: "R1" in m. 1 (and again in mm. 34–36) and "R2" in m. 3 (again in mm.16–18 and 21–23 and combined with "R1" in m. 38). One other subtle harmonic touch that's worth pointing out is the A natural in the guitar and the trombones in mm. 1 and 6. An A♭ would have been more predictable, given the parallel-structure voicings of the two chords that follow.

At letter **A** (m. 26), the main theme (motive "a") is presented by our first instrumental subdivision ("Subdivision 1"), formed by the lead alto, trumpet 2 (open), and guitar. It's a pretty straightforward melody in C minor, harmonized by Cm-D♭Maj7, and for a brief moment we have a feeling of a C minor tonal center being established. This is quickly dispelled in m. 29, when the theme modulates to E major and then to G major (root motion by major and minor thirds). A contrasting motive, "b," appears at m. 33, supported by rhythmic hits ("R2" and "R1"), harmonized by a modulating progression vaguely hinting at E major (by landing on the B7♭5♭9 at the end of m. 36). The rhythmic hits here are played by instrumental "Subdivision 2," consisting of the trombone section, bari sax, piano, bass, and drums.

Essentially, the entire chord progression of both letters **A** and **B** is constantly modulating and nondiatonic (not based on dominant harmony). Rather than attempt a harmonic analysis using Roman numerals, which would be pointless in this case, we've simply indicated the implied passing tonal centers on the score reduction ⒸⓂ⑄, etc. Looking at the indicated tonal centers, it becomes clear that there's a lot of root motion by major and minor thirds and seconds and not very much V-I at all (although we do see a B7–E7sus in mm. 36–38). The abundance of major 7+11 chords and the occasional polytonal sounds (A/B♭ in mm. 30–31, D/E♭ in m. 49, and G/E♭ in m. 64) further enhance the nonfunctional nature of the chord progression. Still, the intro (mm. 1–10) and letters **A** (mm. 26–50) and **C** (mm. 69–96, which is a recap of **A**) begin solidly in C minor, and letter **B** ends solidly in F major (or Dm, mm. 65–67).

What appears to be of more musical interest is the unusual and asymmetrical melodic phrase structure, shifting from three- to two- to four-bar phrases, over a more regular harmonic rhythm (e.g., four bars of one chord per bar in mm. 26–29 followed by four bars of one chord every two bars in mm. 30–33). Of course, there's also the measure of 6/4 (m. 39) and the measure of 2/4 (m. 44), adding yet another level of complexity to the phrase structure.

At m. 40, a new contrasting motive, "c," is answered by a rhythmic hit played by instrumental "subdivision 3," consisting of two sopranos and one tenor sax, three trumpets in harmons, and piano. The **A** section ends with a powerful rhythmic phrase played by "subdivision 4," which is the ensemble in full tutti, minus alto 1, trumpet 2, and the guitar ("subdivision 1"). The melody here consists of a descending fourth motive, actually an inversion of "i" from the intro.

Letter **B** presents us with a release of tension and contrast by reverting to a simpler, more regular phrase structure: two two-bar phrases followed by a four-bar phrase (mm. 51–58 and 59–66). The pickups to motive "d" are reminiscent of the ascending perfect fourths from the intro. More unity is provided by the now-familiar rhythmic motives "R1" and "R2" answering the melodic phrases, first played by the rhythm section alone and then joined by the trombones and saxes.

The real interest at **B** comes from the incredible array of contrasting timbres, with a total of eight different instrumental groupings overlapping and building in intensity throughout this one 16-bar section. First "b" is stated by the bari and trombones 1 and 2 in unison (mm. 50 and 52 and again at mm. 58 and 60—"subdivision 5"). The melody is developed by one alto, one tenor, bari, one trumpet, and two trombones (m. 54—"sub. 6"), immediately followed by two flutes and one trumpet in harmon (mm. 55–56—"sub. 7"), with rhythmic hits played by the bari, trombones, and rhythm (m. 55—"sub. 2"), then the same grouping plus one tenor sax (m. 56—"sub. 8"), and then alto, tenor, bari, three trumpets, trombones, and rhythm (m. 57—"sub. 9"). The rhythmic hits keep building in intensity, next with four saxes, trombones, and rhythm at mm. 65–66 ("sub. 10") and finally four saxes, three trumpets, and rhythm ("sub. 4") at mm. 66–67.

Letter **C** is a recap of **A**, with the first two phrases each elongated and evened out to four bars and with the addition of rhythmic hits played by the bari, trombones, and rhythm ("sub. 2"). Measures 79–95 are an exact repetition of mm. 34–50.

(The following is *not* included in the score reduction although the full score *is* available on the companion website.) The intro now returns as a transition into the trumpet solo (letter **D**). The five-bar phrase is stretched out to a more even six bars, with the trumpet sneaking in and blowing on C Phrygian over the last four bars of the phrase. This happens four times; then there's a 10-bar tag on rhythmic and harmonic material derived from the head, and we're into the extended trumpet solo.

As is often the case with tunes of this level of harmonic and structural complexity, it can be a good idea to simplify the form and harmonic rhythm of the blowing section to make it easier for the soloist to improvise (see Ex. 11-1). Abene chooses this approach for the trumpet solo on "Uncertainty," beginning the solo section with two bars of C minor to two bars of D♭Maj9+11, repeated for a full 16 bars. This is followed by some more interesting changes derived from the tune, but the harmonic rhythm remains pretty consistent and even, with two bars per chord throughout the entire blowing section.

465

Ex 33-2 "Uncertainty" Head Reduction

comp/arr. by Michael Abene

Ex 33-2 "Uncertainty" Head Reduction - 2

467

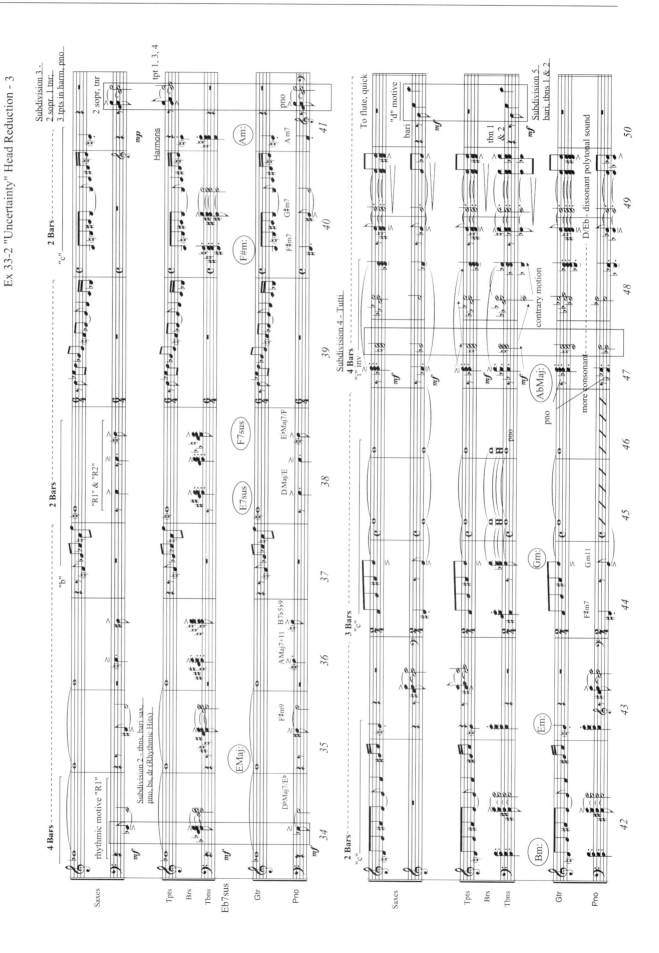

Ex 33-2 "Uncertainty" Head Reduction - 3

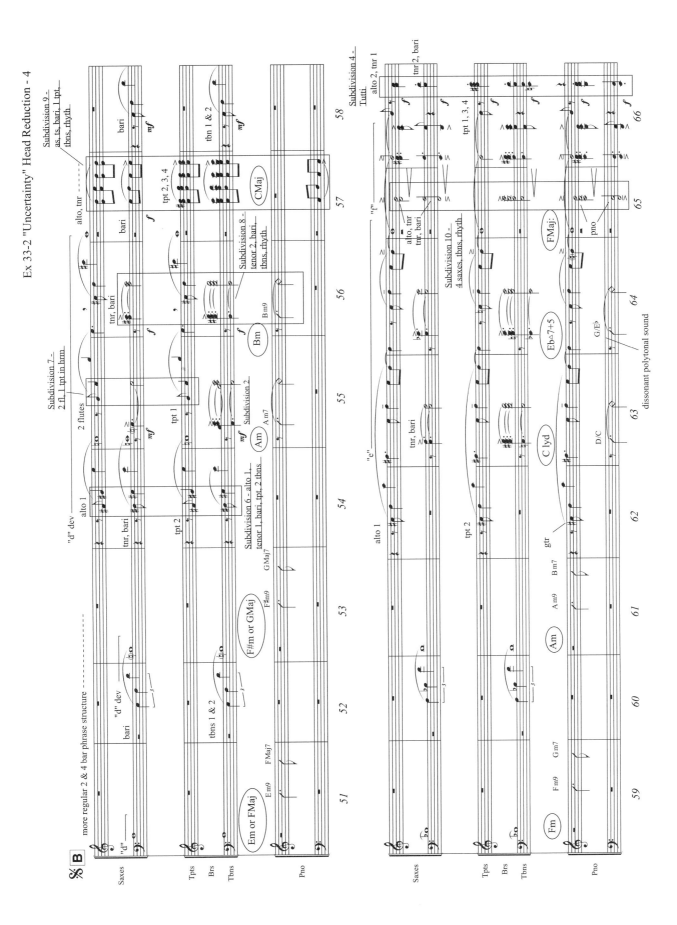

Ex 33-2 "Uncertainty" Head Reduction - 4

Ex 33-2 "Uncertainty" Head Reduction - 5

Ex 33-2 "Uncertainty" Head Reduction - 6

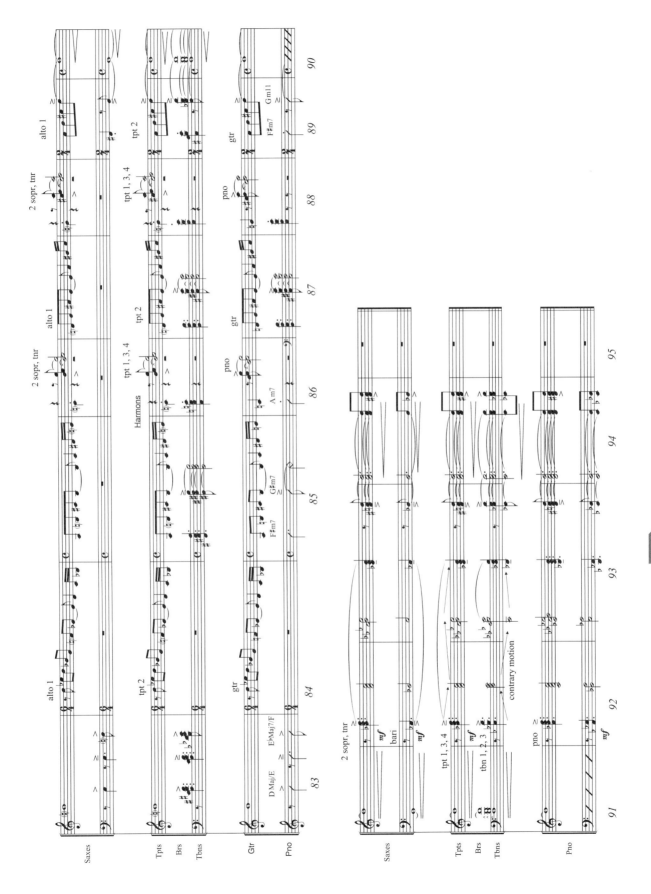

All of this has the effect not only of making things easier for the trumpet soloist but also of providing a welcome release of tension and contrast to the complexity of the tune. The entire band can relax a little and let the solo groove without being too cerebral. The intensity and modern feel is sustained through the use of the Phrygian mode and the ensuing modulating and modal chord changes.

The chart continues with backgrounds entering on the second chorus of the trumpet solo. This is followed by an interesting ensemble section (letter **E**), based on material from the bridge of the tune (**B**). This again includes the use of contrasting instrumental subdivisions consisting of flutes, soprano sax, and various subgroupings of the brass, with lots of interesting counterpoint. Next follows a guitar solo with backgrounds (**F**), which turns out to be a teaser, since the band enters with a rhythmic kicker/transition into the open guitar solo at **G**. The guitar solo follows the same form and chord changes as the trumpet solo at **D**, with the exception that there is only one chorus of guitar solo, with backgrounds entering halfway through the chorus.

Letter **H** is a sax soli based on changes derived from the **A** section of the head. Much of the sax soli, with soprano lead, is in unison/octaves, occasionally voiced in two-note parallel thirds or sixths by alto 2, tenor 2, and the bari. Letter **I** is the shout chorus, which was analyzed in Ex. 31-3. There's a D.S. to **B**, and the chart ends with the intro, restated as a coda, ending with a final Cm9(13) chord. Be sure to listen to the recorded example on the companion website as you study this analysis. The full score is also available for download on the website.

33-5 Analysis of "Art of the Big Band" by Bob Mintzer

Bob Mintzer's arrangement of his original tune "Art of the Big Band," from the 1991 CD of the same name, provides us with an exciting and high-energy example of some more modern arranging techniques (Ex. 33-3). There's extensive use of dissonant, modal, parallel, constant-structure voicings and heavily syncopated melodic figures in the intro. However, the actual melodies, based on motive "a," are actually very tonal, with a bluesy, pentatonic feel. The melodies are made to sound modern by suspending modal, parallel, constant-structure voicings from each melody note and by throwing a low contrapuntal line in the bass and bass trombone under the opening sax voicings. The resultant, somewhat arbitrary, dissonances create a hip, modern harmonic texture.

The actual simplicity of the melody is clearly evident in the guitar part, which doubles the lead alto throughout the first section (mm. 1–24). If we analyze the melody alone, we see that it is made up entirely of notes of the B♭ Dorian mode, with a strong pentatonic flavor vacillating between F and B♭. The phrase structure is very asymmetrical, with some unexpected turns and twists that lend an improvised feel to the whole section. The modern, slightly atonal, harmonic vibe is created entirely by hanging modal, parallel-structure voicings from the melody notes. Each vertical chord voicing played alone sounds consonant (as in "Uncertainty"). However, the resultant, somewhat arbitrary, shifting tonal centers create a kaleidoscopic sense of harmonic ambiguity.

The very first chord played by the saxes, highlighted in m. 1 of the score, consists of a D♭ major triad over a B♭-G♭, defining a B♭ Aeolian mode. This voicing is then repeated exactly, in parallel motion, through the end of m. 24. At m. 25, we have the first of several open blowing sections for Bob and the drummer (Peter Erskine), this time on A♭m7. In fact, the entire intro (mm. 1–49) features the ensemble, alternating with open blowing sections for the tenor, playing only with the drums and written low counterpoint parts played by the bass and bass trombone or bari.

At m. 26, the full brass section enters with the "a" motive, now in D minor and voiced with modal parallel constant-structure voicings in a manner very similar to that of the saxes in the first 24 bars. The first brass voicing in m. 26 is formed by superimposing a B♭ major triad over an A♭ major triad and then adding the G in the trumpets and B♭ in the trombones. The resultant voicing is more dissonant than that played by the saxes, partly because there are seven notes in the chord, compared with five in the sax voicing. More importantly, there are more dissonant intervals—two major sevenths (A♭-G and E♭-D) as well as several major seconds. Also, contained within the voicing is a familiar fourth-chord structure, C-F-B♭-D (from bottom to top), two perfect fourths with a major third on top (see Section 26-1 for more on fourth chords and Section 27-1 for more on constant-structure voicings).

This voicing is again repeated exactly, in parallel motion, by the brass section, through the end of m. 40. The music builds in intensity as the melody becomes more rhythmic and percussive and less lyrical and also through modulating several times (from D minor to D♭ minor to B♭ Dorian). Measure 41 is another open blowing section for Bob, now on B♭/C.

The intro builds to a climax in mm. 42–48, with the brass and sax sections playing in voiced counterpoint (motive "b" and "b" inverted), producing some intense dissonances and polytonal sounds. Each section maintains the exact same parallel voicing structures used in the preceding sections, and the lead lines of each section remain tonal, the brass in D minor and the

473

saxes in B♭ major. The brass and saxes come together harmonically on the E Maj Lydian chord in mm. 47–48. This is followed by one more open blowing section for Bob, this time on G♭Maj7♭5. Notice that the last two ensemble sections of the intro (mm. 34–40 and 42–48) are both seven bars long, helping to increase the tension as we go into the contrapuntal section at m. 42.

Everything comes together as the full rhythm section enters, with a release of tension at m. 50, which we've labeled **A** (there are no rehearsal letters in the original score). The main theme "a" is now clearly stated, in a simplified form, by the saxes in unison/octaves. Despite the key signature of four flats, the tonality is clearly B♭ minor (actually B♭ Dorian, so the key signature of four flats makes sense), and the underlying harmonization is diatonic, complete with a full V-I cadence from m. 57 to m. 58. The one nondiatonic chord is the EMaj9, which functions as a tritone substitution for V of IV. It's interesting to note that there is no key signature in the score through the entire intro, until m. 50.

The material at **A** is made even more accessible by placing it within a symmetrical four-bar phrase structure, which continues all the way through m. 99. This same material, motive "a," is developed for another 16 bars (mm. 66–81), with the melody still played in unison/octaves by the saxes, now transposed and reharmonized but still solidly in B♭ minor. Notice the one-bar displacement of the melody at mm. 71 and 79. Although the harmonic rhythm continues with regular four-bar phrases, the melody now enters on the second bar of each phrase instead of on the first. The entire **A** section (mm. 50–81) is now repeated, adding brass hits, primarily in the form of close position trumpet voicings over open position voicings in the trombones. The guitar continues to double the sax melody throughout this section.

The head comes to a climax at letter **B** (mm. 82–99) with the introduction of the joyful "c" countermelody, played by the four trumpets in unison and supported by close position harmonies in the trombones. Here the saxes play motive "a" as counterpoint to the brass melody, with some diminished scale fills in the spaces at mm. 84–85 and 88–89. This section ends with a modulation to E♭ at the second ending (mm. 98–99), leading us into the shout-like kicker, letter **C** (mm. 100–115). The intensity builds on the repeat of letter **C** with the addition of a contrapuntal part based on "a," played by the saxes in unison/octaves. The counterpoint leads to some interesting polytonal rubs (m. 103) with dense clusters in the brass (mm. 105 and 109). Sixteen bars of saxophone solo are followed by one more repeat of **C**, finally propelling us into the open sax solo at m. 114. Notice how the asymmetrical 14-bar length of **C** adds to the increase of tension leading into the tenor solo.

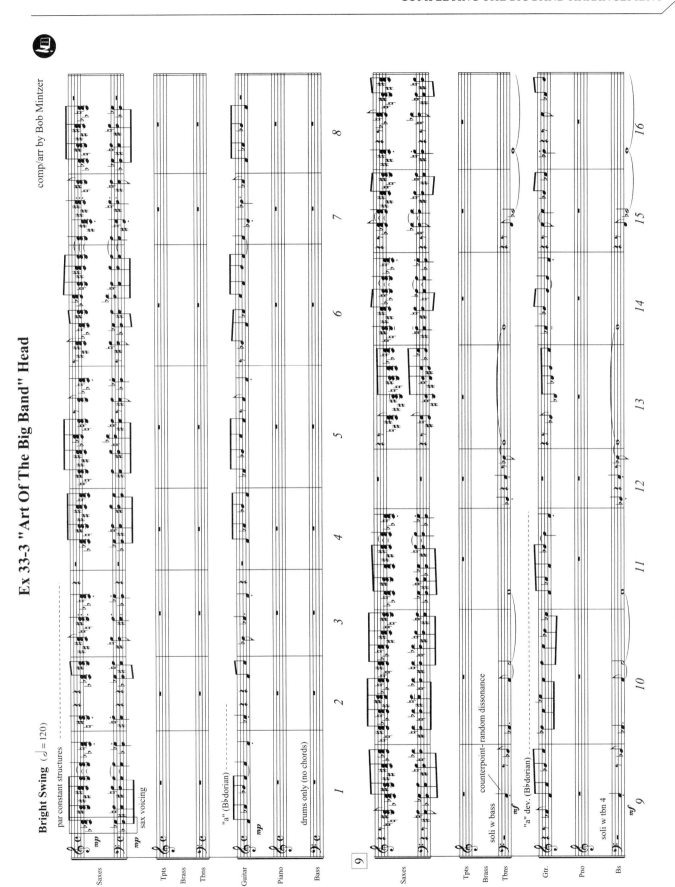

Ex 33-3 "Art Of The Big Band" Head

comp/arr by Bob Mintzer

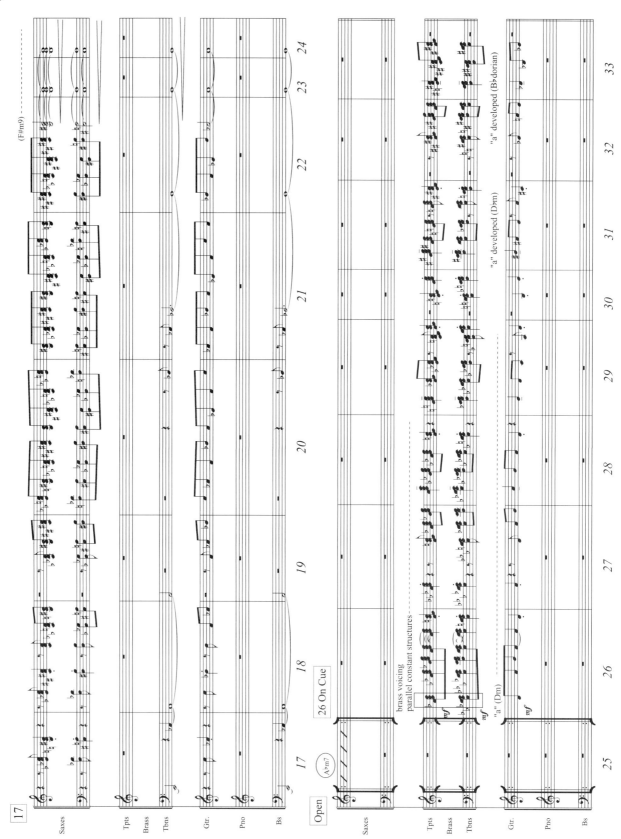

Ex 33-3 "Art Of The Big Band" Head - 2

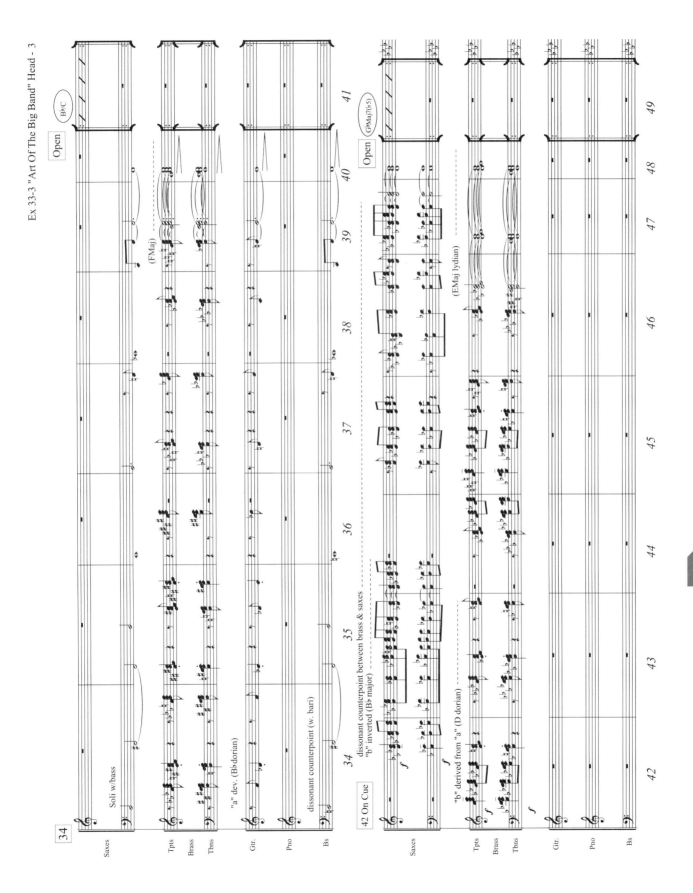

Ex 33-3 "Art Of The Big Band" Head - 3

477

Ex 33-3 "Art Of The Big Band" Head - 4

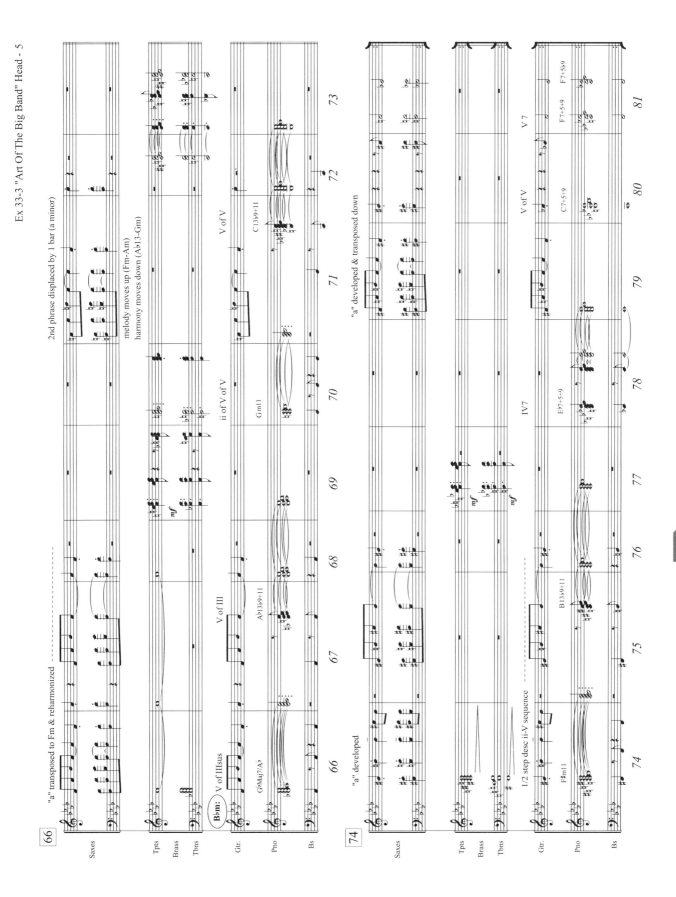

Ex 33-3 "Art Of The Big Band" Head - 5

Ex. 33-3 "Art Of The Big Band" Head - 6

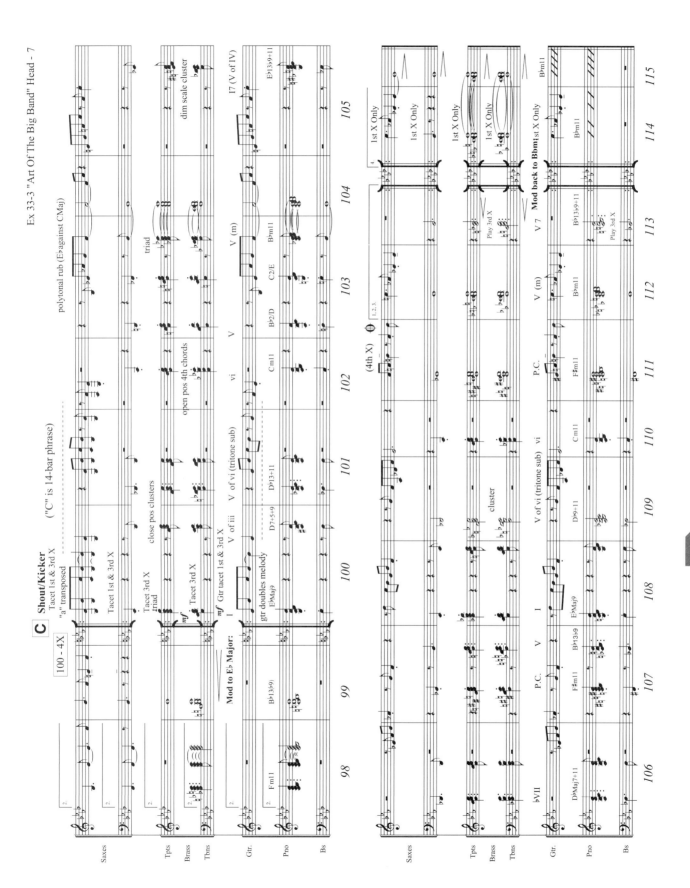

Ex 33-3 "Art Of The Big Band" Head - 7

As is often the case with modern, harmonically complex tunes, the blowing changes are simplified, allowing the soloist more freedom to improvise. In this case, the blowing changes are derived from the beginning of **A** (m. 50), with those changes simply expanded to four bars of Bbm9, four bars of G7+9, four bars of E Maj7+11, three bars of Eb9, and one bar of F7+9. After some backgrounds, there's a D.S. and a coda to an unexpected, short sax soli reminiscent of the intro, winding down to the final sustained Bbm (sus4) chord in the saxes and ending with a single low Bb octave played by the rhythm section. As with the other commercially available examples, we haven't provided a recording of this chart on the website. Try to get hold of a copy of the original recording when studying the analysis. The full score of the head is also available for download from the website.

◊ Special Bonus Score Available on Website! For another great example of a hip, modern sounding big band chart in a more contemporary jazz style, check out "Extra Credit" by the great jazz pianist and composer/arranger Jim McNeely. The score to the head and some ensemble sections of the chart is available for download as Ex. 33-4 on the companion website. As with other commercially available recordings examined in this book, we haven't provided a recording of this chart. The recording is available on the album "Lickety Split" bsy the Vanguard Jazz Orchestra on New World Records, 1997. We once again encourage you to support the great jazz musicians of our generation by purchasing the CD, or at least downloading the tune.

Chapter Summary

In this chapter we examined methods for adding a recap and an ending to the arrangement. We reviewed some important information regarding score and part layouts, instrument transpositions, proofreading, and printing the score and parts. We also provided three contrasting examples of big band arrangements, complete with detailed analyses, illustrated here with score reductions. Be sure to go to the companion website for more detailed study of the complete scores of each example. You should now be ready to put the finishing touches on your own big band arrangement, call a rehearsal, and listen to the fruits of your labor!

◊ **Software Tip:** The final stage of completing a composition with any music notation program is creating the score and part layouts prior to printing. Refer to the website for important information regarding parts and score layout.

Exercises

Use techniques discussed in this chapter.

1. Add a recap and ending to your big band chart.

2. Print out the parts and score for Arranging Project 3. Call a rehearsal, and play through the chart several times. Record it.

3. Listen to the recording with the other musicians. Discuss which parts worked well and which didn't. Make any necessary changes (this usually means taking things out or revoicing sections that may be too thick or dissonant). Print everything out again, and play it again!

4. Close this book and put it on the shelf. Go to concerts and clubs and listen to recordings by the great composers and arrangers. Listen to as much music in as many different styles as possible. Search for your own inner voice, and keep searching until it feels right. Create!

Chapter **34**

Summary of Music Notation Software Techniques

Before concluding our study of jazz composition and arranging in the digital age, we'd like to briefly summarize some of the salient features regarding the use of music software as a compositional tool and its relationship to the creative process. As stated numerous times throughout this book, music notation software is simply another tool, similar to paper and pencil, for expressing and documenting your musical ideas. In Chapters 2, 5, and 15 and in the Software Tips provided at the ends of chapters and on the companion website, we've presented some basic principles, instructions, and tips on how to accomplish the essential tasks necessary to document your ideas and to create professional-looking scores and parts. We've also presented some caveats specific to music technology about things that may occasionally distract from or impede the creative process.

34-1 Summary of Music Notation Techniques and Features

A complete list of the essential techniques necessary for creating scores and parts in any software platform is provided in Section 5-3. Mastering those techniques in any software platform has the potential for greatly facilitating and streamlining the creative process. Following are some of the benefits of using the current versions of notation software.

1. Easy and quick note entry
2. Enhanced management of musical expressions, articulations, and other musical symbols

3. Enhanced management of chord symbols, lyrics, and other text elements

4. Cut, copy, and paste editing

5. Specific timesaving edit techniques, such as "Explode" and "Implode" music

6. Management of instrument transpositions

7. MIDI playback

8. Ability to easily make corrections and revisions through linked score and parts

9. Convenient archiving and transfer of files

10. Desktop publishing capabilities for printing out professional-looking scores, parts, and educational materials

Section 5-5 provided a list of some basic principles of music preparation (just as applicable whether you're using a computer or writing the music out by hand). Observing the basic rules of music preparation will ensure smooth and efficient rehearsals and performances of your music.

Section 5-4 dealt with some of the benefits and dangers of MIDI playback. The chief advantages of MIDI playback include the ability to hear instantly whether melodic and harmonic material is working (chord voicings and polyphony) and to get a sense of the overall flow and structure of the music in a way that's difficult to accomplish at a piano. It can also be helpful for catching mistakes and wrong notes (although *not* a substitute for thorough proofreading). Essentially, the greater the number of staves in a score, the more valuable MIDI playback can be. However there are some significant dangers and traps to watch out for.

1. MIDI playback can all too easily become a crutch, resulting in mental and creative laziness. The highest form of musical creation still requires composer/arrangers to hear things with their "inner ear" and to be able to create without the benefit of MIDI or pianos.

2. With MIDI playback, you're always at the mercy of your sample libraries, which will never sound as good as or be as expressive as real acoustic instruments played by live players.

3. The overtone structure of synthesizers and sampled sounds is different from that of acoustic instruments, so some chord voicings that sound good on acoustic instruments won't work with samples, and vice-versa.

4. It's possible for a computer to play things that would be technically impossible, awkward, or extremely difficult on an acoustic instrument. It's essential to know the ranges and technical limitations of the instruments which you're writing for.

5. It can be difficult and time-consuming to achieve musically expressive MIDI playback with a notation program. Sometimes it's just not worth

the effort, and it can actually become a distraction and an impediment to the creative process.

6. It's easy to write music that is overly complex and impractical for live musicians.

34-2 Comparison of Finale and Sibelius

Finale and Sibelius are both very powerful and complex programs, each capable of accomplishing almost any task required by the average music professional, whether composer, music copyist, or engraver. Initially, Finale appeared to be the more powerful program, with greater flexibility but a more cumbersome interface and steeper learning curve. Over time, the two programs have seemed to move closer together, with Sibelius adding functionality and in some cases outpacing Finale with innovative new features. At the same time, Finale has come a long way in streamlining its interface and becoming more user friendly.

At the time of this writing (December 2010), it's difficult to make any kind of conclusive comparison regarding which program is better, more powerful, or easier to use. However, the following statements can be made with a fair degree of accuracy.

1. Simply because Finale has been around longer, it probably commands a greater share of the market for professional music preparation houses. Virtually any music prep office, whether independent or attached to an orchestra or production company, will accept Finale files. The same cannot be said of Sibelius.

2. Among younger, first-time users, there is probably a skew toward Sibelius, because of the perception (whether accurate or not) that it is easier and faster to use as well as that it is surpassing Finale in terms of the development of new, cutting-edge features.

3. Older users who have been working in one platform or the other for a number of years often exhibit a stubbornness and unwillingness to switch based primarily on a reluctance to spend the time necessary to learn a new piece of software.

4. Since being purchased by Avid in 2006, Sibelius has a larger parent company and may now be able to gain market share through access to greater marketing resources.

5. Both programs have their strengths and weaknesses. Some functions are more powerful and easier to perform in Finale, others in Sibelius. Both programs also have their share of cumbersome or overly complicated features, which can be a source of frustration while working. There is still plenty of room for improvement—and they're working on it!

34-3 Additional Software Tips

We've provided a few additional software tips for both Finale and Sibelius on the companion website. As new versions, features, and shortcuts become available, we hope to keep this a work in progress, with periodic updates to the site. Please refer to the website for the current list.

34-4 Using a Sequencer in Conjunction with Notation Software

There are some situations where a MIDI or digital audio sequencer may be a more appropriate compositional tool than a notation program such as Finale or Sibelius. Please refer to Section 2-4 for an overview and description of the various types of music software.

First of all, some types of music and musical styles are predominantly electronic in nature, relying primarily on electronically produced sounds or on electronic sounds in combination with acoustic or electronically processed acoustic instruments. This includes much contemporary dance music, electronica, techno, certain types of scoring for film and TV, and some abstract electronic jazz and electronic classical music. This type of music often needs no printed score, in which case the software (sequencer or digital audio workstation [DAW], such as Digital Performer, Logic, or Pro Tools, or sound-designing environment, such as Max/MSP or Kyma) becomes both the compositional tool for documenting the music (replacing traditional music notation) as well as the medium for the final realization of the music.

In situations where electronic sound sources are combined with acoustic instruments in performance, it may still be preferable to compose first in a sequencer, with MIDI reference tracks for the acoustic instruments, and then to export the reference MIDI tracks as a "Standard MIDI File" to be opened later in Finale or Sibelius. A score and parts for the acoustic instruments may then be created. It's also possible to first create the score in the notation program and then export that to be opened later in the sequencer or DAW, to work on the electronic elements of the music.

If the music is primarily electronic, with only a few acoustic instrument tracks, it may actually be easier and faster to use the notation functions within the sequencer. Of course, because of the limitations of the notation capabilities in most sequencers, this would be an option only if there's no need to publish a professional-looking score or parts of the music (see Section 2-4).

Finally, if the music is composed for acoustic instruments but you need a musically expressive demo of the music prior to rehearsal or performance, it's still generally preferable (as we've mentioned periodically throughout the book) to create the demo in a sequencer rather than a notation program. There is still much greater flexibility, power, and facility for editing the dynamic and expressive musical features of MIDI, such as control changes (including volume), attack velocity, tempo, and note duration, within a sequencer rather than in a notation program. It's also easier to work with an expanded sound palette using third-party virtual instruments and sample libraries, such as Kontakt and the VSL instrument.

There are three ways to proceed with this scenario, each with its advantages and disadvantages, depending partly on the style of music and background experience of the composer.

1. Create the Score in a Notation Program First—Method 1

You can first create the score in a notation program and then export the file as a Standard MIDI File by going to File > Save As > Standard MIDI File (Finale) or File > Export/MIDI File (Sibelius). Then open the MIDI file in the sequencer or DAW of your choice. The advantage to working this way is that if you're used to composing in the traditional manner by notating the music on score paper or in a notation program, this method will be much easier.

However, there are several potential problems and dangers in working this way. First of all, the notation program is likely to include MIDI controller data (including volume), attack velocities, note placement and duration, program changes and key switching, and tempo changes derived from its default MIDI playback settings, which may not be the best choices for your sequencer. This means you may have to redo much of the volume (controller 7) data, adjust attack velocities, adjust note placements and durations, edit patch changes and key switching to match the sound palette of your sequencer, and revise tempo changes. There are also likely to be some extraneous control changes, such as controller 6, 10, 38, 91, 100, and 101, that will need to be deleted or adjusted. This type of MIDI data generally has no bearing on the functions of the sequencer and may cause playback problems or simply clutter up the edit windows.

One way to simplify this problem is to turn off "Human Playback" in Finale, or set the Performance style (Play > Performance) to "Meccanico" in Sibelius, before saving as a MIDI file. Now, however, there is a different problem, because everything will be quantized to 100%, without any swing feel, and all velocities will be set to the same default values. In either case, you're going to need to spend a fair amount of time working in the sequencer with controller 7, velocities, note placement and durations, and tempo changes in order to get the sequence to sound musically expressive. Also, the tracks may wind up in the wrong order in the sequencer's tracks list.

2. Create the Score in a Notation Program First—Method 2

If you need to start by notating the music in the traditional manner, you can first create the score in a notation program and then print it out, or you can split

489

your screen and enter the music into the sequencer in real time, to a click, one staff at a time. Although this method may at first appear to be more time-consuming, it may actually be the easiest way to create a musical demo of the music quickly when working in this manner.

3. Create the Music in a Sequencer First

You can first create the music in a sequencer. Then export the file as a Standard MIDI File by going to File Menu > Save As > Standard MIDI File (or a similar method—all sequencers will allow you to "Save As" or "Export" as a standard MIDI file). Then open the MIDI file in the notation program of your choice to create a professional-looking score and parts. The advantage to working this way is that if you're used to composing in a sequencer, you'll wind up with a much more musically expressive sequence right off the bat.

Although it might seem quite foreign to some to compose for a jazz big band in a MIDI sequencer *before* notating it, consider that jazz arrangers such as Thad Jones and Willie Smith, among others, frequently composed by copying out the parts without first (or ever) writing out a score. All of the music was always completely formed in their minds. The score to "On a Misty Night" (Ex. 19-1), arranged by Willie Smith for Joe Lovano, was compiled by inputting the handwritten parts into Finale, one staff at a time. There was never a written score! By comparison, composing in a sequencer seems like a luxury. If viewing the music in standard notation helps you to organize your ideas, the notation capabilities in Digital Performer, Logic, Cubase, etc. are adequate in most cases—and you have the advantage of much more musical MIDI playback from the start.

There is one crucial issue to be dealt with before exporting a MIDI sequence to be reopened in a notation program. It's essential to quantize everything, *including note durations*, to 100% strength before saving as a MIDI file. If you don't do this, then when you open the file in Finale or Sibelius you're likely to be confronted with a nightmare scenario of dotted 32nd notes, 64th rests, triplets that should be eighth notes, and vice versa. It's *much* easier and faster to deal with this type of editing in the sequencer than in the notation program; with a little bit of practice, it can be accomplished with a minimum of stress. Be sure to rename the file *before* making these changes, because doing this will eliminate any expressive nuances from your live performance or any expressive editing or quantization you've applied to the sequence.

34-5 Where Do We Go from Here?

As we mentioned at the end of Chapter 2, as the technology continues to advance and as the host computers become more and more powerful, some of the different types of music software have begun to overlap in their functionality. Many of the leading products continue to add astonishing new features with each

490

update, moving toward overlapping functionality that attempts to integrate within one program all of the essential features necessary for music composition, notation, audio recording, and mixing.

One thing we can be certain of: The technology will continue to advance at a breathtaking pace, in ways that we can't even imagine today. Some of the software tips offered in this book may be out of date by the time the book goes to press. Fortunately, the companion website provides a practical means of keeping up to date with technological breakthroughs as they occur.

As we mentioned at the end of Section 5-4, the implementation of "Rewire" capabilities into Sibelius 6, or the incorporation of Sibelius capabilities into Protools since both companies have been purchased by Avid, may very well point a direction for the future development and integration of notation and sequencing software. It seems like a logical step, one that would solve many of the problems described in Section 34-4.

Finally, we'd like to reiterate our underlying philosophical views stated at the end of Chapter 2: For us—the professional musicians and composers, serious music students, music educators, and music hobbyists—technology is a means to an end, not an end in itself. It's essential to maintain your perspective and to keep your focus on that ultimate goal: the beauty and artistry of the music itself.

Chapter Summary

In this chapter we provided a summary of music notation software techniques and features. We also presented a comparison of the two main notation programs, Finale and Sibelius, and offered a few more software tips for each. We then examined some of the issues relating to using a MIDI sequencer in conjunction with a notation program. Finally, we took a look at the likely continuing development of music technology in the future and reiterated some of our philosophical precepts from Chapter 2.

This concludes our study of jazz composition and arranging in the digital age, an examination of the basic musical principles essential to the art of arranging for large and small jazz ensembles, presented within the context of using music notation software. Music is a lifelong study with an infinite number of possible paths. With this book we've attempted to establish some guidelines and direction for one of those paths. We sincerely hope that the information presented here provides you with a practical foundation of knowledge and useful tools for creating jazz compositions and arrangements for various size ensembles. We also hope that the included technical information will help you to navigate the maze of software techniques and options while maintaining your focus on the creative goals.

Use the principles and techniques presented here as a starting point on the journey toward discovering your own unique, creative potential and fulfillment.

And remember: The most valuable music lessons are obtained not from a book, but from listening, practicing, doing, following your own creative instincts, and taking chances! Simply following the rules and principles presented here will not result in the composition of great music. Learn to be your own most rigorous critic, and never settle for the obvious or easy way out. Always keep searching for new solutions and possibilities. Maintain your focus and discipline, and let the music flow through you!

Index

abbreviations and symbols, chord, 164–165
accents, 9, 151
accidentals, 352, 362–363
accompanying soloists, 433–435
active counter-melodies, 127
additional melody notes, 121*m*
African rhythm and melody, 68
alignment conventions, 51–52
altered chord tones, 86, 121*m*
alternate voicings, 94*m*, 96*m*
alto flutes, 24–25, 26*m*
alto saxophones, 23*m*, 24
   See also brass section
analog, described, 5–6
"Analycity" by Richard Sussman
  analysis of, 89*m*
  big bands, 407*m*–409*m*
  mixed combinations, 375*m*
  reharmonization of approach tones, 109*m*
  shout choruses, 232*m*, 233
  soli section, 227*m*–229*m*, 230
    analysis of, 410–411
    big bands, 407*m*–409*m*
antecedent phrases, 69
anticipations, 60
appoggiatura, 152
approach tone reharmonization, 82, 105–117
approach tones
  "Basie sound," 288, 289
  in harmonies, 105
  voicing positions, 90
arrangements
  backgrounds, 144–146
    six horns, 220*m*–221*m*
  big bands, 328–330
    completing arrangements, 453–454
    creative process, 331–332
    scores, 330–331
    workflow concepts, 330–331
  codas/endings, 140, 146, 171–172
    six horns, 237–238
  concept and direction, 131–133
  counter-melodies, 126–128
  creative process, 331–332
  dynamics, 149–150
  endings, 140, 146, 171–172
    six horns, 237–238

form, 133–137
  instrumentation and outlining, 138–139
  outlining and graphing, 137–138
improvisation, 133
instrumentation, 328–330
  and outlining, 138–139
introductions, 140–142
kickers, 140, 142–143, 219*m*
melody development, 76–78, 77*m*
music spacing, 172
outlining and graphing, 137–138
part transpositions, 172–173
polyphony, 126–128
printing, 173
proofreading, 172–173
recapitulations, 134, 137, 171–172
  six horns, 237–238
rhythm section, 161–170
scores
  big bands, 330–331
  and part layouts, 172
  staff, conventions of, 50–51
six horns, 237–238
  backgrounds, 220*m*–221*m*
for soloists, 433–452
transitions, 140, 142–143
workflow concepts, 330–331
See also individual tunes
articulations
  brass and woodwinds, 150–154
  MIDI playback, 158
  proofreading, 454
  software, 269
"Art of the Big Band" by Bob Mintzer,
    475*m*–481*m*
  analysis of, 472–474, 482
  polyphonic big band writing, 396
asymmetrical phrase structures, 70–71
atonal harmonies, 88
atonal sounds, 358, 359, 359*m*, 360*m*
attack velocity, 7, 9
  notation software, 47
audio effects, 10
audio mixes of scores, 312
augmentation, 72, 73*m*
augmented triads, 85, 349
Austin, Patti, 438, 439–440

"Autumn Leaves" by Mercer, Prevert, and Kosma
  counterpoint, 128*m*
    modern, 361*m*
  functional reharmonization, 125*m*
  lead sheet with analysis, 124*m*
  melodic reharmonization, 121*m*–123*m*, 359*m*
  modern counterpoint, 361*m*
  modern reharmonization, 126*m*
  vocal chart, 436*m*–437*m*

backgrounds, 137, 144–146
  focus of music, 34
  six horns, 220*m*–221*m*
balance
  big band, 367–368
  syncopation and notation, 59
  vertical harmony, 87
  woodwind section, 367–368
baritone saxophones, 23*m*, 24
Basie, Count, 264, 288, 316
"Basie sound," 287*m*, 288, 289, 301
  big bands, 455
  brass plus saxophones, 310–311
  and shout choruses, 418, 419, 423
  upper-structure triads, 346
bass clarinets, 26*m*, 27
basses, 163–164
  notation, 167*m*
  ranges, 31*m*
  sounds of, 29
  See also rhythm section
bassoons, 22
  See also woodwind section
bass trombones, 19, 21*m*
beaming, 60, 61*m*
Beirach, Richie, 348, 359
bend notes, 151
big band configuration, 263
big bands
  "Analycity" by Richard Sussman, 407*m*–409*m*
  arrangements for
    completing, 453–454
    creative process, 331–332
    instrumentation, 328–330
    scores, 330–331
    workflow concepts, 330–331
  "Art of the Big Band" by Bob Mintzer, 475*m*–481*m*
    analysis of, 472–474, 482
  "Basie sound," 455
  brass and woodwinds, 368–372
  brass doubles, 365–367
  creative process, 331–332

cross-sectional instrumental subdivisions, 320–324
"Cross-Section" sketch by Richard Sussman, 332–334, 335*m*–336*m*
"Fletcher" by Richard Sussman, 456*m*–458*m*, 460*m*–461*m*
  analysis of, 454–455, 459
form
  elements of, 327
  outlining, 328–330
harmonic concepts (modern). *See* harmonic concepts (modern)
instrumental subdivisions, 315–325
  cross-sectional, 320–324
instrumentation, 328–330
orchestral colors within, 379
polyphonic writing for, 396, 397*m*–401*m*, 402
scores, 330–331
shout choruses, 417–432
soli sections, 405–416
"Uncertainty" by Michael Abene, 466*m*–471*m*
  analysis of, 463–465, 472
upper-structure triads, 345
woodwind and brass doubles, 365–367
woodwind section
  brass, combinations with, 368–372
  dynamics, 367–368
  mixed combinations, 372–378
workflow concepts, 330–331
See also large ensembles
"Bill Bossa" by Richard Sussman, 175*m*–182*m*
  analysis of, 174, 183–185
binary code, 7
block voicing, 201
blowing change modification, 135*m*–136*m*
blues scales in jazz, 67
"Brass Colors" by Richard Sussman, 371*m*–372*m*
brass doubles, 213–214
  big bands, 365–367
brass mutes, 155–158, 158*m*
  comparisons, 371, 371*m*–372*m*
  and woodwinds, 368
brass section, 15, 16–21
  articulations, 150–154
  concerted writing for, 283–298
    low register melody, 286–287, 287*m*
    mid-register melody, 288–294
    open position voicing, 295
    saxophones, combining with, 301–309
    software limitations, 295–297
    voicing principles, 284–286
  constant coupling, 301–302, 302*m*
  large ensembles, 272

low register melody, 286–287, 287m
mid-register melody, 288–294
open position voicing, 295
and saxophones, 203m
    "Basie sound," 310–311
    combining with, 301–309
    contrasting with, 315–316, 317m–319m
scores for small ensembles, 63
shakes, 151
software limitations, 295–297
variable coupling, 303–309
voicing positions - six horns, 203m
voicing principles, 284–286
and woodwinds, 150–154, 368–372
See also individual instruments
Brookmeyer, Bob, 19
bucket mutes, 156

CAI (computer-assisted instruction) software, 12
call and response format, 315
cascading effects, 393, 395m
C extension of the bass, 18
Charles, Ray, 66n
chord abbreviations and symbols, 164–165
chord density, 87
chord function, 86
chord progressions
  in arrangements, 134
  horizontal harmony, 87
chords, 82–86
  diminished seventh chords, 86m
    harmonic concepts (modern), 349
    melodic reharmonization, 121m
    reharmonization of approach tones,
      106, 107m
  by fourths, 340–341, 342m
  quality, changing, 122m
  reharmonization of approach tones, 106, 107m
  roots, 87
  scale derived seventh chords, 84
  scales, 84
  spacing of, 87
  structures of, 348–349
  symbols and abbreviations, 164–165
  by thirds, 82
chord voicings
  for 5-6 horns, 198–203
  harmonic concepts, 82
  vertical harmony, 86–87
Chowning, John, 37
clarinets, 22, 25
  ranges and transpositions, 26m
  See also woodwind section
close voicing position, 90–91, 93m, 95m
  8-piece brass, 285m

5-6 horns, 199m–200m, 201, 203m, 206,
    207m–208m
5 saxophones, 300m
  mixed, 207m
cluster bombs, 349
"Clusters" by Richard Sussman, 350m
cluster voicings, 349
codas, 137, 140, 146, 171–172
  six horns, 237–238
color combinations, 379, 380m
  5-6 horns, 214–216
color tones, 86
Coltrane, John, 24
compositional form in arrangements, 134
computer-assisted instruction (CAI)
    software, 12
computers. *See* software
concert and transposed scores
  software change in, 64
concerted writing for brass section, 283–298
  low register melody, 286–287, 287m
  mid-register melody, 288–294
  open position voicing, 295
  software limitations, 295–297
  voicing principles, 284–286
concert pitch, 15–17
configurations, 48
consequence phrases, 69
consistency conventions, 52
consonance, 87
consonant chords, 83
constant coupling, 301–302, 302m
constantly modulating horizontal harmony, 88
constant structures
  harmonic concepts (modern), 356–357, 357m
  melodic reharmonization, 358, 360m
  soli sections, 411
contrary motion
  melodic motion, 98, 99m
  polyphonic big band writing, 396
  and shout choruses, 418
  soli sections, 407
contrast and variety, 34
  phrase structures, 71
  polyphonic big band writing, 396
  syncopation and notation, 59
Control Change, 8–9
controller, MIDI musical expression, 8–9
Corea, Chick, 34i
counter-melodies
  in arrangements, 126–128
  background parts, 144, 146m
  six horns, 221m
  independent, 361–362
  melody development, 74

counterpoint, 128m, 361m
free, 74, 75m
harmonic concepts (modern), 361–362
See also polyphony
courtesy accidentals conventions, 51–52
crescendo, MIDI controller, 9
cross-sectional instrumental subdivisions, 320,
321m–323m
"Cross-Section" sketch by Richard Sussman
instrumental subdivisions, 321m–322m
workflow analysis of, 332–334, 335m–336m
cup mutes, 156

"Dancing on the Ceiling" by Rodgers &
Hart, 287m
DAWs (digital audio workstations), 10
"Dear Old Stockholm" by Richard Sussman,
293m–294m, 295
brass plus saxophones, 306, 307m–309m
delays, in syncopation, 60
derby mutes, 156
destination tones, 301
diatonic chord progression, 83
diatonic harmony
harmonic concepts, 82
horizontal harmony, 88
melodic reharmonization, 121m
reharmonization of approach tones,
106, 107m
six horns, 205m
digital, described, 5–6
digital audio recording technology, 7
digital audio sequencers, 9–10
digital audio workstations (DAWs), 10
diminished chords, 83
diminished scales, 348–349
constant structures, 357m
"Diminished Scale Structures," 357m
diminished seventh chords, 86m
harmonic concepts (modern), 349
melodic reharmonization, 121m
reharmonization of approach tones, 106,
107m
diminution, 72, 73m
dissonance
and shout choruses, 426, 430
upper-structure triads, 346
vertical harmony, 87
dissonant chords, 83
dissonant intervals, 87
doit, 151
dominant chords
harmonic concepts, 83
modal concepts, 96–97, 97m
upper-structure triads, 345

dominant harmony
harmonic concepts, 83
melodic reharmonization, 122m
reharmonization of approach tones,
106, 107m
six horns, 205m
dominant seventh chords, 67, 83
Dorsey, Tommy, 264
double-diminished chords, 348
doubles, 213–214
big bands, 365–368, 369m–370m, 371
dovetailing entrances and exits, 274–275
downbeats
swing feel, 62
syncopation and notation, 59
"drop-2" voicing positions, 90–92, 95m, 96m
8-piece brass, 285m
5-6 horns, 199m–200m, 201
5 saxophones, 300m
mixed, 207m
drums, 165–166, 169
notation, 167m
in software, 170
sounds of, 30
See also rhythm section
dynamics, 149–150
MIDI playback, 158
woodwind section, 367–368

Earth, Wind and Fire, 66n
economy in music, 34
editor librarian software, 10
effect processors, 12
eighth note interpretation, 58, 60
eight-piece brass, 285m, 286
electric pianos, 27–28, 31m
Ellington, Duke, 264
embellishments, 72, 73m
endings, 137, 140, 146, 171–172
big bands, 453
six horns, 237–238
English horns, 22
See also woodwind section
ensembles
instruments, 15
six horns, 256m–258m
See also large ensembles; small ensemble
writing
euphoniums, 413
"Exercise in Flutility" by Richard Sussman,
376m–377m
expectation and surprise, 35
exposed fifths, 98
expositions, 137, 140
melodic motives, 69

extensions, 72, 73m
  of a trombone, 19
"Extra Credit" by Jim McNeely, 482

Fender Rhodes electric pianos, 27–28
F extension of the trombone, 18
fills, 127
Finale software, 38, 39–40
  drum grooves, 170
  "Explode Music," 116
  layers, 402
  MIDI playback and editing, 47–50
  notation techniques, 41–47
  score and parts layout functions, 189–193
  shortcuts and macros, 158–159
  Sibelius, comparison with, 487
  templates, 196
  user interface, 187–189
  See also software
"Fletcher" by Richard Sussman
  analysis of, 454–455, 459
  big bands, 460m–461m
  head out, 461m–462m
  introduction and head, 318m–319m,
    456m–458m
  kicker reduction, 460m
flugelhorns, 16–17
  ranges and transpositions, 21m
  See also brass section
flutes, 22, 24–25
  "Analycity" by Richard Sussman, 375m
  "Exercise in Flutility" by Richard Sussman,
    376m–377m
  ranges and transpositions, 26m
  See also woodwind section
focus of music, 34
fonts, software, 431
foreground of music, 34
form
  arrangements, 133–137
    instrumentation and outlining, 138–139
    outlining and graphing, 137–138
  and balance, 34
  big bands, 327, 328–330
  elements of
    big bands, 327
    5-6 horns, 213
  5-6 horns, 213, 214–216
  horizontal harmony, 88
  instrumentation (5-6 horns), 214–216
  outlining, 328–330
fourth chord structures, 340–341
free counterpoint, 74, 75m
free reharmonization
  melodic reharmonization, 358–359, 360m

reharmonization of approach tones,
    106, 108m
  six horns, 205m
French Horns, 16–17, 19
  ranges and transpositions, 21m
  See also brass section
full score format, 82
functional reharmonization, 125m

generating parts, notation software, 187–189
Gershwin, George, 438
"Get a Handel on It" by Richard Sussman,
    424m–425m
  analysis of, 423
ghosted notes, 152
glissandos, 151
  of the trombone, 18m
Goodman, Benny, 264
grand staff format, 82
graphs, outlining and, 137–139
guide tones, 144
  in counter-melodies, 127
guitars, 28–29, 161–163
  notation, 167m
  ranges, 31m
  scores for small ensembles, 63
  See also rhythm section

half-step planing, 106
Hammond organ, 28
Handel, George Frederic, 423
harmonic concepts (3-4 horns), 81–103
  chord, building, 82–86
  horizontal harmony, 87–89
  melodic motion, 98–99
  modal concepts of voicing, 96–97
  vertical harmony, 86–87
  voice leading, 98–99
  voicing, standard, 90–96
harmonic concepts (5-6 horns), 197–211
  chord voicings, 198–203
  reharmonization of approach tones, 204–205
  voicing positions, 206–208
harmonic concepts (modern), 339–353
  chords by fourths, 340–341, 342m
  chord structures, 348–349
  cluster voicings, 349, 350m
  constant structures, 356–357, 357m
  and melodic reharmonization, 355–363
    techniques of, 358–360, 360m
  parallel five-voice structures, 357, 357m
  polytonal sounds, 348
  spread voicings, 349–350, 351m
  upper-structure triads, 343m
harmonic innovations from jazz, 67

harmonic rhythms, 58, 63
    in arrangements, 134, 135m, 136–137
harmon mutes, 155
harmony
    and balance, 33
    horizontal harmony, 88
hat accents, 151
hats, as brass mutes, 156
"Have You Met Miss Jones?" by Rodgers
        and Hart
    background parts, 145m
        six horns, 220m–221m
    introductions, 141m–142m
        six horns, 217m–218m
    kickers/transitions, 143m
head of a tune, 137
Henderson, Fletcher, 263–264, 315, 454
hidden fifths, 98
high unison, 273m
homophonic musical textures
    8-piece brass, 285m
    5-6 horns, 199m–200m
    5 saxophones, 300m
    melody development, 74, 75m
    voicing positions, 93m, 95m
hooks, 140, 142m
    six horns, 218m
horizontal harmony, 87–89
host sequencers, 11

"I Could Write a Book" by Rodgers
        and Hart
    alternate voicing positions, 94m, 96m
    analysis of, 69–71, 69m
    brass and sax sections, 203m
    8-piece brass, 285m
    5-6 horns, 199m–200m
    5 saxophones, 300m
    melodic alteration, 73m
    monophonic scoring, 77m
    musical textures, 75m
    standard voicing positions, 93m, 95m
    tessitura, 78m
"I'll Remember April" by Johnston, Raye, and
        De Paul
    constant structures, 357m
    parallel five-voice structures, 357m
    static harmony, 114m
    voice leading, 115m
improvisation in arrangements, 133
independent counter-melodies, 361–362
insertion of chords between melody
        notes, 122m
in stand, brass mutes, 156
instantiation of virtual instruments, 11

instrumental subdivisions, 315–325
    cross-sectional, 320–324
    six-horn arrangements, 247
instrumentation, 138–139, 328–330
    5-6 horns, 214–216
instrument ranges, 15–31
interface, 7
internal resonance, 87, 202
intervals, 82, 87
introductions, 137, 140–142
    six horns, 217m–218m, 240m–244m,
        250m–255m
    transitions/kickers, 143m
inversion, 71, 72, 73m
"I've Got the Articulations & Dynamics Blues"
        by Richard Sussman
    brass and woodwind articulations, 154m
    rhythm section arrangements, 168m
"Ivories Tower" by Richard Sussman
    color combinations, 379, 380m
    mixed combinations, 372, 373m, 374, 378m
    voicing techniques, modern, 341, 344m

Key Switches, 47, 381
key switching, 381
kickers, 140, 142–143, 143m
    reduction, 460m
    six horns, 219m

landscape orientation
    changing to portrait, 43
    printing the parts and the score, 173
    score layout conventions, 50, 80
large ensembles, 263–270
    basic principles, 265
    combining the instruments, 272–273
    melodic development, 271
    melodic phrase structure, 274–275,
        275m–278m
    musical textures, 283
    the scores, 266–267
    sound palette, 265–266
    tune selection, 267
    unison scoring, 273m, 274m, 276m–278m
    vertical harmony, 284
    See also big bands
large ensemble writing, 267
    transposed scores, 266
large form, 134
layouts
    big band, 454
    notation software, 187–189
    scores, 222
librarian software, 10
Liebman, Dave, 359

"Linealogy" by Richard Sussman
    cascade effect, 393, 395*m*
    increasing/decreasing voices, 393,
        394*m*, 395
    line writing, 385, 386*m*–389*m*, 390,
        391*m*–392*m*
line writing
    basic principles of, 383–384
    increasing/decreasing voices, 393, 394*m*
    "Linealogy" by Richard Sussman,
        386*m*–389*m*, 390, 391*m*–392*m*
    polyphony, 383
    procedures for, 384–385, 386*m*–389*m*
lip gliss, 151
long accent, 151
long fall, 151
long note, 151
low interval limits, 87, 92
low register melody, 286–287, 287*m*
low unison, 274*m*
lyric content, 76
lyrics, 435
    See also vocalists

major chords
    harmonic concepts, 83, 84*m*
    modal concepts, 96–97, 97*m*
    symbols and abbreviations, 164
    upper-structure triads, 345
    voicing techniques, modern, 343*m*
mallet (pitched percussion) instruments,
    30, 31*m*
mapping samples, 11
Maria Schneider Orchestra, 366
marimbas, 30, 31*m*
McNeely, Jim, 341
measures, numbering conventions of, 51
mechanical voicings, 90
melodic analysis. *See* individual tunes
melodic development. *See* melody
    development
melodic motions, 68*m*, 99*m*
    harmonic concepts, 98–99
melodic motives, 69–71
melodic phrase structure, 134
    large ensembles, 274–275, 275*m*–278*m*
melodic reharmonization, 119
    "Autumn Leaves" by Mercer, Prevert, and
        Kosma, 121*m*–123*m*, 359*m*
    free reharmonization, 358–359, 360*m*
    techniques of, 119–126, 358
    See also harmonic concepts (modern)
melodic rhythms
    swing feel, 62–63
    syncopation and notation, 59–61

melodic shapes, 68*m*
melody development, 67–80, 271
    and an arrangement, 76–78
    horizontal harmony, 88
    motion, shape and, 67–68
    and motives, 71–73
    musical textures, basic, 74–75
    and phrase structure, 69–71
    shape and motion, 67–68
melody in low register, 286–287
melody in mid-register, 288–290,
    290*m*–294*m*
"Memories of Lives Past" by Michael Abene,
    413*m*–415*m*
    analysis of, 412
Metropole Orchestra, 366–367
middleground of music, 34
MIDI (Musical Instrument Digital Interface),
    6–7, 9–10
    bank, 381
    commands of, 7–8
    history of, 7, 37
    key switching, 381
    messages of, 8–9
    middle C terminology, 19*n*
    new protocols of, 12
    and notation
        history of, 37
        software, 47–50
    playback and chords, 79
    program changes, 381
    stuck notes, 324
MIDI channel voice messages, 8–9
    notation software, 47
MIDI Manufacturers Association (MMA), 12
MIDI messages, 7
MIDI playback and editing, 47–50, 486–487
    dynamics, 158
    piano chords, 129
    swing feel, 62–63
MIDI studio, 7
mid-register melody, 288–294
Miller, Glenn, 264
minor chords
    harmonic concepts, 83, 84*m*
    modal concepts, 96–97, 97*m*
    symbols and abbreviations, 164
    upper-structure triads, 345
    voicing techniques, modern, 343*m*
"Minor Infractions" by Michael Abene,
    250*m*–258*m*
    analysis of, 247–249
minor third substitution
    harmonic concepts, 84, 85, 85*m*
    melodic reharmonization, 122*m*

Mintzer, Bob, 341
  polyphonic big band writing, 396
  soli sections, 411, 412m
minuet form, 134
mixed combinations, 372–378
mixed open positions, 208m
mixed voicing positions, 207m
MMA (MIDI Manufacturers Association), 12
modal concepts of chord voicings, 84, 96–97, 97m
modal harmonies
  chords by fourths, 340–341, 342m
  horizontal harmony, 88
  melodic reharmonization, 123m
modern counterpoint, 361m
modern harmonies, 361–362
modes, 88
modulations
  horizontal harmony, 88
  melodic reharmonization, 123m
  MIDI controller, 8–9
monophonic musical textures, 74, 75m
monophonic scoring, 77m
motion and shape of melody, 67–68
motivic development. *See* melody development
Musical Instruction Digital Interface (MIDI).
    See MIDI (Musical Instrument Digital
    Interface)
musical textures
  5-6 horns, 199m–200m
  large ensembles, 283
  melody development, 74, 75m
  voicing positions, 93m, 95m
    5-6 horns, 199m–200m
music education software, 12
music spacing in arrangements, 172
music stand as mute, 156
mute, MIDI program change, 9
muted brass, 155–158, 213–214
"My Romance" by Rodgers and Hart
  arrangement outline of, 138–139
    5-6 horns, 215–216
  graph of, 139
  no reharmonization of approach tones, 109m
  reharmonization of approach tones,
    107m–108m
  six horns, 205m

natural overtone series, 86, 87
non-diatonic harmonies, 88
non-functional harmonies
  horizontal harmony, 88
  melodic reharmonization, 358, 360m
notation, 59–61
  beaming, 60, 61m
  rhythm section, 167m

notation software, 10, 37–53
  benefits of, 485–486
  configurations, 48
  copyist conventions, 50–53
  generating parts, 187–189
  history of, 37–38
  MIDI (Musical Instrument Digital Interface),
    47–50
  page layout, 187–189
  and sequencers, 488–490
  See also software
Note Off, 8–9, 47
Note On, 8–9, 47

oblique motion, 98, 99m
oboes, 22
  See also woodwind section
octaves
  large ensembles, 274m, 276m–278m
  melodic motion, 98
"On a Misty Night" by Tadd Dameron,
    240m–244m
  analysis of, 238–239, 490
  open position voicing, 295
"One for Thad" by Richard Sussman, 396,
    397m–401m
open, MIDI program change, 9
open position voicing, 295
Open Sound Control (OSC), 12
open voicing positions, 90, 92, 93m, 95m
  chord roots, 87
  8-piece brass, 285m
  5-6 horns, 199m–200m, 201
  5 saxophones, 300m
  mixed, 208m
orchestral colors, 379
organs, 27–28, 31m
OSC (Open Sound Control), 12
outlining, 137–138
  big band, 328–330
  5-6 horns, 214–216
overtone structures, 16n

pads, 144, 145m
  six horns, 220m
page layout, in notation software,
    187–189
panning, MIDI controller, 9
parallel fifths, 98
parallel five-voice structures, 357, 357m
parallel motion, 98, 99m
  reharmonization of approach tones,
    106, 108m
  six horns, 205m
part transpositions, 172–173

passing tones
  "Basie sound," 289
  in harmonies, 105
pedal points, 123*m*
pedals, 140
percussion instruments, 30
  See also rhythm section
perfect fifths, 86
phrase structures, 69–71
phrasing and articulations, 150–154
pianos
  in arrangements, 161–163
    notation, 167*m*
  MIDI playback and editing, 129
  ranges, 31*m*
  scores for small ensembles, 63
  sounds of, 27
  See also rhythm section
piccolos, 22
  ranges and transpositions, 26*m*
  sounds of, 25
  See also woodwind section
Pitch Bend, MIDI channel voice message, 8–9
pitch of instruments, 272
pivot chords, 174
planing, 106
plop, 151
plug-ins, 11
  audio effects, 10
plunger mutes, 156
polyphonic musical textures
  8-piece brass, 285*m*
  5-6 horns, 199*m*–200*m*
  5 saxophones, 300*m*
  melody development, 74, 75*m*
  voicing positions, 93*m*, 95*m*
polyphony
  in arrangements, 126–128
  big band writing, 396, 397*m*–401*m*, 402
  line writing. *See* line writing
  modern harmonies, 361–362
  See also counterpoint
polytonal sounds
  melodic reharmonization, 359*m*
  voicing techniques, modern, 343*m*, 348, 358
portrait orientation
  changing to landscape, 43
  parts layout conventions, 51, 80
  score layout conventions, 50
positions of the trombone, 18*m*
Pratt, Dean, 454
primary chords, 120
primary chord tones, 86
primary harmonization, 120
primary harmony, 119

printing
  arrangements, 173
  big bands, 454
  using notation software, 187–189, 195
Program Change
  MIDI channel voice message, 8–9
    notation software, 47
proofreading arrangements, 172–173
  big bands, 454
protocol, 7
pulse and style, 58–59
punch, 151
pyramid effect, 393, 395*m*

quarter notes, 60

ranges and transpositions, 21*m*, 23*m*,
    26*m*, 31*m*
recapitulations (recap), 134, 171–172
  in arrangements, 137
  big bands, 453
  six horns, 237–238
receive channel, 8
recording and editing software, 10
Redman, Don, 263, 315
register of instruments, 272–273
reharmonization of approach tones, 106,
    107*m*, 108*m*
  "Analycity" by Richard Sussman, 109*m*
  8-piece brass, 286
  5-6 horns, 204, 205*m*, 206
  harmonic concepts, 82
  legend for, 116–117
  "My Romance" by Rodgers and Hart,
    107*m*–108*m*
  repeated notes, 111–112, 113*m*
  six horns, 205*m*
  static harmony, 114–115, 114*m*
  target notes, 111
  3-4 horns, 105–117
  voice leading, 115, 115*m*
    5-6 horns, 206
    5 saxophones, 311
  whole-step planing, 106
rehearsal letter conventions, 51
repeated notes, 111–112, 113*m*
  5-6 horns, 206
repetition, 71, 73*m*
retrograde, 71, 72, 73*m*
retrograde inversion, 71, 72, 73*m*
rhythm and rhythmic notation
  harmonic rhythm, 63
  pulse and style, 58–59
  rhythm basics, 57–58
  score preparation, 63–64

rhythm and rhythmic notation (*Continued*)
  swing feel, 62–63
  syncopation and notation, 59–61
rhythm basics, 57–58
rhythmic alteration, 77*m*
  motivic development, 71, 73*m*
rhythmic comping in backgrounds, 144, 145*m*
  six horns, 220*m*
rhythmic hook, 183
rhythmic unison, 74, 75*m*
rhythm section, 27–31, 161–170
  bass, 163–164
  chord symbols and abbreviations, 164–165
  drums, 165–166
  guitars, 161–163
  "I've Got the Articulations & Dynamics
      Blues" by Richard Sussman, 168*m*
  jazz ensemble instruments, 15
  notation, 167*m*
  pianos, 161–163
  scores for small ensembles, 63
  styles, 169
  See also individual instruments
"Riffology" by Richard Sussman, 316, 317*m*
riffs
  background parts, 144, 146*m*
    six horns, 221*m*
  scoring, 316
rip gliss, 151
rondo form, 134

sample libraries, 11, 269
  notation software, 47
sampler software, 10–11
saxophones, 22
  and brass section
    combining with, 301–309
    contrasting with, 315–316, 317*m*–319*m*
  constant coupling, 301–302, 302*m*
  ranges and transpositions, 23*m*
  scores for small ensembles, 63
  sounds of, 23–24
  variable coupling, 303–309
  voicing positions, 203*m*
  voicing techniques, 299–301
  See also brass section
scalar melodic motions, 68*m*
scale-derived chords
  harmonic concepts, 83
  seventh chords, 84*m*
scoops, 151
score and parts layout functions
  Finale software, 189–193
  Sibelius software, 193–195
Score Music Publishing System, 37

scores
  big bands, 330–331, 454
  harmonic rhythm, 63
  large ensembles, 266–267
  layout of
    big bands, 454
    conventions, 50
    5-6 horns, 222
    part, 172
  preparation, 63–64
  pulse and style, 58–59
  rhythm basics, 57–58
  staff, conventions of, 50–51
  swing feel, 62–63
  syncopation and notation, 59–61
score staff arrangement conventions,
    50–51
SDEs (sound-designing environments),
    11–12
Sebesky, Don, 33, 273
secondary dominant chords, 83
semi-open position, 90, 91–92, 93*m*–95*m*
sequencers and notation software, 488–490
shakes, 151, 152
shape and motion of melody, 67–68
short accent, 151
shortcuts and macros, 158–159
short fall, 151
short gliss, 151
short note, 151
shout choruses, 134, 137, 230–233
  "Analycity" by Richard Sussman, 232*m*, 233
  big bands, 417–432
  contrary motion, 418
  dissonance, 426, 430
  "Get a Handel on It" by Richard Sussman,
      424*m*–425*m*
    analysis of, 423
  recorded examples, 233–234
  software, 234, 431
  and soli sections, 405, 417–418
  "Uncertainty" by Michael Abene,
      427*m*–428*m*, 429*m*–430*m*
    analysis of, 426–431
  "Unithology" by Richard Sussman,
      419*m*–421*m*
    analysis of, 418–419, 422, 423
Sibelius software, 38, 39–40
  drum grooves, 170
  Finale, comparison with, 487
  MIDI playback and editing, 47–50
  notation techniques, 41–47
  score and parts layout functions, 193–195
  shortcuts and macros, 158–159
  templates, 196

user interface, 188–189

voices, 402

See also software

similar motion, 98, 99*m*

simplification, 72, 73*m*

six horns

  backgrounds, 220*m*–221*m*

  ensembles, 256*m*–258*m*

  instrumental subdivisions, 247

  introductions, 217*m*–218*m*, 250*m*–255*m*

  "On a Misty Night" by Tadd Dameron,
     238–239, 240*m*–244*m*

  reharmonization of approach tones, 205*m*

  through-composed form, 237

  voicing positions, 203*m*

slide trombones, 17–18

slow counter-melodies, 127

slurs, 152

small ensemble writing

  harmonic rhythm, 63

  pulse and style, 58–59

  rhythm basics, 57–58

  score preparation, 63–64

  swing feel, 62–63

  syncopation and notation, 59–61

Smith, Leland, 37

Smith, Willie, 238, 239, 490

software, 5–6, 9–13

  accidentals, spelling of, 352, 362–363

  articulations and dynamics, 269

  audio mixes of scores, 312

  drum grooves, 170

  Finale, 38, 39–40

    drum grooves, 170

    layers, 402

    notation techniques, 41–47

    score and parts layout functions, 189–193

    shortcuts and macros, 158–159

    Sibelius, comparison with, 487

    templates, 196

    user interface, 187–189

  fonts, 431

  future development of, 490–491

  key switching, 381

  limitations of, 295–297

  MIDI playback and editing, 47–50,
    486–487

  notation, 37–53, 187–189

    benefits of, 485–486

    history of, 37–38

  notation techniques, 41–47

  and real instruments, 295–297

  score and parts layout functions

    Finale, 189–193

    Sibelius, 193–195

shortcuts and macros, 158–159

shout choruses, 234, 431

Sibelius, 38, 39–40

  drum grooves, 170

  Finale, comparison with, 487

  notation techniques, 41–47

  score and parts layout functions, 193–195

  shortcuts and macros, 158–159

  templates, 196

  user interface, 188–189

  voices, 402

soli section, 234

templates, 196

user interface, 187–189

See also MIDI (Musical Instrument Digital
  Interface)

soli sections, 137

  big bands, 405–416

    creating, 406–407, 407*m*–409*m*, 410

    "Memories of Lives Past" by Michael Abene,
      413*m*–415*m*

    analysis of, 412

  recorded examples, 233–234

  and shout choruses, 405, 417–418

  with six horns, 225–230, 245*m*–246*m*

  "Swangalang" by Bob Mintzer, 411, 412*m*

soloists

  accompanying, 433–435

  arranging for, 433–452

  brass section, 16–17

  composing for

    brass section, 16–17

    woodwind section, 22

  woodwind section, 22

sonata form

  in arrangements, 134

  classical music, 69

song form, 134

soprano saxophones, 23–24

  ranges and transpositions, 23*m*

  See also brass section

sound-designing environments (SDEs), 11–12

sound palette, 265–266

sound sets, 48

"Spreads" by Richard Sussman, 351*m*

spread voicings, 349–350, 351*m*

staccato articulations, 151

standard voicings, 90–96

Standford University Artificial Intelligence
  Laboratory, 37

static harmony, 114–115, 114*m*

  5-6 horns, 206

stopping of a French Horn, 19

straight mutes, 155–156

stuck notes, 9, 324

style
   horizontal harmony, 88
   pulse and, 58–59
   rhythm section, 169
suspended sounds, 123m
sustain pedal, 9
"Swangalang" by Bob Mintzer, 412m
   analysis of, 411
swing feel, 58, 59, 62–63
   brass and woodwind articulations,
      153m–154m
symbols and abbreviations, chord, 164–165
symmetrical phrase structures, 70–71
symmetry and asymmetry, 35
syncopation, 58, 59–61
   motivic development, 71
   notation, 61m
   rhythm section arrangements, 166
synthesizers, 27–28, 31m
synthetic scales, 67

target chords, 120
   "Basie sound," 288, 289
target notes
   in harmonies, 105
   melodic reharmonization, 120
   reharmonization of approach tones, 111
target tones
   "Basie sound," 289
   brass plus saxophones, 301
   voicing positions, 90
"Tautology" by Richard Sussman, 113m
templates, software, 196
tenor battles of soloists, 133
tenor saxophones, 24
   ranges and transpositions, 23m
   See also brass section
tenor trombones, 17–18
   ranges and transpositions, 21m
   See also brass section
tension and release phrasing, 34–35, 71
tenuto, 151
tessitura of instruments
   in arrangements, 76, 78m
   large ensembles, 273
   melody development, 74
Thad Jones - Mel Lewis Orchestra, 264
theme and variations in arrangements,
   134, 136
"There Will Never Be Another You" by Harry
   Warren and Mack Gordon, 206, 207m
through-composed form, 134
   for six horns, 237
timbre of instruments, 272–273
tonal centers, 88

tonal music, 67–68
tonic chords, 83
transitional passages, 137
transitions, 140, 142–143
transmit channels, 8
transpositions, 15–31
   big bands, 454
   concert pitch instruments, 15–17
   concert scores, 52–53
      software change in, 64
   instruments
      brass instruments, 16–20
      for concert pitch, 15–17
      woodwind section, 22–27
   large ensemble writing, 266
   motivic development, 71, 73m
tremolo, 151
triads, 82
trigger of a trombone, 19
trill, 151
tritones
   harmonic concepts, 83, 85, 85m, 86
   melodic reharmonization, 122m
trombones, 16–18
   scores for small ensembles, 63
   See also brass section
trumpets, 16–17
   ranges and transpositions, 21m
   scores for small ensembles, 63
   See also brass section
truncation, 72, 73m
tubas, 16–17, 20
   ranges and transpositions, 21m
   See also brass section
tune analysis. See individual tunes
tune form, 134
tunes
   constructing introductions, 140, 141m
   large ensemble writing, 267
   transitions/kickers, 143m
turn, 151
turnarounds, 140, 141m
   six horns, 217m
"12-Bar Blues" by Richard Sussman,
   290m–292m
   brass plus saxophones, 304, 305m

"Uncertainty" by Michael Abene
   big bands, 466m–471m
      analysis of, 463–465, 472
   shout choruses, 427m–428m, 429m–430m
      analysis of, 426–431
unison, 74, 75m
   large ensembles, 273m, 274m
unison scoring, 276m–278m

"Unithology" by Richard Sussman
    instrumental subdivisions, 323*m*
    large ensembles, 275*m*–278*m*
    shout choruses, 419*m*–421*m*
        analysis of, 418–419, 422, 423
unity in music, 35
upbeats, 59, 62
upper structure chord tones, 86
upper-structure triads, 343*m*, 345–346, 347*m*
"Upper-Structure Triads" by
    Richard Sussman, 347*m*

valve trombones, 19
vamps, 140
variable coupling, 303–309
variety and contrast in music, 34
vertical harmony, 86–87
    large ensembles, 284
vibraphones, 30, 31*m*
Village Vanguard Orchestra, 366
virtual instruments, 7, 10–11
virtual samplers, 11
vocalists
    arranging for, 433–452
    "Autumn Leaves" by Mercer, Prevert, and
        Kosma, 436*m*–437*m*
    the lyrics, 435
    "Who Cares?" by George and
        Ira Gershwin, 441*m*–450*m*
        analysis of, 438–440
voice leading
    5-6 horns, 206
    5 saxophones, 311
    harmonic concepts (3-4 horns), 98–99
    reharmonization of approach tones,
        115, 115*m*
voicing brass section, 284–286
    melody in low register, 286–287
    melody in mid-register, 288–290,
        290*m*–294*m*
    mistakes, common, 292*m*
voicing positions
    8-piece brass, 285*m*
    5-6 horns, 199*m*–200*m*, 201, 203*m*, 206,
        207*m*–208*m*

    5 saxophones, 300*m*
    harmonic concepts, 90–96
    mixed, 207*m*, 208*m*
    modal concepts, 96–97
    open, 295
    six horns, 203*m*
voicing principles, 284–286
voicing techniques
    "Ivories Tower" by Richard Sussman, 341, 344*m*
    modern, 343*m*, 345–346, 347*m*, 348, 358
    for saxophones, 299–301
    See also harmonic concepts (modern)
Voltaire, 332
volume, MIDI controller, 9

"Waiting" by Richard Sussman, 135*m*–136*m*
WDR Band, 366, 423, 438
"Who Cares?" by George and Ira Gershwin,
    441*m*–450*m*
    analysis of, 438–440
whole-step planing, 106
"Woodwind Doubles" by Richard Sussman,
    369*m*–370*m*
woodwind section, 22–27, 213–214
    articulations, 150–154
    balance, 367–368
    big bands
        brass, combinations with, 368–372
        doubles, 365–368, 369*m*–370*m*, 371
        dynamics and balance, 367–368
        mixed combinations, 372–378
    brass, combinations with, 368–372
    doubles, 365–368, 369*m*–370*m*, 371
    dynamics and balance, 367–368
    jazz ensemble instruments, 15
    large ensembles, 272
    mixed combinations, 372–378
    trill or tremolo, 151
    See also individual instruments
workflow concepts
    big bands, 330–331
    "Cross-Section" sketch by Richard Sussman,
        332–334, 335*m*–336*m*
    score layouts, 222
Wurlitzer electric pianos, 27–28